Goddesses in World Culture

Goddesses in World Culture

Volume 1
Asia and Africa

Patricia Monaghan, Editor

 PRAEGER

AN IMPRINT OF ABC-CLIO, LLC
Santa Barbara, California • Denver, Colorado • Oxford, England

Library of Congress Cataloging-in-Publication Data

Goddesses in world culture / Patricia Monaghan, editor.
  p. cm.
Includes bibliographical references and indexes.
ISBN 978-0-313-35465-6 (set : alk. paper) — ISBN 978-0-313-35466-3 (ebook)
1. Goddesses. I. Monaghan, Patricia.
BL473.5.G64   2011
202′.11409—dc22   2010017298

ISBN: 978-0-313-35465-6
EISBN: 978-0-313-35466-3

15 14 13 12 11   1 2 3 4 5

This book is also available on the World Wide Web as an eBook.
Visit www.abc-clio.com for details.

Praeger
An Imprint of ABC-CLIO, LLC

ABC-CLIO, LLC
130 Cremona Drive, P.O. Box 1911
Santa Barbara, California 93116-1911

This book is printed on acid-free paper ∞

Manufactured in the United States of America

Contents

Introduction

Patricia Monaghan

Any museum in which great art is exhibited includes statuesque women, some nakedly beautiful, some clothed in symbols of power and prestige. Some bear names of historically known goddesses, like Isis and Hera, Xiwang Mu and Epona, but others remain nameless or are labeled as "fertility figures" or "ancestor idols." The earliest of these artworks go back to the dawn of humanity's emergence in the Paleolithic or Old Stone Age, approximately 35,000 years ago. The latest might be only a few years old, crafted by an artist in one of the many lands where feminine divinity is still honored.

Goddesses have been part of human culture for millennia. They appear not only in visual art but also in literature, both oral and written. At times they are clearly divine powers such as Greek Athena in *The Iliad* or White Buffalo Calf Woman in the sacred stories of the Lakota. Or they may be disguised and diminished, appearing as queens and other heroines: Guinevere in the legends of King Arthur and Vashti in the Hebrew scriptures. Alternatively, they may be so removed from cultural centrality that they have become figures of folklore, appearing in children's stories as the fierce witch Baba Yaga in Russian tales or in local legend to explain names of places, as does the Irish cow of abundance, the Glas Ghaibhleann.

These powerful female figures also appear in religious rituals and liturgies. In some cases, the rituals remain only in historical records, for worship of the goddess in question died out or was suppressed. Such is the case with the great goddesses of Greece and Rome, known now only through ancient literature and archaeological remains. No one alive has seen a man castrate himself with a stone knife in honor of the Magna Mater, the "great mother" Cybele, or seen the vast procession of worshipers seeking initiation into the mysteries, threading their way to the shrine of Greek Demeter at Eleusis. The number of goddesses lost to history through deliberate persecution is impossible to know, although historical evidence points to the elimination of some divinities such as Berecynthia in Gaul, known only through documentation that her wagon-borne procession ceased when the Christian Martin of Tours destroyed all her images and threatened her followers. In other cases, as with many indigenous peoples around the globe, colonization and forced conversion, together with destruction of culturally important sites and monuments, have meant that the name and mythology of the goddess have been lost to history.

But in many cases, goddess rituals are still celebrated today. Such is the case with Divali, the Indian feast of the goddess of wealth, Lakshmi, which is part of the yearly cycle of Hindu devotion in Chicago as well as Calcutta. In Ireland the old Celtic feast of the goddess Brigit continues to be marked on February 1; although she now appears as a Christian abbess and saint, the same holy wells are visited in her honor as when she was acknowledged as divine. Finally, some goddesses are honored in reconstructed rituals, such as that dedicated to Isis in Southern California or those to Diana across the United States. Far removed in time and place from earliest worshipers, these new devotees create rituals; they walk to the Pacific Ocean rather than to the Nile, wearing gold lamé rather than hand-woven linen, chanting the name of Isis the all-mother; or they join in drum circles on a midwestern farm and call down to Diana to empower their daily lives. Even more startlingly, a worldwide movement to honor Celtic Brigit's ancient fire worship exists entirely online; people who never see or speak to each other share a living vigil by a virtual flame.

When scholars address the role of the feminine in religion today, they do so most frequently from the point of view of monotheistic religions. Annually, hundreds of articles and books, both learned and popular, address questions of the status of women in Judaism, Christianity, and Islam. But an underlying question arises among scholars who question how women can ever be equal in religion based on a single male divinity. Although orthodox believers argue that such a god represents all humanity, male and female, others point out that monotheism is almost invariably associated with a male clerical hierarchy whose edicts impact the lives of countless voiceless women. While the presence of a goddess within a religion is no guarantee of better status for women, her absence provides an opportunity for oppression. In countries that offer a vote to their citizens, only two do not allow women to vote: Saudi Arabia and Vatican City, both centers of monotheistic patriarchal religions.

Monotheism is based on a male divine image. The opposite is not, however, true. There is no known case of a monotheistic religion based on a goddess; all religions where goddesses are honored employ both male and female imagery in describing divinity. Scholars of goddess religion have argued that by creating a "god/nongod" dualism, monotheisms encourage an exclusionary and divisive worldview. When "woman" is placed on the side of "nongod," spiritual gender segregation can result, with women excluded from religious power.

Yet even within monotheisms, images remain of powerful women: mothers, sisters, lovers, warriors. Although not accepted as divine, these figures hold much the same place in art and narrative as goddesses in nonmonotheistic cultures do. Christianity deliberately adopted the images and symbols of powerful goddesses for saints and the Virgin Mary. Slavic Europe still honors many "black Madonnas" in areas where the black-skinned earth goddess Mokosh was once worshiped; when the Spanish conquered Mexico, the figure of Aztec Tonan was absorbed into the Christian Guadalupe. Such goddess-like figures often attract more popular devotion than the official male divinity, as is suggested by the fact that more Catholic churches in America are named for the Virgin Mary than for her divine son.

These volumes offer an introduction to the ways in which images of the feminine divine have appeared in world culture. Rather than attempting to discuss only the best-known figures in world religion, the chapters address figures of varying centrality within their cultures. Sedna, the "great food-dish" who assures survival to the Inuit, appears here, but so does Sôlmundae Halmang, a Korean goddess who exists only in place-name stories of the island of Cheju. Some goddesses suggest a bridge between several cultures; the Matronae, for instance, were honored in Roman-occupied areas where Celtic and Germanic peoples lived and thus reveal some of all three cultures; and Cinderella, familiar to readers from Germanic fairy tales, is shown to have come originally from Asia by way of Egypt. Some cultures that are especially rich in goddess lore, such as India, are represented by more than one chapter, while due to limitations of space, other cultures are not covered. In every case, the figure is not intended to represent all aspects of the female divine in a specific culture; rather, each offers an illuminating view of a culture's views of the feminine.

Similarly, the chapters exemplify a variety of methods for goddess study, from new translations of liturgical hymns to the living goddess

Lakshmi to interpretation of archaeological remains in examination of the related Egyptian goddesses Bast, Sekhmet, and Hathor. Among the methods employed by the authors of these chapters are ethnography, textual analysis, and visual reconstruction. Several authors are primarily poets and bring a trained poetic sensibility to the examination of goddesses, such as Greek Helen and Mexican Guadalupe. Others employ a psychological framework, especially relying on archetypal theories articulated by Carl Jung and Toni Wolff in examining the feminine divine. Many of the contributors deliberately select or create cross-disciplinary methods in order to better define and describe their topics. The writers themselves include both women and men from various religious and ethnic backgrounds. Within these volumes are Christians and Mormons, Jews and pagans, women in religious orders and those who follow indigenous religions. Some approach their subjects as devoted followers of the goddess in question, others as disinterested observers, but all employ critical analysis in discussing their subjects.

Volume 1 discusses figures from Asia and Africa. Here several important Hindu divinities are found, including the wealth-goddess Lakshmi and the death-dancer Kali. As well as orthodox Hinduism, this volume includes discussion of goddesses from pre-Hindu traditions, the "village goddesses" known only with a limited geographical area and perceived as protectors of both land and people. In the nearby lands of Tibet and Nepal, female Buddhist figures appear who hold great power, both spiritual and political. Similar imagery is found in China, where the "goddess of mercy" Guanyin melds an indigenous tradition with images from the immigrant Buddhism. In Japan and Korea, contributors describe geographically located goddesses who are seen as embodied in the land itself. In Egypt and Africa scholars attest to important female divinities whose influence continues despite recent attempts to discourage their worship.

Volume 2 discusses goddesses from the eastern Mediterranean and Europe. Goddesses of the Babylonians and the Assyrians, such as Inanna-Ishtar and Nisaba, testify to the power and prestige such deities had among people of the lands that are now Iraq and Iran. Another chapter describes the controversial Asherah, now believed by many scholars of the Old Testament to be an original primary divinity of the Hebrews, consort to Jehovah. That a now-monotheistic religion may have once honored a goddess is unsettling to some believers, but contemporary archaeological evidence points to monotheism as having been created during the Babylonian captivity. Similarly, the figure of Mary

Magdalene, either a saint or sinner (or both) in Christian legend, is shown to hold the power of earlier goddesses despite being positioned within a monotheistic religion, while Lilith, "Adam's first wife," shows how female power was demonized with the rise of monotheism. In Europe, despite a common assumption of an overarching "Western way of thinking" that upholds linear and patriarchal values, our authors reveal an ongoing and powerful substrata of goddess worship. Even such an apparently familiar figure as Helen of Troy is revealed to descend from a powerful earth divinity. From the Celtic lands, evidence of several important goddesses appears in iconography and literature, suggesting the power of the feminine in that ancient culture, while in the Germanic culture we find a number of similarly powerful figures including the fate-goddesses called Norns who sit at the foot of the world-tree and control human destiny. In the Alps, place-names and legends hold in memory an ancient goddess of the white peaks, whose worshipers may have included the "Ice Man" found sacrificed on her glaciers.

Volume 3 brings together myths of Australia and the Americas. The volume begins with reflections on goddesses of Australia, including an indigenous figure rarely discussed in scholarly literature and the unnamed goddesses who appear in pre-Aboriginal rock art; these chapters only graze the surface of a rich and complex goddess mythology in the world's most ancient continent. The volume then explores some of the goddesses of North, Central, and South America. These range from White Buffalo Calf Woman, whose myth is today used to inspire a new generation of Lakota with reverence towards living women, to the frightening snake-skirted Aztec goddess Coatlicue, whose visage can be seen in magnificent ancient art. Several chapters reflect the syncretic impulse that led, in Mexico and the Caribbean, to the emergence of figures that include aspects of ancient goddesses under the guise of Christian figures. The volume also includes chapters on contemporary American interpretations of goddess myths: the adoption of Roman Diana as the matron divinity of women's religious groups in America, the self-creation as a goddess of a Wiccan priestess, the creation of a temple to Egyptian Sekhmet on the western American desert. The volume also includes commentary on the use of goddess imagery by contemporary American writers, whose projects of reclamation suggest the importance of the feminine divine to the creative artist.

Were all the world's important goddesses to be discussed in such depth, dozens more volumes would be needed; were we to add the intriguing but lesser-known divinities, the volumes would cover many shelves. Goddesses and goddess-like figures have been known in every culture and every era. Their stories and images offer an immense variety of possibilities for ways to interpret women's realities. They speak both to men and to women about human as well as divine potential. These volumes offer a glimpse of the richness of goddess mythology throughout the world and, it is hoped, will inspire more such efforts as well as more general awareness of the diversity of approaches possible in study of such mythic figures.

1

Lakshmi: Hindu Goddess of Abundance

Constantina Rhodes

Let me contemplate the goddess Lakshmi,
Adorned with sparkling ankle bracelets
And charming toe-rings,
Playfully holding a lotus in her hand.

O Lakshmi, bright one, exalted one,
Wielder of conch, discus, and mace,

Bestower of all success,
Grant me a boon.[1]

Traditionally in India, and nowadays across the globe, people from a wide range of cultural backgrounds and geographic regions worship Lakshmi, beloved goddess of wealth, abundance, happiness, beauty, well-being, good fortune, and every type of prosperity. She is goddess to rural villagers and to big-city dwellers, to the humble of means and to multimillionaires. Men, women, and even children actively seek her favor. Her devotees can be comfortably bold in their worship: as the opening verses demonstrate, the goddess is enjoined to grant a boon, a gift given by a deity, usually in exchange for an offering. Offerings to this goddess usually consist of bright flowers, sweets, succulent fruits, fragrant oils and incense, money, and songs—all of these embodying and mirroring back to the goddess her own essence of sweetness and joy.

Lakshmi is a goddess of this earth, this life, this society, this round of cyclical existence. When her devotees need to acquire or to successfully maintain the things that make life in this world easeful and enriching, they turn to Lakshmi. They pray for success with exams and careers, finding a spouse, the birth of children, and the expansion of bank accounts. Lakshmi provides life's bounty—good health, a pleasant place to live, an abundant flow of income, successful personal relationships, and a meaningful spiritual life. Lakshmi oversees all four "goals" or "wealths" (*caturartha*) that Hindu scriptures recognize as the recipe for a satisfying life: physical pleasure and enjoyment (*kama*), material wealth (*artha*), harmonious relationships (*dharma*), and spiritual liberation (*moksha*). Stepping back to view a perspective beyond the individual, Lakshmi is the very foundation of life, that which makes the individual attainment of these goals possible. This chapter shows how Lakshmi, the auspicious essence of abundance and prosperity itself, takes form as abundance and prosperity in the world and in the personal lives of her devotees.

The Primordial Lotus Goddess

Long before songs praising Lakshmi were written down, ancient Indian visual art was replete with lovely and graceful motifs of lotuses rising from pools of water and of nymph-like figures curling lithely around tree trunks. Other images depict a female figure seated on a lotus, bearing in her hands blossoming lotuses and tender shafts of freshly sprouted grain. This same figure is sometimes flanked by plump elephants that shower her with water from belly-round urns. These images depict the primordial lotus goddess, earliest form of the Indian mother goddess, beneficent deity of life force, fertility, and glorious abundance. Worshipers recognized the earthly form of the goddess as something very much of the natural realm and yet not quite of this world, a hybrid apparition of a radiantly beautiful woman embodied in all living things, but especially in the sacred lotus. Like all forms of life, the form of the goddess begins in the waters.

The earliest of these images were created some 4000–5000 years ago by the artists of the Harappa civilization of the Indus River Valley, in modern Pakistan.[2] The iconographic records from ages past have no written indications of her name, but when the sacred texts begin to recognize this deity in song, she is called upon with a variety of names that reiterate her images, among them Kamala, Ambuja, Padma, and Padmini, all of which mean "lotus." Thus it is that in the opening verse of the *Lakshmi*

Sukta (*Hymn to Lakshmi*), one of her earliest songs of praise, Lakshmi is addressed and identified as the lotus goddess Padmini:

> Most lovely goddess Padmini
> With lotus face
> And lovely lotus-petal eyes,
> O you who cherish the lotus,
> O you who cherish the world,
> O goddess whose heart pervades the universe,
> To your lotus feet I bow.[3]

As the hymn continues, each part of the goddess's body—her eyes, lips, limbs, and so forth—is said to consist of lotus petals. She sits on a lotus, dwells within the lotus, bears lotuses in her lotus-hands, and indeed is the inner essence of the lotus. This is a hyperreality; the parts do not add up to make ordinary sense, nor are they expected to. As such, this is a more potent form of the goddess, less specifically manifest, yet containing every possibility, for as the unfolding petals expand outward, they express the goddess's essence in form, replicating the entire multilayered universe, which itself is the very body of the primordial lotus goddess. Her divine essence is understood to dwell in that form, and her worshipers see the lotus not as a symbol but as an embodiment of the goddess. The lotus flower in full bloom is seen as an expression of the abundance, beauty, purity, gracefulness, mystery, and revelation of this goddess.

Just as her many epithets address this goddess as the foundation of the world, so too has the lotus persisted as a pan-Indian image that represents the wellspring and support of the creation. The lotus seat serves as the foundation upon which the gods rest in their embodied forms when they become manifest upon the earth, thereby serving as an intricate link between the earth and the realms of heaven. It is an image that extends beyond Hindu iconography to that of Jainism and Buddhism, for the lotus seat that supports the images of the Buddha has been taken far beyond the motherland to become established in the sacred arts of virtually all of the Buddhist countries.

The Goddess of Abundance: Shri's Essence, Lakshmi's Form

The Vedas or "wisdom books" are the earliest scriptures of the Hindu tradition, dating to 1200 BCE or even earlier. These texts hold hymns to the various Vedic gods and mysterious forces; among these are invocations to attract the presence of Shri, which translates as "splendor," "glory," "majesty," "brilliance," and "the divine power of auspiciousness." Shri is the power of life and vitality, and that which is touched by Shri becomes radiant with health, wealth, well-being, abundance, and bounteous prosperity. The radiant force of Shri can dispel the darkness of misfortune, decay, and poverty.

Shri is an abstract quality, and although as a feminine noun the term carries the connotation of a divine feminine force, it is not yet associated with any particular form or personification of divinity. Rather, there is a magnificent ambiguity in the term, for "splendor" is recognized as taking the form of wherever it manifests, as in the blossoming abundance of the earth, the life-giving waters, bounteous grains, and fatted cattle. Shri is identified also in the auspicious workings of society: in the peaceful and prosperous kingdom of a righteous king; in the abundant circulation of gold and commercial exchange; and in harmonious relationships, strong families, and loyal friends, colleagues, and attendants. In the Vedic consciousness, the stability of the universe (*rita*) depends upon the attraction and maintenance of the elusive Shri. Indeed, all that is auspicious—the luxuriant bounty of the earth, the resonant chanting of sacred songs, the virtuous actions of regents, indeed, every type of prosperity—is inextricably linked as *shri* and is propitiated to become graciously manifest on earth and in the affairs of society.

By the late Vedic period, when the scintillating and auspicious qualities known as *shri* come to be recognized as manifesting in a particular form, they are also called *lakshmi*, literally an imprint, a sign, an expression, or a display, that is, a specifically recognizable manifestation of *shri*. This divine force is now recognized as embodied in the world not only as an abstract quality but also as a deity, and, in particular, as a goddess, a personification of the abundance, prosperity, splendor, and beauty that have long been recognized as desirable qualities in life. The songs now sing of shri (Shri, capitalized when referring to the personalized goddess) and lakshmi (Lakshmi), sometimes as two independent goddesses, and at other times as one and the same goddess.[4] In all of her attributes of abundance and splendor, the goddess of prosperity eventually comes to be known by an abundant array of names, all of which lend further dimensions to the human perception of her identity.

In later Indic literature, the world has exploded into myriad expressions of form. The Puranas are a group of texts composed from approximately 200 BCE to 1000 CE, a period that also produced the two great epics of India, the *Ramayana* and the *Mahabharata*. The expansive, elaborate cosmology of the epics and Puranas extends through eons of time and vast stretches of space, describing cycle upon cycle of world-creation, world-preservation, and world-dissolution. Here Lakshmi becomes established in the religious imagination as the goddess of abundance and prosperity whose personification blends with the identities of the primordial lotus goddess and the Vedic Shri, culminating in the form of a gracefully smiling, scintillatingly beautiful woman with long, dark, unbound, flowing hair.

In what is perhaps her best-known birth-story, Lakshmi emerges fully grown from the Ocean of Milk.[5] In this lengthy and complex story, the warring gods (*deva*s) of heaven and the demi-gods (*asura*s) of the underworld reluctantly join forces to regain the *amrita*, or elixir of immortality, which has been cast into the ocean. Both sides engage in a massive tug-of-war, churning the vast milk-ocean to force its contents to the surface. Some of these are deadly and others kindly. The contest continues as all watch for the emergence of the lost elixir. Finally they behold the auspicious sight of the magnificent Lakshmi rising out of the sea-foam. Lakshmi, goddess of abundance, prosperity, and all auspiciousness, bears the precious urn of immortal elixir.[6] The goddess's appearance is cause for jubilant rejoicing in the three worlds, as harmony is restored to the inhabitants of heaven, earth, and the netherworlds alike.

In the epics and Puranas, Lakshmi is closely affiliated with Vishnu, lord of world preservation, and together they serve as sustainers of the universe. They constitute the quintessential divine couple, existing as a singular energy that expresses itself in the complementary aspects of divine male and divine female. It is the unified image of Lakshmi and Vishnu that also sets the paradigm for the bride and groom in the Hindu wedding ceremony.

In world-cycle after world-cycle, Lakshmi and Vishnu descend from Vaikuntha, their heavenly abode, to restore harmony in the creation. Each of these "descents" (*avataras*; hence the English word *avatar*) takes a different form that constitutes the basis of another cycle of stories. When Vishnu descends to earth as Rama, Lakshmi accompanies him as Sita; when he appears as the dwarf, she is the lotus; when he takes form as Krishna, she expresses the *aishvarya* ("majestic") aspect of her essence as Rukmini, his queen in Mathura, and the "sweet" aspect of her essence as Radha, his beloved *gopi* ("milkmaid") in the magical realm of Vrindavana.

So too does Lakshmi express herself through auspicious embodiments of prosperity that are independent of Vishnu—as cows, horses, gold coins, precious gems, brightly colored flowers, sprouts of grain, and literally in every female. In the *Praise-Song for the Lotus Goddess* (*Kamala Stotra*), for example, the gods proclaim:

> You exist as little girls in their childhood,
> As young women in their youth,
> And as elderly women in their old age. . . .[7]

Lakshmi, Embodiment of the Four Wealths (*Caturartha*)

Songs from the epics and Puranas invoke Lakshmi for all manner of wealth, abundance, prosperity, harmony, and well-being. And so it is that these songs extol the goddess of prosperity as embodied in the four types of blessings that, when addressed together, are said to create a life of balance and harmony: *kama* (pleasure and enjoyment), *artha* (material prosperity), *dharma* (virtuous conduct and harmonious relationships), and *moksha* (spiritual liberation).

The four "goals" or "wealths" operate as a continuum, for a well-balanced life enjoys the blessing of Lakshmi in many aspects of existence. The first three goals, specifically world-affirming, are most readily apparent in their associations with Lakshmi as the goddess of prosperity, yet the wealth of Lakshmi is the full and harmonious infusion of Lakshmi's abundance, culminating in liberation from attachment. In the worship of the goddess, one must first embrace the world, glorifying it as a manifestation of divine essence. Before liberation can be attained one must live well in the world and yet grasp its hidden meaning, having evolved to the awareness by which Mahamaya—the goddess as "Great Illusion"—is recognized as both the one who veils and the one who reveals the truth of existence.

Lakshmi as Kama: The Wealth of Pleasure

Kama is pleasure, delight, sensuality, sexuality. It is the passion that incites idea toward form. It is the pulse and the impulse of nature, deeper than thought or intention, which ignites the spark of procreation, ensuring the continuance of life from one generation to the next. Lakshmi is golden-skinned and scintillating, the exciter of passion, arousing the first stirrings of the sexual energy necessary to propagate life and expansion. Lakshmi is extolled as Pradyumnajanani, "mother of the god of love," by the poet of the *Prasannavarada Shri Lakshmi Stotra* (*Song for Lakshmi, Gracious Bestower of Blessings*).[8]

Kama ranges from eroticism to the pleasurable appreciation of beauty in all of its aesthetic subtleties. Lakshmi is manifest in every perceivable aspect of the material world, in its variegated fragrances and pungencies, in its array of *rasas* ("savors" or "flavors"), and in all that expresses the pulse of divine energy as it ripples through the world. When the senses are enlivened, they heighten one's experience of the goddess's presence, for one's capacity for sensual receptivity is the very same that allows for the reception of Lakshmi's grace.

Through her expression of kama, Lakshmi becomes Radha, the beloved of Krishna, whom she meets for secret love-play in the intoxicating realm of the Vrinda forest. Her essence is recognized in lush, green vegetation sprouting from the moist earth, in the brilliant colors and intoxicatingly sweet fragrance of blossoming flowers, and in the languid waywardness of vines as they grow entangled with luxuriant abandon. The kama aspect of Lakshmi is abundantly lovely, graceful, fragrant, moist, and sensuous, and she expresses herself in the vegetation of the forest as much as in the intertwined bodies and souls of lovers. In *Shri Daivakrita Lakshmi Stotra* (*The Heavenly Gods' Praise-Song for Lakshmi*), the celestial ones celebrate Lakshmi in her glorious display of such forms:

> In Goloka,
> You are the goddess more dear to Krishna
> Than life itself,
> His own Radhika.
> Deep in the forest,
> Deep in the Vrinda forest,
> You are mistress of the mesmerizing rasa dance.
>
> In the boughs of the sacred *bhandira* tree,
> You are Krishna's desire.
> In the sandalwood forest you are Candra,
> In the grove of sweet yellow jasmine you are Viraja,
> And on the hundred-peaked mountain you are the lovely Sundari.[9]

Ecstatic in their union of hearts, bodies, and souls, and mournfully depressed when forced into separation, Radha and Krishna (that is, embodiments of Lakshmi and Vishnu) represent that which Vaishnava theologians interpret as a perfect paradigm for the soul's longing for and blissful union with the divine. Passion, drama, exasperation, delight: all of these are expressions of the soul's journey in the world.

Lakshmi as Artha: Material Wealth and Prosperity Consciousness

More than any of her other aspects, Lakshmi is most widely identified and worshiped as the goddess of material prosperity. She is the quintessential embodiment of *artha* or material wealth. Her qualities of fluidity and expansiveness take form as money and its circulation in society. It is no surprise that merchants are among her most ardent devotees, and many business establishments in India grace their premises with private shrines to the goddess. Lakshmi's most important festival, Divali (the "festival of lights"), is also the occasion for closing out financial books and beginning a new fiscal year. This is also the only time that gambling is encouraged, as if to test one's faith in the blessings of Lady Luck.

There is a luxuriant gracefulness about Lakshmi's wealth. As an expression of her own nature, it springs from the source of her being and pours forth bounteously. Thus is Lakshmi lauded for her generosity, and her sacred images display her with open hands from which pour forth unending streams of gold coins. The easeful, life-giving currents of gold, of water, of fructifying rains, and indeed of any form of energy are all variations on the same image of Lakshmi's bestowal of prosperity. In some images, elephants lustrate the goddess with streams of water, increasing the magnitude of bounty and also illustrating an important point—that the goddess of plenty herself enjoys replenishment. Thus does the cycle continue propitiously.

Invocatory songs address Lakshmi with a variety of epithets, among them, Dhanada (*da*, "bestower" of *dhana*, "wealth"). The term *dhana* incorporates an expansive definition of prosperity: abundance, luxury, comfort, happiness, good health, well-being, material wealth, harmonious relationships with friends, family, and community, and a meaningful spiritual life. Lakshmi is also called Vasudha ("yielder of wealth"), referring to the goddess as the bounteous earth. *Vasu* is the wealth of the land and the abundant life that it yields. It is also the material wealth of the earth's hidden treasures—the precious metals, minerals, crystals, and gemstones that lie beneath its surface—as well as the mysterious treasures of the forests and in the depths of the sea.

When they pertain specifically to "wealth" in the human sphere, the material aspects of dhana and of vasu are specifically called artha, the wealth that may be counted or demonstrated or used in the currency of exchange—property, valuables, treasures, possessions, money, and the like. Just as Lakshmi is a visible expression of shri, so too is artha a material expression of the goddess's energy as money or material wealth.

Attracting and maintaining wealth, however one interprets it, entails an attitude, a state of mind, quite literally a state of consciousness that aligns with the consciousness of the goddess. The poet of the *Prasannavarada Shri Lakshmi Stotra*, for example, seeks the ability to attract wealth as well as to discover the state of consciousness that produces it:

> Consumed by dire poverty,
> I am breathless with anxiety and fear.
> In this impossibly painful state,
> I am drawn to your side.
> O Lakshmi, Ocean of Compassion,
> Bestow wealth,
> And guide me to a state of prosperity.[10]

Prayers to Lakshmi ask for material abundance and at the same time for the conscious awareness to dwell in that state of prosperity, which is a state of consciousness, a state of engagement with the wealth-energy of the goddess. The energy of this goddess is the energy of prosperity itself—effulgent, sparkling, ever-active—and to dwell in this is what truly empowers the supplicant.

The material prosperity denoted by the term *artha* does not necessarily resonate with the wider aspects of abundance that the term *dhana* carries. While Lakshmi is most certainly the source of artha, it is significant that she is never addressed as *artha-da* ("bestower of money"), and only rarely is she supplicated to grant artha by itself. Rather, she is addressed as *dhana-da* ("bestower of wealth") and consistently invoked for the more expansive designations of material wealth as an expression of the goddess's limitless abundance, of which artha is but a finite part. Material wealth is one thing; the energy that creates and sustains material wealth is quite another. It is this that the wise seek of the goddess; they request that the goddess bestow not only the material expression of wealth, but that she draw them into alignment with the limitless source of all prosperity.

So too does Lakshmi's abundance resonate with elegance and harmony, manifest through the multifaceted aspects of life on earth. Those who seek her favor are reminded that an overly zealous attention to any one of the four aims of life to the exclusion of the others may create an imbalance that may actually send Lakshmi fleeing. An unbalanced pursuit of Lakshmi may inadvertently result in attracting her inauspicious sister Atula ("Unbalanced") instead.[11]

Lakshmi as Dharma: The Wealth of Virtue and Right Relationships

There are many ways to translate the term *dharma*: "virtue," "virtuous conduct," "harmonious relationship," "religion," "etiquette," "religious duty," "communal obligation," "social consciousness," "balanced way of life," "living in right relationship," and even "doing the right thing." Because its meanings are so variously nuanced, it is often left untranslated or translated with different terms according to context. In general, dharma is the energy governing relationships—with oneself, with one's beloved, with one's children or family or community, with one's natural environment, and with the gods. It is for this reason that dharma may sometimes be described in terms of obligatory actions, and the scriptures designate codes of etiquette that range from good manners to religious canons and ritual observances. Dharma is the harmony of interconnectedness that preserves creation.

The auspicious preservation of the entire creation reflects harmony and happiness on the personal level. Lakshmi's association with dharma, therefore, informs one's appropriate and successful relationships with others. This is why Lakshmi is so often approached by those seeking a spouse, good home, steady income, and other such aspects of life. In *Devaraja Indrakrita Lakshmī Stotra* (*Lord Indra's Song for Lakshmi*), the lord of the gods praises Lakshmi with these words:

> O Most Fortunate One!
> It is always through your propitious glances
> That men obtain wives and children,
> As well as homes,
> Loyal friends,
> Bountiful harvests,
> And every type of prosperity.[12]

Lakshmi as Moksha: The Wealth of Spiritual Liberation

Lakshmi is extolled as the goddess whose bright auspiciousness infuses the creation with kama, artha, and dharma. Together these three constitute a unit and are qualified as *bhukti* ("enjoyment" or "relishing" of the world). The fourth and final component is *moksha* (also called *mukti*), or release from worldly attachment. As well as providing the foundation for its delights, Lakshmi is the final refuge, the transport to liberation from attachment to the world. Devotees of the goddess are not forced to choose between "spirituality" and "materiality," and in fact to do so would be to disregard the magnificent arena of the goddess's essence. The goddess is invoked for both spiritual and material blessings, for she is the material and spiritual substratum, the platform upon which everything rests and moves; she is the experience of life and she is the wisdom to see past life's vicissitudes. Indeed, one of her best-known epithets in this regard is *bhukti-mukti-pradayini* ("bestower of worldly enjoyment and spiritual liberation").[13]

In this more expansive aspect, Lakshmi is also known as Mahalakshmi ("Great Lakshmi"). She is also glorified as Mahamaya ("Great Illusion"), speaking from a vision of the entirety of the creation and the engagement of living in it, through it, and beyond it. So too is she addressed as the origin and essence of all space and time, Mahakali, as well as the great goddess Mahadevi. It is she who oversees the movement and measuring (*matra*) of time and circumstance, who constitutes it entirely and is yet beyond it, presenting herself not only as the Great Illusion, but also as the Resplendent Wisdom, Sri Vidya, who fosters liberation. Just as she is the veil of illusion that keeps one from recognizing the truth behind appearances, so too is she the means to liberation—the one who removes that veil. The release from the cyclical existence in *samsara*, then, comes from the same goddess who sanctions the world and embellishes it, even mesmerizing one to enjoy attachment to it for lifetime after lifetime. To the one who views kama, artha, dharma, and moksha as disparate endeavors, the illusion of Maya can be tormenting. To the wise, all of this is the majesty of the goddess's creation, unveiled. Again, Lord Indra extols the goddess:

O Auspicious One,
You are sacrificial knowledge,
Supreme knowledge,
And secret, mystical knowledge.
You are knowledge of the higher Self,
O Goddess,
And you are the one who confers liberation.

You are metaphysics,
You are the three Vedas,
You are the arts and sciences,
And you are the purveyor of justice.
O Goddess, the entire world,
With all of its pleasing and displeasing forms,
Consists of your essence.[14]

Is Lady Luck a Fickle Goddess? Lakshmi and Alakshmi the Inauspicious

If Lakshmi brings balance, harmony, abundance, wealth, and a sense of security, she is nonetheless also known as Cancala ("fickle" or "restless"). The sense of security can be just that—a sense, perhaps an illusion—when its true nature is not understood and approached properly. Even Indra, lord of the gods and regent of heaven, learns the hard way that disrespecting the goddess of wealth, even if unconsciously, leads to loss of her favor. How, then, can Lakshmi be sought for security when she herself is cancala: wavering, unsteady, about to leave without a moment's notice? Certainly, Lakshmi is beseeched to be steadfast and to leave behind the restless aspect of her nature as the capricious Lady Luck.

What happens when one does not succeed in attracting and sustaining Lakshmi's favor? Just as the *presence* of auspicious abundance is personified, so too is its *absence*. What is it that takes up residence in Lakshmi's stead?

From very early times, if the auspicious were to be invited into one's presence, it was deemed necessary first to take action to dislodge the presence of the inauspicious or at least to take precautions against its arrival. Before the Vedic fire sacrifice (*yajna*) was performed, the forces of inauspiciousness were invoked outside of the sacred precincts and specifically admonished to stay far from them. The elaborate ritual of the *rajasuya* ("royal coronation"), for example, includes the conscious expulsion of Alakshmi in her form as the inauspicious goddess Nirriti ("cosmic disorder") by attracting her with sacrifices offered at a desolate area, facing south, the direction of death, keeping her far from the auspicious abode of the king and the sacred precincts where Shri Lakshmi would be worshiped.[15]

As the personifications of Lakshmi develop, so too do the forms of Alakshmi. In the epic literature, the embodiment of misfortune and inauspiciousness is also called Daridra ("poverty"[16]) as well as Akirti ("ill repute"), Atula ("unbalanced"), and Jyeshtha ("elder" or "eldest"). The latter name refers to Alakshmi as Lakshmi's elder sister, for when the cosmic Ocean of Milk is churned to bring forth the lost elixir of immortality, all that is inauspicious is born together in a group, followed by the birth of the auspicious, the first of whom is Lakshmi.[17]

Lakshmi and Alakshmi never reside in the same place, for that which attracts one repels the other. Alakshmi is said to be frightened away by

the sound of sacred chanting and the sweet smell of incense. She is said
to be drawn instead to homes "where the family members argue constantly with one another," where "neither Shiva nor Vishnu is honored
ceremonially," where the inhabitants are "deluded," "lethargic," "glutton-
ous," and "neglectful of the home," where "guests are not cared for appro-
priately," and where "adults partake of food in the presence of children
without feeding them as well." The extensive exemplification of Alakshmi's
whereabouts demonstrates the ways in which the inauspicious may pervade
worldly existence, manifesting in all four of the "wealths." In her aspect as
Atula, she manifests as either the extreme denial of or the obsessive indul-
gence in pleasure.[18] As Daridra, she embodies not only the lack of material
goods but also the greed that springs from miserliness, hoarding, and fear
that there is never enough; she is poverty of the spirit and poverty of the
creative imagination. Akirti entails the neglect of dharma, the observance of
which fosters respect, and she attaches herself to one who shuns responsibilities toward the home, family, ancestors, community, and the gods.

The continued invocation of Shri Lakshmi, especially through the
chanting of sacred songs, is said to keep away the inauspicious Alakshmi
in any of her forms. Thus Lord Indra sings:

> Alakshmi, repository of penury and strife,
> Never gains entrance into those homes
> Whose inhabitants offer songs to Shri.[19]

Successfully Engaging the Goddess of Abundance

Lakshmi and Alakshmi are opposites, each bearing the kernel of the
other's name and identity. Auspiciousness and inauspiciousness cannot
inhabit the same space, but they can be very close. Seemingly without
warning, Alakshmi may appear where Lakshmi once stood. In part this
has to do with Lakshmi's cancala nature: as she can be "fickle" and
"capricious," her invocatory verses therefore beseech her not only to
arrive but to stay, to be "steadfast." If Lady Luck is fickle, the message
is that the acquisition of wealth, of glory, of Lakshmi herself, is part of a
continuous movement of energy, an evocation of the fluid qualities of
the goddess. To receive the blessings of this goddess, one must be able to
step into her effervescent energy field. The "steadfastness" of Lakshmi
must be invoked and generated continuously. Lakshmi flees when the
movement and intention of the polishing, of stirring her up, lose their

momentum, forgotten to laziness, apathy, fear, hoarding, circumstances of decay; when one's actions and thoughts, whether through neglect or default, become aligned and hide behind the opaque and stagnant energy of Alakshmi.

The seeming paradox of steadfastness and movement may be explained through Lakshmi's quality of *sattva* ("dynamic equipoise"). This is the ebullience, not frozen stagnancy, that comes from the harmonious balancing of pleasure, wealth, and sacred ceremony. She dwells in the giving and receiving of gifts, of nourishment, and of pleasure; in the commercial exchange of goods and services; and in the ritual exchange of offerings and boons. Therefore, when Lakshmi is called Cancala, this recapitulates the bright and sparkling quality of her presence: that which is scintillating may be difficult to capture, but it is exquisitely enticing. It is in resplendence that the true nature of Lakshmi expresses itself, ever pulsating with the essence of life. One attracts Lakshmi by engaging in her energy. And one sustains Lakshmi by engaging in the conscious awareness, appreciation, and invocation of her presence.

Notes

1. "Meditation for Visualization of the Deity," from the *Shri Mahalakshmi Hṛidayam* ("The Secret Heart of Lakshmi"). The translations of these verses and all others in this chapter are original translations of the author. For the complete Sanskrit texts of these songs and their translations, see Constantina Rhodes, *Invoking Lakshmi: The Goddess of Wealth in Song and Ceremony* (Albany: State University of New York Press, 2010).

2. Detailed discussions of the early iconography of the Indian lotus goddess may be found in a number of excellent sources, such as (listed alphabetically) Ananda K. Coomaraswamy, *Yaksas: Essays in the Water Cosmology*, rev. ed., edited by Paul Schroeder (Delhi: Oxford University Press, 1993), 155–160; S. K., *Elephant in Indian Art and Mythology* (Atlantic Highlands, NJ: Humanities Press, 1983), 19–24; David Kinsley, *The Goddesses' Mirror: Visions of the Divine from East and West* (Albany: State University of New York Press, 1989), 53–70; David Kinsley, *Hindu Goddesses: Visions of the Divine Feminine in the Hindu Religious Tradition* (Berkeley: University of California Press, 1986), 19–22; Curt Maury, *Folk Origins of Indian Art* (New York: Columbia University Press, 1969), 101–126; Miranda Shaw, *Buddhist Goddesses of India* (Princeton, NJ: Princeton University Press, 2006), 94–109; O. P. Singh, *Iconography of Gaja-Lakshmi* (Varanasi: Bharati Prakashan, 1983), 24–58; D. C. Sircar, *Studies in the Religious Life of Ancient and Medieval China* (Delhi: Motilal Banarsidass, 1971), 94–104; *Vāstu Śāstra*, ed. and trans. Shukla, 311–312; and Zimmer, *Myths and Symbols*, 90–102.

3. *Lakṣmī Sūkta* (*Hymn to Lakshmi*), 1; Rhodes, *Invoking Lakshmi*.

4. For details of the independent identities of the two goddesses in the Vedic period, see Gonda, *Aspects of Early Visnuism*, 176–225.

5. The earliest and most complete version of this story occurs in *Vishnu Purana*.

6. The Sanskrit word *amṛta* and the English word *immortal* are close cognates.

7. *Praise-Song for the Lotus Goddess* (*Kamalā Stotra*), 8; Rhodes, *Invoking Lakshmi*.

8. *Song for Lakshmi, Gracious Bestower of Blessings* (*Prasannavaradā Śrī Lakṣmī Stotra*), 10. Pradyumna is an incarnation of Kāmadeva, born to Lakshmi and Vishnu in their forms as Rukmini and Krishna.

9. *The Heavenly Gods' Praise-Song for Lakshmi* (*Śrī Daivakṛta Lakṣmī Stotra*), 6, 7; Rhodes, *Invoking Lakshmi*.

10. *Song for Lakshmi, Gracious Bestower of Blessings*, 17; Rhodes, *Invoking Lakshmi*.

11. Atulā and other aspects of the inauspicious will be discussed below.

12. *Lord Indra's Song for Lakshmi* (*Devarāja Indrakṛta Lakṣmī Stotra*), 9; Rhodes, *Invoking Lakshmi*.

13. See, for example, *Eight Verses Praising Mahalakshmi* (*Mahālakṣmyaṣṭakam Stotram*), 4.

14. *Lord Indra's Song for Lakshmi*, 5, 6; Rhodes, *Invoking Lakshmi*.

15. Kane, *History of Dharmaśāstra*, vol. 2, pt. 2 (1941), 1215, and vol. 3 (1946), 79.

16. *Gautamī-mahātmya* 67, 2–3 (pt. 4 of the *Brahma Purana*).

17. *Linga Purana* 6.1–7, 15–18.

18. Ibid., 6.8–14, 38–42, 69b–75.

19. *Lord Indra's Song for Lakshmi*, 31, 32; Rhodes, *Invoking Lakshmi*.

Bibliography

Sanskrit Texts and Translations

Brahma Purana. Translated by a Board of Scholars. Ancient Indian Tradition and Mythology Series, vols. 33–36. Delhi: Motilal Banarsidass, 1985–1986.

Linga Purana. Translated by A Board of Scholars. Ancient Indian Tradition and Mythology Series, vols. 5–6. Delhi: Motilal Banarsidass, 1973.

Sri Laksmi Upasana. Edited by Pandit Rajesh Dixit. Delhi: Dehati Pustak Bhandar, *samvat* 2032 [CE 1974/1975].

Vastu-Sastra: Hindu Canons of Iconography and Painting. Vol. 2. Edited and translated by D. N. Shukla. New Delhi: Munshiram Manoharlal, 1993.

Vishnu Purana: A System of Hindu Mythology and Tradition. Translated by H. H. Wilson. Calcutta: Punthi Pustak, 1961.

Secondary Sources

Bailly, Constantina Rhodes. "Auspicious Glances: Decoding the Magnificent Paradox of Hindu 'Idol Worship.'" *Mythosphere: A Journal for Image, Myth, and Symbol* 2, no. 3 (2000): 269–283.

Bailly, Constantina Rhodes. "The Majestic Essence of Sweetness: Exploring the Radha-Laksmi Relationship." *Journal of Vaisnava Studies* 10, no. 1 (Fall 2001): 27–50.

Bailly, Constantina Rhodes. "Sri-Laksmi: Majesty of the Hindu King." In *Goddesses Who Rule*, ed. Elisabeth Benard and Beverly Moon, 133–145. New York: Oxford University Press, 2000.

Coomaraswamy, Ananda K. "Early Indian Iconography: No. 2, Sri-Laksmi." *Eastern Art* 1 (1928–1929): 175–189.

Dhal, Upendra Nath. *Goddess Laksmi: Origin and Development.* 2nd rev. ed. Delhi: Eastern Book Linkers, 1995.

Gonda, Jan. *Aspects of Early Visnuism.* 2nd ed. Delhi: Motilal Banarsidass, 1969.

Kane, P[andurang] V[aman]. *History of Dharmasastra: Ancient and Mediaeval Religious and Civil Law.* 5 vols. Poona [Pune]: Bhandarkar Oriental Research Institute, 1930–1958.

Kumar, P. Pratap. *The Goddess Laksmi: The Divine Consort in South Indian Vaisnava Tradition.* Atlanta: Scholars Press, 1997.

Narayanan, Vasudha. "The Goddess Sri: Blossoming Lotus and Breast Jewel of Visnu." In *The Divine Consort: Radha and the Goddesses of India*, ed. John Stratton Hawley and Donna Marie Wulff, 224–237. Boston: Beacon Press, 1982.

Zimmer, Heinrich. *Myths and Symbols in Indian Art and Civilization.* Edited by Joseph Campbell. Bollingen Series 6. Princeton, NJ: Princeton University Press, 1972.

2

Kali: Goddess of Life, Death, and Transcendence

June McDaniel

The Hindu goddess Kali is a strange and mercurial figure. She is portrayed as a terrifying death goddess and a nurturing mother, a black hag at the battlefield and a young and innocent girl. In northwestern India she is thin and ugly, while in West Bengal she is voluptuous, with large eyes and full lips. In some areas of India, she is a tribal and village goddess who protects a group of people or a geographical region, and an ancestress who grants the desires of her people. She is also a yogic goddess of death and transcendence, who gives the gift of liberation to her followers. The tantric Kali dances at the cremation ground, wearing her necklace of skulls and belt of human hands, while the devotional Kali gives blessing and protection, and entrance into heaven, from beneath a crown of white solapith and layers of gold tinsel and flowers. She is eternal yet ever changing. These perspectives on Kali exist throughout Hindu Shaktism, the worship of the goddess in India.

Origins of the Goddess

The word *Kali* comes from the Sanskrit term for "black," *kala*. Most historians find the origin of the goddess Kali in the Sanskrit great tradition, which involves the most ancient texts of India, understood as revealed by the gods and written by sages. In the Vedic texts, Kali has been associated with the goddess of night Ratri and with the terrible Nirrtidevi of the Satapatha and Aitareya Brahmanas, who is black and fond of cremation grounds. The name Kali is first found in the *Mundaka Upanishad*, one of the major Upanishads or Vedic commentaries, where Kali is the name of one of the seven tongues of the sacrificial fire or *yajna*. Her first mention as a deity is in the *Kathaka Grihya Sutra*, another Vedic commentary. The dating of these commentaries is much debated, but a rough estimate might be 1000–500 BCE. Kali is described in the *Mahabharata*, seen by Asvatthama when he entered the Pandava camp at night to kill the soldiers. She had bloodshot eyes and four arms, wore red garlands, carried nooses, and was terrifying in appearance.

A major source for Kali's myths and stories is the set of Hindu sacred texts known as the Puranas. Again, their dating is subject to scholarly debate, but most scholars estimate their writing as somewhere between 400 CE and 1400 CE. In the *Agni* and *Garuda* Puranas, Kali is described as giving success in war and conquest of enemies. In the *Bhagavata Purana*, she can give sons and also revenge. According to the *Vayu Purana*, the god Shiva was of twofold nature, both male and female. Shakti or his female nature also had two aspects: one half was black and the other half white. The black or fierce nature included such goddesses as Kali, Durga, Chandi, Chamunda, Bhadrakali, and Bhairavi, while the white or peaceful nature included Uma, Gauri, Parvati, Maheshvari, Lalita, and Annapurna. The fierce forms became important as part of the Kali tradition, and the goddess or Devi in fierce form is seen in such medieval texts as the *Markandeya*, *Skanda*, *Devi*, *Garuda*, and *Shiva* Puranas, as well as such tantric encyclopedias as the *Tantrasara* and the *Saradatilaka*. In the *Vamana Purana*, the goddess Parvati (called Kali by her husband Shiva because of her dark complexion) grows angry and does austerities to rid herself of this dark aspect. She becomes Gauri, the golden one, while her darker aspect becomes the battle goddess Kaushiki, and later Kali.

Kali is described as an emanation from the goddess Durga in the Chandi or Devi Mahatmya section of the *Markandeya Purana*. When Ambika (Durga titled as "Divine Mother") became angry at her enemies, her face became dark as ink, and Kali emerged from her forehead. She was armed with a sword and noose, and a skull-topped staff, wearing a garland of skulls, and clad in a tiger's skin. She was terrifying, with her tongue lolling out and her deep-sunk reddish eyes; she filled the regions of the sky with her roars. She devoured the hosts of the *asuras* or demons, the enemies of the gods. Many stories of Kali's origin are variants of her emanation from the anger of the warrior goddess Durga in this text.

According to the *Mahabhagavata Purana*, Kali chose to incarnate as the god Krishna. Shiva had told Kali that he had a desire: he wanted to make love with Kali in a male form and himself in female form. This could best be done by his being born as a female and her being born in male form. Kali kept this in mind. When Brahma came to her and worshiped her as the goddess and asked her to get rid of such demonic tyrants as Kamsa and Duryodhana—for they were disturbing the goddess Earth—she agreed to become incarnate on earth. She would be born as Krishna and save earth from the demons. Shiva could then be incarnate as Radha, Rukmini, and other of Krishna's wives and consorts, and he could get his wish fulfilled.

In the *Linga Purana*, Shiva asks Parvati to destroy the demon Daruka, who could only be killed by a woman. Parvati enters Shiva's body and takes the poison that is stored in his throat from the time when he saved the earth by swallowing the poison that arose with the churning of the Ocean of Milk at the beginning of time. With this, she is transformed into the terrifying Kali. Accompanied by destructive spirits (*pisacas*), she attacks Daruka and his armies. Kali defeats them, but gets so angry in the battle that she threatens to destroy the world. Shiva comes to calm her, and the world is saved. Also in the *Linga Purana*, Kali is part of Shiva's army as he goes off to defeat another demon. She wears skulls and an elephant hide, holds a trident, and drinks the blood of demons. She is called the daughter of the mountain god Himalaya, thus linking her with Parvati and Uma.

This kinship to Himalaya is seen much later on in the *agamani* and *vijaya* songs of the 18th and 19th centuries. These poems and songs describe the difficult marriage of Himalaya's daughter, variously called Kalika, Uma, and Parvati, to her husband Shiva. Shiva does not stay at home with his wife, but rather goes off to the mountains to dance wild dances with his weird followers, take *bhang* (a form of hashish), and drink alcohol. He is not willing to get a job, so his wife is poor and lonely. In these songs Kali becomes a sympathetic figure, a neglected wife who tries to retain her happiness and her honor. In their humanizing of Kali, the *agamani* and *vijaya* songs show the later influence of devotional Shaktism.

Kali in Later Literature

In early Sanskrit literature generally, Kali is negative and devouring. Bana's *Harsa-carita* describes her as black like the charcoal of the funeral piles and covered with blood, eager to swallow all creation as a mouthful. The *Khila Harivamsa* focuses on a goddess fond of meat and wine, worshiped by Adivasi and low-caste groups, and in Bhavabhuti's *Malatimadhava*, a terrifying goddess is described who is worshiped with human sacrifice. She is dark and violent (*ugra*) and dances a mad dance of death with Shiva at her temple by a burning ground. In the seventh-century drama *Kadambari* by Banabhatta, the dark goddess Chandi (associated with Kali) was worshiped by the Sabara tribal people.

In the Hindu tantric texts, Kali becomes a goddess who demands much but gives much. The *Yogini Tantra*, the *Kamakhya Tantra*, and the *Niruttara Tantra* call Kali the greatest of the wisdom-forms of Mahadevi, the great goddess, and the *Niguma Kalpatara* and the *Picchila Tantra* describe her mantra as the most powerful of all mantras. The *Mahanirvana Tantra* calls her the original form of all things, Adya Shakti Kali, the "Kali of Primordial Power." The tantric texts place great emphasis on the many forms of the goddess.

Forms and Images of Kali

Kali is worshiped in several major ways in India. The first and probably oldest type of Kali worship is found in rural areas of India; it may be called folk or tribal Shaktism. It involves the worship of both tribal goddesses (often in the form of an old woman or ancestress) and local Hindu goddesses (especially those understood to exist within natural forms, such as rocks and rivers, which are believed to be forms or manifestations of Kali). These goddesses are amoral and often dangerous, and require propitiation by worshipers. But once they are shown proper respect, they become benevolent and willing to help their worshipers. This form of Kali may possess a medium, usually female, or appear in dreams. The goals of this type of worship tend to be the healing of disease or discord in the group, fertility, protection from danger, and the ability to prophesy and to exorcize troublesome spirits and ancestors.

The tribal Kali, dark and powerful, may be worshiped as a *gramadevata* ("village goddess") or an ancestress. She is sometimes dangerous and threatening, sometimes protective. Kali may appear in the form of an old woman, whose knowledge is reflected in her years, as well as the forms of mother and warrior. As mother she grants fertility and happiness; as warrior she grants protection from death and threat; as old woman she teaches tribal traditions and gives revelations.

Another form of Kali worship is seen in tantric or yogic Shaktism. Kali is reached by meditation and visualization, and by ritual worship, making use of mantras, *mudras* or hand positions, and *yantras* or visual diagrams, usually understood to be symbolic maps of the spiritual worlds. Yogic practice is often involved, especially in Kundalini yoga, a form of yoga in which the energy centers of the body or chakras have associated deities, colors, and powers. There are two major subtypes of this strand, here called folk or popular tantra, and classical or scholastic tantra.

In folk or popular tantra, the emphasis is upon ritual practice, direct experience, and pragmatic results. Kali gives supernatural abilities (*siddhi*) and power (*sakti*), and she appears to the practitioner in the forest or burning ground. She gives the gift of supernatural power. In classical or scholastic tantra, the Kali is symbolic of liberation (*moksa*) and is understood to be a personification of infinite consciousness (*brahman*). She is able to grant the classical *tantrika* or practitioner the gift of omniscience (*brahmajnana*) or liberation, as well as spiritual insight and knowledge. Her forms, whether beautiful or terrifying, are understood to be illusory, a part of her play of illusion. Classical tantra has a strong literary focus, and the term "*tantra*" refers primarily to a set of texts. The major Bengali school of classical tantra is known as the Kali-kula, or lineage of Kali. The goal of classical tantra tends to be liberation from rebirth, and knowledge of ultimate truth or *brahman*.

Love of Kali

The third and most widespread style of Kali worship is that of Shakta devotion, or Kali *bhakti*. In medieval times, Shaktism was a small religion practiced by groups of tantric yogis, until the puranic texts popularized the powers and adventures of the goddess, and later poetry portrayed her as beautiful and loving. The 18th-century *bhakti* poets described her as a loving mother and a young girl, and devotional worship grew around these images. Devotees began to worship Kali with passionate intensity. She became Kali Ma ("Mother Kali"), the universal mother or innocent girl, who may be frightening on the outside but is inwardly loving and compassionate. Shakta devotion also values intense love of the deity rather than simple obedience. There are three subtypes of Kali devotion.

The first subtype is emotional *bhakti*. In this type, the goddess has a variety of roles: mother, child, friend, lover. She expects passionate devotion and dependence from her worshipers, who are most often described as her children. The most intense love is not romantic love, but rather parent/child love, according to Bengali Shaktas or followers of the goddess. Some devotees begin with fearing her terrible forms but end up loving her when they see the sweetness within her. The devotee loves passionately; he or she swings between elation and depression, loving the world because the goddess is present there or hating it because she has not appeared. The ideal attitude is total dependence on the goddess, with love evoking divine vision or *darshan*, in which goddess and devotee meet and recognize each other. Many miracle stories show Kali's love toward her chosen devotees. She grants salvation and entrance into her heaven to those who love her, and she appreciates their poetry and songs. Worship may be on a small scale, with household altars and family ceremonies, or it may be on a larger community scale, with elaborate shrines, jeweled statues, and sacred food piled high at festivals such as Kali Puja. Devotees tell the stories of the goddesses and read from the Puranas, or meet to sing *kali kirtana*, hymns to Kali. Devotional poets such as Ramprasad Sen popularized this form of Kali worship.

The second subtype of Kali devotion is political Shakta *bhakti* or Shakta nationalism. In this type, the goddess represents the land. She is Mother India, Bharat Mata or Bharat Devi. She is like the folk goddess who represents the village, but on a larger scale. She calls upon her children to rescue her when the land is in trouble, and they do so by protest, war, revolution, or other political activities. From the mid-19th century, the goddess has become a symbol of Indian nationalism, the Divine Mother who is herself the land of India. Kali has been particularly linked with the city of Calcutta.

The third subtype of Kali worship is Shakta universalism. In this approach Kali is a loving mother who is also infinite consciousness. Though the mother is the chosen symbol for this mystical state, understood to be identical to *brahman* or the ocean of consciousness, other deities and symbols may also represent it. In the 20th-century literature of this tradition, Kali is more frequently described as a philosophical concept than as a person. Shakta universalism has been strongly influenced by the 19th-century Bengali saint Ramakrishna Paramahamsa of Dakshineshwar and his disciple Vivekananda. It is still an important perspective among Shaktas outside of India, especially in the United States. Modern popular Shaktism echoes this universalist sentiment, saying that the ultimate aim of all religions is the same. Though Ramakrishna stated that all religions of the world were valid paths to the divine reality, and all forms of the deity were equally legitimate, he preferred Kali. Though all forms of religious rituals ultimately lead to the same state, he preferred worship of the goddess.

Visualizations of the Goddess

Kali takes on many forms in Hindu tradition. Her name means "black" or "dark-colored," and her darkness is associated with both death and time. Her most popular images are dark ones: as the four-armed Dakshinakali and the ten-armed Mahakali. As dark can cover a range of colors, Kali's statues and pictures are often colored dark blue, sometimes purple, as well as black. Her eyes are red, her hair hangs loose, and her tongue juts out of her mouth. She may be naked or wearing a tiger skin, and she usually has a skirt of human arms and a necklace of human heads. Jackals and snakes may accompany her, and in one popular image she stands upon the corpse of the god Shiva. In her four-armed form, she carries a sword, a trident, a head, and a bowl or skull-cup. In her ten-armed form, she also has ten heads and ten legs. Each object she carries represents a power that she possesses.

The many visualizations or *dhyanas* of Kali describe different aspects for the devotee to contemplate. In the tantric encyclopedia *Tantrasara*, the four-armed Kali is described as smiling and full of blood, with three red eyes, and she stands on Shiva's heart. He is lying like a corpse, yet he is involved with her in reverse or *viparita* intercourse, in which the woman is above the man. In another visualization in the *Tantrasara*, Kali wears a sacred thread that is a snake, she is drunk on alcohol, and she is standing within a cremation fire. In other descriptions she is soaked with a shower of nectar, wearing matted hair, and making a loud roaring noise. Sometimes she stands on a human corpse, and sometimes she stands on Shiva as a corpse. In the *Kalika Purana*, she is a young and beautiful goddess riding a lion, four-armed, and holding a sword and blue lotuses.

A few of the more popular forms and names include fierce Dakshina-kali (or Shyamakali), who has four hands, a garland of heads, black skin, and stands naked on Shiva with corpses as earrings and a belt of hands. Smashanakali is similar, but surrounded by jackals and yoginis, and wears a snake as a sacred thread. Siddhakali has three eyes, drinks nectar from a skull, has deep blue skin and the sun and moon as earrings. Mahakali has five faces, each with three eyes. She holds a spear and trident, a bow and arrows, and a sword and shield. Guhyakali is the color of clouds, with a snake necklace, a crescent on her head, a smiling face (some sources give her ten faces), Shiva as a child at her feet, and behind her (or above her head) the thousand-headed serpent king. Chamundakali has a pleasant face, holds a sword and long bone topped with a skull, a noose, and human head, wears a tiger skin, and sits upon a corpse. She is also worshiped in the form of a yantra or symbolic geometrical form.

Like Krishna in the *Bhagavad Gita*, Kali also has a universal form (*virat rupa* or *visvarupa*). The universal form of a deity is his or her aspect as greatest deity of the cosmos, representing all worlds and all powers. In the

Kurma Purana, Kali/Parvati revealed her universal form to her father, Himalaya. As her father was frightened, she assumed her original form, with the fragrance and complexion of a blue lotus. In the *Devi Mahatmya*, she expanded her form to frighten the demon Mahishasura.

According to one popular story, while sitting at the burning ground the Shakta sage Krishnananda Agambagisha had a vision of the goddess Kali. She told him that Shakta tantra in Bengal flowed like an underground river that was becoming polluted, and he needed to cleanse it. He was to worship and popularize a new form in which to worship her. When he asked which form he was to worship, she told him that it would be the image of the first woman that he saw the next morning.

When he awoke at dawn the next morning and walked toward the Ganges River, he saw a woman with dark skin at the entrance of her hut. One foot was on the step of her hut, the other was on the ground. Her right palm was full of cow dung, and she held her hand to make sure that the cow dung did not fall, a position that had the fingers in the mudra or hand position of fearlessness. Her left hand applied a coat of wet mud onto the wall. Her dark hair hung long, and she wore a short sari. When she saw Krishnananda standing in front of her, she stuck her tongue out in embarrassment and turned away. This became a very popular image of Kali, with an image of Shiva lying under her feet added later on.

The meaning of Shiva lying at Kali's feet has been much debated. The popular view is that Kali is a good wife who touched Shiva with her foot accidentally, a violation of respect and purity, and she is embarrassed at this breach of etiquette. Some Shaktas say that Shiva fell at the goddess's feet in wonder when he saw her create and destroy the world. And at the end of time, Kali dances upon the corpse of the world and the power of time, thus she dances upon Shiva in his form as a corpse. In the *Mahanirvana Tantra*, Shiva calls Kali the source of the world, the origin of all form, formless yet with form, the Supreme Adya Kali who existed as darkness before the beginning of things. She is the creator, preserver, and destroyer of the universe, and the source of the power of the gods. According to Samkhya philosophy, Shiva represents *purusha*, pure potential that cannot act. He needs *prakriti*, an active force that gives birth to all and accomplishes all, to generate creation. Kali represents the creative force, bringing the universe into existence, yet is linked to Shiva as manifest action is linked to its potential being. Shiva also represents *Brahman*, pure consciousness, while Kali is *Sakti*, action and creation, or *Maya*, the power of illusion.

In these cases Shiva is usually portrayed as the husband of Kali. In Kerala, however, Shiva is Kali's father, who gave birth to her in a ray of light from his third eye. In Kali's form as Tara at Tarapith, she nurses the infant Shiva, giving him her breast milk to save him from death by poison. Shiva is thus in the role of her child. According to other stories, when Kali does a dance of destruction and is about to destroy the world, Shiva becomes a crying infant, and Kali stops her dance to feed and care for him.

While the goddess Kali traditionally threatens order and stability, she also represents a transcendent order; thus her roles and images vary. In the texts she is ugly, with a black and emaciated body, matted hair, and snakes, but in her statues and posters she is young and beautiful, with flirtatious eyes, large breasts, a narrow waist, and a big smile. She may be deep blue, sky blue, or even white, with delicate pink hands and feet; all are beneficent and auspicious forms of the goddess. For many Shaktas, this beautiful form is her real and inner form, with the ugly image existing only to frighten the unworthy. If you are her enemy or do not respect her, the black Kali of the burning ground will take revenge. But if you are devoted, she is the beautiful white Kali, whose graceful form will come to you at the time of your death, and she will smile lovingly as she takes you to Kalisthan or Manidvipa (the Island of Jewels) to dwell on her lap forever.

As a devotional goddess, Kali is mother of the universe and the beloved parent of those who worship her. She is a loving deity, and her dark side is justified by the presence of death in nature; Kali represents what is true, not what people would like to see. She is described as loving, sweet, and compassionate in the poetry written about her in the Bengali Shakta tradition. She is also capable of saving her devotees from their own karma, their difficulties due to bad actions in previous lives, sweeping them out of the ghostly worlds between incarnations and taking them to her paradise.

In the *Mahabhagavata Purana*, Kali's heaven of Kalisthan is full of jewels and surrounded by walls with four gates in the four directions. In the middle is a lion throne, full of gold and jewels. The goddess sits on it, served by sixty-four yoginis. Toward the north is a forest full of flowers and singing birds, and in the east is a lake full of golden lotuses and other flowers. According to the *Devi Bhagavata Purana*, Kali's heaven is only open to women. During earthly worship, the devotee should give offerings to brahmins, young girls and boys, the public, and the poor, seeing all of them as forms of the goddess. When the worshiper dies, and he goes to Kali's heaven of Manidvipa, he must take on the form of a woman to enter, in order to echo the form of the goddess. No men are allowed in the goddess's heaven.

Adya Shakti Kali and the Mahavidyas

A popular form of Kali worshiped in Calcutta is Adya Shakti Kali, or Kali as primordial power. Adya Shakti Kali is also present in some tantras, especially the *Mahanirvana Tantra*. Because she devours Kala or time, she is Kali, the original form of all things, and because she is the origin of and devourer of all things, she is called Adya Kali. She is without beginning yet the beginning of all, creator, protector, and destroyer. She is worshiped on the new moon night, with the *pancamakara* or five forbidden things—meat, fish, wine, parched grain, and ritual sex. The worshiper is believed to gain wisdom and wealth and strength, and to attain all of his or her desires. According to some modern worshipers of Adya Shakti Kali in West Bengal, she is a *yuga devi*, a goddess of the apocalypse. Now it is the *kali yuga*, the age of iron that represents the end of the universe and the close of time, and the presiding goddess is Adya Shakti Kali, who revealed herself late in the *yuga* to preside over the great disasters of the end-times.

The Adya Shakti form of Kali that has been popularized is primarily a tantric form of the goddess. There are many tantric forms of Kali. The *Tantraloka* lists 13 forms of the goddess, while the Tantrasara mentions nine forms. However, the ten major tantric forms of the Kali are known as the Mahavidyas. The Mahavidyas, or wisdom goddesses, are usually understood to be forms or emanations of the goddess Kali. They are specialized for gifts in certain areas, and each has her own priests who have one Mahavidya form as personal deity (*istadevi*). Kali is the most important Mahavidya in the Kali-kula tradition. The ten Mahavidyas are forms of the goddess Shakti, Kali, or Sati, and were said in the Puranas to have originated at the time of Daksha's great mythical sacrifice.

According to the *Brihaddharma Purana*, the goddess Sati's father was having a great public sacrifice, and he did not invite Sati or her husband. Sati wished to go to the sacrifice, and her husband Shiva did not want her to go. Fire flashed from her third eye, and she was transformed into Kali (or Shyama, the dark one). When he saw this, Shiva was terrified, and he tried to escape. However, the emanated forms of Sati blocked all of the ten directions. These forms were the ten Mahavidyas. A longer description comes from the *Mahabhagavata Purana*. According to this text, when Daksha's daughter Sati was not invited to her father's sacrifice and wanted to go anyway, Shiva told her it would cause great trouble and refused to allow her to go. To emphasize her desire to go, she split into ten terrifying forms, frightening him into agreeing that she should go. It was at this sacrifice that Sati committed suicide, with her death as the distant origin of the later practice of *sati* or "suttee," as the early British literature spelled it.

According to various sacred texts of the Kali-kula tradition, Kali gives both pleasure and liberation during the Kali yuga. She is worshiped by gods and sages, and her worship is necessary for any spiritual accomplishments. The *Tararahasya* states that seeking liberation without worshiping Kali is like trying to satisfy hunger without eating, or like trying to see oneself in a mirror while keeping both eyes closed. As a sea is vast compared to a river, so Kali is vast compared to the other deities, and all of the Mahavidyas which were generated from Adya Kalika also exist eternally within her. While Kali is black to earthly eyes, she is radiant in her true form, which is great brilliance (*mahajyoti*).

The Pan-Indian Kali

As a goddess who is both pan-Indian and local, Kali has many titles and associated stories. Traditionally, in West Bengal she is worshiped as Dakshinakali or Tara, in Kerala as Bhadrakali or Bhagavati, in Kashmir as Tripurasundari, and in Nepal as Guhya Kali. These deities may be equated with Kali or understood as each other's manifestations or emanations.

In Kerala she is the warrior goddess Bhadrakali, a form of Bhagavati, the great goddess who is both benign and ferocious. She is independent, said to have come from Shiva's third eye when it flashed with destructive fury. Kali is associated with the South Indian goddess Kottavai, who rides her tiger into the battlefield. She is a protector who appears in possession dances and speaks through male oracles, and her stories are told in dramatic plays. Her major dramas follow the story in the *Linga Purana* of her conquest of the demon Darika in a swordfight. However, in the Kerala version, Darika's widow curses Kali with smallpox, and Kali's statue is usually dark with white smallpox marks along with fangs and snakes. She is a virgin, associated with heat and the dry season, and she is worshiped with teak resin and sandalwood paste to cool and calm her. Bhadrakali is also the cause of epidemic disease in Kerala.

In the Panjab area of northwestern India, Kali is a form of Seranvali, the lion-rider. She is the mother goddess whose forms are light (as Vaishno Devi) and dark (as Kali Devi). Kali is a fierce and independent goddess, also called Amba, Durga, and Kalkattevali, a title associated with the Kalighat temple in Calcutta and goat sacrifice. She is associated with jackals and the cremation grounds, but is gracious and can give gifts and blessings.

In the Vindhya hills of central India, Kali is an aspect of the great goddess, or Adi Shakti Mahadevi. Her major form is called Vindhyavasini. She is associated with Uma and the dark goddess Kaushiki, and worshiped through readings of the Devi Mahatmya. As Kali, she is offered goats and chickens in sacrifice and gives both liberation and earthly happiness. She is understood philosophically as Mahakali, the great mother who is the origin of the world.

In Sri Lanka, off the southern tip of India, Kali's role has expanded with the civil war that has been ongoing there since the 1980s. Traditionally, Kali was worshiped in temples by priests, and she would possess certain practitioners (called deity dancers or *tevyam atumakkal*). She would appear in various local forms, such as Pattirakaliyamman and Virammakali. With the civil war, there are more vows to the goddess, and increased austerities (such as walking on beds of hot coals, and piercing the body with iron fishhooks and small tridents). Kali's presence is believed to instill courage and make people better able to deal with the tragedies of war. Kali is understood to be the best deity to help people respond to violence.

Shakta Theology

Theologically, understandings of the identity and origin of the goddess differ. Some Shakta traditions say that all goddesses are manifestations of the same great goddess, Adi or Adya Shakti, or Parama Shakti, while others say that the many goddesses are separate and unique, or sometimes that they are manifestations of one or more gods. There is Shakta monism, in which all phenomena are the parts of the goddess, whose deepest nature is *brahman* or universal consciousness. There is Shakta monotheism, in which all other deities are aspects or emanations of a single goddess who has created the universe. There is Shakta dualism, in which the divine couple made up of Shiva and Shakti constitutes the primordial deities. There is Shakta polytheism, in which many goddesses hold great power and sometimes compete for power and devotees with other goddesses or with male gods. And there is Shakta henotheism, where many goddesses are recognized as legitimate, but one is most powerful. This central goddess is often called Mahadevi, the great goddess. In many tantras Kali is the primordial or most authentic form (*svarupa*) of the great goddess.

One of Kali's most famous devotees was Ramakrishna Paramahamsa of Dakshineshwar. Ramakrishna was a priest of the goddess Kali who saw her as the Cosmic Mother. He was born in the village of Kamarpukur, West Bengal, in 1836. He became a priest, worshiping in the grove of five sacred trees behind a Kali temple, and he had intense religious experiences that included paralysis, burning sensations, and the experience of beings entering and leaving his body. He said that visions came to him constantly, and that for six years he was unable to shut his eyes or sleep. He experimented with various forms of nontraditional spiritual practices and had visions of Kali as a goddess with a baby to which she had given birth, and a sword with which to kill it—a goddess of creation and destruction. According to some of his biographies, at one point he decided to commit suicide, and he had a vision of Kali that became well known. Ramakrishna had picked up a sword with which to kill himself, for the goddess would not appear to him. This threatened suicide motivated her to appear, in the form of a great ocean of consciousness, with shining waves rushing at him from all sides. He was caught up in it and experienced a state of pure bliss in which he felt the presence of the goddess.

Ramakrishna continued to have visions of Kali. As priest, he saw her statue as alive, and he would laugh and dance with it, joke with the statue and hold its hands, and lie down next to it at night. Sometimes he identified himself with Kali, and he would decorate himself with flowers and sandal paste. His employers and relatives thought that he was mad and tried different strategies to cure him: Ayurvedic medicine, exorcism, even a prostitute in case the madness was due sexual frustration. They also arranged a marriage for him with a young girl. However, his visions and trances continued. Ramakrishna practiced a variety of tantric rituals under the instructions of Bhairavi Brahmani, a woman who felt that his states of apparent madness showed sainthood. He also practiced Vaishnava rituals and later fell into extended trances under the teaching of the Vedantin Totapuri. He also briefly practiced Islam and Christianity. However, he remained a Shakta and a priest of Kali all his life, dancing and talking with the goddess, and acting as her beloved son. Many of his actions and statements echoed those of Ramprasad Sen, an earlier Bengali Shakta devotee.

Kali Outside India

Understandings of the goddess Kali outside India have changed over time. Kali was first described in the 17th- and 18th-century writings of travelers, missionaries, and merchants from Europe who had visited India. She was generally portrayed in negative terms, emphasizing her dark and frightening statues, the practice of animal sacrifice, and her association with the Thuggee criminal group. Later writers were more disturbed by tantric rituals associated with Kali, especially those involving sexuality. Some writers exaggerated and sensationalized her worship, coming up with the more imaginative understandings of Kali and her worship now termed "Orientalism." Such writers variously understood Kali as a symbol of primitive savagery or of "Eastern" wild sexuality and devil worship. Writers interested in the historical development of religion associated her with deities from other cultures, especially the goddesses of ancient Europe and the eastern Mediterranean.

However, greater interest was inspired in the late 19th century by the lectures of Swami Vivekananda, a disciple of Ramakrishna. He interpreted Shaktism and Vedanta for new followers in the United States and Europe, emphasizing the symbolic nature of Hindu ritual and its universal appeal. In the early 20th century, Sir John Woodroffe wrote about tantra under the pen name Arthur Avalon. He interpreted Kali and tantra generally through a Vedanta perspective, with sexuality as symbolic rather than literal, and he described Shakta tantra as a useful philosophical approach. Later in the 20th century historians of religion, art historians, psychologists, poets, and anthropologists explored Kali traditions.

An alternative scholarship of Kali may be found in modern New Age sources, such as magazines, books, artwork, and Web sites. In these sources Kali is reinterpreted for a largely non-Indian audience. She becomes a personification of female destruction and rage, or of uninhibited sexuality, or a figure of the dark universal unconscious. In these adaptations, traditional ritual is no longer required, and Kali becomes a new deity with new forms of activities and stories. She represents a transcendence of limiting ideas like purity and impurity, sin and acceptable social behavior; she rebels against patriarchal religions and their rules. She overcomes the fear of death and instinct and gives a positive side to anger, sexuality, and intense emotion. In New Age Shaktism, Kali is associated with the dark goddesses from various religions: the Greek Hecate and the Gorgons, the Celtic Mórrigan, and the Babylonian Anath. She is a major figure for Shakti Wicca and some of the new Indo-Pagan traditions.

Thus Kali appears in many forms: terrifying goddess of death and night, tribal goddess of fertility, yogic goddess of transcendence, devotional goddess of love and mercy, the anger of Durga and the love of Shiva. For her devotees she is a protector from danger, guide of the soul in the afterlife, the mythic great goddess, and modern *tabula rasa* for archetypes and projections. She represents a living goddess tradition for modern feminists and an ancient figure of life and death.

Bibliography

Bhattacharyya, Narendranath. *History of the Sakta Religion.* New Delhi: Muhshiram Manoharlal, 1974.

Caldwell, Sarah. *Oh Terrifying Mother: Sexuality, Violence, and Worship of the Goddess Kali.* New Delhi: Oxford University Press, 1999.

Dasgupta, Sasibhusan. *Bharater Sakti-Sadhana O Sakta Sahitya.* Calcutta: Sahitya Samsad, 1960.

Erndl, Kathleen M. *Victory to the Mother: The Hindu Goddess of Northwest India in Myth, Ritual, and Symbol.* New York: Oxford University Press, 1993.

Hawley, John Stratton, and Donna Marie Wulf. *Devi: Goddesses of India.* Berkeley: University of California Press, 1996.

Jagadiswarananda, Swami, trans. *Devi Mahatmyam (Glory of the Divine Mother).* Mylapore: Sri Ramakrishna Math, 1953.

Kinsley, David R. *Hindu Goddesses: Visions of the Divine Feminine in the Hindu Religious Tradition.* Berkeley: University of California Press, 1988.

Kinsley, David R. *The Sword and the Flute: Kali and Krsna, Dark Visions of the Terrible and the Sublime in Hindu Mythology.* Berkeley: University of California Press, 1975.

Kumar, Pushpendra, ed. *Mahabhagavata Purana.* Delhi: Eastern Book Linkers, 1983.

McDaniel, June. *The Madness of the Saints: Ecstatic Religion in Bengal.* Chicago: University of Chicago Press, 1989.

McDaniel, June. *Offering Flowers, Feeding Skulls: Popular Goddess Worship in West Bengal.* New York: Oxford University Press, 2004.

McDermott, Rachel Fell. *Mother of My Heart, Daughter of My Dreams: Kali and Uma in the Devotional Poetry of Bengal.* New York: Oxford University Press, 2001.

McDermott, Rachel Fell, and Jeffrey J. Kripal, *Encountering Kali: In the Margins, at the Center, in the West.* Berkeley: University of California Press, 2003.

Sen, Dineshchandra. *The Bengali Ramayanas.* Calcutta: University of Calcutta Press, 1920.

Vijnanananda, Swami, trans. *Sri Mad Devi Bhagavatam.* New Delhi: Munshiram Manoharlal, 1977.

Warrrier, A. G. Krishna, trans. *The Sakta Upanishads.* Madras: Adyar Library and Research Center, 1967.

3

The Goddess Ganga: Her Power, Mythos, and Worldly Challenges

Kelly D. Alley

Water and rivers have held sacred value in religious and cultural traditions around the world since the dawn of civilizations. In India all rivers are feminine, and many are important goddesses in the Hindu traditions. Two of the most eminent river goddesses are the Ganga and Yamuna rivers; they share the values and characters of other goddesses in the Hindu traditions in that they are benefactors to the world, to humans and to all life. These goddesses are worshiped by Hindus across India and the world and in return have nourished civilizations and fed the cradle of Hindu and Buddhist pilgrimage culture in India for millennia.

Some of the most important centers of spiritual learning and healing have thrived along the banks of the Ganga and Yamuna rivers. At the Himalayan headwaters of the Ganga and of her sister goddess the Yamuna, sacred shrines at Tapavan, Gomukh, Bhojbasa, Gangotri, and Yamunotri mark the sources of the goddess's sacred power. These are sacred sites located up in the Himalayas and access to some of them requires rigorous hiking and high-altitude camping. The shrines of Kedarnath and Badrinath are the most visited and celebrate their position in the upper reaches of these watersheds. They draw pilgrims throughout the year and are sometimes visited by processions of devotees that make the long journey from the home villages. Farther downstream in the Ganga

Figure 3.1 The goddess of India's most important river is Ganga, whose sustaining powers are embodied in the waters of the river Ganges. Like other important water sources throughout the world, the Ganges is now endangered from overpopulation and resulting pollution. (Copyright Hrana Janto.)

basin are Uttarkashi, Rishikesh, and Haridwar, large towns that accommodate great numbers of pilgrims for important annual festivals. Along the plains lie Allahabad (whose ancient sacred name is Prayag) at the confluence of the Ganga and Yamuna rivers, and farther downstream on the Ganga the sacred city of Banaras. The sacred complex of Nadia is important for the history of Sanskrit learning and contemporary Krishna worship and Kalighat houses a temple dedicated to the goddess Kali. Along the river Yamuna are the sacred complexes of Paonta Sahib, Vrindavan, Mathura, Gokul and Bateshwar, all known for the presence of powerful gods and deities. Inland within the Ganga basin lie Vindhyachal and the Buddhist sites of Gaya, Rajgir, and Nalanda; these are reached by village roads that wind alongside paddy fields. At the pilgrimage centers

that border the two sacred rivers, pilgrims worship the goddesses Ganga
and Yamuna and carry away their water for worship and purification rituals in temples and in homes.[1]

According to the Hindu view, the sacred is not detached from the material (*bhautik*) realm of ecology and the built environment, but provides a
context for understanding the truth of the physical world. In general,
Hindu interpretations of sacred space describe intersections and conjunc-
tions between divine power and the physical world. Along the Ganga River
pilgrimage sites bring out the divine power of the goddess through
empowered physical spaces and by intersections of these spaces with the
flow of the river herself. In this way, Hindu mythologies and sacred texts
weave together understandings of sacred and natural ecology as if there
were no separation between them, at the same time portraying the encompassing power of the sacred to invigorate the natural and physical worlds.

To Hindu devotees, Ganga is a goddess who absolves worldly impurities and rejuvenates the cosmos with her purificatory power. She is a
mother who cleans up human sin and mess with loving forgiveness. Her
sister, Yamuna, is also a mother who sustains and provides, but Yamuna
is more concerned with the blessings of this life than Ganga, whose role
is purification and preparation for death.[2] Ganga's immanent form as
water (*jala*) is used as the central element of Hindu ritual practice, and
ablutions or *snan* in the early morning hours are crucial for residents
and pilgrims in sacred cities along the river. Hindus immerse the ashes
or bones of the cremated in the Ganga to ensure their safe journey to
the realm of the ancestors. When used for *puja* (offerings to deities),
Ganga's sacred water purifies and centralizes the connection between
sacred and material realms. Devotees carry Gangajala in jugs to temples
across India and the world to perform *jalabhisek* (pouring of Gangajala
over a Siva *linga*) and other rituals. Ganga is often associated with the yogic
culture of the ascetics who seek release from this world, while Yamuna is
associated with the loving devotional traditions that seek enjoyment in this
life. The popular phrase, "Bathe in Ganga, drink Yamuna" (*Ganga snan
Yamuna pan*) indicates the central role that both ritual and consumption play
in the sacred and very public uses of these rivers in the past and today.

In sacred places, Hindu devotees revere the goddess and seek blessings
from her by undertaking the ritual of *arati*, a ceremonial offering of fire
enacted when devotees stand on the riverbank, wave an oil lamp and
other sacred objects in her presence, and sound bells, gongs, drums, and
conch shells to bring forth her power. While worshiping Ganga's power, a
devotee can receive a part of this power by chanting *mantras* or formulaic

phrases understood as verbal codifications of sacred texts. Singing also accompanies the last rites of the arati ceremony.

Ganga is inscribed in temple sculpture and art as a purifier, mother, sustainer, and daughter or co-wife of Siva, one of three main gods in the Hindu pantheon, worshiped for his extreme powers to create and destroy. Ganga is often depicted coiled in his locks of hair. She descended from heaven in her liquid form through his locks to avoid flooding the earth with her power. Devotees recite eulogies to both goddesses from the Hindu sacred texts, particularly in the Ramayana, Mahabharata, the Puranas, and Mahatmyas. One of the oldest sacred texts, the Rig Veda, describes Ganga's character as a life force and goddess. In the epic *Mahabharata*, Ganga takes anthropomorphic forms as daughter of Bhagiratha, the mortal who prayed for Ganga's descent to earth; as mother of Bhisma, the father of the Pandavas and Kauravas; and wife of Samtanu, the great king of Hastinapura in the epic. As three of her familial forms, these are characterizations of her that speak about her worldly deeds and values. Theological notes in puranic inscriptions cite the powers she can offer devotees and outline how a bath in Ganga cures ailments, makes impure people pure, and leads to *moksa* or final liberation. These prescriptions are linked to the ritual practices of ablution and arati through behavioral gestures and verbal admissions of sentiment.[3]

Many of the stories of Ganga's descent from heaven relate the main events of the Ganga-avatarana, a chapter in the Ramayana. Following the general storyline from the Ramayana, Hindus describe how a devotee named Bhagiratha called Ganga down to earth to purify the ashes of King Sagara's 60,000 sons. When King Sagara reigned across northern India, he periodically reaffirmed his power by sending a horse out across the territory. If the horse roamed free and returned safely, the King's sovereignty was re-established. But on one occasion, the horse was captured by a *rsi* (renouncer and monk) meditating on the banks of the Bay of Bengal. Sagara sent his sons out to recapture the horse, but they never returned. The rsi, outraged at their audacity, had burned Sagara's sons to the ground with his rage and left their ashes smoldering.

In a lesser-known telling of Sagara's exploits, the king had initially wanted daughters, rather than sons, as blessings from God. Sagara was hoping to gain daughters to give away in marriage through a meritorious practice known as *kanyadan*. As one swami, or Hindu religious leader, put it:

There was once a jackal in a forest who gave his daughter in marriage to another jackal in another forest. After some time this jackal went to visit his daughter. The forest was a big one and he thought the forest was their whole house. So he didn't want to eat or drink anything in that forest. He was adhering to the principle very strictly [that food and gifts were not to be taken from the other family in exchange for the daughter]. When he was coming back to his forest, he died on the way. When he died he became a human being and he remembered his past life, that he was a jackal and that by giving one daughter in marriage and observing the rules he became a King, a human being. Suppose, he thought, I do such sacrifice of *kanyadan* with 60,000 . . . and he calculated: by doing one kanyadan how much merit, by doing two how much? By doing 60,000, he could become the King of the Gods! To have 60,000 daughters, however, was not humanly possible so he thought, let me pray and get divine grace. Ultimately he found that God was pleased with him and told him he could have whatever he wanted. But by that time the King of the Gods had become jealous because he thought this man might take his position. So he went to the Goddess Saraswati, Goddess of learning and wisdom, and told her to go and sit in the mortal's mind. The God told her: he is going to ask for *putri* [daughter]. Tell him instead of *putri* to ask for *putra* [son]. So the King was doing penance and the God was pleased with him and asked, What do you want? The King replied, I want 60,000 *putra*. His intention was for *putri*! But he asked for sons and that is how Sagara got 60,000 sons. Instead of giving them in marriage and getting merits he trained them in warfare.[4]

In all versions of this story, King Sagara's sons were finally liberated by the penance of the king's descendant, Bhagiratha, who had achieved sufficient power through his devotional penance to impress on Lord Brahma that he be granted one wish. Bhagiratha wished for Ganga to descend to earth and purify the burning ashes of his ancestors with her liquid form. Brahma agreed and poured Ganga out of his jug and onto the locks of Lord Siva. From there, she descended down the peaks of the western Himalayas and followed Bhagiratha across the plains of northern India to the site where the burning ashes of his ancestors lay. At that spot, Ganga purified them by her touch before flowing into the Bay of Bengal.

Another descent story, from a treatise of the medieval period called the *Bhagavata Purana*, relates how Vishnu in his incarnation as a dwarf asked for three strides from Bali, the lord of the universe. Thinking the dwarf's stride would be limited, Bali granted the wish. But then the dwarf (who was really Vishnu) grew many sizes larger and extended his three legs across this world, the heavens, and the netherworld in the strides allotted by Bali. The toe of one foot scratched the highest tip of the cosmic egg encapsulating this world and out of this crack Ganga flowed and washed down Vishnu's foot. The verse relates how in the descent of rivers from the cosmic realm, the sins of the world are washed away.

In the sacrifice performed by Bali, the Lord (Vishnu) himself appeared as Trivikrama. Standing there on the ground, he wanted to measure three feet of land donated to him by Bali. He covered the whole of the earth by his right foot. He raised the left foot to measure the heavenly regions by his foot-step, the upper crust of the shell of the cosmic egg got cracked by the nail of the big toe of his left foot. Through that opening rushed in the stream of waters, covering externally the cosmic egg. While washing the lotus-like feet of the Lord, she (the water of the stream) became reddish by the pollen-like dust (on the Lord's feet). She washed away the dirt, in the form of the sins of the whole of the world, by her touch, and yet she herself remained pure (unpolluted by sins).[5]

After washing over Vishnu's foot, Ganga descended onto the head of Lord Shiva who contained her powerful flow with his locks of hair. In this way, Ganga's descent is intricately related to Brahma, Vishnu, and Shiva, the three main gods of the Hindu pantheon, and Ganga herself is called *tripathaga* (the union of three paths or aspects). On *pancganga ghat* in the pilgrimage place of Banaras, priests and pilgrims perform arati every day at sunrise and sunset and sing the following *stuti* (hymn):

Salutation, darsan, puja removes sin (*pap*)
King Bhagirath did this for the well being of humanity (*lokkalyan*)
Giver of devotion, liberation, peace, and freedom
King Bhagirath did this for the well being of humanity
Auspicious deeds and service done
King Bhagirath did this for the well being of humanity
Remover of distress, danger and provider of wealth
King Bhagirath did this for the well being of humanity
Knowledge of Brahman, *yajna*, complete understanding
King Bhagirath did this for the well being of humanity
Karma, knowledge and devotion (*bhakti*)
King Bhagirath did this for the well being of humanity
Ramanandi, free from all worldly attachments,
was made the teacher of Vaishnav
Sarvodaya, Siva in this world, auspicious, all being, transcendent.

Devotees celebrate Ganga's purificatory power and abiding grace in the festivals of Ganga Dasahara and Ganga Saptami. However, the performance of ritual and the celebrations of festivals do not have any effect on her purificatory power. Rituals are not powerful enough to purify Ganga in a kind of feedback process because devotees see Ganga's purity as part of a more holistic process of cosmic order and balance. This is an order in which humans should strive to live harmoniously.[6] Although saints are able to generate the power to purify Ganga in return, many say that the average individual has no such power.[7] Still, pleased by their efforts, Ganga blesses the faithful, purifies their minds and souls, and grants a devotee's wishes if requests are made with pure faith. As one merchant working on Dasasvamedha ghat in Banaras put it, "People who do bathing, meditation, and ritual worship (*snan*, *dhyan*, and *puja*) of Gods and Goddesses, this is understood as our history and knowledge." Dumont and Pocock pointed out, and this is found in the *Brahma Purana* as well, that one must be pure to approach gods and goddesses.[8] Although humans cannot reach the purity of the divine, there is some expectation that purity is a condition for that contact to be beneficial.

Purification by Ganga

There are two views in current popular discourse about whether Ganga can purify an impure person. One view argues that an impure person cannot become pure simply by bathing in her waters at a sacred place; rather, individuals must engage in the more holistic purifying process of committing the soul to Shiva. The other states that by reciting the name of Ganga, one gains mastery over sin, by taking *darsan* (auspicious sight) of her one achieves well-being, and by performing *snan* one purifies 70 generations. The "Ganga Stuti," a eulogy sung to Ganga, communicates these themes. In Banaras, at the time of Ganga *Maha arati* (great arati) performed on the day of Kartik Purnima (the full moon day concluding the month of Kartik) pilgrim priests sing this stuti:

> From the place where the lotus foot of the Lord, where Bhagirath did great *tapasya* (ritual austerities), Ganga poured out from Brahma's jug into the locks of Siv-Shankar.
> She then descended to earth on a mountain of countless sins.
> Tulsidas says open your two eyes and see how naturally she flows as a stream of nectar.
> Those who take her name in memory will get *mukti*, those who do *pranam* (prayer) will arrive at God's place.

Those who come to the banks of Ganga will find heaven, those who see
the waves of emotion will get *moksa.*

O Tarangani (Ganga), your nature is this, what God has given to you.

O Bhagirathi (Ganga), I am full of sin and dirtiness. I believe you will
give me *mukti* (liberation) and a place at your feet.

This *stuti*, written by the famous poet Kavi Keshav, communicates
themes similar to those in the "Ganga Lehari," a poem written by Jagannath in the 19th century. For mortals, Ganga is a vehicle to *moksa*, the
transcendent, and is the transcendent herself.

In sacred cities in the Ganga basin, master narratives of Ganga's purificatory powers and the unrequited love of Yamuna are tenable as personal and family convictions; they are reproduced through occupations
(*pesa*) and everyday ritual practices. The narratives tend to disregard material, everyday, and this-worldly oscillations in favor of the eternal and
transcendent. Devotees will point out that Ganga's purificatory power
can outlast a great deal of assault from the human and material worlds.
For them, her eternal and transcendent powers bring out the true essence
of creation. Her sister Yamuna's love and compassion can turn misconduct into worship and bring humanity back from the brink of disaster.
These and other sacred values affirm the importance of these rivers for
human and all life and bring religious practices with their core beliefs into
modern narratives of environmental decline.

Ganga and Modern Environmental and Hydropower Designs

In *Water and Womanhood*, Feldhaus argues that when interacting with
rivers, many residents of the state of Maharastra stress a river's female
attributes over her purificatory powers.[9] But Ganga is unlike many of the
other Hindu goddesses in that she does not react to or retaliate against
human misconduct or even human overconsumption. Devotees will say
that Ganga is a good mother who cleans up the messes her children make
and forgives them lovingly. In this way, she cleans up other kinds of dirtiness people bring to her, excusing them with maternal kindness. When
men speak, however, they will tend to accentuate the powerful aspects of
motherhood generated through reproduction less and focus instead on
her selfless cleaning and forgiveness. This attribution of motherly duties
to Ganga may be part of a gendered strategy (that has support in the
sacred texts or *sastras*) to associate women's responsibilities with these
tasks. It is also a reflection of what women are already doing: nourishing
and cleaning up after children. In this way, Ganga cleans up the messes of
the whole of humanity, selflessly and lovingly.

Devotees living in the Ganga basin may also invoke the scientific notion of water quality and the modernist notion of the microbe to support the master narrative of Ganga's sacrality. Many argue that if kept in a jar or glass at home for years and years, sacred Ganga water will never "spoil" or "develop bacteria." It will never develop the kind of bacteria that breeds in mineral water or tap water: an unidentified microbe found only in Ganga may be responsible for the river's incredible self-purifying capacity. Ganga possesses the microbe to eat up material pollution at a fantastic rate. But the nature of this microbe is ultimately a spiritual issue: why does Ganga possess it? She uses the material microbe to carry out purifying functions, and in the process the ecological and biological processes highlighted by modern science are eclipsed by her more powerful cosmic cycles.

For pilgrim priests (*purohit* or *panda*) who live and work on sacred spaces along the river, the river Ganga is a goddess who possesses the power to absorb and absolve human and worldly impurities. In a fashion cited in the *Visnu Purana*, she is able to wash over the impurities of the world like she washed over the foot of Lord Visnu on her descent to earth.[10] Using this transcendent power in the contemporary context, pilgrim priests and other devotees will say that Ganga can stave off the degeneration of contemporary society without defiling herself. They argue that since she remains pure and fertile, she should be worshiped by devotees and pilgrims through ablutions, meditation, and worship (snan, dhyanas, and puja).

By contrast, some devotees have referred to Ganga's capacity (*ksamta*) to purify as if to suggest that there is some kind of upper limit to her power. They suggest this when referring to her "capacity" (*ksamta*) to take away worldly dirtiness and impurity. Some residents acknowledge that agricultural, industrial, and human wastes are negatively impacting the Ganga, even when they cannot or will not define the nature of that impact.

Since the 1980s the government of India has planned and executed river action plans to prevent intrusion of raw wastewater into rivers. The aim has been to divert wastewater for treatment before routing the treated water back to rivers. The government of India moved through British, Dutch, Japanese, and Australian donors to fund the first and second phases of the first river program, the Ganga Action Plan. From this sprung other river action plans (the Yamuna and Gomati plans at first) that were designed to collect municipal, state, and central funds and build and operate wastewater diversion and treatment systems in important river basins. During this period, the understanding was that public uses of rivers, and in particular Hindu ritual uses, required pollution prevention schemes to improve water quality, especially in religious bathing areas. References to the religious importance of the Ganga and Yamuna rivers, in particular, lined the policies of the Ganga and Yamuna action plans from the outset and pictures of religious worship framed many government publications and websites.

In academic and government research and policy reports on these plans, scientists and government officials also evoked religious meanings of the Ganga to justify the utility of water-quality studies and sewage-treatment systems. While officials generally dismissed any relevant connection between ecology as it is known through science and the cosmic theory of Ganga's origin and essence, officials did not cast off religious symbols and narratives as if they had no valence among the wider public. This is evident in a report on the Ganga Action Plan prepared by scientists at Patna University; one author began by quoting a Sanskrit *sloka* (verse) by Valmiki. Other reports followed, fitting data on the physico-chemical and biological profile of the river into a larger cosmic framework. One paper in the report began with a Sanskrit sloka and then provided an English translation of it.

Papapahari duritari tarangdhari durpracari girirajguhavidari
jhan karkari haripadrjovi_ari ganmyam punatu satant subhkari vari

Let the pure murmuring waters of the Ganga, which removes the evil, destroys the sin, takes away the dust from the feet of (Lord) Hari (of Haridwar) and runs in waves to far distances, having pierced through the depths of the Himalaya, cleanse (us) ever—Valmiki

The next *sloka* heading the section on hydrological characteristics of the Ganga gave the scientific document a literary charm but left open the possibility of a transcendent power beyond natural ecology.

*Bhagirathi sukkdayini matasvab jalamahima nigame khyat_*
Naham jane tab mahimanam stra_i kripamayi mamkshanam

Oh Mother Bhagirathi (Ganga), the source of delight! Your wondrous waters are well known in the books of knowledge. I can not fathom your greatness. Deliver me from my ignorance, oh merciful one!—Sankaracarya

Following this theme, a report titled "Ganga, the Most Self-Purifying River" explained that Ganga has a mystical transcendent quality that befuddles even the most serious scientists. The biochemist who authored the report called Ganga the most "naturally purified" river. He wrote:

> During a water quality survey of Ganga and Yamuna, several interesting phenomenon [*sic*] were observed which played a significant role in the natural purification of these rivers. The rate of exocellular polymers, excreted during the endogenous growth phase of the various species of bacteria, vary considerably by reducing the BOD [biochemical oxygen demand] and hence turbidity. The interaction of exocellular polymers present in the rivers with the colloidal matter present in sewage results in a very rapid and significant reduction of the BOD. The data analysis has shown that Ganga has the highest BOD rate constant value and the reaeration rate constant value, both of which are higher by an order of magnitude than the thus far reported values [for any river]. The coliform organisms are also found to reduce significantly in very short times. The findings have been reasoned to suggest that Ganga is the most naturally purified.[11]

More recently, researchers have been looking at ways to define this sacred power through the functions of phages, bacterial strips that reside in the river and degrade other bacteria rapidly and effectively. This follows from the long-standing argument of biochemists who claim that Ganga carries a high bacterial load but is able, by aeration, to reduce these levels in a very short time. These native scientists have also pointed out that scientists from overseas recognize the Ganga's special "pathogen killing properties" and admit that an explanation of the sources of its unique electro-chemical properties is hard to produce.

All these approaches show attempts to reconcile the sacred meanings of the river with the modern understanding of water pollution. This is not an easy reconciliation and conceptually, at least from the Hindu point of view, it is not possible. With some semantic shifts, however, devotees do admit that Ganga may be dirty.[12] But they will quickly follow that she can never be impure (using different words and concepts for dirtiness and purity). Her purity is a sacred power and it is ultimately transcendent while dirtiness is a worldly condition brought on by human misconduct.

As projects for public health and modern sanitary engineering, the river pollution-prevention schemes along the Ganga and Yamuna rivers aimed to restore water quality to bathing standard (now called Class B status), safe for public access and especially for ritual and multipurpose bathing. The first river action plans were consolidated under the National River Conservation Directorate (NRCD) in the Ministry of Environment and Forests, and this body carried along the water quality model in its pollution prevention programs. In the first 10 years, officials in the NRCD started to construct treatment and diversion facilities with state and local authorities and made additional plans to build facilities along all the major waterways in the country. However, after plans were drawn up the costs escalated, and funds from local and state coffers became harder to fully procure. Attempts were made to develop cost sharing with state governments, but the central government's projects have since been starving for the substantial funding they need.

In late 2004, after almost 20 years of the Ganga Action Plan, facilities were in a dilapidated state in key cities along the sacred river. Most treatment plants were not running constantly; some plants were partially closed, and many employees had gone without pay, some for months. British projects had been completed, the Indian government terminated the Dutch as project donor, and the Japan Bank for International Cooperation sought ways to salvage its investments. Not only was the population larger than when the first large treatment plants were built in 1985–1996, under the Ganga Action Plan, but the public was more wasteful of water as well as consumer goods including plastics and other toxic substances. Surface waters were being polluted by industrial and metropolitan waste including pesticides and heavy metals. Even with such problems, the plants did not provide sufficient uninterrupted electricity, as key parts were missing that would have permitted expensive facilities to function efficiently.

Unfortunately, today most projects remain starved for funds and only the minimal work at infrastructure building is addressed. Meanwhile public uses of rivers and ritual practices continue to grow. Citizens are not barred from religious bathing at sacred sites, but the physical/chemical quality of the river water they use is significantly affected by upstream diversions, urban and industrial effluents, runoff and more. These effluents change the quality and experience of use, even if they do not go so far as to undermine religious devotion to the river goddess or worship practices more broadly. While the belief in the sacred purity of the Ganga may override all this, public river uses do bring citizens into direct contact with untreated effluent and wastewater, contacts that bring on human health and ecological consequences.

Water quality, watershed ecology, and ecosystem services are all affected by the increase in intensive uses of river water and river beds as effluent channels. Peer-reviewed scientific research has documented the rise in levels of fecal coliform, bacteria, pathogens, and metals in rivers and the deterioration of water quality—in terms of biochemical oxygen demand (BOD) and dissolved oxygen (DO)—for fishing and public uses. Yet these "pollution" considerations appear almost outdated now, as citizens and officials shift the public-water discussion in India and elsewhere more passionately to the possibilities of transferring surplus water from one basin to another. The emerging interest in transference—entailing contracts on distribution and consumption across agricultural, urban, and industrial users—appears to be shadowing the problem of pollution and in India the importance of the cultural practice of bathing in a sacred river. The water-quality model is giving way to a water quantity (flow, water potential) model, as statements about the growing needs of agriculture, industries and cities increasingly eclipse the importance of public uses and religious rituals in public policy. In the process, national policies are moving from a focus on river basins to visions of national water grids and hydro projects that transfer rivers in networks of canals. More recently in India this vision of transference has focused more tightly on the last water rich frontier, the tributaries to the Brahmaputra and Ganga rivers in the northeastern states of India, and a market model of water use is taking over an older state centric, populist model. Water in rivers is now being auctioned off to the highest bidder through dam and canal contracting, and then most of the work is outsourced to private companies. This means that the significant public user group of river goddess worshipers may be slipping into invisibility in water-allocation equations and policies on a river's "ecosystem services." Stakeholders who use unpriced services such as water for religious bathing appear more and more like liabilities in reports and policies—they are "impacts"—and like the villagers resettled from a dam's reservoir catchment they may not be considered stakeholders with a right to a share of project benefits or access to future water.

This is a point Vandana Shiva has made very clearly in her book, *Water Wars*.[13] Policies that expand water privatization are changing the fundamental notion of water from a sacred power (and a goddess) to a natural and fully marketable resource. It is only since the constitutional changes of the late 1970s that water has been "policied" as a basic human right in India. However, religious and cultural traditions have made the Ganga and her waters sources of sacrality and purity for much longer, and these traditions have served important use values not just for Hindus but for all basin residents as well. These sacred values guaranteed access to river waters for all residents of the river basin and for all visitors during auspicious days marked on the Hindu calendar. The slow erasure of religious definitions from the calendar of total uses in river policies can be considered an "enabling condition" for the phase-out of public, unpriced uses. This is occurring as the interest in rivers for irrigation or hydropower gains more official and public attention and projects that treat wastewater and generally improve water quality for the general public go underfunded.

The goddess Ganga of today is positioned between long-standing religious and cultural traditions that give her power, purity, and a central role in the cosmic order and modern market and state interests that aim to redistribute water to specific users. Bets are being made now about the future value of water, by companies, banks, and governments, some of whom function under the assumption that water will be privatized and that its market value will rise.

This may very well happen up until the point that hydrological forces and river ecosystems reassert their natural powers and create problems for techno-engineering approaches. Or as Hindu devotees would have it, this may occur up to the point that the goddess reasserts her encompassing power and reclaims herself as the genetrix of the universe and the provider of all that comes forth on earth.

Notes

1. See Kelly D. Alley, *On the Banks of the Ganga: When Wastewater Meets a Sacred River* (Ann Arbor: University of Michigan Press, 2002), and D. Haberman, *River of Love in an Age of Pollution* (Berkeley: University of California Press, 2006).

2. Alley, *On the Banks of the Ganga*; Haberman, *River of Love*.

3. C. Dimmit and J. A. B. van Buitenen, *Classical Hindu Mythology: A Reader in the Sanskrit Puranas* (Philadelphia: Temple University Press, 1978).

4. Interview with a servant of a well-respected religious leader.

5. *Bhagavata Purana*, Skandha 5 17.1, translated and annotated by G. V. Tagare, pt. II (Skandas 4–6) (Delhi: Motilal Banarsidass 1976), 716.

6. See also C. J. Fuller, "Gods, Priests and Purity: On the Relation Between Hinduism and the Caste System." *Man* (n.s.) 14 (1979): 460, and C. J. Fuller, *The Camphor Flame: Popular Hinduism and Society in India* (Princeton, NJ: Princeton University Press, 1992), 76.

7. See also K. Vatsyayan, "Ecology and Indian Myth," in *Indigenous Visions: Peoples of India, Attitudes to the Environment*, ed. India International Centre (Delhi: India International Centre, 1992).

8. P. V. Kane, *History of Dharmasastra*, vol. 4 (Poona [Pune]: Bhandarkar Oriental Research Institute, 1958), 63–64.

9. Anne Feldhaus, *Water and Womanhood* (New York: Oxford University Press, 1995).

10. *Bhagavata Purana* 5.17.1.

11. D. S. Bhargava, "Ganga, the Most Self Purifying River," paper presented at the International Symposium on Water Resources Conservation, Pollution and Abatement, December 11–13, Department of Civil Engineering, University of Roorkee (Delhi: Sarita Prakashan, 1981), 233.

12. Kelly D. Alley, "Idioms of Degeneracy: Assessing Ganga's Purity and Pollution," in *Purifying the Earthly Body of God: Religion and Ecology in Hindu India*, ed. Lance Nelson (Albany: State University of New York Press, 1998), 297–330.

13. Vandana Shiva, *Water Wars: Privatization, Pollution, and Profit* (Cambridge, Mass.: South End Press, 2002).

Bibliography

Alley, Kelly D. "Idioms of Degeneracy: Assessing Ganga's Purity and Pollution." In *Purifying the Earthly Body of God: Religion and Ecology in Hindu India*, ed. Lance Nelson. Albany: State University of New York Press, 1998.

Alley, Kelly D. *On the Banks of the Ganga: When Wastewater Meets a Sacred River*. Ann Arbor: University of Michigan Press, 2002.

Bhagavata Purana. Translated and annotated by G. V. Tagare. Part II (Skandas 4–6). Delhi: Motilal Banarsidass, 1976.

Bhargava, D. S. "Ganga, the Most Self Purifying River." Paper presented at the International Symposium on Water Resources Conservation, Pollution and Abatement, December 11–13. Department of Civil Engineering, University of Roorkee. Delhi: Sarita Prakashan, 1981.

Dimmit, C., and J. A. B. van Buitenen. *Classical Hindu Mythology: A Reader in the Sanskrit Puranas*. Philadelphia: Temple University Press, 1978.

Feldhaus, Anne. *Water and Womanhood*. New York: Oxford University Press, 1995.

Fuller, C. J. *The Camphor Flame: Popular Hinduism and Society in India*. Princeton, NJ: Princeton University Press, 1992.

Fuller, C. J. "Gods, Priests and Purity: On the Relation Between Hinduism and the Caste System." *Man* (n.s.) 14 (1979): 460.

Haberman, D. *River of Love in an Age of Pollution*. Berkeley: University of California Press, 2006.

Kane, P[andurang] V[aman]. *History of Dharmasastra: Ancient and Mediaeval Religious and Civil Law*. 5 vols. Poona [Pune]: Bhandarkar Oriental Research Institute, 1930–1958.

Shiva, Vandana. *Water Wars: Privatization, Pollution, and Profit*. Cambridge, Mass.: South End Press, 2002.

Vatsyayan, K. "Ecology and Indian Myth." In *Indigenous Visions: Peoples of India, Attitudes to the Environment*, ed. India International Centre. Delhi: India International Centre, 1992.

4

Village Goddesses: Vernacular Religion in Orissa

Elinor Gadon and Rita Ray

The cult of the village goddess, the *gramadevi* or *thakurani* as she is popularly known in the state of Orissa in eastern India, is an age-old institution whose roots are prehistoric, reflecting a worldview that is prepatriarchal. In the centuries, perhaps millennia, before the brahmanic Hinduism spread throughout the subcontinent, most indigenous peoples worshiped a Mother Goddess. While there are several major goddesses in the Hindu pantheon—Lakshmi, Durga, and Kali are examples—they are part of the male-dominated religion and served by male priests. The tradition of the village goddess, by contrast, is folk religion in which there are no temples, Brahman priests, mantras (codified prayers), or canonical images. Brahmanic Hinduism did not come to Orissa until the sixth century. The tradition of the much older village goddess comprises popular, vernacular Hinduism. The villagers address this goddess as *Ma*, Mother.

Orissa has more than 51,000 villages. According to the belief system of the residents, the foundation of each village was only possible when the goddess's power was clearly felt in a particular locality, be it in a tree, a rock, an anthill, or a hilltop. There is an identifiable place with special energy, considered auspicious, which the local population identifies as the goddess. She is found at one end or the other of the village, protecting its territory. Her presence delineates the boundary of the village of which she is the reigning authority. This energy is always female. In fact, the settlement is structured as if the village was the extended womb of the gramadevi and she gave birth to it.

Her foremost responsibility is to ensure regeneration, typically characterized as the continuity of life, both human and nonhuman. She signifies peace and order in the village and interacts directly with the villagers in order to promote their well-being. Her protection is limited to the physical and emotional security of the inhabitants of her territory and acts against the entry of evil spirits into the boundaries of the village. She also safeguards the villagers when they cross her territorial boundaries and go out in the course of everyday activities.

She represents human survival—the well-being of their children, the continuity of life, and the success of crops dependent on favorable weather conditions as well as the fertility of the soil. Their lineage should be secure for, if she is honored, people should not be bothered by barrenness or the death of children. She places humans in harmony with nature, reaffirming their connection to it. The tree, for example, a manifestation of the goddess, is a symbol of regeneration. The tree splits open and reveals her presence. The stone is numinous. She does not want a roof over her head because it disconnects her from nature. The villagers believe that she comes out of the earth. The gramadevi is also a source of justice. In their constant struggle to set things in order, the villagers look to her for the restitution of justice.

Her ethos is essentially that of the indigenous pre-Indo-European culture that perseveres as the foundation of the villager's worldview. From earliest times there was a tradition of village mothers who were concerned with the facts of daily life, propitiated to ward off calamities. Orientation was to the primary needs of humanity and awareness of social reality.[1]

Both iconography and tradition point to this model as the archetypal picture of the feminine principle, the objectification of a perspective that perceives all life-sustaining power as essentially female and implicitly equated with nature and its processes, and with the vehicle of that very energy, the female principle, as the ultimate reality. The deep-rooted influence of a mother-oriented worldview, in terms of an all-pervading female principle of creation, persisted in religion and rituals though the ages.[2]

The gramadevi is generic; she is always present in the tree, the rock, the anthill. Although there are many variations of her origin stories, all have a common thread. While her place of origin is fixed, her power moves around the village territory routinely to check on the well-being of her villagers. She is a reality in their lives, a real presence, vibrant and alive. She is the symbol of motherhood in Orissa.

Unlike the gods and goddesses of the high Hindu pantheon who are supernatural beings, she does not create miracles but facilitates earthly things. She does not promise but will try to meet the villagers' needs and answer their queries. Her behavior and actions are human. The villagers see her as an elderly wise woman and hear her talking to them. They hear her soft, womanly voice answering "yes" when they call. She has no consort or husband. All villagers—men, women, and children—relate to her as mother. In Oriya culture, all females, including young girls, elderly women, and newborn girl children, are addressed as *Ma*. The villagers want to be protected in ways that their own mothers could not do for them in a patriarchal society. Families are almost completely mother-centric. The village is considered a family. In the village the goddess has an important role in minimizing the abuses of patriarchy. Her superiority is not in the sense of hierarchy but of wisdom and knowledge.

The goddess speaks to them, through dreams, intimately connecting them to the land, the place where she stays, and with the people who live there. She is not worshiped with prescribed ritual and prayers but interacted with. The villagers communicate directly with her through dialogue, usually at night while asleep. They call this "dreaming" but it is more like having a vision. They do not have to call her because surrendering to her is giving over the self. Men who only see her in her fierce form do not readily submit to her. Women, however, find her a comforting presence. Like a force of nature the village goddess can be benevolent but also, at times such as epidemics or natural disasters, destructive.

For the villagers, the bringing of the disease is not malevolent; an outbreak of smallpox, for example, is seen as the goddess emerging. They firmly believe that Ma's emergence is neither good nor bad but that she wished to come and everything will have to be done her way. This is not to be confused with the concepts of ritual purity and pollution so central to brahmanic Hinduism. The conventional definitions of malevolence and benevolence are dualistic and do not capture the essence of the *gramadevi*. She brings the disease, she is the disease, and she cures the disease.

There are no prescribed, obligatory rituals. There are no priests; she does not need to be awakened by special prayers like the brahmanic deities. There are no texts, no hymns of praise; the structures of communication are more direct. What is important is dialogue. Whoever is in difficulty has a direct conversation with her. She is not worshiped but experienced through her energetic presence. She communicates directly to the villagers through a dream that usually comes at night, a time when the boundary between human and divine is lowered. Through dreams she answers the village's questions and offers solutions to problems that must be obeyed. The "dream" is not a dream in the conventional sense but rather an expression of an inner consciousness, a manifestation of needs, a visionary creation of the imagination. The villagers access their subconscious through the person of the *devi* but from the point of view of the culture she is the protagonist, a virtual reality that sustains them and enables them to confront the ongoing crisis in their lives. Their belief and trust in her reinforces their existence.

The two key rituals through which her powers function are *kalisi* (prophecy and healing) and *bali* (blood sacrifice). The *kalisi* is a traditional healer and oracle who while in a state of possession is the living representative of the *gramadevi*. She shows up once or twice a year in the body of a living person who embodies Ma through trance and her thoughts are channeled through him or her. When it is a man, he dresses in a sari like a woman and is referred to as *Ma*. The *kalisi*'s dream is a communal omen dreamt by the whole community. She predicts the fortunes of the village for the coming year. Will there be an epidemic, a flood, a drought? Will there be a good crop? Are there injustices silently going on? The *kalisi* acts for the general good and sets the moral tone of the village.

Bali or blood sacrifice is an integral part of the *gramadevi* tradition. Blood is the basis of her sustenance, something she needs for her very survival. She must have an ongoing supply of energy so that she can regenerate it for the people. The villagers believe that she needs blood to fertilize the fields. But for the rural peasants, regeneration of the earth and the family are interconnected, and so *bali* is given for the good of the community. They offer blood for regeneration, for the security of their lineage as well as the success of the crop. Blood sacrifice continues, although now it is illegal in most parts of India because of pressure from the central government. The substitution of an innocuous vegetable like the pumpkin belies the understanding of the power of blood. Blood cannot easily be replaced; pumpkins do not bleed.

The seeds that the *gramadevi* has planted are deeply rooted in the soil of Orissa but with the combined forces of brahmanization and globalization, her hold on the indigenous cultural ethos is weakening. But wherever the tradition exists in its primal form, it continues to protect nature and the indigenous culture.

Notes

1. N. N. Bhattacharya, *History of the Shakta Religion* (New Delhi: Munshiram Manoharlal Publishers, 1974), 111.

2. Ibid., 16.

Bibliography

Bhattacharya, N. N. *History of the Shakta Religion*. New Delhi: Munshiram Manoharlal Publishers, 1974.

Brighetti, Francesco. *Sakta Cult in Orissa*. New Delhi: D. K. Print World, 2001.

Eschmann, Anncharlotte. "Hinduization of Tribal Deities in Orissa: The Shakta and Shaiva Tradition." In *The Cult of Jagannath and Regional Traditions of Orissa*, ed. Annecharlotte Eschmann, Herman Kulke, and Gaya Charan Tripathi. New Delhi: Manohar, 1986.

Gold, Ann Groodzins, and Bhoju Ram Gujar. *In the Time of Trees and Nature, Power and Memory in Rajasthan*. Durham, NC: Duke University Press, 2002.

Kulke, Hermann. "Tribal Deities at Princely Courts: The Feudatory States of Central Orissa." In *Kings and Cults: State Formation and Legitimation in India and Southeast Asia*. New Delhi: Manohar, 1993–2001.

Mallebrein, Cornelia. "Creating a 'Kshetra': Goddess Tarini of Ghatgaon and Her Development from a Forest Goddess to a Pan-Orissan Deity." *Journal of Social Sciences* 8, no. 2 (2004): 155–165.

Padel, Felix. *The Sacrifice of Human Beings*. New Delhi: Oxford University Press, 2000.

5

Mariamma: Cosmic Creation Goddess

Judy Grahn

Much has been written about the great goddess, especially as a feature of the Neolithic era in areas of Europe and Africa. What exactly is a great goddess, that is, what makes a goddess tradition "great"? Does such a deity continue to exist? This chapter suggests that a village deity of South India, Mariamma, both fulfills and provides some interesting criteria for such a supposition.

Mariamma, whose name is transliterated into English variously as Maryamma, Mariamman, and Mariammon, is a feature of the South Indian landscape. Her innumerable temples are located in the five southern states. These include Tamil Nadu, which covers the tip of India; two states directly above that each border a sea, Andhra Pradesh on the east coast and Karnataka on the west; and parts of Kerala, which lies in a strip along the west coast roughly in the same location in relationship to India that California has to the United States. While in the past, knowledge about this goddess surfaced from within local, economically poor, and even socially rejected communities, her worship has spread to other parts of the world and across all economic groups.

When first encountered, Mariamma may seem supremely unimposing, described since at least 19th-century accounts as part of the "little tradition" of deities and commonly considered as "a smallpox goddess" called upon only in cases of outbreak of illness, as distinct from the major tradition, the pantheon of Vedic deities who have dominated in written thought. Mariamma at first appears to be essentially local, a *grammadevata*

Figure 5.1 In rural villages across India, but especially in the state of Orissa, local divinities called "village goddesses" are honored as mother-protectors of each settlement and its inhabitants. Such goddesses are rarely known outside their immediate area but some common features can be found in traditions associated with them. (Copyright Hrana Janto.)

(village goddess) who serves primarily as a "boundary goddess" for village life. Yet, among others, two notable Indian scholars, Karin Kapadia and Pupul Jayakar, have each subverted this diminutive view. Jayakar refers to Mariamma as "the mighty goddess" while Kapadia, who lived with and became friends with people of the village of Auruloor in Tamil Nadu, and who calls Mariamma a "great goddess," reports that the villagers think of their Mariamma as no less than "the autonomous ruling power of the universe."[1]

If Mariamma is not only "mighty" but also "great," in the sense of ruling the cosmos, then surely she may fit criteria to be considered as a "cosmic goddess," if that is an appropriate term. Dictionary definitions of the term *cosmic* cover quite a bit of territory. Cosmic is of or related to the universe, especially as distinct from planet Earth. Cosmic is infinitely or inconceivably, expanded, and is of, related to, or concerned with abstract spiritual or metaphysical ideas. And cosmic is characterized by greatness, especially in extent, intensity, or comprehensiveness.

On the surface this seems ample enough; however, on closer examination, this definition is quite deficient, not nearly full enough to encompass all that Mariamma is, even in the brief exploration of this chapter. To begin with, the viewer's own positionality needs to be part of what is "all," and so, rather than positing that "universe" is "distinct from earth," the idea of "cosmos" needs to encompass *both* earth and a greater, knowable (or unknowable) universe. Second, a more holistic statement would be that spiritual or metaphysical ideas can be *embodied* as well as abstract. Mariamma is an earth goddess, marking the boundaries of each village of whom she is the *place*. An example of how this idea is manifested is that during worship of her, craftspeople make Mariamma's head, of clay or another substance, and place it on the ground; the earth is her body. The village thus lives upon and within her, as the precinct of existence.

In support of Mariamma as a great goddess, let us first consider her multiple forms and characteristics, including some that associate her with sky as well as earth. Her name, Mari, is frequently translated as "rain" though it also can mean much more; it can mean "to change"[2] or "to pour down." An earlier writer on South India reported *Mari* to mean "the power" or *sakti*.[3] *Amma* is a generic goddess term in India meaning "mother." She is maternally nurturing, and she is also dreaded Marai, goddess of destruction in north India found in the burial grounds.[4]

On a memorable soft evening sitting on the porch of his home in the state of Kerala in the southwest corner of India, Ayappan Panniker, distinguished poet and professor, gave the interpretation of Ma-ri as "who pours down," emphasizing that this quality refers to "anything at all that pours down," not only, most obviously, rain, but also presumably locusts, the grain harvest, a plague, water, blood, birthing fluids, tears, sweat. Smallpox, in its heyday her signature disease, is a condition she inflicts; she takes it upon herself until it spills over; and she is the smallpox itself. So part of her "cosmic" character is that she is not remote, she is as close as the earth, and as fluids and bumps on bodies; and she manifests also as what is pouring from above, from the heavens.

The dynamic implications of the immanence of her being, that she "pours down," is illustrated by an origin story of the building of one of her temples.[5] Several centuries ago, in a village named Mannadikonam, outside Kerala's capital city of Thiruvananthapuram, a landowner hired a woodcutter to fell a tree. While the woodcutter was working, the landowner, who was beneath the tree, fell into an unconscious state. The woodcutter brought water, and when the man awoke he halted the cutting and sent for a religious astrologer and other landlords. A sacred astrologic reading revealed the presence of Muthumariamman, described in the account as "Dravidian mother goddess": Mariamma. "Dravidian" refers to South Indian language and cultural groups who are pre-Indo-European. The determination was that a temple must be constructed if the tree was to be cut, and this was done. So the goddess acquires attention by knocking worshipers out at times, and reveals her desires through astrological readings connecting the position of the stars with intimate, local affairs on earth.

Immanence is one of the primary qualities of any Indian goddess, and especially so the "dark" goddesses Kali and Mariamma, who are called "dark" not only for their fierce aspects but also because their powers pour through devotees and carefully prepared practitioners such as the *velicha-pads* (shamans, also called *matangis*) in oracular and mystical trance-states in which they speak for, or otherwise embody, the goddess. Mariamma's immanent power can "possess" a woman, man, or child, causing the person to sing, dance, lurch or roll about, become oracular, speak truth to authority, prophesize, or give other indications of altered states of consciousness. While women and girls are open to the immanence of the goddess, and especially when they are menstruating or have their menarche, men and boys prepare more elaborately to open themselves, and frequently this preparation involves bloodletting of some kind, especially body-piercing rituals.[6]

Mariamma's Physical Manifestations

In addition to her form as a head made of clay or metal, Mariamma frequently takes the form of a small standing stone, a stone that is alive and "bleeds." Recently, since blood sacrifice has been outlawed, the stone is painted with red lines, though in former times it would have been drenched with blood of chickens or goats, with which she is fed. Now the red is likely from turmeric dye or other red plant substances.

As village goddess of South India, Mariamma takes a multiplicity of forms. Besides stone and rain, she appears as a sacred tree, an ant mound, a flame, a single grain of rice, a clay or bronze head, a maiden, and a plague of smallpox, chickenpox, or cholera. In her iconography and other depictions she is a handsome, serious woman who holds a crescent-shaped sickle or a fisher-people's trident, among other objects. She dresses in red, for the most part, though yellow is also her prominent color, and she sometimes wears blue clothing. She is beautiful in her human form, often with a black face, often white, or with a red complexion, a white forehead, draped in flowers and crowned with a diadem. In poster art, Mariamma in her form as a young dignified woman is frequently seated with one leg crossed, her pleated red skirt lush and flowing. Her feet are large and sometimes yellow. In areas close to Kerala she may also be visually portrayed as ferocious, standing and with blue skin, protruding eyes and tongue, fangs (*dharmstra*), and holding a sword and decapitated head in her hands. She is compassionate, tender, and protective, self-disciplined, magical, fiercely vigilant, blood-drinking. Depending on context, she wears a garland of flowers, a garland of neem leaves, a garland of sheep, a garland of skulls. Geometric forms, triangle, square, and hexagon, are hers, as is the crossroads.[7]

The poet Panniker said that the villagers after harvest take a single grain of rice, and dress it as Mariamma. He held his thumb and forefinger a centimeter apart while his other hand wrapped imaginary thread to depict the delicate, ritual act of dressing the tiny goddess in her red rice form, his face reflecting wonder. Mariamma's forms then, range through the realms of nature, from the distant constellations to the tiny seed of grain, and she is both aniconic as a living stone and iconic as a beautiful woman. Her stories tell even more about her manifestations.

Mariamma's Creation Story

Mariamma plays a major role in several of South India's most marvelous sacred stories. One of these is her own creation story, collected and published by Pupul Jayakar. The story begins at the very beginning, that is to say, the opening of human consciousness and the capacity to name the world. In the beginning there were only two elements, water and light. Then the goddess decided to manifest in the form of a woman: Mariamma. "Before the existence of hills or trees or fields or plants there was only water. In the midst of this existed the great world light." The anthropomorphic form of Mariamma was born of this cosmic light meditating on itself, for eons. In her human form she immediately grew to womanhood and the desire for a man companion arose within her. As she wandered in a garden near an anthill, a jasmine bough bent over her, and the lady plucked a flower and said, "This will be my love." The virgin goddess took the jasmine flower and placed it within a lotus blossom that floated on the surface of the water. Then, with the magic powers held within her, the goddess transformed herself into a bird and settled upon the lotus, brooding over the jasmine flower. The sacred bird, pregnant from the flower, laid three eggs within the lotus. From one egg was born the heavens, the sun and moon, the stars, and all the encircling sea. From the black speck within the egg was born Shiva, Vishnu, and Brahma. From the second egg were born earth beings, including snakes and demons. The third egg was addled.[8] The story clearly shows Mariamma as a bird goddess, and the bird goddess as a creator of the cosmos, laying in her eggs the beings of the heavens and earth, and of all potentiality. In the remainder of the Mariamma creation story recorded by Jayakar, the goddess loses her youth and sexuality after her son Shiva tricks her into giving him her third eye. She then decides to fight the demons she herself created; their destructiveness coalesces into the mythic form of the buffalo, whom she sets out to destroy. Mariamma's vulnerability shows in this portion of her creation story, as the roaring breath of the buffalo sends her running, and she dives down into the ant mound, an underworld of snakes. "Meanwhile, the goddess descended into the bowels of the earth, reaching the land of the serpents, and found the *siddhas*, masters of magic and mantras. With an army of ninety million *siddhas*, and chanting incantations, the ancient one marched up in the upper world. The thunderous river of the magical sounds reached the buffalo demon, who immediately died."[9]

The ending of Mariamma's creation story, as related by Jayakar, is often associated with the mother goddess Durga of North India. A more complexly woven story involving Mariamma comes from South India. This version, called Darikavadham, or "the killing of Darika," usually centers on the goddess Bhadrakali. The demon Darika begins as an extremely pious man, a devotee of the gods Shiva, Vishnu, and Brahma. He is so loyal to them that they award him a boon, and he asks for immortality. Given this gift, he launches campaigns of every sort of social transgression. In their failure to stop him the gods realize that Darika turned down the gods' offer of protection from the power of the feminine. Therefore, they arm seven wives of the Vedic male pantheon who sally forth against the demon; one of them strikes him with her trident. To everyone's horror, every drop of his blood produces a thousand more versions of himself. At this point Shiva creates a goddess, Bhadrakali, dedicated to the killing of Darika. She rolls her long tongue out as the surface of the earth, to drink the blood, every drop, as Darika dies. A variant of this story, told by an attendant/priestess[10] of the Mariamma installation, or shrine, at the Srji Khurumba Bhagavathi Temple at Kodungallur, implicates the feminine as well as the masculine. In her account, Mariamma has taken the role of Darika's wife, and it is her mantra (sacred chanted syllables) that keeps his power in place. Before Bhadrakali can engage Darika in battle she must first steal the mantra from Darika's wife, and she achieves this through trickery. Following Darika's demise, the two powerful goddesses, Bhadrakali and Mariamma, then fight each other, but through the compassion of each, they achieve a peaceful coalition, such that both coexist in the same temple.

Mariamma emerges from her creation story as a deity who takes responsibility for the harm done by her own creations, since the "demons" emerged from one of her cosmic eggs. In her north Indian story she kills the buffalo demon with devotional prayers and chants. In South India in one of her earthly forms she is someone who marries the demon and keeps him in place, and so must herself be overturned, but through compassion between herself and another goddess, she is transformed. She is what she creates, and she is its problems, its solutions, its destruction, and its reconstitution. In a sense she creates the buffalo, fights the buffalo, subdues the buffalo, and is the buffalo.

The most primal imagery that leaps out of her creation story, however, is her connection to bird and snake, both of which she embodies. Sacred birds occupy Mariamma's iconic and ritual territory. The living sacred bird called "Garuda," a member of the kite family, circles over the festival of Bharani at Kodungallor Bhagavathi Temple, which is also called the "cock festival" for its former practice of chicken sacrifice, and large white plaster roosters adorn the gates at one entrance to the seven acre temple grounds. An installation of Mariamma stands in the western corner of the temple yard. While this temple is best known for the installation of Bhadrakali, not Mariamma, a very particular bird ritual is part of the worship of Mariamma in many of her own temples. This is a ritual called "hook swinging" or *thukkam*. Men who perform this prepare for months prior to being dressed and painted as the Garuda bird, and swung high in the air by hooks inserted through the flesh of their backs. Interestingly, practitioners say they are in such a trance state that the piercing does not hurt. The myth explaining the South Indian ritual is part of the Darika-vadham story of the goddess destroying the demon, and the bird is "drinking the blood," as an offering to Mariamma.[11]

In her form as a bird goddess of creation, Mariamma laid an egg with sky elements, then another egg with earth elements, including snakes. Later in the story she flees the fiery breath of the buffalo by running down into an ant mound, where the snakes live. Some Mariamma temples are built over ant mounds, which are understood as manifestations of her; in these temples, snakes are revered and their icons given offerings of eggs. In a well-known story in which Mariamma takes the role of the woman named

Renuka, she had the power not only to form water up into the shape of a pot, but also to coil a living snake into a roll to place on her head and hold the pot while she carried it. In some of her icons and devotional paintings, Mariamma is depicted holding a cobra in one hand, has a protective covering of cobra heads, and is accompanied by stone sacred snakes called Nagas. She can appear to a devotee in the form of a living snake,[12] for the serpent is an integral part of Mariamma's being.

Both snake and bird motifs in goddess iconography occupy territory that is extremely old. Marija Gimbutas identified icons in the area she called "Old Europe."[13] The icons are of female body characteristics united with characteristics of birds or snakes, and dated as early as the Upper Paleolithic, or late Stone Age of Europe, from 10,000 to 40,000 years ago. It seems entirely possible that Mariamma's associations with these motifs could be that old as well.

As a creation myth, her story reflects the development of human consciousness present in many other grand creation stories, using elements of water, light, plants, bird, and eggs. From the eggs come differentiation of moon from sun, and a range of creations from the stars in the sky to snakes under the ground. From the separation into three eggs derives the distinction between sky and earth, and also beneficial and malevolent elements or beings. If this would later be storied as good versus evil, there is no reason to believe that the earliest tellers of this story saw one egg as better than the other. The third or "addled" egg is intriguing, a place kept for incompletion, for miscarriage, or evolutionary trial and error. And this egg, too, was laid by the mother.

The goddess is not expected to be omnipotent. For instance, she may be the giver of smallpox but she is not in control of it; rather she takes on the smallpox herself and then sometimes the illness overflows from her. Moreover, living through the pox may be a boon, as the meaning of an illness depends on outcome, not fixed belief that it must be negative. So the goddess does not appear to determine outcomes or to be omnipotent.[14] She is not dichotomized, and while in everyday practice she is usually understood as the sympathetic, nurturing, and protective mother, in her stories she has other, more complexly constructed roles. In the next story, Mariamma takes the part of a woman who seems symbolic of the centuries-ago assimilation of a then-new upper caste, the patrilineal Brahmins, with the older residents of South India, the Dravidians. So while she is extremely old, Mariamma also emerges as an assimilative factor, capable of continually changing creation, and a part of evolutionary turning.

Assimilating and Reconstructing Caste and Gender

In the state of Kerala, a prominent creation story currently is that of Renuka. She is the mother of the culture hero, Parasurama, who is credited with having created the entire state of Kerala by throwing his ax into the sea, land appearing everywhere the ax flew along its northward course. This frequently told story revolves around Renuka but sometimes fails to mention the crucial detail that she is a form of Mariamma. Renuka is married to Jamadagni, a sage and a jealous man, with whom she has a number of sons—four or five, depending on the version of the story. Renuka is so very chaste in her thoughts, and so austere and disciplined in her habits, that these practices give her a mystical power, especially with the element of water. When she goes to the river to fetch water, she does not need to carry a pot. Variants of the story say that she takes river mud and makes a pot without need to dry the clay or fire it to keep its shape. One particularly magical version relates how she can roll up the water itself and form it into its own pot, carrying it home on her head.[15]

One day, Renuka's attention was caught by some sexual frolicking in the water as she passed by. Various descriptions describe the frolickers as a married couple, young men and women, or simply young men; sometimes they are *ghandarvas*, sexual creatures dangerous to maidens, who fly about in the sky. The amorous antics of these beings distracted her focus, and she began to fantasize about them. These thoughts broke her internal chastity, held in place through austerities, and thus she lost her powers, including the power of carrying water without a clay pot. When she arrived home, ashamed at this loss, she faced a husband who knew at once that the lost capacity was a consequence of loss of chastity. Her patriarchal husband was so enraged at her "infidelity" that he ordered her sons to kill her. One by one the oldest sons refused, and in his rage the jealous sage burned each of them to ash. When Parasurama, the youngest, returned home, he was aghast at the sight of his burned brothers; he thought about the situation and then he agreed to his father's desire.

Parasurama killed his mother by beheading her. Variants of the story place this murder in various locations, especially because of the crucial detail that the youngest son, Parasurama, killed not only his mother, who was of high caste (Brahmin) but also, by accident, simultaneously beheaded a low-caste (Dravidian) woman. Variants of the story give different communities (Chella, Cakkilicci, Pariah) and occupations (leatherworker, washerwoman, field worker) to this woman, as well as different locations for the murders. One interesting explanation places the beheading inside a menstrual hut, where the young woman was in seclusion. Renuka ran in, chased by Parasurama, who in the confusion of darkness accidentally beheaded both of the women.[16] On the return of his bloody handed youngest son, the father gave him a boon—any wish. Parasurama asked that the whole family be restored to life. Reluctantly, the father agreed to keep his word. The older sons immediately arose from their ashes back to life, though their ordeal had rendered them eunuchs.

Parasurama put his Brahmin mother and the other woman back together, but in his confusion he mixed the heads. The body of the out-caste and the head of the Brahmin became the goddess Renuka/ Mariamma. The body of the Brahmin and head of the outcaste became the goddess Matangi, who is currently a goddess whose temples welcome everyone, a characteristic of many lower-caste temples. In the Renuka story, as in her guise as Darika's wife in Darikavadham, Mariamma is mar-ried to a patriarchal principal, believed by many to have been brought through Indo-European invasions of India from the areas of the Caspian and Black seas. The exchange of heads and bodies implies an assimilation of the patriarchal and patrilineal systems into the matrilineal matrix of a number of South Indian communities. A new goddess figure grew from it—Renuka, who following her husband's death threw herself onto his funeral fire in sacrificial offering and became the goddess Mariamma, worshiped as Renuka, frequently in the form of a clay or cast metal head with flames around it. Matangi, an older Dravidian goddess who once took the form of an elephant,[17] now also became a new goddess who grew from the Brahmin body united with the outcaste woman's head. As one scholar has stated the dynamic, "when Parasurama puts his mother's head on the Untouchable woman's body, he has reconstructed the god-dess to include all levels of social hierarchy. She is now not only his mother but is everyone's mother. Thus the goddess and her devotees mutually construct the other."[18]

Parasurama's brothers, left as eunuchs in the family struggle by their refusal to participate in their father's matricidal rage, are not abandoned by their mother. Mariamma doesn't stop with the accommodation to the patrimony of Parasurama and his father. She also takes the form of a third goddess, Yellamma (or Ellamma) who, according to several versions of her story, is worshiped by Renuka's loyal older sons. Their eunuch status is taken literally, and Yellamma's temple in Savadatti village near Belgaum in the state of Karnataka today is known as a sanctuary for transgendered people and other sexual categories outside the param-eters of normative society.[19] Hence not only is an inclusivity of social stratification part of Mariamma's province, inclusivity of sexual stratification is as well. Worshipers bathe in the beautiful water of three ponds, and into very recent times came to the temple naked underneath a draping of leaves of the neem tree, sacred to goddess Mariamma. In one manifestation Yellamma rides upon the back of a handsome chicken—once again, here is the bird goddess. In yet another story of creation through the laying of cosmic eggs, Yellamma takes the form of a hen.[20]

The devotion of transgendered people of all descriptions to goddess Yellamma at the temple in Savadatti is one aspect of androgynous qualities in the goddess herself. Karin Kapadia has a different perspective for the androgynous nature of Mariamma, one that perhaps carries meaning for women as a category. Kapadia argues that the widely known androgyny of the Shiva-Shakti balance in Vedic pantheon does not actually give women the fullness of their being. She argues that in the Vedic view, "Wisdom or Knowledge is gendered as male," and held to be superior to "Power or Energy, which is gendered as female. Wisdom controls and directs the exuberant creativity of Power." She goes on to say that only men become divinely possessed by the goddess, in this system, and therefore "only men can thus join Wisdom to Power, women are forever separated from Wisdom."[21]

Kapadia, who engaged with villagers of Auruloor in the South Indian state of Tamil Nadu, and thus with an indigenous Dravidian, not a Vedic, system, found they consider Mariamma

> entirely "complete," for she is the Supreme Deity herself. . . . She is the autonomous ruling power of the universe—and she is—to the people of Auruloor—as infinitely wise as she is powerful. We will have no difficulty understanding this female representation of Supreme Deity if we do not essentialize gender. For in the popular, common understanding of God in Auruloor, God/Maryamman is female in her powers but also male in her infinite wisdom. She is supremely wise, beneficent, good, and tender—though she is also angry with sinners and destroys the wicked. She is God Herself—both female and *implicitly* male. So she, too, is androgynous in gender.[22]

A "Great Goddess" Who Is Local as Well as Cosmic

As a village goddess, Mariamma is the earth itself. Potters and smiths make an image of her head, which then sits directly on the ground; the village is her body, and the villagers live within her; she keeps and protects the boundaries of the village. In this setting, her cosmology is experiential. But to live within the body of the goddess is to be within the allness of her "world," however largely or locally this is imagined. Within her boundaries devotees pour out their hearts to her in her form as a stone, and lay offerings of flowers and red powder at her feet in her form as a sacred tree. In rural areas villagers continue to offer sacrifices to her, of buffalo, sheep, goats, and chickens. To maintain and attain prosperous, healthy families, women offer her rice porridge, bending over outdoor flames, and through piercing rites boys, men, and some women solicit healing from her. All are equally welcome in the temples where she resides as an ant mound.

She is inherently local, with deep rural roots. Yet the religion of Mariamma has spread far beyond the village. Her worship is contemporary and rapidly growing; because of the diaspora of Indian peoples, especially Tamils, Mariamma temples thrive in Singapore, Malaysia, Vietnam, Australia, South Africa, and increasingly in urban centers.

To return to the opening question, "What is a great goddess?" in considering the complexity of Mariamma, a great goddess might be said to encompass the following criteria:

1. She is "cosmic" in the expanded sense of being both in the earth and in the universe.
2. Her presence is manifest through extreme lengths of time past in human history, yet still thriving in present time. She is local, yet spans geographic space.
3. Her worship crosses boundaries of class, gender, and other social distinctions.
4. She is multiple in form, including elements, species and so on.
5. She has a cosmic creation story.
6. Ethical, as well as spiritual and metaphysical ideas attach to her, which are both embodied and abstract.
7. She is autonomous yet in community, not subservient to a male god, and not alone either; other deities coexist with her and she is intrinsically androgynous.
8. She is interactive with evolutionary forces; because her tradition is mostly oral, and her practices not under a central authority, she has the additional wisdom of plasticity and engagement.

While the scope of this definition is beyond the limits of this chapter, enough points hopefully have been touched on through Mariamma's stories and characteristics to suggest the range of her presence. She travels through historic time, not fixed in the past. She assimilates and recreates class and marriage systems, as well as definitions of gender. The Mariamma of archaic stone, of Neolithic bird and snake, coexists in practice as well as myth with the political developments of patriarchal marriage systems and of cross-caste gender identifications. She assimilates, living out her name, "to change." As Renuka, the goddess is married to the upper strata, yet as Mariamma she diligently safeguards the villages of the most modest of workers. As Renuka, she is the ultimate in faithful wives; while as the wife of the demon Darika she is partnered with the most self-serving of men. As Yellamma she extends open arms to gender outcastes and those in sexually defined and socially reviled situations. As warrior she protects against evil, and as mother she heals, nourishes, and cherishes her devotees; as earth, rice, and rain, she provides.

Mariamma can be thought of as "cosmic" because of her very evident antiquity and geographic spread, perhaps as one of many "earth goddesses" whose name includes the syllable "Ma." The definition of *cosmic* includes having qualities that are beyond the earth, encompassing the heavens and the universe. Mariamma certainly does this in her creation story. She can be thought of as "cosmic" because of the complexity of her imagery, the range of her forms—bird of sky and snake of earth; buffalo of death and rice of life; stone fed with blood and tree fed with flowers; flame as well as shaper of water; ant mound of underground activity and egg of cosmic creation spilling out the stars, sun, and moon. She seems to embody the development of human understanding of the elements of sky, water, fire, earth, and to stretch across eons of evolutionary time. Her stories are overtly cosmic—a grand creation myth, which morphs into intersections with patriarchal developments, and implies in its local details moral imperatives of ecological protection, compassion, justice, and peacekeeping.[23] At the same time, in the same space, she is intensely personal and present, a listener who is not omnipotent yet who does her best to help her devotees. She seems to be continually interactive with evolutionary process. What more could one ask of a deity?

Notes

1. Pupul Jayakar, *The Earth Mother: Legends, Goddesses, and Ritual Arts of India* (San Francisco: Harper and Row, 1990), 187; Karin Kapadia, *Siva and Her Sisters: Gender, Caste and Class in Rural South India* (Boulder, CO: Westview Press, 1995), 160.

2. N. E. Craddock, "Anthills, Split Mothers and Sacrifice: Conceptions of Female Power in the Maryamman Tradition," Ph.D. diss., University of California at Berkeley, 1994, 51.

3. Henry Whitehead, *The Village Gods of South India* (New York: Garland Publications, 1980), 29.

4. Jayakar, *The Earth Mother*, 188.

5. Satheesh Bose, personal correspondence, 1998.

6. Judith Rae Grahn, "Are Goddesses Metaformic? An Application of Metaformic Theory to Menarche Celebrations and Goddess Rituals of Kerala and Contiguous States in South India," Ph.D. diss., California Institute of Integral Studies, San Francisco, 1999, chap. 5.

7. Jayakar, *The Earth Mother*, 188.

8. Ibid., 40–41.

9. Ibid., 41.

10. Grahn, "Are Goddesses Metaformic?," chap. 5 and appendix C. The storyteller's name is Saraswathiama Thevaravattath.

11. Wilmore Theodore Elmore, *Dravidian Gods in Modern Hinduism* (Whitefish, MT: Kessinger, 2003), 37; Jeffrey A. Oddie, *Hindu and Christian in Southeast India* (London: Routledge/Cuzon, 1993).

12. Mahalakshmi Ganghadaran, personal communication, 1998.

13. Marija Gimbutas, *The Language of the Goddess* (San Francisco: Harper and Row, 1989), chaps. 1, 14.

14. Elinor Gadon, "The Village Goddess," unpublished manuscript.

15. Craddock, "Anthills, Split Mothers, and Sacrifice," 48.

16. Wendy Doniger, *Splitting the Difference: Gender and Myth in Ancient Greece and India* (Chicago: University of Chicago Press, 1999), 207–208.

17. Amarananda Bhairavan, author, personal communication, 2005.

18. Craddock, "Anthills, Split Mothers, and Sacrifice," 188.

19. K. L. Kamat, "The Yellamma Cult," posted July 31, 2000; updated February 10, 2009, http://www.kamat.com/kalranga/people/yellamma/yellamma.html; Firoze Shakir, "Devadasi Hijda of Yellamma," http://www.hijdaeunuchblog.html.

20. Craddock, "Anthills, Split Mothers, and Sacrifice," 42.

21. Kapadia, *Siva and Her Sisters*, 159–160.

22. Ibid., 160.

23. Grahn, "Are Goddesses Metaformic?"; Dianne Jenett, "Red Rice for Bhagavathi/Cooking for Kannaki: An Ethnographic/Organic Inquiry of the *Pongala* Ritual at Attukal Temple, Kerala, South India," Ph.D. diss., California Institute of Integral Studies, San Francisco, 1999.

Bibliography

Craddock, Norma Elaine. "Anthills, Split Mothers, and Sacrifice: Conception of Female Power in the Maryamman Tradition." Ph.D. diss., University of California at Berkeley, 1994.

Doniger, Wendy. *Splitting the Difference: Gender and Myth in Ancient Greece and India.* Chicago: University of Chicago Press, 1999.

Elmore, Wilbur Theodore. *Dravidian Gods in Modern Hinduism*. Whitefish, MT: Kessinger, 2003.

Gadon, Elinor. "The Village Goddess." Unpublished manuscript.

Gimbutas, Marija. *The Language of the Goddess*. San Francisco: Harper and Row, 1989.

Grahn, Judith. "Are Goddesses Metaformic Constructs? An Application of Metaformic Theory to Menarche Celebrations and Goddess Rituals of Kerala and Contiguous States in South India." Ph.D. diss., California Institute of Integral Studies, San Francisco, 1999.

Jayakar, Pupul. *The Earth Mother: Legends, Goddesses, and Ritual Arts of India*. San Francisco: Harper and Row, 1990.

Jenett, Dianne. "Red Rice for Bhagavati: Pongala Ritual at Attukal Temple in Kerala, India." *ReVision* 20, no. 3 (1998): 37–43.

Jenett, Dianne. "Red Rice for Bhagavati/Cooking for Kannaki: An Ethnographic/Organic Inquiry of the *Pongala* Ritual at Attukal Temple, Kerala, South India." Ph.D. diss., California Institute of Integral Studies, San Francisco, 1999.

Kamat, K. L. "The Yellamma Cult." Posted July 31, 2000; updated February 10, 2009. http://www.kamat.com/kalranga/people/yellamma/yellamma.htm.

Kapadia, Karin. *Siva and Her Sisters: Gender, Caste, and Class in Rural South India*. Boulder, CO: Westview Press, 1995.

Oddie, Geoffrey A. *Hindu and Christian in South East India*. London Studies on South Asia 6. London: Routlege/Cuzon, 1993.

Shakir, Firoze. "Devadasi Hijda of Yellamma." Posted March 29, 2008. http://www.hijdaeunuchblog.html.

Whitehead, Henry. *The Village Gods of South India*. New York: Garland Publications, 1980.

6

Durga: Invincible Goddess of South Asia

Laura Amazzone

The great mother goddess Durga astride her tiger, brandishing eight to eighteen arms each carrying a distinct weapon or tool, is one of the most ubiquitous images in South Asia today. She is stunningly beautiful: her long dark hair cascades down her back and over her shoulders; each arm is adorned with bangles and decorated with hennaed tattoos; golden earrings dangle from her ears and are connected on one side to a delicate chain that leads to a ring in her nose. A garland of orange and yellow marigolds flows over her breasts. The folds of her sari enhance her sensual feminine features, and intricate symbols patterned on natural objects are portrayed on her feet.

Durga radiates great confidence and authority. She is formidable and fearsome: four of her hands hold a scythe, a spear, a trident, and a club. She is beneficent, generous, and reassuring: three other hands hold a conch shell, a lotus, and a discus, while another gives the *mudra* or hand gesture of "Fear not, I will protect you."

The sacred objects Durga carries in each of her eight to eighteen hands carry the power to create and destroy. Symbolically they serve as guides and tools for use in enduring the inevitable cycles of death, destruction, and suffering as well as life, blossoming, and joy. For example, Durga's knives are not to be used for violence, but are a symbol of liberation. The knife is a tool that cuts away; it severs or excises that which no longer serves, whether it is a destructive belief, an unhealthy relationship, or a

Figure 6.1 Goddess Durga on the final day of the Durga Puja, Vijaya Dashami, Kathmandu, Nepal. (Photograph courtesy of Laura Amazzone, 2006.)

toxic situation. Her sword also points to helping focus and draw from the discriminating wisdom that is necessary in life—particularly to those committed to a spiritual path. All the sharp weapons Durga carries cut through obstacles that impede progress and clear the path for spiritual growth.

Often she carries a shield for protection, a bow for determination and focus, and an arrow for penetrating insight. When she holds a bell, it is to be used to invoke mental clarity and to clear the air of negativity. When her fingers play with a string of beads (*mala*), her worshipers are reminded of lessons on concentration and spiritual growth. The club she wields can be used to beat a new path, and the three-pronged trident pierces through the veils of the past, present, and future and teaches about birth, life, and death. The conch shell represents the vibratory powers of manifestation, while the lotus refers to both spiritual and material abundance. The skull or severed head, a common motif also associated with Durga in her fiercest of forms, represents the ego and all the ways it can enslave.[1] The mind conceives of situations as bad or good, positive or negative, while Durga shows the paradoxical nature of reality and the divine unity behind all existence. Both negative and positive are part of her inseparable force.

The goddess's name, Durga, means "fortress" and expresses her unconquerable, unassailable, and invincible nature.

History of the Goddess

Durga appears in benevolent and terrifying forms throughout her history. She is both the all-devouring and all-nurturing mother. In the ancient world, the goddess was conceived as responsible for the generative and creative as well as destructive aspects of existence. Throughout her evolution she takes on various epithets or names that describe the different functions for which she is responsible. The different names and attributes associated with a specific form of goddess define the vast terrain of earthly and cosmic experience that she has governed since ancient times. Although she appears in thousands of names and forms, within the Hindu worldview she is ultimately one goddess.

Earliest evidence of the goddess today known as Durga in South Asia goes back to the Saraswati Valley Civilization approximately 3500 BCE, but there is ample evidence of mother worship throughout the ancient and indigenous world. The goddess astride her lion or tiger is a common motif.[2] From earliest times the feline has been one of the sacred vehicles and power animals of the goddess. The goddess's association with the tiger and other animals demonstrates shamanic connections and an understood interrelationship between the animal and human world. Trees and plants also were believed to contain spirit, and qualities found in the goddess Durga can also be traced to these nonhuman forms. The goddess is also portrayed as a vegetative goddess and in this manifestation she is called Sakhambari. In her early vegetative form, the goddess is depicted with legs open, yoni exposed and a pot with a blossoming plant where her head would be. In this manifestation the generative powers of the *yoni* (vulva and uterus) are understood as synonymous with the earth.[3]

Myriad forms of this goddess are worshiped in aniconic form as uncut stone or geometric designs as well as anthropomorphic representations throughout South Asia. Villages often have a central deity that shares similar characteristics and/or iconography with Durga; however, these goddesses are called by specific, regional names. Others host the ubiquitous image of Durga slaying the buffalo-headed demon, or simply Durga on her tiger with her eight to eighteen arms. Ritual practices in villages and more remote places often are based on ensuring the fertility of land. There is a strong identification of earth with woman. The connection between women's bodies, specifically a woman's menstrual and reproductive cycle with the lunar and agricultural cycle, is an important focus of worship in the earth-based and female-centered Shakta and later tantric traditions. The Shakta tradition, known in its earlier historical appearance as Kaula, is one of the earliest sects of the Hindu tradition.[4] Within it, the goddess is understood to be the supreme force behind all existence. Reverence for the female principle as divine is evident in contemporary ritual implements and objects throughout South Asia. The symbolic origin of many of these ritual objects can be traced back to the Saraswati Valley civilization.

The highly creative, peaceful, and egalitarian Saraswati Valley civilization existed around the now underground Saraswati River and extended over half a million square miles.[5] Controversy over the results of archaeological findings remains a heated dispute within scholarship today. Nevertheless, the undeniable presence of thousands of female figurines and seals that exhibit a pictographic script suggest a sophisticated ancient culture that honored the power, beauty, and immanent divinity of the female. Many scholars contend that Durga's earliest form can be traced at least to this civilization, if not earlier.[6]

Mythic and ritual texts throughout written history also demonstrate the longevity of this goddess. Durga's evolution from earth goddess to warrior goddess can be traced through the texts and witnessed in the temple iconography. Beginning around 1300 BCE in the Rig Veda, the oldest of India's sacred texts, the goddess continued to appear in primordial forms such as Vac (Speech), Ushas (Dawn), and Ratri (Night). However, she is not conceived as the supreme force behind all existence as she is in the early Saraswati Valley civilization. In the post-Vedic period, from the fourth century CE onward, the Upanishads give little attention to goddesses except in their role as saviors to men. No longer were goddesses powerful, fierce, and autonomous. Instead, Hinduism continued to develop in part by linking male deities such as Vishnu and Shiva to the local female divinities and claiming them as wives (700 BCE–100 CE). Nevertheless, the female-centered Shakta tradition continued to thrive in some parts of the subcontinent. By the second century CE, images of powerful goddesses in stone, especially of Durga slaying Mahisuramardini, the buffalo-headed demon, began to appear. The mythic narration of Durga's epic battle with this shapeshifting demon is expressed in the *Markandeya Purana* (300–600 CE) and also through the Durga Saptshati, a collection of 700 hymns glorifying the goddess.

Durga's most famous textual appearance lies in the *Devi Mahatmya*, a fifth-century text that narrates the story of her mythic battles with the *asuras* or demons. This Shakta text focuses on three manifestations of goddess: Saraswati, Lakshmi, and Kali, as expressions of the generative, sustaining, and destructive qualities of existence. Other epithets, which speak to the varied nature of goddess, appear throughout the myth.[7] This text does not need to explain the goddess's supremacy; to a Shakta, goddess *is* supreme. In fact, she is also referred to as Adya Shakti, the primordial power of all existence.

Myth of the Goddess Durga

The following is adapted from the Devi Mahatmya:

It has been said that when life becomes full of suffering, when no relief seems to be within reach, when forces threaten to destroy one's very existence, it is then that the universal mother goddess Durga will appear to her devotees and free them from the forces that bind them to their anguish. Although the male gods have their place within the universal scheme of things, there are times when it is only the divine female force who can respond to the desperate call of those that need her.

In the timelessness of her ultimate reality there is a demon known as Mahisuramardini or Durgama, the shape-shifting buffalo demon, who visits the land of the gods and asks the God of Creation for a boon. Brahma is wise enough to know a demon should not be given the gift of immortality, but he does agree to grant Mahisa's second request: that he die only at the hand of a woman.

Off the demon goes, determined to conquer the universe. For over a thousand years, the demon and his ruthless armies wage war in every realm of the cosmos. Finally, the lesser gods summon the holy male trinity. The gods of destruction, preservation, and creation—Shiva, Vishnu, and Brahma respectively—meet to devise a plan to stop the demons. Not only are they too late, but also they do not possess the natural power that is necessary to stop the violence and restore balance on the earth. It is only the divine mother goddess who pervades the entire universe, and who ultimately is the force behind these gods' own existence, who can stop them. But will she come? Yes: she will always come when called.

Ambika, mother of the universe, appears on her mighty tiger bearing weapons the gods have given her as gifts. Never before had a more beautiful and powerful being existed. Undaunted by the thought of battling this vicious demon and his minions, the goddess roars in delight at the task before her. Her laughter sends a tremendous echo across the skies and causes tremors in all the worlds. Mahisa and his demon armies are shocked that there is still another power that they must reckon with. When Mahisa learns it is a goddess, he is delighted for he mistakenly thinks he is more powerful than she. The demon king Mahisa orders two of his most repulsive demon generals to do whatever it takes to bring her to him. He has decided that a woman of such beauty is meant to be his possession. He then sends them off to find the beautiful goddess who is waiting for them in the Himalayas. Ambika has taken the form of Parvati, the beautiful mountain goddess with skin as dark and rich as the earth. When the demons find her, they are dumbstruck by her radiant beauty but remember their mission and attempt to regain control of themselves. "If you even dare refuse," they tell her as they snicker and burp, "we have been told to drag you by the hair."

"Oh really?" the goddess replies. "But I will only marry the man or god who can defeat me in battle."

The demons laugh and joke with each other about how easy it will be to fight her. After all she is only a woman! The goddess listens to them carry on but soon becomes bored by their ridiculous egos. She lets out a long sigh that stirs the trees across all the lands, then points her finger at them. The rays of the sun reflect off of her faceted carnelian ring and for a brief second blind the demons' sight. They do not even have a chance to be alarmed, for as she shakes her finger flames stream out its tip and annihilate the demons.

So ends the first of three battles of the great mother goddess.

The Next Battle with the Demon

When Mahisa learns that two of his most beloved generals have been tricked by the goddess he is outraged. He sends his army of hundreds of thousands of demons to defeat her. They descend upon the mountains where she is waiting for them and then transforms herself into one of her fiercest forms: Chandika, the angry goddess with her three eyes that can see past, present, and future. However, Mahisa has another trick that cleverly keeps him in power. With every drop of blood that falls from the demons, another demon springs up from the blood. Enthralled by his own cleverness,

Mahisa watches the battle from his palace. His pride grows by the second, and he feels increasingly certain that even the supreme mother of the universe cannot defeat him. The battle wages on and more and more demons appear with every drop of blood that is shed.

The goddess knows she must change her tactic. She decides to call on her own powerful army of female warrior deities and summons the eight Matrikas ("mother goddesses") who leap from her third eye onto the battlefield. The Matrikas send out ululating war cries that stop every demon in his tracks. Arrows fly through the air and before the demons' blood can even fall to the earth, one of the Matrikas, Kali Chamunda, unrolls her long snaky tongue and laps up every single drop.

Furious that he is no longer winning, Mahisa throws a temper tantrum. He calls out to Chandika and accuses her of cheating. He demands that she take back her army and promises he will do the same. It is time for a duel between the two of them.

Knowing that the Matrikas are only aspects of herself, the mother of the universe, the goddess inhales, and her sweet breath draws them back inside her luminous body.

The Final Part of the Battle

For a moment all is silent as Ambika waits for Mahisa to appear. Behind her, a river of blood from the felled demons streams across the land. Above her, the gods cautiously peek through the clouds eagerly waiting for the next epic drama to unfold. Finally, Mahisa comes storming onto the battlefield in his form of a buffalo kicking up mountains as he charges at her. Ambika punches away the mountains with her ringed fists. The demon shakes with fury and transforms into an elephant. In his elephant form he comes barreling at her with every intention of trampling both the tiger and the Goddess. But she is too quick for him and throws a noose about his neck just as he attempts to slay her tiger with his tusk. Again the demon changes form. He becomes a lion and lunges at her. Ambika raises her sword and chops off his head, but the demon turned lion now assumes the form of a man. The goddess and her tiger roar together as they leap onto the man's chest and force him to the ground. Mahisa shape-shifts back into his original form of half-buffalo/half-man just as she pierces his chest with a trident in one hand and lops off his head with a scythe in another. The terrible demon cries out in pain and fury, then falls lifeless to the ground. As she stands with one foot on his torso proudly holding his severed demon head in one of her hands, Ambika decides that from then on whenever her devotees call her to help them with any difficulty she shall be called Durga.

The gods are elated and join Durga on the battlefield to celebrate her victory. Durga blesses each and every being and promises to return whenever they need her aid. She reminds them that it is only the fiercely compassionate goddess, the supreme mother of the universe, who can take on the demons in all their insidious forms and win. "Remember that just as each of you and every other being is part of me," she tells them, "so too is every demon part of my great body. This is my sacred and most mysterious play."

She turns to leave on her majestic tiger, then suddenly stops. There is one more promise she wishes to make. She assures the assembly that if they call on her and create ritual festivities, she will come every year in the fall and give her blessing of balance between the forces of light and dark, day and night. She will come and battle any *asuras* (demons) with her fierce gaze of measured intent. She will always come to liberate the oppressed. She will always come to remind her devotees to awaken the fierce creative force of goddess within themselves.[8]

Interpreting Durga's Myth

There are many layers of interpretation of this myth. Historically, it can be understood as a commentary on the confrontation between two peoples with varying belief systems. Psychologically, this appears as the internal battle with the asuras or demons of greed, shame, fanaticism, ignorance, corruption, hatred, and so forth. Philosophically, it can be interpreted as a spiritual guide for the evolution of consciousness. But perhaps, most significantly in this day and age, the myth offers a powerful model of female authority that comes to offer liberation from restrictive societal convention and the cruelties that come with oppressive religious dogma. Durga in her various forms is not submissive or subservient but autonomous, strong and fierce. She has nurturing and sensual qualities; however, her beneficent qualities are not in the service of men or the support of the status quo. There is much to learn from a myth that venerates the female as divine. As Vidya Dehejia points out,

While the myths surrounding the Great Goddess have not thus far been interpreted to serve as women's empowerment, today's new generation of women may indeed reinterpret the message of the myths to provide them with a degree of freedom and power . . . [I]t would indeed be gratifying to see women on the Indian subcontinent draw from the tradition of the Great Goddess to redefine their status within society and to consider the many options inherent within those myths that might be used to revalidate and revalue their position.[9]

Other literature such as the puranic texts, which tell the life, powers, and accomplishments of certain divinities and their followers, show the reemergence of fierce and independent goddesses as a powerful indomitable primal force from the fifth century into the Middle Ages. In the temple iconography from the eighth to 16th centuries one witnesses the syncretism that occurred over the ages. However, thanks to Shakta and tantric practitioners in Bengal, Assam, Nepal, Orissa, and South India, the goddess in her wild, unfettered form still remains strong and popular. The goddess's most common names appear in the Puranic texts: Durga, Kali, Lakshmi, Saraswati, the Matrikas, and so forth.

Durga is also mentioned in the famous Indian text *Mahabarata* (400 BCE– 400 CE) through her association as a warrior goddess with Krishna and Arjuna in their battles. She also appears in the popular epic narrative the Ramayana (600–400 BCE). In some parts of India the annual Durga Puja focuses on Durga's victory over the demon king Ravana.

Philosophy of the Shakta Tradition

In the Shakta tantra tradition goddess Durga is conceived as the supreme force behind all existence. Not only does she appear in anthropomorphized forms of certain energies, she also has an ethereal and philosophical presence as *Shakti* (power), *Maya* (illusion), and *Prakriti* (phenomenal reality). Shakti is the creative, dynamic power that pervades the universe while Shiva, her male counterpart, is the receptive foundation upon which she acts. As the force known as Maya, Durga creates a veil of illusion that challenges one's perception of the world. From this perception, the material world is illusory—both real and unreal. It is the goddess herself who conceals and reveals all realities. All forms of existence and every action of every being are her *lila* or play. All existence, whether it has a form or has not yet come into being, is understood to be goddess. Durga herself is the universal body of the seen and unseen worlds. As Mahamaya, or the great illusion, she holds the mystery of creation and destruction. The concept of Prakriti or the goddess as phenomenal reality comes from the Samkhya school (fourth century CE), which describes the universe as comprised of three strands or universal qualities called *gunas*: *sattva* (purity), *rajas* (activity), and *tamas* (lethargy).[10] Prakriti is inseparable from its complementary aspect known as Purusha, a principle of consciousness that is described as inactive and male. Purusha is often used to refer to the worldly self and Prakriti to the ground upon which the world becomes manifest. Shakti, Maya, and Prakriti are philosophical concepts found throughout different schools of Vedic and Tantric literature that express the goddess as cosmogonic and cosmological reality.

Samkhya, Shakta, and other ideologies of the Tantra tradition demonstrate how goddess can take a form and also can be formless. Tantra is a yogic path of integration. It is a path that embraces opposition and paradox. It involves practices that attempt reconciliation between disparate parts or thoughts. Tantra works to heal all dichotomies; particularly the dichotomy of spirit and matter, which has been so prevalent in the West. In tantrism all reality is seen as one. This oneness must be realized through the integration of all dualities; male and female, active and passive, higher and lower, good and evil, joy and sorrow, birth and death, pure and polluted, divine and human.

Tantrism arose in the early Middle Ages (eighth century CE) as a response to limiting orthodox practices within the Hindu and Buddhist traditions. There are at least sixty-four tantric schools, and while many "share a common sexual paradigm to portray the relationship between the manifest and unmanifest worlds, they are not philosophically uniform."[11] The Shakta tantra tradition, in which Durga is most firmly situated, honors the unifying force of all existence as goddess and promotes a nondual view of reality. The nondual perspective within Shakta tantrism emphasizes the complementary nature of all tensions and opposites rather than viewing them as dualistic or separate. Therefore, the inner *Cit* or consciousness of a human being is also a microcosmic reality of the greater macrocosmic whole.

Durga herself is the ultimate consciousness of the universe. She is both creator and destroyer, mother of life and death. Durga is the female sacred force that influences and informs everything. She pervades all that is good as well as all that is evil and ignorant, so that she can remove the darkness and provide light and knowledge. She reveals the truth underlying all falsehood. World struggles, sorrows, and distress are relieved through her grace. Ultimately she cannot be defined. She knows no beginning or end. All comes from her and returns to her, emerges from her and dissolves into her.

Collective Forms of Durga

In the *Devi Mahatmya*, eight Matrikas spring out of Durga's forehead to help her wage battle with the demons. When the demon general accuses her of cheating, she calmly calls the Matrikas back within herself and takes him on by herself—and wins. The Matrikas can be understood as aspects of Durga that, like other goddesses, rule over or assist with a specific sphere of existence. Since their earliest anthropomorphized appearance on a Saraswati Valley civilization seal, these goddesses have been worshiped in groups of seven or eight goddesses.[12] Although this grouping of goddesses later became individually named a variation of one of the male gods (Brahmani, Maheswari, Kaumari, et al.), they, in all likelihood, were originally regional goddesses who protected the community from illness and natural calamities. Historically, and even today outside of Shakta circles, they are primarily feared and equated with chaotic and impure aspects of existence. However, from a Shakta tantric perspective, the powers associated with their elemental and uncontrollable natures can be harnessed and utilized for practices that liberate ordinary consciousness and allow for a deeper sense of union with the goddess within. The Matrikas' relationship to the four cardinal directions and intermediary directional points offers protection and also emphasizes the undeniable presence of goddess both around and within any given space. These goddesses are also tied to specific places in the local geography, for example, cremation grounds, crossroads, hilltops, sacred groves and forests. They are also known to protect the threshold of various states of consciousness: dreaming, sex, pregnancy, birth, menstruation, and death.

The eight Matrikas, like Durga herself, defy conventional expectations of femininity. Instead of being restricted to submissive and subordinate roles within institutionalized marriage and motherhood, these goddesses are wrathful and fearsome, nurturing and seductive, beautiful and grotesque. They embody the full spectrum of the female psyche and offer a model of femininity that is empowered and liberated, autonomous and creative.

Other collective forms of Durga include the Nava or Nine Durgas. Sometimes their names are conflated with those of the Matrikas, but they have specific functions and modes of ritual worship of their own.

While the Matrikas are understood to be protectors of a place and the boundaries of consciousness during experiences such as birth, menstruation, dreaming, sex, and death, the Nine Durgas govern time and movement. They are connected to the natural cycles of the year, specifically the agricultural cycle as well as the reproductive cycle of women's bodies. Moreover, they have a direct association with nine specific plants and the seven major planets and two nodes of the moon, demonstrating the goddess's singular and communal governance over both earthly and cosmic existence.

Another collective form of Durga are the Yoginis. Durga is sometimes worshiped as the queen of the Yoginis, which includes *chakras* or circles of 49, 64, or 81 goddesses. These *chakras* sometimes contain the Matrikas and Navadurgas within the larger fold of goddesses. The Yogini groupings are numerologically related to the numbers 7, 8, and 9, which multiplied by itself becomes a group of 49, 64, or 81 Yoginis. In Hindu and Tantric philosophy the numbers 7, 8, and 9 have mystical associations with the creation and ordering of the universe. The Yoginis are complex and multifaceted expressions of female power, authority, and divinity. The term *Yogini* refers both to goddesses and living female practitioners. Tantric rites around the Yoginis relate to subduing the restlessness of the mind, confronting fears, and using the powers generated from sexual practices as well as from substances considered socially and culturally taboo, for example, alcohol and certain foods, to help expand consciousness. Each of these collective forms of Durga emphasizes the Shakta understanding of goddess as the one and the many.

Durga Puja: Annual Festival to the Great Goddess

Each autumn Durga's mythic battle is reenacted through ritual, storytelling, dance, and worship across the Hindu world in a festival known as Dashain in Nepal and Navaratri or Durga Puja in other parts of South Asia. The Durga Puja is one of the most important religious festivals in the Hindu world. Millions come together to worship god as mother Durga.

For ten days and nine nights the *Sri Chandi* is recited, hymns to the goddess are sung, and temporary shrines holding freshly constructed straw and clay *murti* (statues) of the goddess are ritualistically placed throughout cities and towns. The first three days are devoted to Kali, and rites are performed for removing obstacles and letting go of the old. On the next three days, Lakshmi is honored and rites celebrating the vegetative world are performed. On the final three days Saraswati, goddess of purity and wisdom, is revered. Practitioners place their tools, books, work objects, and other daily utensils on the altar and ask for the goddess's blessing. All are seen as aspects or forms of Durga.

Throughout the lunar-based festival, the Asta Matrikas and the Navadurga are worshiped as a collective form of Durga. Revered as protectors of space and time, they are danced at midnight in the main squares of the three medieval kingdoms of the Valley: Kathmandu, Patan, and Bhaktapur. While each of these goddesses is honored on individual days of the festival, they are ultimately understood as various forms of Durga.[13]

The final day of the festival, Vijaya Dashami, celebrates Durga's victory over the demonic forces. With her victory a new cycle begins. Although the goddess is returning to her mountain abode, she is always within reach. Devotees know they can always call on the divine mother when they need assistance.

Regardless of which stream of Hinduism one encounters in the various texts or temple iconography, the power of goddess in some manifestation is always evident. Durga appears in infinite forms and guides her devotees through the challenges and triumphs of life. The unbroken, varied, and ubiquitous expression of her invincible power unequivocally affirms Durga's longevity and omnipotent presence in the consciousness of South Asians for millennia.

Notes

1. For a comprehensive analysis of ten of Durga's tools and weapons see Babaji Bob Kindler, *The Ten Divine Articles of Sri Durga: Insights and Meditations* (San Francisco: Sarada Ramakrishna Vivekananda Associations, 2001).

2. Asko Parpola, *Deciphering the Indus Script* (Cambridge: Cambridge University Press, 1994), 254.

3. Carol Radcliffe Bolon, *Forms of the Goddess Lajja Gauri in Indian Art* (Delhi: Motilal Banarsidass, 1997).

4. N. N. Bhattacharya, *History of the Shakta Religion* (New Delhi: Munshiram Manoharial Publishers, 1996).

5. Ibid., 12.

6. See ibid.; Katherine Anne Harper, *The Iconography of the Saptamatrikas: Seven Hindu Goddesses of Spiritual Transformation* (Lewiston, NY: Edwin Mellen Press, 1996); Thomas Coburn, *Devi Mahatmya: The Crystallization of the Goddess Tradition* (Delhi: Motilal Banarsidass Publishers, 1984).

7. Thomas B. Coburn, *Encountering the Goddess: A Translation of the Devi Mahatmya and a Study of Its Interpretation* (Albany: SUNY Press, 1991).

8. "Myth of the Goddess Durga," adapted version from Laura Amazzone, *Durga: Empowering Women, Transforming the World* (Lanham, MD: Hamilton Books, 2010). Reprinted with permission.

9. Vidya Dehejia, "Encountering Devi," in *Devi: The Great Goddess Female Divinity in South Asian Art* (Washington, DC: Arthur M. Sackler Gallery, 1999), 134.

10. Tracy Pintchman, *The Rise of the Goddess in the Hindu Tradition* (Albany: SUNY Press, 1994), 68.

11. Constance A. Jones and James D. Ryan, *Encyclopedia of Hinduism* (New York: Facts on File, 2007), 438.

12. Harper, *Iconography of the Saptamatrikas.*

13. For more about Durga, the Matrikas, and the annual fall festival, see Laura Chamberlain, "Durga and the Dashain Festival: From the Indus to Kathmandu Valleys," *ReVision: Journal of Consciousness and Transformation* 25, no. 1 (Summer 2002).

Bibliography

Amazzone, Laura. *Durga: Empowering Women, Transforming the World.* Lanham, MD: Hamilton Books, 2010.

Bhattacharyya, Narendra Nath. *History of the Shakta Religion.* New Delhi: Munshiram Manoharial Publishers, 1996.

Bolon, Carol Radcliffe. *Forms of the Goddess Lajja Gauri in Indian Art.* Delhi: Motilal Banarsidass, 1997.

Chamberlain, Laura K. "Durga and the Dashain Festival: From the Indus to Kathmandu Valleys." *ReVision: Journal of Consciousness and Transformation* 25, no. 1 (Summer 2002).

Coburn, Thomas B. *Devi Mahatmya: The Crystallization of the Goddess Tradition.* Delhi: Motilal Banarsidass Publishers, 1984.

Coburn, Thomas B. *Encountering the Goddess: A Translation of the Devi Mahatmya and a Study of Its Interpretation.* Albany: SUNY Press, 1991.

Dehejia, Vidya. "Encountering Devi." In *Devi: The Great Goddess Female Divinity in South Asian Art.* Washington, DC: Arthur M. Sackler Gallery, 1999.

Harper, Katherine Anne. *The Iconography of the Saptamatrikas: Seven Hindu Goddesses of Spiritual Transformation.* Lewiston, NY: Edwin Mellen Press, 1989.

Jones, Constance A., and James D. Ryan. *Encyclopedia of Hinduism.* New York: Facts on File, 2007.

Kindler, Babaji Bob. *The Ten Divine Articles of Sri Durga: Insights and Meditations.* San Francisco: Sarada Ramakrishna Vivekananda Associations, 2001.

Kinsley, David. *Hindu Goddesses: Visions of the Divine Feminine in the Hindu Religious Tradition.* Berkeley: University of California Press, 1998.

Parpola, Asko. *Deciphering the Indus Script.* Cambridge: Cambridge University Press, 1994.

Pintchman, Tracy. *The Rise of the Goddess in the Hindu Tradition.* Albany: SUNY Press, 1994.

7

Kumārī: Nepal's Eternally Living Goddess

Jeffrey S. Lidke

The word *kumārī* comes from the ancient East Indian language of Sanskrit and means "young girl, virgin." Throughout India, Nepal, and other regions of South Asia there is a strong and longstanding ritual tradition—evidence of Kumārī worship dates back to the origins of India's oldest scripture, the Veda (circa 2000 BCE)—in which prepubescent girls are venerated as incarnations (*avatāra*) of the divine feminine, called Devi or Sakti. During the Hindu festival of Navarārtri or "Nine Nights," it is still a common practice to select young girls to embody the goddess as kumārīs for the course of the festival. There are also major centers of Kumārī practice at the Indian temples of Kāmākhya, Assam; Kanyakumari, Tamil Nadu; Kanya Devi, Punjab; and Karani Mata, Rajasthan; as well as several temples in the Kathmandu valley, Nepal. While the traditions at each of these sites have their unique histories and practices, they all share in common the understanding that the ritual worship of select young virgin girls makes possible the descent to earth of the divine feminine presence. This chapter focuses on the kumārī traditions of the Kathmandu valley, Nepal, as they are among the strongest and most thoroughly documented of the many South Asian kumārī traditions.

Eleven Kumārīs live in the Kathmandu valley, spread throughout the three primary cities—all former kingdoms—of Kathmandu, Patan, and Bhaktapur. The specific focus of this chapter is the Rāj or Royal Kumārī of Kathmandu. While in times past there were also royal Kumārīs in Patan and Bhaktapur, the Rāj Kumārī of Kathmandu has been the

Figure 7.1 The Royal Kumārī of Patan as she appeared in 1996. Young girls, chosen through a series of ritual tests, serve as living incarnations of goddesses in Nepal. Traditionally associated with hereditary kingship, the institution of the Kumārī is undergoing change since the dissolution of royal power. (Photograph by Jeffrey S. Lidke.)

national Kumārī since the unification of the Kathmandu valley in the 18th century under King Pṛthivī Nārāyan Śāh. Consequently, the institution of the Kathmandu Rāj Kumārīs has received primary adoration, interest, and study of the Nepalese faithful and scholars alike in recent decades and provides an excellent case study not just for Kumārī traditions in Nepal, but throughout South Asia as a whole.

Kumārī's Divine Identities

The beginning of the 21st century has been a complex and profoundly interesting time in the history of the Kathmandu Rāj Kumārī because Nepalese kingship, the institution that established the Kumārī tradition, became a monument of the past. On May 28, 2008, Nepal officially established itself as a parliamentary democracy with the first meeting of the Constituent Assembly and the stepping down of former king Gyanendra. This death of Hindu monarchy in Nepal was one significant consequence of a Maoist-led twelve-year civil war that took over 13,000 lives throughout the country and led to tremendous political, social, and cultural upheaval. In the wake of this war, there emerged a strong and growing antireligious sentiment among many Nepalese who came to accept the position that religion—particularly the Hindu and Buddhist religions practiced by Nepal's kings over the past centuries—had been an instrument of economic, political, social and cultural dominance by the elite.[1]

This sentiment was no place more evident than in the supreme court case that called for an end to the institution of the royal Kumārīs.[2] From the perspective of the nonreligious in Nepal, the Kūmārī is the living fossil of antiquated institution linked to political and economic systems of repression. From the perspective of the faithful, the Kūmārī is the supreme goddess, called by many names, but most popularly known as Mā Durgā. It is this latter perspective—of faith and devotion—that this chapter seeks to map out.

Taleju-Durgā: The Goddess as Invincible Power

The logical first step in this regard is an investigation of the goddess most frequently identified with the Nepalese Kumārī: Taleju. The word *Taleju* is derived from the indigenous Newar language and translates approximately as the "Goddess of the High Temple," which indicates her status as the chosen deity of Nepalese kings dating back to the 14th century when this goddess likely first migrated to Nepal from northern India.[3] Why was Taleju revered by Nepal's king? The answer to this important question partly resides in her being identified not just as a particular goddess, but as Mahā Devī, the great goddess, and therefore, according to the tradition, unlimited in power. In particular, Taleju is commonly identified as the "fierce emanation of Durga," one of the most popular forms of the great goddess in South Asia.[4] Durgā is venerated in homes and temples ranging from the southern tip of Kerala in India to the Himalayas of Nepal. Whereas many forms of the divine feminine in South Asia have very specific and therefore limited powers, Durgā is understood to be the embodiment of all powers. Her creation myth, recounted in the Devīmahātmya, emphasizes this very point.

In an age long ago, the Devīmahātmya informs its audience, the gods were engaged in a battle with a terrible demon named Mahiṣa who received, through penance, the boon of invincibility from the creator god, Brahmā. As a result, no single god could defeat him and Mahiṣa, driven by the hunger for power, was quickly becoming lord of all the three worlds. Desperate, the lesser gods went to the highest heaven, called

Vaikhuṇṭa, and beseeched there the assistance of Vishnu and Shiva, the two mightiest of the Hindu gods. Seeing that the situation was dire, these supreme leaders devised a brilliant military plan: create a "weapon" that was the combination of the powers of all the gods. This plan was actualized by means of all the gods generating their internal energy (*tapas*) and projecting it simultaneously into a single field of power. From that combined field of power emerged the goddess Durgā, bearing the weapons of the gods in her multiple arms, three-eyed, riding a tiger, and proclaiming herself to in fact not be a product of creation but rather the original source of creation.

Mysteriously uncreated, yet designed for a clear militaristic purpose, Durgā proceeded to do battle with the invincible demon Mahiṣāsura. The demon assumed multiple forms in attempting to defeat the goddess, but each time she was victorious. Finally, he assumed the form of a buffalo (in Sanskrit *mahiṣa* means "buffalo") but Durgā stunned him with the brilliance of light emanating from her body and then beheaded him with her sword, forever earning the name Mahiṣāsuramārdinī, the "Slayer of the Buffalo Demon."[5]

As a slayer of invincible enemies, Durgā is identified not just as *a* goddess, but as *the* goddess, called Mahā Devī or "great goddess." Consequently, she is understood to be the source of and to contain all other goddesses within her. For this reason, the Kumārī, Durgā's living incarnation (*avatāra*) on earth, can and is addressed by the names of other popular Hindu goddesses, such as Kālī, Pārvatī, Tripurasundarī, and Ambikā.

The identification of the Nepalese royal Kumārīs with Mahā Devī reveals a key facet of her identity and function as a living divinity: she is the embodiment of a power (*śakti*) that protects the nation against any and all enemies of state. To understand how a small virgin girl can embody such awesome power, one must take into account the ritual ideology and practice that undergirds the Kumārī institution. It is ritual that transforms the young virginal girl into a divinity capable of destroying all enemies.

Vajradevi: The Kumārī as a Buddhist Wisdom Deity

The Kumārīs' identity is by no means shaped solely by traditional Hindu theology and myth. The central power of the Kumārī institution is that it functions as a ritual mirror in which Nepal's multiple ethnic groups see reflected their respective cultural values. For Newar Buddhists Kumārī is a living embodiment of the Vajrayāna Buddhist deity Varjayoginī, "The Adamantine (*vajra*) Female Yogi (*yoginī*)," known more commonly in Nepal as Varajdevi, "The Adamantine Goddess."[6] To initiates of Varjayāna Buddhism, the Kumārī-as-Vajrayoginī is revered as Buddhahood or perfect enlightenment itself. As described in numerous Paddhatis and depicted in traditional Newar art, Vajrayoginī is naked, red-skinned, dancing with ankle bells, adorned with a garland of skulls, holding a skull bowl in her left hand and a crescent blade in her right.[7] To Buddhist initiates, Vajradevi is a wisdom *ḍākinī*, the female liberator whose function is to assist those on the meditative path to awakening.[8]

The male consort of Vajradevi is Cakrasamvara, "The Binder of the Wheel," frequently depicted with a blue-colored body, four faces, and twelve arms, each holding a particular ritual implement. When represented as a united "father-mother" deity (*yab-yum*) Cakrasamvara and Vajradevi symbolize the fullness and completion of enlightenment. This identification of Kumārī with the female principle of liberation in Buddhist Tantra indicates what initiates themselves see as the secret and highest purpose of the Kumārī institution: to manifest into the inherently restrictive temporal realms of society the energy and wisdom of timeless transcendence.

Kumārī and the Ritual Technologies of Tantra

The technologies that transform virgin girls into divine Kumārī's stem from Tantra, a system of ritual practice and related ideologies that date back to the fourth century. The Tantric tradition—which cuts across the divide between Hindu and Buddhist—assumes that all of existence is an unfolding of a singular conscious energy or śakti that manifests itself according to a precise geometrical and acoustic pattern termed *mandala* ("territory"). The universe itself is the grandest of mandalas, being the cosmic emanation of śakti. Within the cosmic mandala, śakti replicates itself an infinite number of times in a way akin to what modern physicists term *fractals*—self-replicating patterns in which the macro-form and micro-form are identical. This "fractal logic" is captured in the tantric dictum "as in the universe, so in the body." In other words, from the perspective of Tantric practitioners, called Tāntrikas, the body is a replica of the universe. If there is infinite power in the universe—and Tāntrikas believe there is—then infinite power also resides within the body. The key, then, is to access and harness this power.[9]

Girls designated to serve as Rāj Kumārīs are selected because their young, virginal bodies are deemed qualified to serve the nation as vessels for this harnessing of divine power. Through ritual they are temporarily transformed into that cosmic power that is depicted mythologically as Durgā/Taleju and iconographically as that mandala structure whose perfect interwoven forms are the power-patterns that protect the region—at the cosmic, bodily, and state levels—from all enemies.

In order for the ritual empowerment to be successful, first the selection team must appoint a worthy candidate. There are a number of requirements linked to the selection of Kumārīs. A committee of religious officials, including the Bāha Guruju or chief royal priest, the priest of Taleju, and the royal astrologer, conducts the selection. Additionally, in times past the king was invited to suggest potential candidates. Candidates for the Rāj Kumārī are selected from the Newar Śākya caste of silver- and gold-smiths, which claims links to the family of the historical Buddha. Candidates must demonstrate that they are free from disease and other bodily imperfections, including the loss of blood or teeth. Passing this stage, the potential Kumārī is examined for the "thirty-two perfections" which include a list of apparently idealized female bodily attributes, such as "thighs like a deer," "eyelashes like a cow," as well as dark black hair and eyes, and well-formed, complete teeth. However, recent Royal Kumārī, Rashmila Shakya, clarifies in her fascinating biography—a primary inspiration for this chapter—that these perfections actually astrological references. It is the horoscope, far more than the physical body, that must be free of any indications of conflict with the horoscope of the reigning king.[10] Any incompatibility would give rise to serious reflection on whether or not the right candidate had been found.[11]

This emphasis on compatibility sheds light on the key function of the Kumārī: to empower the king. It is for this reason that the tradition claims the chosen candidate innately demonstrates the attributes ascribed to the great goddess in her various textual sources. Such attributes are said to be particularly exemplified during the ten-day festival of Dashain, particularly on the Kālrātri, or "black night," when 108 buffaloes and goats are sacrificially offered to the Royal Kumārī as an emanation of the goddess Kālī. It is commonly believed that a final test transpires in the central Taleju temple. There, the candidate exhibits her goddess nature by remaining tranquil even in the presence of the bloody, severed heads of buffalo slaughtered that day. According to Allen, these heads are illuminated by candles while masked dancers engage in a ritual dance around the candidate. If she does show fear, then the next candidate is sought and tested. However, if she continues to demonstrate the attributes of the goddess, then she is destined to be Nepal's next Royal Kumārī. "Having passed all the tests," Allen writes, "the child will stay in almost complete isolation at the temple, and will be allowed to return to her family only at the onset of menstruation when a new goddess will be named to replace her."[12]

Rashmila Shakya explains that the purpose of these particular rituals has less to do with whether or not the selected human candidate literally experiences no fear, but rather that she be represented in such a way. Whatever their own individual experience, the function of the ritual is to manifest a being who is transcendent to fear. For it is this fearlessness that the king himself must actualize as his nation's leader.

The Fulfillment of Wishes

The technologies that transform virgin Nepalese girls into living conduits of these real unseen powers are described in sacred ritual texts called Paddhatis, which detail ritual prescriptions for daily worship, festival worship, and worship for specific intentions, such as the power to win an election. Of these three types of ritual the most common and most important is the daily ritual. Once the Kumārī is chosen, she must be ritually purified each day so that she can be an unblemished vessel for Taleju. The heart of the ritual is the placement of the Kumārī on a ritual seat shaped in the form of a mandala while a Tantric priest worships her with special body postures (*mudrā*s) and liturgical formulae (*mantra*s) that empower her body to be a living manifestation of what the Paddhatis call the Goddess of Universal Form (*viśvarūpa-devī*).[13]

At the completion of each daily ritual, it is understood that the power of the supreme goddess (*parādevī*) fully resides in the human form of the Royal Kumārī and that therefore she deserves the official title of Taleju, identifying her as the king's own sovereign deity. Affectionately, the Royal Kumārī is commonly called by the members of her inner circle as Dyāh Meiju, Newar for "Mother Deity." As a Mother Deity it is believed that the Kumārī can transmit power or śakti directly into the bodies of those devotees who come to have her audience (*darśana*). For this reason, every day, after the daily ritual, the Royal Kumārī receives the faithful in her inner chambers for a brief period, providing an opportunity for direct contact with living divinity. In other words, the ritual is the medium of transformation. Through ritual a human girl becomes the microcosmic embodiment of the goddess. In this way, as Alexis Sanderson has noted, ritual makes the impossible possible.[14]

The Kumārī is a medium through which the goddess Taleju disseminates her divine nature throughout Nepal, which the faithful perceive as her own body writ large as geopolitical space. For the Tāntrika who has been initiated into the system of the mandala, the entire country of Nepal is perceived as the body of divinity. This is because Nepalese Tāntrikas operate according to a kind of inside-out logic that situates the origin-point of "objective" space within the consciousness of the witnessing subject. In other words, from a Tantric perspective, the universe adapts itself to each individual's perception of reality. The Kumārī is for this reason called the "Wish Fulfilling Cow" (*kāmadhenu*) for like that mythic being she too functions to bestow the desires of the nation's citizenry.

In order to assure that the Kumārī maintains this desire bestowing power, the Royal Kumārī priest—established in correct posture (*āsana*) and proper breathing regimen (*prāṇāyāma*)—begins his daily worship of the Kumārī with the construction of an internalized image (*dhāraṇā*) and meditation (*dhyāna*). The image he constructs in his mind is called the Śrī Yantra and is considered by Nepalese Tāntrikas to be the most sublime representation of the supreme goddess (*parādevī*). Once constructed, he meditates on the small point in its center, called *bindu*, which represents the center point of the cosmos out of which flows the creative source of all being. Then, through a special technique of empowerment by means of self-touch, called *nyāsa*, he begins to instill the beings and powers of this internalized mandala in his own limbs, inscribing himself with the wisdom of the mandala (*maṇḍala-vidyā*) and making himself a worthy vessel to worship the goddess. After thus encoding his body, he opens his eyes and receives the darśana of the Kumārī as Taleju herself, that female deity who is the very soul of the cosmos, his nation, and his very being.

At this point the priest proceeds to worship the feet of the goddess, receiving from them the divine blessing, prasāda, that for centuries was carried daily directly to Nepal's kings for their daily consumption. After visually mapping the Śrī Yantra across the entire body of the Kumārī, the priest then, without disrobing her, focuses this image specifically on her womb, or *yoni*, for it is here that the goddess yields her greatest power: that of creation itself. Having transformed the Kumārī into Taleju by projecting his internalized vision of the Śrī Yantra onto her, the Tantric priest receives the blessings of her transformed divine presence. The consumption of prasāda in the tangible form of eggs, sweets, and other food items is the ritual evidence that this reciprocal transformation had indeed occurred. Through this blessed food, the power generated by this inside-projected-outside transformation of perceptual space is immediately actualized by the yogic realization that the "objective" world is nondistinct from the internal continuum of consciousness.

Through this process of ritual consumption the goddess creates a stirring, or vibration, within the microcosmic bodies of the ritual participants as well as within the mesocosmic plane of social space. This stir is her *spanda*, the subtle vibratory pulse that is manifested as the acoustic body of the mandala. As the power of cosmic emission (*visarga-śakti*), this pulse makes possible the projection of the goddess onto her own screen as the śrī Yantra. As the power of individual-awakening (*śakti-pāta*), this pulse stirs the dormant *kuṇḍalinī-Śakti* and brings about the internal ascent of the goddess within the body of the *yogin*. As the power that stabilizes and invigorates the social-mandala, this pulse stirs through the various ritual performances and musical traditions that serve as conduits for disseminating the goddess's acoustic body.

The Core Identity: Divine Pulsation

Through her rhythmic sound body, the goddess enlivens the mandala. The Thami shamans of Dolakha in eastern Nepal worship Taleju through music, seeking possession by the goddess through the sounds generated by their drumming and the repetitive chanting of her many sacred names. Similarly, the Ha Bāhāh priests of the Patan Kumārī tradition worships the Kumārī through the ritualized sounds of his litany accompanied by drumming. The link is a pan-Asian technology of producing deity-possession through the ritualized production of sound.[15] In Nepal the classical canonical traditions of the Tantra intermingle with indigenous shamanic traditions, interconnected through technologies of deity-possession rooted in the ritual performances that harness the transformative power of sound.[16]

In this way, Nepal's divine Kumārī is many things at once, a foundation in many senses. As a servant to the state, her work symbolizes commitment to the nation's institutional complex, formerly embodied concretely by her master, the nation's king, whose initiation into goddess Tantra qualifies him to be both a servant and master of divine śakti. For this end, the Kumārī becomes his divine consort, serving as the goddess of the heights (Taleju) whose incarnational body (*avatāra-deha*) makes possible the transmission of unlimited power into the land of her residence.

Although the king does not visit the human form of the Kumārī on a daily basis, it is key to the well-being of the nation that the king encounter the spiritual essence of his chosen goddess at the start of every day. For this reason, ritual offerings, called *prasād*, from the daily worship of the Kumārī are brought to the king's royal priest who in turn offers them to the king.

The Kumārī in History: The Intersection of Eternity and Time

According to the Nepalese dynastic chronicles, Gopālarāja-Vaṃsāvalī, in 1192 CE King Lakṣmīkāmadeva,

> thinking that his grandfather had acquired so much wealth and conquered the four quarters of the world through the aid of the Kumārīs, resolved to do the same. With this intention he went to the . . . [palace] of Lakshmī-barman, [where] he erected an image of Kumārī and established the Kumārī-pūjā.[17]

After the reign of King Lakṣmīkāmadeva we continue to find inscriptions mentioning the worship of Kumārīs by kings. Both the Kaumārī-Pūjā (1280 CE) and the Kumārī-Pūjā-Vidhana (1285 CE) describe the worship of the Kumārī by the king and equate the Kumārī with the king's personal deity (iṣṭa-devatā), highlighting her paradoxical role as both the king's political servant and his revered deity.[18]

Trailokya Malla, who reigned in the independent kingdom of Bhaktapur from 1562 to 1610, is credited with establishing the institution of the Kumārī in each of the three Malla kingdoms. The accounts of this historical event are illuminating, as they highlight the institution's links to mystico-erotic traditions of Tantra, which view sexual union (maithuna) as an integral aspect of the Tantric path. Paralleling the classical mythology of Śiva and Pārvatī, Trailokya and the goddess were playing dice. The king longed for intimate contact with his iṣṭa-devī, who consequently scolded him and said that he could only communicate with her through a girl of low caste.

Perhaps the most significant historical example is King Prthivī Nārāyan Śāh (1723–1775). The historical accounts of his life reveals the intimate relationship of Tantra to kingship and the ways in which the institution of the Kumārī, while clearly embodying an anthropo-contingent power dimension, also comes to symbolize theo-contingent power. While king of Gorkha, a region in western Nepal, Prthivī Nārāyan arduously practiced the Tantric yoga of Bālā Tripurasundarī, "The Beautiful Young Goddess of the Three Cities." After he had practiced Tantric sādhana for twenty-five years, this child goddess appeared to him and granted him the boon that he would conquer and unite the Kathmandu Valley.[19] Prthivī Nārāyan and his troops entered Kathmandu on the day of Indra Jātra, the occasion when the Kumārī bestows her divine approval upon the king. At the time of Prthivī Nārāyan's surprise attack, the then-king of Kathmandu, Jaya Prakāś Malla, was preparing to receive the Kumārī's blessing. Swiftly and unexpectedly Pṛthivī Nārāyan rode into the royal courtyard and bowed before the Kumārī, who unhesitatingly blessed him. In that moment, popular legend goes, the king of Gorkha became king of Nepal in a swift act of power that was the result of both political strategy and divine grace won through years of arduous devotion to the Goddess.

The most recent chapter in the history of the Royal Kumārī institution is one filled with tragedy and the demise of monarchy in Nepal. On June 1, 2001, King Birendra Shah Dev and several members of his family were murdered at the Narayanhity Royal Palace in Kathmandu. While the official report is that the king's own son, Dipendra, shot his entire family before putting the gun to himself in a drugged state of rage, many Nepalese to this day believe that the massacre was orchestrated by the king's brother, Gyanendra, who came to power with the death of his brother and his entire family.[20] According to Sthaneshwar Timalsina, there were signs that the Royal Kumārī did not favor King Gyanendra. When he came for her audience, it is said that one of the daggers in the inner sanctum of her residence fell auspiciously to the floor, heralding, some believe, the demise of King Gyandendra himself.[21]

Conclusion: The Benefits of a Living Goddess

With Gyanendra now forced from office and the centuries-old institution of kingship officially extinct in Nepal, critics of traditional culture have argued that there is no point in having a Royal Kumārī if royalty in Nepal is no longer a living tradition. However, important voices from within the tradition have argued passionately for the wisdom of keeping Kumārī alive. Deepak Shimkhada writes:

> By doing away with venerated, age-old customs, elements of the new Nepali government and some human rights organizations may be going down the path to wiping out their culture, history, and identity as Nepalis. Cultural identity is more important than political identity. As we move toward assuring essential human rights for all, we should preserve those customs that make us who we are. As a Nepali, I certainly hope that the newly elected government in power will think twice before abolishing cultural traditions that add value to the country's heritage and prestige, and bring financial gain to the country through tourism. Although Kumari was traditionally associated with the throne, she does not have to disappear just because Nepal has voted to abolish the monarchy. Judging by

the situation on the globe all heads of states could do with the blessings of a living goddess. The people of Nepal, who need and seek peace, harmony, and reconciliation, need Kumari's blessings more than ever.[22]

Shimkhada's impassioned plea highlights the centrality of the Royal Kumārī as a cultural tradition over and above its historical links with kingship in Nepal. In so doing he explicitly invokes the deeply held belief that the Kumārī is a living source of blessing power, a source capable not only of impacting affairs of state, but bringing a state of well-being to a troubled people. In this regard his sentiments echo a long-standing and deeply abiding belief that Nepal's living goddess, as a Kumārī, embodies a wisdom and power transcendent to the mortal frames that are her temporary embodied home.

Notes

1. Marie Lecomte-Tihouine, *Hindu Kingship, Ethnic Revival, and Maoist Rebellion in Nepal* (New York: Oxford University Press, 2009), 149–154.

2. Balkrishna Basnet, "Injustice Within an Esteemed Practice," in *Sancharika Feature Service* 8, no. 6 (2005): 1–4.

3. Brownen Bledsoe, "An Advertised Secret: The Goddess Taleju and the King of Kathmandu," in *Tantra in Practice*, ed. David White (Princeton, NJ: Princeton University Press, 2000), 195–205.

4. Rashmila Shakya and Scott Berry, *From Goddess to Mortal: The True Life Story of a Former Royal Kumari* (Kathmandu: Vajra Publications, 2005).

5. Thomas B. Coburn, *Devīmahātmya: The Crystallization of the Goddess Tradition* (New Delhi: South Asia Books, 2002).

6. Mary Slusser, *Nepal Mandala: Cultural Study of the Kathmandu Valley*, vol. 1. (Princeton, NJ: Princeton University Press, 1982), 314–315.

7. See Miranda Shaw's illuminating discussion of Vajrayoginī in her *Buddhist Goddesses of India* (Princeton, NJ: Princeton University Press, 2006), 357–386.

8. For an excellent and detailed analysis of the Dakini, see Judith Simmer-Brown, *Dakini's Warm Breath: The Feminine Principle in Tibetan Buddhism* (Boston: Shambhala, 2001).

9. Jeffrey Lidke, *The Goddess Within and Beyond the Three Cities: Śākta Tantra and the Paradox of Power in Nepāla-Mandala* (New York: Edwin Mellen Press, 2010).

10. Shakya and Berry, *From Goddess to Mortal*, 15–18.

11. Indra Majupuria and Patricia Roberts, *Living Virgin Goddess Kumari: Her Worship, Fate of Ex-Kumaris and Sceptical Views* (Lalitapur, India: Craftsman Press, 1993), 26–29.

12. Michael Allen, *The Cult of Kumari: Virgin Worship in Nepal* (Kathmandu: Mandala Book Point, 1975), 24–26.

13. *Kanyārūpasarvabhūtā pūrakadehinī devī*, Tripurasundari Paddhati, Nepal National Archives, 21.3–21.5.

14. Alexis Sanderson, "Mandala and Āgamic Identity in the Trika of Kashmir," in *Mantra et Diagrammes Rituels dans L'Hindouisme,* ed. Andre Padoux (Paris: CNRS, 1986), 210.

15. Mircea Eliade, *Shamanism: Archaic Techniques of Ecstasy* (Princeton, NJ: Princeton University Press, 1972).

16. Surendra Bahadur Shahi, Christian Rätsch, and Claudia Müller-Ebeling, *Shamanism and Tantra in the Himalayas* (London: Thames and Hudson, 2002).

17. Daniel Wright, *History of Nepal: With an Introductory Sketch of the Country and People of Nepal,* translated from the Parbatiya by Munshi Shew Shunker Singh (New Delhi: Asian Educational Services, 1993), 157.

18. Allen, *The Cult of Kumari*, 16; cf. Slusser, *Nepal Mandala*, 311.

19. L. F. Stiller, trans., *Prithvinarayan Shah in the Light of the Dibya Upadesh* (Kathmandu: Himalayan Book Centre, 1989), 40–41.

20. "Nepalese Royal Family," http://en.wikipedia.org/wiki/Nepalese_royal_massacre.

21. Oral communication, San Diego, CA, July 2008.

22. Deepak Shimkhada, "The Future of Nepal's 'Living' Goddess: Is Her Death Necessary?" http://www.asianart.com/articles/kumari/index.html#4.

Bibliography

Allen, Michael. *The Cult of Kumari: Virgin Worship in Nepal.* Kathmandu: Mandala Book Point, 1975.

Basnet, Balkrishna, "Injustice Within an Esteemed Practice." *Sancharika Feature Service* 8, no. 6 (2005): 1–4.

Bledsoe, Brownen. "An Advertised Secret: The Goddess Taleju and the King of Kathmandu." In *Tantra in Practice,* ed. David G. White, 195–205. Princeton, NJ: Princeton University Press, 2000.

Coburn, Thomas B. *Devīmahātmya: The Crystallization of the Goddess Tradition.* New Delhi: South Asia Books, 2002.

Eliade, Mircea. *Shamanism: Archaic Techniques of Ecstasy.* Princeton, NJ: Princeton University Press, 1972.

Gregson, Jonathan. *Massacre at the Palace: The Doomed Royal Dynasty of Nepal.* New York: Hyperion, 2002.

Huntington, John C., and Dina Bangdel. *The Circle of Bliss: Buddhist Meditational Art.* Chicago: Serindia Publications, 2003.

Lecomte-Tilouine, Marie. *Hindu Kingship, Ethnic Revival, and Maoist Rebellion in Nepal.* Oxford: Oxford University Press, 2009.

Lidke, Jeffrey. *The Goddess Within and Beyond the Three Cities: Śākta Tantra and the Paradox of Power in Nepāla-Mandala.* New York: Edwin Mellen Press, 2010.

Majupuria, Indra, and Patricia Roberts. *Living Virgin Goddess Kumari: Her Worship, Fate of Ex-Kumaris and Sceptical Views.* Lalitapur, India: Craftsman Press, 1993.

Sanderson, Alexis. "Mandala and Āgamic Identity in the Trika of Kashmir." In *Mantra et Diagrammes Rituels dans L'Hindouisme,* ed. Andre Padoux, 169–214. Paris: Éditions du Centre National de la Recherche Scientifique, 1986.

Shahi, Surendra Bahadur, Christian Rätsch, and Claudia Müller-Ebeling. *Shamanism and Tantra in the Himalayas.* London: Thames and Hudson, 2002.

Shakya, Rashmila, and Scott Berry. *From Goddess to Mortal: The True Life Story of a Former Royal Kumari.* Kathmandu: Vajra Publications, 2005.

Shaw, Miranda. *Buddhist Goddesses of India.* Princeton, NJ: Princeton University Press, 2006.

Simmer-Brown, Judith. *Dakini's Warm Breath: The Feminine Principle in Tibetan Buddhism.* Boston: Shambhala, 2001.

Slusser, Mary. *Nepal Mandala.* Vol. 1. Princeton, NJ: Princeton University Press, 1982.

Stiller, L. F., trans. *Prithvinarayan Shah in the Light of the Dibya Upadesh.* Kathmandu: Himalayan Book Centre, 1989.

Wright, Daniel. *History of Nepal: With an Introductory Sketch of the Country and People of Nepal.* Translated from the Parbatiya by Munshi Shew Shunker Singh. New Delhi: Asian Educational Services, 1993.

8

Dakini: The Goddess Who Takes Form as a Woman

Vicki Noble

The Tibetan Buddhist Dakini is a representation of untamed female freedom. She is dynamic and moving, expressing a sense of the unexpected. Her appearance often precipitates a shock or disruption, having the effect of derailing one's ordinary mind from its routine tracks. She liberates practitioners from ego fixations and seemingly intractable problems. The arrival of the Dakini releases blockages in the energy field and melts frozen patterns, so that the mind is suddenly ajar and something new can enter. Dakinis are often connected to the phenomena of synchronicity and inexplicable coincidents of fate. As Tsultrim Allione wrote, "[T]he dakini appears at crucial moments. These encounters often have a quality of sharp, incisive challenge to the fixed conceptions of the practitioner."[1]

Dakinis are particularly associated with Dzogchen Buddhism, known as the path of instantaneous awakening, sometimes called "the path of no path" because the awakening can happen to anyone, at any time, without the necessity of any special techniques or austere practices. Although Dzogchen practitioners may not be Buddhist, it is with Tibetan Buddhism that Dzogchen is most frequently associated. A typical Dzogchen practice is to lie on the ground, relax, and stare at the sky, watching the clouds go by—noticing the way thoughts come and go in the mind, arising and dissolving back into emptiness. The goal is spontaneous presence, for which the Dakini is a representation.

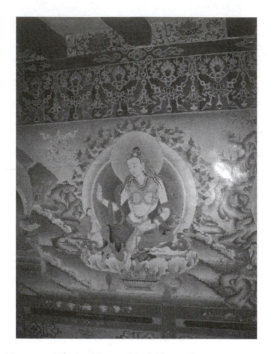

Figure 8.1 Mural image of Yeshe Tsogyal in Tibet's Samye Monastery. (Photograph taken by Vicki Noble in 2007, all rights reserved.)

The word *Dakini* is associated most strongly with Tibetan Vajrayana or Tantric Buddhism, established in the remote Himalayas during the eighth century CE through the legendary collaboration of a famous magician, Padmasambhava, and a local princess, Yeshe Tsogyal. *Dakini* is a Sanskrit word whose inferred meaning has been borrowed from and equated with the Tibetan word *khandro* ("sky goer" or "one who moves through space"); *dakini* and *khandro* are often used interchangeably. But unlike *dakini*, with its derived counterpart male form (*daka*), *khandro* has no such twin and stands alone as a female being who moves through emptiness or space—a kind of Tibetan fairy goddess or, as June Campbell named her in her book, a "traveller in space." The word *khandro*, Campbell says, "is quite a unique word, with no male equivalent, and would seem to have arisen not out of the Sanskrit background of Tantra . . . but apparently from the shamanistic roots of Tibet itself."[2]

Spirit flight, where the invisible spirit body detaches from the physical in order to ascend to upper worlds or descend to the underworld for healing or soul-retrieval, is a well-understood feature of traditional shamanism around the world.[3] Since earliest times, supernatural shamanistic females engaging in the ecstasies of soul flight have been depicted as having the capacity to "move through space" like birds. The famous "Land of the Dakinis," called Odiyana or Uddiyana, referred to as a "country of women" in Tibetan historical and Tantric texts, would have been a place of women spiritual leaders. The name translates to mean "vehicle of flying." Imagine an entire country of women who fly—gifted shaman women and magical priestesses—and the powerful yogis who accompany them. It is from that mythohistoric realm that the famous yogi Padmasambhava is said to have originally flown into Tibet with a retinue of Dakinis in order to subdue the demons (wild and fierce nature spirits and spirits of the land who resisted the new religion) and anchor Buddhism there for good. Miranda Shaw mentions several Indian scholars who "suggest that Tantra (both Hindu and Buddhist) originated among the priestesses and shamanesses of matrilinear tribal and rural societies."[4]

Winged women and bird goddess figures abound in many places around the world and through eons of time, going all the way back to the Paleolithic period (ca. 30,000 BCE) where they are part of the earliest human art. Hybrid bird-women, hugely pregnant, dance with the animals on a ceiling in the cavern at Pech Merle in the south of France.[5] From the later Neolithic period, more than 100,000 female figurines have been unearthed from Old Europe alone, a large percentage of them depicted with wings or as pregnant birds; significantly, many are covered with an ancient extinct script.[6] Egyptian vulture goddesses with arms raised predate 3000 years of dynastic empire in northern Africa. Intricate and colorful bird women in flight are embroidered on ancient remarkable textiles found wrapped around mummies in Peru and Bolivia, from extinct Andean cultures known to have practiced shamanism. These figures all qualify as female "traveler(s) in space." The Dakini, although historically dated to eighth-century Tibet, descends from a much more ancient strata of female supernatural beings reaching far back to earliest human cultural origins.

Linguistic and archaeological evidence shows that until fairly recently shamanism was a collective function of the human female group. Even in the 20th century, a Russian ethnographer surveying shamanism across Siberia wrote: "The woman is by nature a shaman" and "women receive the gift of shamanizing more often than men."[7] The oldest word for shaman actually means "female shaman" and connects to words for "earth goddess" and "mother earth," as well as to those indicating the two bear constellations, Ursa Major and Minor. Words for "male shaman" came into being later, after the tribes had migrated away from the place of origins.[8]

Techniques used by shamans are similar to those found in the lore about Indian yoginis, whose "extraordinary powers" were "often of a magical and yogic nature." Some of these powers include "complete control over breathing and other bodily functions, levitation . . . and control over living creatures."[9] Although myriad forms of Buddhism are found in East Asia, the Tibetan Vajrayana path is the only Tantric one. With its mantras, drums, trumpets, cymbals, and bells, it is noisily shamanistic ("employing nonordinary states of consciousness"), clearly distinguishing it from "quietist" or "clerical" traditions such as Zen or Theravadin. "Lamas in Tibet function as shamans," says Samuel. Indo-Tibetan scholar David Snellgrove equates Vajrayana with "Mantrayana (Way of Spells)," meaning the "application of spells to a particular aim." He believes these spells were part of the Vajrayana tradition transmitted to Tibet from Central Asia and India, specifically mentioning Khotan and Kashmir.[10]

The Silk Road

Central Asian trade routes linked China and India with the Mediterranean for as much as four thousand years.[11] These much-traveled routes provided an exceptional channel for the migration of peoples and the cross-cultural exchange of ideas, symbols, and artifacts that ultimately must underlie any serious investigation of the Dakini in Tibet, Nepal, and India. Deborah E. Klimburg-Salter points out that in addition to Indian sources, Tibetan Buddhist art "shows the influences of India, China, Iran, and the Mediterranean."[12] A long and rich lineage of Afro-Eurasian female shamanism left traces along the Silk Routes:

> This ancient female lineage began in the Neolithic (if not earlier) and included priestesses of the Aegean Bronze and Iron Ages (the Maenads), the shaman women of Central Asian tribes such as the Cimmerians, Scythians, Sauromatians, and Saka (to name only a few), and the cemetery-dwelling yoginis and wandering "dakini witches" of India and Tibet. Furthermore this lineage includes the Scandinavian "Valkyries," Irish "Banshees," Iranian and Tocharian mummies of the Tarim Basin.[13]

John Vincent Bellezza confirms this ancient underground stream when he refers to certain "extinct" Tibetan female sisterhoods that provide "evidence suggesting the existence of a matriarchal culture and the supremacy of female deities in prehistory."[14]

Excavation of burials found near the Black Sea and all the way east to the Altai Mountains have unearthed high-status women covered in gold, often wearing elaborate headdresses, with the mirrors and portable altars that defined their spiritual leadership, as well as other burials with weapons that indicate that the women were warriors. Many were buried with one leg bent at the knee, in the typical "dakini pose" so well known in Tibetan iconography. Some of these were the Sauromatians (sixth century BCE) and Sarmatians (fifth–fourth centuries BCE) living along the Don and Volga rivers in southern Russia, who have been dubbed "Amazons" by the archaeologists who found them. The word *amazon* was believed in ancient times to mean "without a breast"; however, "most modern linguists seem to agree that the word *Amazon* actually comes from a Proto-Indo-European term meaning "no-husband-one."[15] These communities with their matrilineal social organization were distinguished from their male-dominated neighbors by their lack of patriarchal marriage.[16]

American archaeologist Jeannine Davis-Kimball collaborated on a Russian dig at Pokrovka (near the border of Kazakhstan), where she and her Russian partner discovered the burials of numerous shaman priestesses as well as high-ranking warrior women. Perhaps even more interesting is the fact that all the women in the tribe—regardless of status or specialization—were buried at the center of their mounds, suggesting a matrifocal social base.[17] These nomadic Amazon tribes were not exclusively women, but were rather tribes of men and women *governed* by women, and these women were nobody's wives.

Tibet in the Eighth Century CE

Although today Tibetan Buddhism is associated with the pacifism preached by the Dalai Lama and practiced by contemporary Tibetans, this was not always the case. By the mid-first millennium CE, Tibetan warriors controlled a great empire including much of China and central Asia. By the eighth century CE, Islam was invading Khotan from the west, sending Buddhist monks from there fleeing into Tibet.[18] Pre-Buddhist pagan or tribal peoples all along the Silk Route were disrupted and in some cases annihilated by this invasion from the west, at the same time that the Chinese were invading Tibet from the east. By the time Buddhism was anchored as the state religion, Tibet had vastly expanded its territory by conquering many oasis towns along the trade routes. Oasis towns like Khotan, Kucha, and Dunhuang were sophisticated places where Buddhism had already flourished by the time Tibetans conquered the cities and assimilated their knowledge—and perhaps their pacifism as well.

Some of these oasis sites had been settled more than a thousand years earlier during the Bronze and Iron ages by migrants from the Black Sea region—Caucasoid peoples with blue eyes and blond hair, who brought with them the arts and tools of weaving when they settled in the Tarim Basin.[19] Bronze and Iron age burials recently discovered at some of these sites include mummified "shaman priestesses" wearing high pointed hats, and tattooed others wearing red woolen garments like those worn by Tibetan monks and nuns today.[20]

Barber presents evidence that these migrants may be genetically or linguistically related to those who left from the same point of origination in the Caucasus but traveled west to Crete and the Mediterranean, carrying the same distinctive weaving tools with them. In Minoan Crete during the late Bronze Age an amalgam of the Afro-Eurasian shaman priestess flowered, known by then as the Maenads or wild women. Given the many common themes, such as funerary rituals and magical practices, tattoos, ecstatic dance, and the use of intoxicating fermented beverages, Maenads might be seen as a Mediterranean version of Indian Yoginis and Tibetan Dakinis, or the other way around.[21]

Some General Understandings of the Dakini

In her exuberant descriptions of the Dakini, Miranda Shaw emphasizes "flights of spiritual insight, ecstasy, and freedom from worldliness granted by the realization of emptiness." Shaw translates the name to mean "women who revel in the freedom of emptiness" and relates the poetry of various Dakinis known by names like Victorious-Minded Woman and Wings of Breath, or Blissful Corpse-Eater and Dakini Lion-Face—names, she says, that celebrate the "exhilarating sense of freedom from the prison of ego" and the release of "experience into a dance of energy, a sparkling, incandescent display of light and color, sound and awareness, that shimmers momentarily like a magician's illusion in the open space created by the simultaneous dissolution of self and other." This dissolution of boundaries between self and other is a primary Buddhist goal. Shaw says, "A wild, playful, unpredictable quality erupts when experience is released from its predetermined patterns."[22]

Lama Tsultrim Allione calls Dakinis "mystical female beings who may appear in dreams, visions, or human form. . . . In Dzog Chen traditions dakinis, female spiritual forces, are an absolutely integral part of the teachings." The Dakini, she says, "represents the ever changing flow of energy with which the yogic practitioner must work in order to become realized. She may appear as a human being, as a goddess—either peaceful or wrathful—or she may be perceived as the general play of energy in the phenomenal world."[23] Allione, an American teacher, was recently recognized in Tibet as a Lama and an emanation of Machig Lapdron, Tibet's most famous Dakini. She takes a psychological approach when working with students in relationship to the Dakinis, developing original methods for contemporary women and men to investigate and invoke the Five Dakini Families of a traditional Tibetan Mandala. More recently she has adapted the Chöd practice of offering one's body as a feast for invisible beings, particularly those with whom there is some karmic debt from the past.[24] Discussing the iconography of a red wrathful Dakini, Vajravarahi, Allione remarks that the image "could be an inspiration to women in our culture," which lacks such images of the feminine. "Our culture has clearly discouraged women from claiming their feminine potency," she states.[25]

Is the Dakini a Woman or Not?

Khandro, that explicitly gendered supernatural female, is depicted in a variety of peaceful and wrathful forms, often paradoxically fierce and erotic at the same time. Traditionally, in her efforts to alleviate suffering in the world, she is known to take form as a human woman. Not all women are Dakinis, but any woman, at any time, might be. This trait is the locus of a rift that has occurred in scholarly expositions of the Dakini, especially those written by women scholars in the last two decades. Some women eagerly embrace the concept of the Dakini as a welcome and much-needed icon of female liberation, one that can be utilized by contemporary women for the purposes of gaining confidence, raising self-esteem, and finding a sense of the sacred mirrored back in the same gender.[26] Others have seized on the Buddhist concept of "no gender" to argue that any personal identification with the Dakini as a particularly female form is delusional and, at worst, can be considered a harmful act toward Tibetan lamas and Tibetan Buddhist tradition, as well as a cultural appropriation. Judith Simmer-Brown makes the extreme charge that a feminist critique of the largely male perspective in Buddhism and/or any so-called appropriation of the Dakini as a symbol of female power "threaten(s) the integrity of the transmission of Buddhist teachings."[27]

A confluence of Buddhist philosophy and postmodern analysis has taken place in America, bringing to the fore the idea of "no self" and, in an even more particular way, "no gender" presuming that any sense of oneself as male or female is entirely constructed and has no inherent reality. This position is given expression by Simmer-Brown, who chooses "to speak of the 'feminine,' not of the 'female.'" The Dakini, she argues, is "a symbol but not an archetype; as feminine in gender but not a conventional female."[28] This abstraction from bodily existence, this apparent recoiling from women and nature, is at the heart of every feminist critique of Tibetan Buddhism.

Yet Tibetan Tantric Buddhism uses as its central methodology "deity yoga," the visualization of a divine image with which the practitioner is expected to identify and merge. The goal is to develop a quality of "divine pride," not to be confused with ordinary pride or arrogance, so that through becoming an excellent practitioner, one can benefit other beings. When Tibetan lamas first arrived in the United States and began teaching their traditional practices, the only images were male ones, the Buddha and Guru Padmasambhava, the famous yogi mentioned earlier who anchored Buddhism in Tibet. The arrival of Tara and eventually the Dakinis has been experienced as a boon to many female practitioners, especially feminists. But the accusation of "essentialism" has been leveled at women practitioners who choose to perceive the Dakini, in her form as an actual human woman, as a helpful mirror image. Women who take the Dakini as a personal role model report finding their imaginations stretched and their sense of possibility enlarged to include power, mastery, autonomy, and active personal agency—male prerogatives that have been mostly absent from the socialization process of many contemporary women.

Simmer-Brown feels "gender wars," as she refers to feminist critiques, have "completely missed the point of the fundamental teachings of Tibetan Buddhism in general and the Dakini tradition in particular." Yet she goes on to describe, paradoxically, how the "lore" of the Dakini "provides genuine support for women practitioners . . . to develop confidence, perseverance, and inspiration in their meditation practice."[29] She explicitly aligns herself with the writing of Jan Willis, who says about the Dakini that, although she appears most often in female form, she is not actually female, and against Miranda Shaw who insists and celebrates that she is.

Many women students and practitioners are grateful to Tsultrim Allione for speaking about the primal female experiences of pregnancy, birthing, raising, and even losing children—while at the same time making the effort to keep a spiritual practice active. "There is a natural infusion that takes place," Allione writes, "when feminine experience enters and reflects on traditions that have been dominated by men for many centuries." Speaking frankly about the dilemma of motherhood, she writes that there is "always a tension between my desire for the cave and the demands of the kitchen sink." She admits that through becoming a mother, she "irrevocably left the realm where compassion for all beings is visualized from a retreat cabin."[30] Allione shares her personal journey—with its joys and sorrows, descents and rebirths—as a way of relating to and benefiting her students: her early commitment to Buddhism and her ordination as a nun, followed by her taking on marriage and household life, the loss of her child, and the ongoing creative process of pulling out teachings that arise out of real life experiences as a woman.

Vajrayogini: Quintessential Dakini

The most famous and all-encompassing Dakini is the red, naked Vajrayogini, considered to be the queen of Vajrayana Buddhism itself. Shaw refers to her as "the foremost female Buddha."[31] Simmer-Brown says her most important manifestation is as a *yidam* ("meditation deity") visualized in Vajrayana practice who represents "awakening, in peaceful or wrathful form corresponding to the practitioner's nature." Having a yidam and doing practice in relation to the deity, she says, "binds the practitioner irrevocably to the enlightened sanity within."[32] Shaw sees Vajrayogini as the most significant yidam for women and says, "Vajrayogini repeatedly states that she reveals herself in and through women," announcing in one of the Yogini-tantras, "Whenever in the world a female body is seen, that should be recognized as my holy body." For women, Shaw says, "the relationship with Vajrayogini is one of identity. Women must discover the divine female essence within themselves. This should inspire self-respect, confidence, and the "divine pride" that is necessary to traverse the Tantric path. . . . This pride is an antidote to self-doubt." Finally, she sums up: "Vajrayogini takes form so that women, seeing enlightenment in female form, will recognize their innate divinity and potential for enlightenment."[33]

Vajrayogini's forms are varied, with three characteristic poses expressing the dynamism of this potent and preeminent Dakini. In the first, somewhat mild one, she stands facing front and stepping out into action, ready to actively benefit beings like a Bodhisattva. In the second, she stands with feet apart, knee bent, in something like the "warrior pose" in yoga, with a skull cup raised to the sky in her left hand and a Dakini's crescent knife in her right. The skull cup is filled to overflowing with menstrual blood, which she drinks. She wears bone ornaments, including necklaces, breast ornaments, and apron, and a necklace of skulls or human heads. Finally, in a classic dancing pose with one leg raised, she seems to shape-shift into her alter ego: the wrathful, erotic goddess Vajravarahi, an aspect or expression of Vajrayogini with a boar's head poking out the side or top of her head. In her most wrathful form, Vajrayogini becomes the Black Dakini, Tröma Nakmo ("angry woman") as she destroys the demons of doubt and fear, and all other ego fixations.

Vajrayogini is closely connected with Yeshe Tsogyal, the female cofounder of Tibetan Buddhism with Guru Padmasambhava and the one who hid the treasures so that later reincarnated *tertons* ("treasure-finders") could find and disseminate them. Yeshe Tsogyal is said to be an emanation of Vajrayogini and her standing posture ("stepping out") is the same, as is her special syllable, BAM (or VAM, depending on the transliteration). Yeshe Tsogyal's autobiography, which was discovered and revealed as a *terma* ("treasure") several hundred years ago, has been translated into English three different times and is available for contemporary students of Tibetan Buddhism. It includes the following narrative, in which she says that she reached the brink of death in her advanced meditation retreat and called out to "the Teacher": "Then I had a vision of a red woman, naked, lacking even the covering of bone ornaments, who thrust her *bhaga* against my mouth, and I drank deeply from the copious flow of blood. My entire being was filled with health and well-being, I felt as strong as a snow-lion, and I realized profound absorption to be inexpressible truth."[34] It would seem that the essential female bodily substance, menstrual blood, is shown here to be the nourishment *par excellence*. At the very least it is a striking metaphor for female-to-female direct transmission in a lineage of wisdom, in this case from the deity to a Dakini in human form.

David Gordon White, an expert in Hindu Tantra, says in another context, "When the template is the body of a naked maiden and the medium her sexual or menstrual discharge, we are in the presence of the Tantra of the old Hindu 'clans' (the Kula, or Kaula) and their inner and East Asian Buddhist Tantric homologues." White has emphasized in much of his work the extreme importance of the "sexual fluids" in early tantric practice in India, which was later "cleaned up, aestheticized, and internalized in different ways."[35] White's descriptions of the yoginis in the early Indian tantric practices seem to resonate with the visual representations of Dakinis in Tibetan practice. For example, he writes that a "horde of wild goddesses . . . attracted by offerings of mingled sexual fluids, would converge into the consciousness of the practitioner, to transform him, through their limitless libido, into a god on earth." He describes practices of Kaula, a Tantric sect of practitioners belonging to a clan lineage, as taking place in cremation grounds and involving "the communal consumption of blood, flesh, wine, and sexual fluids." Later, the "bliss of sexual orgasm" replaced the earlier rites as the way to "godhead."[36] This single-minded focus on orgasm can be seen in contemporary versions of Tantra imported to the United States and available in profitable weekend workshops.

Regarding Yeshe Tsogyal's visionary experience of receiving and ingesting Vajrayogini's blood, White's material grounds the story in ancient tradition. "The cosmic force that activates and energizes every facet of tantric practice—that originates from the womb of the Goddess and passes through every link in the chain of transmission . . . is ultimately nothing other than a stream (*ogha*) or flow (*scrotas*) of sexual fluid." And to this day, he says, the tantrikas in Assam "identify their 'lineage nectar' (*kulamrta*) with the goddess's menstrual fluid or the commingled sexual fluids of Siva and the Goddess." Assam, according to White, is also one of the regions where historians have reported a Kingdom of Women that could equate with the earlier-mentioned Oddiyana or Land of the Dakinis. In a discussion on the "tantrika's favorite sexual partner," an outcaste woman or *Dombi*, he says she "was most prized for the transformative powers of her menstrual blood," which he calls "the most powerful fluid in the universe."[37]

Elizabeth English investigates the red Queen of the Dakinis through references in earlier Indian texts, such as the Yoginitantras, which describe arcane magical practices; many of these have been incorporated into Tibetan Buddhism. One text English uses refers to her as the mother of "those with secrets," or initiates.[38] She details the mandala practices, symbols, mudras, accoutrements, and mantras belonging to Vajrayogini, along with those for her close sister-emanations, Vajravarahi and the Black Dakini, including food offerings to the five deities of the mandala. A mandala is a diagram meant to be read as a three-dimensional image seen from above, which marks the four cardinal directions and the center and functions as a transformative healing technology. Mandalas predate the Vedas, having been depicted in many locations since at least Neolithic times, and thus have their origins in the more ancient indigenous strata of female-based rituals.

Describing Vajrayogini's "thirteenfold Mandala" as a *mahasukhacakram* ("circle of great bliss"), English says that the fivefold central mandala is referred to as the *bhagah* ("vagina").[39] Likewise, Shaw describes how the "inner anatomy of a woman's sexual organ is seen as a mandala" and that the "center of the mandala radiates out from the cervix, or innermost point of the vulva." These meditations are sometimes imagined as expanding out and becoming large enough to "embrace the world and all living beings." Whatever way the mandala is precisely done, Shaw points out that it is understood to emanate from the central point, the cervix, "which is where the woman focuses her attention for this meditation."[40]

Mandala: Dakinis of the Four Directions and the Center

Mandala practices utilized in Tibetan Buddhism, at the very core of the Vajrayana or Tantric tradition, predate Buddhism by millennia. The ritual of positioning oneself in the center of a circle, then squaring the circle by marking off the four cardinal directions and often splitting those in two as well, appears to have been widely practiced in ancient times, and even up to the present in many places. Abundant images and representations of distinct mandalas are found in Old Europe, Asia, South America, Africa, and so on. Lepinski Vir, the oldest Neolithic site in Europe, was established as a mandala which is also a calendar of the seasonal cycles.[41] The so-called Aztec Calendar Stone found in Mexico City is an image of the mandala/calendar. The Inca Cross, ubiquitous in Peru, resembles the mandala shape found in Nepal and Tibet.

The purpose of the mandala practice, also true of many deity yoga practices, is to link up the mind mandala (the "pledge") with the invisible sacred mandala of deities or the Five Great Mothers (the "knowledge") that is understood to exist on another plane—and then bring them together in a potent dynamic fusion. The vibrational activity known to contemporary Wiccan practitioners as "drawing down the moon,"[42] Tibetans call *akarsanam* ("drawing down"), relating to the act of summoning the deity into a mandala. In Bronze Age Crete this religious epiphany was depicted on numerous sealstones in which priestesses with their arms raised bring down a figure of the goddess who hovers above the altar. Even Islamic mosques are built with four gates in the four directions; these are predated by the mandala-shaped fortresses at the Bactria-Margiana Archaeological Complex sites all along the Silk Road from the Bronze Age (ca. 2300 BCE). Allione calls the mandala a "primal centering tool" that "interfaces between the yet-to-be-perfected world, or encumbered emotions, and the dimensions of luminosity of the sacred ideal world."[43]

The use of the mandala in Tibetan Buddhism may be almost entirely devoted to recalling the ancient woman-honoring underpinnings of the religion as it came to be identified in the last 1200 years. The Buddha himself is said to have "touched the earth," thereby authorizing his own enlightenment by referring back to the ancient religion of the great goddess. Moreover he said, "I follow the ancient path," by which Reginald Ray says he "meant to show a 'way back' to a more fundamental experience of human life than the one evolving in his day."[44] Female Buddha-like figures formed of clay have been found on the islands of Naxos and Crete dating from 6000 BCE, in Anatolian sites from the same time period, and on the island of Malta from the fourth millennium BCE.[45] Any one of these could function as a stand-in for Tibet's illustrious Prajnaparamita, the Mother of the Buddhas.

Perhaps the most interesting story of a Tibetan Dakini is that told about the Supine Demoness, whose body was pinned down by the placement of Buddhist structures designed to keep her from indulging in the free-ranging activities in which she engaged prior to the anchoring of Buddhism in Tibet.[46] Unlike the snake at Delphi or the sea serpent Tiamat of Sumer, the invading hero did not kill the demoness of Tibet. Instead she was harnessed by being staked to the ground through the placement of Buddhist structures, such as stupas and monasteries, which held her in place without killing her. The risk was that she might someday escape. It would seem that with the brutal Chinese invasion in 1950 that sent Tibetan lamas dispersing to the four corners of the globe, and the destruction of Buddhist structures all over Tibet, the demoness has been set free.

Notes

Portions of this chapter are adapted from Vicki Noble, "Dakini: The Goddess Who Takes Form as a Woman," *MatriFocus* 8, no. 3 (2009), http://www.matrifocus.com/BEL09/nob.

1. Tsultrim Allione, *Women of Wisdom* (Ithaca, NY: Snow Lion Publications, 2000), 114.

2. June Campbell, *Traveller in Space: In Search of Female Identity in Tibetan Buddhism.* (New York: George Brazillier, 1996), 145.

3. Mircea Eliade, *Shamanism: Archaic Techniques of Ecstasy* (Princeton, NJ: Princeton University Press, 2004).

4. Miranda Shaw, *Passionate Enlightenment: Women in Tantric Buddhism* (Princeton, NJ: Princeton University Press, 1994), 6.

5. Vicki Noble, *Shakti Woman: Feeling Our Fire, Healing Our World* (San Francisco: HarperSanFrancisco, 1991), 137.

6. Darrell S. Gundrum, "Fabric of Time," *Archaeology* 53, no. 2 (March–April 2000): 46–51.

7. M. A. Czaplicka, *Aboriginal Siberia: A Study in Social Anthropology* (London: Oxford University Press, 1914), 244.

8. Vicki Noble, *The Double Goddess: Women Sharing Power* (Rochester, VT: Inner Traditions, 2003), 91.

9. Vidya Dehejia, *Yogini Cult and Temples: A Tantric Tradition* (Delhi, India: National Museum, 1986), 8.

10. Geoffrey Samuel, *Civilized Shamans: Buddhism in Tibetan Society* (Washington, DC: Smithsonian Institution Press, 1993), 4, 9; David Snellgrove, *Indo-Tibetan Buddhism: Indian Buddhists and Their Tibetan Successors* (London: Serindia Publications, 1987), 360.

11. Andre Gunder Frank, *The Centrality of Central Asia* (Amsterdam, Netherlands: V. U. University Press for Centre for Asian Studies, 1992), 30.

12. Deborah E. Klimburg-Salter, ed., *The Silk Route and the Diamond Path: Esoteric Buddhist Art on the Trans-Himalayan Trade Routes* (Los Angeles: UCLA Art Council, 1982), 21.

13. Noble, *The Double Goddess*, 91.

14. John Vincent Bellezza, *Divine Dyads: Ancient Civilization in Tibet* (Dharamsala, India: Library of Tibetan Works and Archives, 1997), 308.

15. Martin E. Huld, Karlene Jones-Bley, Miriam Robbins Dexter, and Angela Della Volpe, eds., *Proceedings of the Fourteenth Annual UCLA Indo-European Conference: November 8–9, 2002*, Journal of Indo-European Monograph Series 47 (Washington, DC: Institute for the Study of Man, 2003), 93.

16. Vicki Noble, "From Priestess to Bride: Marriage as a Colonizing Process in Patriarchal Conquest," in *The Rule of Mars: Readings on the Origins, History and Impact of Patriarchy*, ed. Cristina Biaggi (Manchester, CT: Knowledge, Ideas and Trends, 2005), 197.

17. Jeannine Davis-Kimball, *Warrior Women: An Archaeologist's Search for History's Hidden Heroines* (New York: Warner Books, 2002), 49.

18. Snellgrove, *Indo-Tibetan Buddhism*, 352.

19. Elizabeth Wayland Barber, *The Mummies of Urümchi* (New York: W. W. Norton, 1999).

20. J. P. Mallory and Victor H. Mair, *The Tarim Mummies: Ancient China and the Mystery of the Earliest Peoples from the West* (London: Thames and Hudson, 2000).

21. Noble, *The Double Goddess*.

22. Shaw, *Passionate Enlightenment*, 38, 19, 93, 95.

23. Allione, *Women of Wisdom*, 92, 103.

24. Tsultrim Allione, *Feeding Your Demons: Ancient Wisdom for Resolving Inner Conflict* (New York: Little, Brown, 2008).

25. Allione, *Women of Wisdom*, 112.

26. Noble, *Shakti Woman*.

27. Judith Simmer-Brown, *Dakini's Warm Breath: The Feminine Principle in Tibetan Buddhism* (Boston: Shambhala Publications, 2001), 6.

28. Ibid., 40, 11.

29. Ibid., 7.

30. Allione, *Women of Wisdom*, 38, 39.

31. Shaw, *Passionate Enlightenment*, 28.

32. Simmer-Brown, *Dakini's Warm Breath*, 140, 141.

33. Shaw, *Passionate Enlightenment*, 41.

34. Keith Dowman, *Sky Dancer: The Secret Life and Songs of the Lady Yeshe Tsogyel* (London: Routledge and Kegan Paul, 1984), 71.

35. David Gordon White, ed., *Tantra in Practice* (Princeton, NJ: Princeton University Press, 2000), 11.

36. David Gordon White, *The Alchemical Body: Siddha Tradition in Medieval India* (Chicago: University of Chicago Press, 1996), 4, 137.

37. Ibid., 138, 309.

38. Elizabeth English, *Vajrayogini: Her Visualizations, Rituals, and Forms (A Study of the Cult of Vajrayogini in India)* (Boston: Wisdom Publications, 2002), 28.

39. Ibid., 187.

40. Shaw, *Passionate Enlightenment*, 159.

41. Ljubinka Babovic, *The Mystery of Lepenski Vir: The Image of the Sun Deity from the VIIth Millennium B.C.* (Belgrade, Serbia: National Museum, 2008).

42. Margo Adler, *Drawing Down the Moon: Witches, Druids, Goddess-Worshippers, and Other Pagans in America* (New York: Penguin Compass, 1979).

43. Allione, *Women of Wisdom*, 50.

44. Reginald Ray, *Indestructible Truth: The Living Spirituality of Tibetan Buddhism* (Boston: Shambhala Publications, 2000), 2.

45. Noble, *Shakti Woman*, 151.

46. Janet Gyatso, "The Supine Demoness," in *Feminine Ground: Essays on Women and Tibet*, ed. Jan Willis (Ithaca, NY: Snow Lion Publications, 1987).

Bibliography

Adler, Margo. *Drawing Down the Moon: Witches, Druids, Goddess-Worshippers, and Other Pagans in America*. New York: Penguin Compass, 1979.

Allione, Tsultrim. *Women of Wisdom*. Ithaca, NY: Snow Lion Publications, 2000.

Babovic, Ljubinka. *The Mystery of Lepenski Vir: The Image of the Sun Deity from the VIIth Millennium B.C.* Belgrade, Serbia: National Museum, 2008.

Barber, Elizabeth Wayland. *The Mummies of Urümchi*. New York: W. W. Norton, 1999.

Bellezza, John Vincent. *Divine Dyads: Ancient Civilization in Tibet*. Dharamsala, India: Library of Tibetan Works and Archives, 1997.

Campbell, June. *Traveller in Space: In Search of Female Identity in Tibetan Buddhism*. New York: George Brazillier, 1996.

Czaplicka, M. A. *Aboriginal Siberia: A Study in Social Anthropology*. London: Oxford University Press, 1914.

Davis-Kimball, Jeannine. *Warrior Women: An Archaeologist's Search for History's Hidden Heroines*. New York: Warner Books, 2002.

Dehejia, Vidya. *Yogini Cult and Temples: A Tantric Tradition*. Delhi, India: National Museum, 1986.

Dowman, Keith. *Sky Dancer: The Secret Life and Songs of the Lady Yeshe Tsogyel*. London: Routledge and Kegan Paul, 1984.

Eliade, Mircea. *Shamanism: Archaic Techniques of Ecstasy*. Princeton, NJ: Princeton University Press, 2004.

English, Elizabeth. *Vajrayogini: Her Visualizations, Rituals, and Forms (A Study of the Cult of Vajrayogini in India)*. Boston: Wisdom Publications, 2002.

Frank, Andre Gunder. *The Centrality of Central Asia*. Amsterdam: V. U. University Press for Centre for Asian Studies, 1992.

Gundrum, Darrell S. "Fabric of Time." *Archaeology* 53, no. 2 (March–April 2000): 46–51.

Gyatso, Janet. "The Supine Demoness." In *Feminine Ground: Essays on Women and Tibet*, ed. Jan Willis. Ithaca, NY: Snow Lion Publications, 1987.

Huld, Martin E., Karlene Jones-Bley, Miriam Robbins Dexter, and Angela Della Volpe, eds. *Proceedings of the Fourteenth Annual UCLA Indo-European Conference: November 8–9, 2002*. Journal of Indo-European Monograph Series 47. Washington, DC: Institute for the Study of Man, 2003.

Klimburg-Salter, Deborah E., ed. *The Silk Route and the Diamond Path: Esoteric Buddhist Art on the Trans-Himalayan Trade Routes*. Los Angeles: UCLA Art Council, 1982.

Mallory, J. P., and Victor H. Mair. *The Tarim Mummies: Ancient China and the Mystery of the Earliest Peoples from the West*. London: Thames and Hudson, 2000.

Noble, Vicki. *The Double Goddess: Women Sharing Power*. Rochester, VT: Inner Traditions, 2003.

Noble, Vicki. "From Priestess to Bride: Marriage as a Colonizing Process in Patriarchal Conquest." In *The Rule of Mars: Readings on the Origins, History, and Impact of Patriarchy*, ed. Cristina Biaggi, 187–206. Manchester, CT: Knowledge, Ideas and Trends, 2005.

Noble, Vicki. *Shakti Woman: Feeling Our Fire, Healing Our World*. San Francisco: HarperSanFrancisco, 1991.

Ray, Reginald. *Indestructible Truth: The Living Spirituality of Tibetan Buddhism*. Boston: Shambhala Publications, 2000.

Samuel, Geoffrey. *Civilized Shamans: Buddhism in Tibetan Society*. Washington, DC: Smithsonian Institution Press, 1993.

Shaw, Miranda. *Passionate Enlightenment: Women in Tantric Buddhism*. Princeton, NJ: Princeton University Press, 1994.

Simmer-Brown, Judith. *Dakini's Warm Breath: The Feminine Principle in Tibetan Buddhism*. Boston: Shambhala Publications, 2001.

Snellgrove, David. *Indo-Tibetan Buddhism: Indian Buddhists and Their Tibetan Successors*. London: Serindia Publications, 1987.

White, David Gordon. *The Alchemical Body: Siddha Tradition in Medieval India*. Chicago: University of Chicago Press, 1996.

White, David Gordon, ed. *Tantra in Practice*. Princeton, NJ: Princeton University Press, 2000.

9

Tara: Savior, Buddha, Holy Mother

Miranda Shaw

Tara is the most beloved goddess of the Indo-Himalayan Buddhist world. She is revered as a divine mother who watches over all beings and acts in myriad ways to deliver them from suffering and lead them to enlightenment. Her name means both "Star Lady" and "She Who Carries Across" (that is, "Savioress"). Like the northern star after which she is named, Tara is a beacon and guiding light for those tossed on the stormy seas of life. She helps her worshipers cross the ocean of worldly existence (*samsara*) and safely reach the other shore: *nirvana*, ultimate peace, liberation. Tara is endowed with exquisite beauty and unlimited saving powers, an irresistible combination that has endeared her to laity, monastics, and yogic specialists alike over the centuries.

There are many stories of the origins of Tara. The most popular tells of her birth from Avalokiteshvara, the Lord of Compassion. According to this widely circulated oral account, Avalokiteshvara was overcome by the feeling that his eons of efforts had barely diminished the seemingly infinite miseries of living beings. His tears of merciful sorrow gathered into a lake on which a lotus blossomed. From the lotus arose Tara, lovelier and more beauteous of heart and mind than all the lotuses in the universe combined. She assured the compassionate lord that she would share his mission to liberate the world from suffering. As this legend evolved in Tibet, Avalokiteshvara is said to have shed two tears. His left teardrop transformed into Green Tara and the right turned into White Tara.

Figure 9.1 One of the most beloved figures in Tibetan Buddhism is Tara, the divine in female form who offers compassion to all humanity. White Tara. Contemporary Newar painting by Amrit Karmacharya. (Photograph courtesy of Miranda Shaw.)

This story, however, only tells of Tara's manner of revelation in the current age. A fuller version recorded in the 16th century by Taranatha traces the beginning of her journey to the distant past, when she was a human princess named Jnanacandra ("Moon of Knowledge"), an ardent follower of the Buddha of that era. When the princess set her aspiration on full enlightenment, some monks urged her to pray to be transformed into a man so she could progress more rapidly toward her goal. The princess retorted that they were fools indeed if they did not know that duality is an illusion and that in reality there is no such thing as a man, woman, self, or person. She vowed to remain in a female body until all living beings are established in supreme enlightenment. Princess Jnanacandra devoted herself to spiritual practice, gaining profound wisdom and meditative mastery. She became so skilled at the arts of liberation that every morning before breakfast she released millions of beings from their worldly obsessions, and she repeated the feat each evening. Thus, she gained the name Tara. For the next ninety-five eons, Tara continued to liberate beings and strive for full perfection. Eventually, her efforts were crowned with

Buddhahood. All this took place before her appearance in the present age through the intermediacy of the Lord of Compassion.

Tara made her historical debut in India in literary and artistic works dating from the seventh century CE. A lotus-bearing female in sixth-century stone reliefs may have been a precursor of Tara, but it was in the seventh century that Tara was first mentioned by name in Buddhist writings and became definitively identifiable in artistic representations. She initially appeared as an attendant of Avalokiteshvara and as one divinity among many who might be invoked through ritual and meditation. Very rapidly, however—possibly in a span of decades—Tara rose to become an object of reverence in her own right. Writings of the seventh and eighth centuries celebrate her as a supreme savior vested with all enlightened qualities and powers. Buddhist masters of this period proclaimed her to be not only a Buddha but also the highest embodiment and expression of Buddhahood. Such early and influential devotees as Suryagupta, Candragomin, and Akshobhyavajra recognized in Tara the essence of the body, speech, and mind of all Buddhas. They proclaimed her to be identical with ultimate reality and exalted her as a transcendent figure whose being encompasses all things, all living beings, and infinite time and space.

Tara soon became the focus of an immense theological enterprise. Her cosmic nature and supreme status made her the Buddhist equivalent of Mahadevi ("great goddess") who was emerging as an object of Hindu devotion during the same period (seventh and eighth centuries). Like Hindu counterparts such as Durga, Kali, and Lalita, who rose to the status of supreme goddesses at this time, Tara inspired a vast corpus of theological works, devotional poetry, and hymns that celebrate her beauty, perfections, and unfailing response to prayer.

After her introduction to the Indian Buddhist world in the seventh century, Tara remained important in that setting until the fall of Buddhism to Muslim invaders in the 12th century. Tara survived, however, in the Buddhism of Tibet and Nepal. In Nepal she retained an enduring niche from the seventh century to the present. In Tibet she gained greater significance than she has held in any other setting.

Iconography of Tara

In the simplest and apparently original version of her iconography, Tara may be depicted in a standing pose but is most commonly seated on a lotus, with her right foot extended forward, elegantly cushioned by a lotus flower, poised to spring into action on behalf of her petitioners.

Her right hand rests on her knee with the palm facing outward, in the classical Indic gesture of bestowing blessings and granting prayers. Her left hand, raised to the level of her heart, delicately clasps the stem of a blue lotus that blossoms above her left shoulder. Tara is envisioned as the epitome of feminine beauty and grace, with a moonlike face, gentle smile, lustrous black tresses, and shapely figure. She is splendid with a jeweled crown, precious adornments, fine silks, and colorful swirling scarves. There is wide variation in the treatment of her anatomy and proportions. Her face may be slender and dimpled with deeply modeled contours or round and wide with shallowly carved features. Her body may be youthfully lissome or amply plump, while her torso may be gracefully curving or regally erect. She embodies the feminine bodily ideals of the geographically and culturally diverse peoples who have revered and portrayed her.

Tara is envisioned as green in her most popular and widely encountered epiphany. This form was known in India simply as "Tara" but came to be designated as Droljangma ("Green Tara") in Tibet. Tara's green hue is a key to her symbolic significance and appeal, visually evoking her kinship with the world of nature. The green hue of her body suggests that plant sap—replete with healing, regenerative, and transformative energies—flows in her veins. Her body resembles a curving lotus stalk, beginning with the stem of the lotus beneath her right foot, curling upward along her leg and through the trunk of her body, continuing as the lotus shoot she holds in her hand, whose flowering blossom appears to grow from her body. Tara is customarily adorned with flowers and endowed with an aureole of blossoming lotus plants. In paintings, she is often framed by a canopy of trees that burgeon with fruit, flowers, and jewels, as nature brings forth its bounty in her presence. She may also be seated on a lion throne adorned with elephants, stags, and crocodilian creatures, incorporating the animal realm into her purview. Tara's manner of portrayal casts her in the role of Mother Nature, sitting at the center of lavish creation as its generative source and personification.

The ongoing appeal of Tara over the centuries and in differing cultural regions is attributable in large part to the encompassing nature of her ministrations. One would be hard pressed to find any need—be it physical welfare, healing, or spiritual salvation—for which Tara is not supplicated. Her worship crosses lay and monastic lines and spans devotional, ritual, and esoteric yogic practices. Practices to elicit her blessings and benefactions proliferated as each generation added new Tara meditations, liturgies, and rituals to the corpus, a process that continues to this day.

Calling upon Tara

One of the hallmarks of the Tara cultus is her direct and immediate accessibility to anyone who calls on her. Whereas many deities of the Buddhist pantheon figure largely in the practices of monastic and yogic specialists and the rituals they perform on behalf of the laity, Tara is a goddess of the people who requires no priestly mediation. Anyone may call on her by intoning her ten-syllable mantra, *om tare tuttare ture svaha*. Other popular observances include making an offering before an effigy, uttering a simple prayer, or calling the goddess to mind in a time of duress. Tara's answer to prayer is said to be as unfailing and swift as a mother attends to the cry of an only child. Like a mother, too, Tara considers no concern of her children to be beneath her interest. She attends to the physical, emotional, and spiritual well-being of her supplicants in whatever way they may require.

One of Tara's main roles in India and Tibet is reflected in her title as Ashtamahabhaya Tara ("Liberator from the Eight Great Fears"), so-named after the eight mortal perils from which she offers rescue: lions, elephants, fire, snakes, thieves, drowning, captivity, and demons. Stories abound of her interventions to save imperiled devotees from these deadly dangers. In Tibet the First Dalai Lama established a set of mental, emotional, and spiritual states that correspond to the eight outer dangers: the lion of pride, elephant of delusion, fire of anger and hatred, poisonous snake of envy, thieves of false views, chains of greed, floodwaters of desire, and demons of doubt. This set of correspondences remained in place as a formulaic expression of the versatility vested in Tara as a liberator from all inner and outer threats to wellbeing.

Special concerns of women also fall within Tara's purview. She figures in protective rites for mothers during and immediately following pregnancy and for newborn infants. The Tara mantra is pronounced over water, butter, amulets, and medicinal mixtures to consecrate them for use in anointing expectant mothers and newborns. Tara has even been reported to help a woman conceive without the assistance of a male.

Tara as Miracle-worker and Savioress

Tara is renowned as a worker of miracles. Her powers as a savior are heralded in written and oral accounts of her miraculous interventions and extraordinary benefactions. A collection of such tales, mainly set in India, was compiled by Taranatha in his *Golden Rosary* anthology. These stories describe Tara's deliverance of devotees from danger, disease, and disaster. Many a fortunate has been snatched from the proverbial jaws of death. She variously protects individuals, caravans, armies, and entire villages. A number of stories devolve on salvation from the aforementioned eight great fears, as Tara calms rampaging beasts, quenches fire, quells floods, turns back thieves, releases from prison, and turns venomous snakes into floral garlands. Rescue from poverty, restoration of social standing, and conferral of kingship also figure in the legendry. The petitioner in question need not be a devotee of Tara or even Buddhist. One finds many instances in which a person with no special claim on her attention finds him- or herself in dire straits and simply calls on the holy mother for deliverance, eliciting a miracle.

The repertoire of oft-told tales gathered by Taranatha yields many interesting themes. For instance, a vision of Tara or the sound of her voice may accompany her visitation and offer assurance of her blessings. She may manifest in dreams to impart spiritual guidance or crucial advice. Her benefactions include the conferral of supernatural powers, such as invisibility, location of buried treasure, attaining the elixir of eternal youth, aerial and subterranean travel, the ability to conjure food and wealth, and command of serpents and spirit-beings. Such powers find emphasis in tantric settings and are elicited by the recitation of her mantra.

Tara presides over a paradise known in Tibetan as Yuloku ("Land of Turquoise Leaves.") This celestial realm is the afterlife destination of devotees who are fortunate enough to be reborn in her presence. There they remain until they attain enlightenment, without again taking rebirth in the realms of suffering. Tara presides over her heaven from a many-tiered, jeweled mansion in a verdant woodland of gem-garlanded trees and strolling peacocks. In the garden is a lotus pool where new arrivals surface amid the blossoms. This is their manner of birth into Tara's paradise, where celestial musicians, dancers, and celebrants raising victory banners greet them. The sky is filled with angelic hosts bearing offerings to Tara and waving parasols and streamers, heralding the arrival of those whose spiritual journey came to such glorious fruition. Through their intensity of practice or sheer devotion to the goddess, they have merited rebirth in her heaven, where they will dwell until they become Buddhas and traverse the universe liberating others from suffering.

Visual Representations of Tara in Art

The outpouring of devotion inspired by Tara has given rise to a profusion of visual representations. She is the subject of virtually countless works of art in every medium, from tiny talismans and small-scale portable effigies to large stone stele and bronze statues installed in public worship spaces. Simpler effigies cast in clay and inexpensive metals were and still are mass-produced to meet an ongoing demand. The molds used for such castings can be skillfully carved without putting the cost of the reproductions beyond the reach of those of limited purse. More elaborate statuary of costly materials would be fashioned for royalty, wealthy temples and monasteries, and other prosperous patrons. A finely modeled piece may be rendered even more luxurious by the addition of gold and silver gilding, turquoise and coral insets, precious stones, and lapis lazuli and other colored pigments. In the case of paintings, too, the quality and scale range from small, rapidly executed portraits to large, elaborately detailed compositions accented with gold paint. Thus, Tara images are accessible to votaries regardless of their resources.

One of the fascinating aspects of Tara worship is the miraculous power attributed to her icons over the centuries. Buddhist annals tell of several famous statues in India that oozed a nectar with the power to cure leprosy and other diseases. One statue in a monastery sprouted a vessel that generated enough coins to support hundreds of monks for decades. A painting of Tara came to life and gave her jewelry to a poor woman begging alms to pay for her daughter's wedding. A number of statues changed direction or location, burst apart, consumed food offerings, and, in the recent case of a sculpture in Nepal that fell into the hands of a smuggler, became too heavy to lift at the airport and was recovered. Most in evidence are talking statues and paintings, known in India, Tibet, and Nepal. Many Tibetan temples boasted a talking effigy. Thus, Tibetan pilgrimage guides and temple handbooks are replete with the locations and legends of talking images. The repertoire of stories of Tara's miraculous statues and dramatic rescues and healings continues to expand in Nepal and wherever Tibetan Buddhism has spread.

As her primary hierophany, Green Tara is the one most frequently encountered in artistic representations from India and beyond. As a fully enlightened being, however, Tara generates multiple bodies and sends them throughout the universe to help the beings who can benefit from her ministrations. She assumes different colors and even varied types of bodies to appear in the manner most suitable for diverse times, places, and audiences. Thus, she appears in a huge number of iconographic forms, in addition to the popular and widely practiced Green Tara. She emanates manifestations in every sacred color of the Buddhist spectrum: red, yellow, blue, green, and white. Tara appears not only in many colors but also in a wide spectrum of bodily forms. She may appear with two, four, six, eight, twelve, or as many as one thousand arms and in a variety of moods that express her diverse saving activities and liberating powers. She can change bodies as easily as humans change clothing, and she can manifest multiple and indeed limitless bodies at one time. To express this concept, there are paintings that show a central Tara surrounded by smaller versions of herself, representing bodies that she sends forth to do her saving work. Paintings of this genre may show Tara with one hundred, several hundred, or even more than a thousand replicas of herself. These numbers metonymize her infinite manifestations, portraying her as a goddess who is omnipresent, filling the universe with her nectar of mercy, ever available to answer prayer and respond to need.

Liturgy of the Twenty-One Taras

The Twenty-One Taras are an important set of Taras in Tibetan Buddhism. The source of the assemblage is a liturgy titled *Twenty-One Praises of Tara and Their Benefits*, a lengthy but nonetheless popular prayer that many Tibetans recite daily to invoke the holy mother's blessings and protection. Each verse describes a different quality or power of Tara in her many aspects: serene, blissful, blazing, laughing, mocking, conquering, destroying, and triumphal. She emerges in these verses as a formidable figure who overcomes all evils and dangers and commands universal worship. The *Twenty-One Praises* gave rise to twenty-one forms of Tara that correspond to the verse themes. The Twenty-One Taras are greatly favored as an artistic subject. The group may be featured in single paintings or relief carvings, depicted in sets of twenty-one paintings or statues, or added to representations of other forms of Tara, arrayed around her in the sky.

A form of Tara that was introduced in India and remains important in Himalayan Buddhism is White Tara (Sita Tara in Sanskrit, Drolma Karmo in Tibetan). White Tara has two arms and is seated on a white lotus with her legs crossed in the meditative pose. Her right hand displays the gesture of divine generosity; her left is held at her heart. Each hand clasps a lotus plant bearing buds and a fully opened flower, indicating that she nurtures beings at every stage of spiritual development to the full perfection of Buddhahood. A distinctive aspect of White Tara's iconography is the possession of seven eyes. In addition to the third eye of omniscience on her forehead she has four "wisdom eyes," on the palms of her hands and soles of her feet. Thus, in Nepal she is known as Saptalocana Tara ("Seven-Eyed Tara").

White Tara figures primarily in meditations and rituals devoted to healing and longevity, a specialization for which she is extremely important in Tibetan Buddhism. A painting or statue of the goddess may be commissioned to secure the blessing of good health and long life for oneself, a family member, or a religious teacher. The white light that forms her luminous body is attributed with the power to purify negative karma and conditions that have resulted in illness or even impending death. In a beautiful healing meditation in which she figures, the light radiating from her body is separated into its component colors and crystallized into layered spheres of light. The inner orb is white, followed by successively larger spheres of golden yellow, ruby red, sky blue, emerald green, and indigo. Each hue is attributed with a different healing property. The white light pacifies illness, negative karmic forces, and causes of death. The golden light increases the life span, merit, glory, and mental acuity. The red light grants dominion over "the three worlds," that is, all that is below, on, and above the earth. The sky-blue light eradicates problems and obstacles caused by demons, enemies, poisons, and misfortune. The green light bestows magical and supernatural powers, while the deep-blue or purple light reinforces these attainments. This meditation may be performed on one's own behalf or for the benefit of another. The intended recipient is envisioned at the center of the rainbow spheres of healing light.

Tara in Tibet

Although Tara was clearly an important and popular deity in late Indian Buddhism (eighth through 12th centuries), she had not attained the zenith of adoration that she garnered in Tibet, where her worship attained the status of a national cult, unifying the religiosity of laity and monastics across all the sectarian traditions. Tibetans claim a special relationship with Tara. The origin myth of the Tibetan people was revised in the 14th century to incorporate Tara as divine progenitress. The legendary monkey demon and rock ogress to whose union the Tibetans traced their descent were identified as incarnations of Avalokiteshvara and Tara. Thus, the holy mother Tara was cast as the mother of the Tibetan people in a literal sense, as their biological ancestress. Moreover, the two wives of the first Buddhist king of Tibet, Songtsen Gampo, are regarded as emanations of Tara. Princess Bhrikuti-devi from Nepal and Wen-cheng from China, both devout Buddhists, imported votive images, texts, and artisans and influenced their husband to promote their faith, thereby altering the course of Tibetan history. The earliest Buddhist architecture, icons, and translation efforts in Tibet date to their seventh-century reign. The Nepalese princess is recognized as White Tara (or as Bhrikuti, a white manifestation of Tara) and the Chinese princess as Green Tara. Thus, Tara is exalted both as mother and as a divine patron whose compassion has shaped the history of the Tibetan nation.

Tara is a pervasive presence in Tibetan cultural life. Her icons are encountered at every turn, in temples and homes, along roadsides and in rural chapels, and worn as an amulet or in a miniature shrine attached to a sash or belt. Colorful flags imprinted with Tara mantras and prayers spread praises and supplications of the holy mother through the atmosphere, carried on the wind. The ten-syllable mantra of Tara is a favored prayer, counted on the rosaries that Tibetans customarily carry. The most popular hymn to Tara is the *Twenty-One Praises*, discussed above. The hymn figures in the morning and evening liturgies at monasteries throughout the Tibetan Buddhist world. Buddhist children memorize the rather lengthy prayer at an early age and subsequently recite it in a variety of contexts, as a private and familial votive practice and at public ceremonies.

Worship of Tara is woven into the fabric of Tibetan cultural life. Folk traditions abound, such as masked dramas enacting her miraculous interventions, a tradition undergoing revival now in diaspora. There are also priestly rites that may be performed in a monastery or private home on request, to generate merit and invoke Tara's blessings. Such ceremonies, which feature offerings and recitation of Tara texts, mantras, or prayers, may last one night or, in the case of the "Hundred Thousand Tara Prayers," three months. Laypersons often prefer to employ nuns rather than monks for this service, on the belief that the Tara rites and prayers of female monastics are more effective, with the fortuitous result that Tara rituals may generate crucial income for a nunnery.

Tara also has a role in Newar Buddhism, that is, the Buddhism of Nepal, which is practiced by the indigenous Newar population rather than by Nepalis, who descend from later Hindu arrivals to the Kathmandu Valley. Green Tara is known in Nepal as Arya Tara ("Noble Tara" or "Holy Tara"). Her white form is called Saptalocana Tara ("Seven-Eyed Tara") as explained above. Images of the goddess are ubiquitous, appearing in homes and among the statuary and relief carvings so abundant in Newar shrines and temple complexes. Tara is a popular subject, too, for Newar painters and sculptors. Many of the most exquisite representations of Tara in collections around the world are Newar creations, produced for use in Nepal and for Tibetan, Chinese, and Mongolian patrons.

Tara has an enduring niche in the Newar pantheon as an object of devotion and invocation. She is recognized as a Buddha and as the consort of Amoghasiddhi, one of the five Buddhas of the Five-Buddha (Panca-Jina) mandala that is a mainstay of Newar ritual life. As a being of infinite wisdom and compassion, Tara may be invoked and worshiped for a range of blessings, while her primary role at present is that of healing deity. In cases of serious illnesses or even of mild conditions that have not yielded to medical treatment, it is common for the family of the afflicted to enlist priests to perform a Satva Vidhana Tara Puja. The ritual features rows of 108, 360, or 1000 small candles made of flour, bowls of water, flickering butter lamps, and cups filled with rice and a coin. This glittering assemblage is embellished by a colorful array of food offerings, jasmine flowers, peacock feathers, greenery, and green vegetables and fruits such as green apples, melons, bananas, and mangos.

Another important Newar Buddhism observance is the Tara Vrata. A Vrata is a type of practice in which the participants fast and maintain a state of ritual purity in order to invoke the energies of a deity into the sacred ceremonial space and within themselves. The Tara Vrata is a one-day rite that can be held whenever a priest or sponsors desire to hold one. Fliers publicize the event, and anyone who wants to do so can participate. The Vrata might be undertaken to express piety, purify karma, or fulfill a specific wish or need. In accordance with Tara's primary role in the Newar context as a healing deity, her Vrata is associated with healing. The Tara Vrata can be undertaken to secure one's own good health and long life or be performed on behalf of someone with a serious medical condition. The women who make up a majority of the participants wear green in honor of Arya Tara. Each woman brings the supplies she will need for the ritual. The offerings feature the color green. One of the special preparations is hand-molded jewelry made of rice dough. The women fashion beaded necklaces, bracelets, finger-rings, and toe-rings and paint them green with a homemade vegetable dye.

The Tara Vrata may be held in any temple courtyard, but two of the favored sites are Itum Baha and Tara Tirtha. The Itum Baha temple complex includes a shrine that houses the most famous Tara image of Nepal, a large bronze statue of White Tara. The shrine marks the spot where Tara descended from the Himalayas to the north (that is, Tibet) and appeared in person to dispense Buddhist teachings. The statue is as known as "The Great Peaceful White Tara Who Turned the Wheel of Dharma." This icon is sufficiently renowned that Tibetans in Nepal frequent the shrine to render homage. Tara Tirtha is a cremation ghat on the bank of the Bagmati River where Tara has appeared to bless her devotees in dramatic ways. Therefore, Tara Tirtha is held to be an auspicious place to perform the Vrata or simply to meditate, pray, and make offerings to the goddess.

In sum, although Tara is not one of the major divinities of the Newar pantheon, she is nonetheless revered in Kathmandu Valley. Her presence is felt throughout the art, architecture, ritual life, and sacred landscape of the country.

Tara emerged to historical view in the seventh century and is still highly revered throughout the Himalayan Buddhist world today. The theological edifice surrounding Tara lays stress on her embodiment of such lofty and transcendent principles as nondual wisdom, universal compassion, and ultimate liberating power. Her persona, however, is redolent with the richness of the earth as she sits on a lotus throne in a verdant, harmonious landscape, the very image of the benevolent face of Mother Nature. Her visual association with nature has no doubt enhanced her psychological and emotional appeal as a maternal figure who nurtures and sustains life in a manner akin to the nourishing abundance and spiritual potency of nature. Tara encompasses the starry heavens, the teeming oceans, the flowering planet. As the Star Lady, she shines in the firmament as a guiding light. As savioress, she guides her devotees across the perilous seas of life. As the lotus-bearing goddess, she tends the universe as if it were her garden, nurturing beings from the budding of aspiration to the full bloom of enlightenment.

The Buddhist tradition celebrates motherhood in many ways and through a range of female divinities, but in no case is motherhood more complete or exalted than in the case of Tara, the ultimate embodiment of mother love. Her maternal tenderness, bolstered by the omniscience and powers of Buddhahood, has made her the supreme and most beloved savior of the Buddhist pantheon. The cornerstone of her character is her role as a liberator who saves her devotees from any peril, be it physical, emotional, or spiritual. This tender and powerful motherhood has enshrined her in the hearts of millions of South Asian and Himalayan Buddhists over the centuries. Tara continues to garner new devotees across the globe, as Tibetans sent into exile by the genocidal Chinese occupation of their country bring their faith to new constituents in the Asian, European, and North and South American countries where they have settled.

Bibliography

Beyer, Stephan. *The Cult of Tara: Magic and Ritual in Tibet.* Berkeley: University of California Press, 1973.

Landesman, Susan. *The Great Secret of Tara*. Delhi: Motilal Banarsidass (forthcoming).

Lewis, Todd T. "Mahayana *Vratas* in Newar Buddhism." *Journal of the International Association of Buddhist Studies* 12, no. 1 (1989): 109–138.

Rinpoche, Bokar. *Tara: The Feminine Divine*. English ed. San Francisco: Clear Point Press, 1999.

Rinpoche, Khenchen Palden Sherab, and Khenpo Tsewang Dongyal Rinpoche. *Tara's Enlightened Activity: An Oral Commentary on* The Twenty-one Praises to Tara. Ithaca, NY: Snow Lion Publishing, 2007.

Shaw, Miranda. *Buddhist Goddesses of India*. Princeton, NJ: Princeton University Press, 2006.

Willson, Martin. *In Praise of Tara: Songs to the Saviouress*. London: Wisdom Publishing, 1986.

10

Guanyin: Goddess of Embodied Compassion

Betz King

Guanyin embodies the essence of compassion. *Embodied* is a multifaceted term meaning "to incorporate, incarnate, or personify." Incorporating bodhisattvas and goddesses from many traditions into a unified whole, this goddess incarnate is invested with the principles of mercy and compassion. She personifies these principles in human form as the princess Miao Shan, who made great sacrifices during her mortal lifetime. A synthesis of her many creation myths is followed by methods for interacting with the principles represented by this merciful goddess.

Guanyin is commonly referred to as the "goddess of compassion and mercy" but she began as a celestial bodhisattva. This holy title describes one who has reached enlightenment and is free from *samsara*—the endless wheel of birth, death, and rebirth—but chooses to remain incarnate until all beings are likewise free. Compassion is a threefold phenomenon, composed of an awareness of suffering, a desire to relieve suffering, and the execution of plans intended to do the same. This was embodied within Guanyin. She was aware that others still suffered, she desired to relieve their suffering, and she renounced her own spiritual transformation in order to bring all beings to enlightenment. This selfless act established Guanyin as a favored champion of the people.

Figure 10.1 Kindly Guanyin is a boddhisatva, a being near to becoming a Buddha. In her case, she elected to remain available to help suffering humanity, for which it is known as the boddhisatva of compassion. *Guanyin of the Southern Sea (Nanhai Guanyin)*, Chinese, 11th/12th century, Liao Dynasty (907–1125). Wood with multiple layers of paint, 95 × 65 inches (241.3 × 165.1 cm). (The Nelson-Atkins Museum of Art, Kansas City, Missouri. Purchase: William Rockhill Nelson Trust, 34–10. Photo credit: Jamison Miller. Reprinted with permission.)

Avalokitesvara and Guanyin

Guanyin is the synthesis of divinity and merciful action, but she was not the first to express this embodied form of compassion. Buddhist holy books are replete with stories of earlier bodhisattvas who performed similar feats. One is of particular interest when considering Guanyin's origins. Buddhism is a nontheistic religion that refutes the concept or worship of a creator God. Buddhism acknowledges the existence of gods or devas who could help when invoked, but considers them mortal and trapped in samsara. The historical Buddha taught about salvation in a series of sermons known as *sutras*. One of the best-known, the Lotus Sutra, tells of "a compassionate Buddha who sends forth the light of enlightenment and salvation to the whole world."[1] "The Universal Gate," chapter 25 of the Lotus Sutra, is devoted to a bodhisattva named Avalokitesvara, "the lord who hears the cries of the world." Avalokitesvara was the embodiment of compassion, and his life was "dedicated to the salvation of others and to becoming a Buddha only in some far distant eon."[2] Described as androgynous in presentation and mannerism, Avalokitesvara is portrayed in many early statues and drawings in effeminate, though still masculine, form. He also possessed decidedly maternal propensities to protect the weak, heal the sick, and assist in matters of pregnancy and childbirth. Avalokitesvara could assume any form necessary to help those who called upon him and granted "compassion wondrous as a great cloud, pouring spiritual rain like nectar, quenching all the flames of distress."[3]

In 406 CE a renowned translator named Kumarajiva completed what has become the most favored translation of the Lotus Sutra in China. In it, the Sanskrit name of Avalokitesvara was translated into the Chinese name of Guanshiyin, "hearer of the cries of the world," thus rendering the bodhisattva gender neutral. Portrayed as masculine through the Tang dynasty (618–907 CE), Guanyin was regularly depicted as a female by the eighth century, and by the 15th century Guanyin was completely feminine.[4]

Hypotheses regarding this transformation are many. It is likely that Guanyin is an evolution of an earlier goddess. In the 15th century BCE, the indigenous shamanic religion of China recognized a divine being called the Queen Mother.[5] Buddhism was introduced into China during the latter half of the Han dynasty (220–206 BCE) and continued to grow through the first 600 years of the Common Era, as did the native Taoism. During this time, Confucianism became the state ideology of China, leaving both Buddhism and Taoism to compete for resources and patronage.[6] By the second century CE, Taoism was the primary religion of China. Having assimilated the earlier practices of shamanism, Taoism acknowledged female deities, including the "Queen Mother of the West" described in Max Dashu's chapter within this volume.

In hopes of appealing to the native Chinese people, Buddhism engaged in the practice of ko-i, a method of teaching Buddhist concepts by pairing them with Taoist terms and ideas.[7] It is possible that the Taoist Queen Mother and the male Avalokitesvara were paired together for teaching purposes, resulting in Guanyin's arrival. Recognition of the need for a feminine divinity may also have inspired the growing Mahayana tradition of Buddhism to borrow the increasingly popular Hindu Goddess Tara. Sixth-century Tibetan Buddhists believed Tara to be the *sakti*, or consort, of Avalokitesvara. Born from one of his tears, she was also considered a bodhisattva of compassion. Some believe that Guanyin is a combination of the male Chinese Avalokitesvara and the female Hindu Tara.[8]

Guanyin's popularity spread across China in the seventh and eighth centuries. By the time of the Song dynasty (960–1279 CE), she had taken on attributes of other regional female deities, with evolutions as the previously mentioned Hindu Tara, as well as Japanese Kwanon (often depicted as male), Vietnamese Quan Am, and Taiwanese Ma-tsu.

Images of Guanyin

There are many iconographic depictions of Guanyin. The Lotus Sutra references thirty-three different forms, eleven each for the worlds of heaven, sky, and earth.[9] Some of the best known include the White-Robed Guanyin, the Royal Ease Guanyin, Guanyin of the Sea (and other water-based depictions), the Thousand-Armed Guanyin, and the Princess Miao Shan. In each, her clothing, posture, and surroundings are symbolic, as are the objects that she is shown with. Some are common to the religious art of the time, while others originate from the myth of her transformation from human to immortal. A full telling of this myth is in the next section.

In the most popular portrayals, Guanyin is quite young and beautiful. As the White-Robed Guanyin, she is clothed in a simple white robe; at other times she is dressed in colorful skirts, tops, and jewelry. The Royal Ease Pose shows Guanyin seated. Her right knee is raised, and her right arm rests upon it, while her left leg and arm remain down in a relaxed position. This pose gives a glimpse into Guanyin's disregard for traditional feminine expectations, for while she is regarded as especially helpful to women, she is tethered to no man or child. Guanyin also resists easy categorization as feminine in less common depictions as a great warrior, armed with weapons and shields.

Many forms show Guanyin on or near the water. Guanyin with Fish Basket carries a basket of fish on her arm, while Guanyin of the South Sea is shown on P'u-t'o Island. Floating on a lotus flower, walking among the waves, sitting on a rock contemplating the sea or slaying a dragon, these images are dear to sailors and seafarers, who call upon her for protection and safe journeying. Guanyin is sometimes portrayed with a thousand arms and hands reaching out in compassion. In each hand, an eye watches over the suffering of the world.

As a bodhisattva, Guanyin has vowed to lead all beings to enlightenment, and the items she is portrayed with are symbolic of this awakening. In some depictions, Guanyin holds a string of beads, reminiscent of the Buddhist mala or the Christian rosary. These beads symbolize the importance of chanting and prayer as tools for enlightenment. At other times she carries the Lotus Sutra, which details the path to enlightenment. She is often shown pouring water from a vase. The water represents compassion, which Guanyin pours onto all who are sick and suffering. The weeping willow branch is a similar emblem. Flexible, yet strong, it represents Guanyin's grace under pressure, femininity, and compassion. It can also be used in exorcisms and shamanistic contacts with the spirit world.[10]

In many images, Guanyin holds or is surrounded by lotus flowers. The lotus flower is an important symbol in Buddhism, representing the purity of mind necessary to achieve enlightenment. Just as the lotus grows from the dark, muddy sediment of the pond, humans begin in the darkness of ignorance and fear. The lotus flower opens only when it reaches the light of day, just as the blossoming of the human mind occurs only with enlightenment.

When portrayed with a child or children, Guanyin expresses a mother's compassion. In this form, which has much in common with the Christian images of the Virgin Mary with the infant Christ, she is the patroness of women, pregnancy, and safe delivery. The peacock—one of Guanyin's companion animals—sometimes accompanies her in statues and pictures. This is due in part to a legend in which Guanyin transformed a simple bird into a beautiful peacock with a thousand eyes on his tail-plumes, to help her keep watch over the feuding animals of earth.[11]

Many of the aforementioned tools and objects come together in a great statue located on the south coast of China's island province of Hainan. Standing 108 meters tall and the third tallest statue in the world, the statue is fashioned with three faces—one facing inland and the other two seaward—that represent Guanyin's blessing and protection of China and the whole world. One face shows Guanyin holding the Lotus Sutra. In the next she is shown with a string of mala beads. She holds a lotus flower in the third. Circling the halos of the three faces are the words *Om mani padme hum*, one of the prayers said to invoke Guanyin. These three facets express Guanyin's commitment to enlightenment, which is also captured in her many myths and legends.

Before exploring the best known of Guanyin's stories, it is useful to review the basic principles of Buddhism, known as "The Four Noble Truths." The First Noble Truth, reflecting on the ever-changing nature of life, tells that health, relationships, finances, possessions, ideals, and beliefs change throughout life. Avoidance of these changes is impossible, and attempts to avoid these changes cause suffering. The Second Noble Truth states that suffering is caused by attachments to people, places, and things, and the desire to avoid pain. The Third Noble Truth offers reassurance that it is possible to achieve liberation from suffering, and the Fourth Noble Truth directs the seeker to follow an Eight-Fold Path of virtues leading to enlightenment.

The rigors of daily survival left Guanyin's followers little time for religious study. While they could see that life was filled with suffering and desired to be free from it, applying the principles of the Eight-Fold Path to their daily lives was difficult. The male Buddha was sometimes more intimidating than accessible, and enlightenment could take many lifetimes to achieve. Since storytelling has been used throughout time to teach otherwise esoteric principles, stories of Guanyin were created in which she expressed the virtues of the Eight-Fold Path in ways to which people could more easily relate.

The best known of Guanyin's legends involve her ascent from human to divine. There are many of these transformation myths, each tailored to a particular belief system or geographic region. Most involve a young princess named Miao Shan whose compassionate nature causes her to suffer the wrath of her angry father, the king.

The Princess Miao Shan

Miao Shan was the third daughter born to a king and his queen. At her birth, a beautiful light enveloped her and the smell of apple blossoms filled the air. Many at the court thought these signs were proof that Miao Shan was holy, but her parents, hoping for a son, were disappointed and did not recognize her true nature.

Miao Shan was an unusual little girl. The comfort of the royal palace did not impress her, and she did not care to be treated as a princess. Her concern for the well-being of insects, animals, and people took up a great deal of her energy, and she spent much time in prayer and meditation. As she and her sisters grew older, her father was eager to marry them off. He arranged marriages for the older sisters without any difficulty, but Miao Shan did not wish to marry. She wanted only to bring healing to those who suffered and did not see how this would be possible if she were tied to a man and expected to run a household. Miao Shan begged her father to let her join a nearby convent, where she could live the contemplative life she desired.

The king allowed Miao Shan to enter the nunnery but ordered the abbess to make her life difficult, hoping that his daughter would change her mind and return home to marry. Miao Shan was sent to the kitchens and given the jobs that no one else wanted. At first, she completed these tasks with good cheer, but eventually they became too much for her. Fortunately, divine forces interceded. Animals and other deities were sent to assist Miao Shan. Together they completed the assigned tasks and more.

When the king realized that he could not break his daughter's spirit, he ordered her captured and killed. As his soldiers stormed the nunnery, they showed no mercy for any in their way, including the women Miao Shan had come to love as spiritual sisters. Her heart broke as she watched the monastery go up in flames, trapping the nuns in certain death. In desperation she called upon Buddha and received the inspiration to prick the roof of her mouth and spit blood into the air. Instantly the skies filled with clouds and rain extinguished the fires. The nunnery and its occupants were safe but Miao Shan was not, for the king ordered that she be brought home and executed immediately.

Hands bound behind her back, Miao Shan was led into the public square to be beheaded. Again, divine forces intervened. As the sun hit the blade of the executioner's sword, it shattered. He tried to strangle her, but as she fell to the ground, a great tiger leapt upon the platform, carried her lifeless body to the woods, and gave her a pill of immortality. It freed her from her physical body and allowed her to enter the realm of immortal beings. There she witnessed the eighteen Buddhist Hells, where she saw tortured souls whom she was compassionately moved to save. Her earnest prayers liberated the suffering and transformed hell into a paradise. Miao Shan was returned to her mortal body.

Some stories credit the Emperor of Hell with returning Miao Shan to her physical body, while others credit Buddha. Most stories agree that she was given a magical peach upon her reincarnation and that she was returned to the island of Mt. P'u-t'o, one of four great mountain chains that represent the elements of earth, water, fire, and air. Mt. P'u-t'o, located off the Chinese mainland, is associated with water. There, Miao Shan continued to pray and meditate until she achieved enlightenment and was released from the cycle of birth, death, and rebirth. Choosing to forgo this release in service of liberating all beings from suffering, Miao Shan achieved her full bodhisattva nature. She remains associated with the sea and the moon, and the isle of Mt. P'u-t'o has become a place of pilgrimage to her.[12]

While Miao Shan was pursuing enlightenment, her father had grown very ill. All his power and wealth could not buy a cure for his illness. Near death, he was visited by a monk, who informed him that "the arm and eye of one who is without anger" could be made into a medicine that would save his life.[13] The king and his queen were at first horrified by the idea of dismembering someone; eventually, in selfish desperation, they grew willing to try. However, they knew of no one who was both without anger and willing to give up an eye and an arm. The visiting monk said that he knew of such a person, a divine being who had obtained perfection and resided on the island of Mt. P'u-t'o. He assured them that she was without anger and would grant their request. A messenger was sent to the island to make the king's plea.

The messenger returned with the necessary ingredients—the arm and eye of one who was without anger—and the monk made the healing potion. He gave it to the king who drank it and was instantly returned to good health. When he tried to thank the monk, the monk advised him to thank the one who had sacrificed her eye and arm. So the king, queen, and their court made their way to Mt. P'u-t'o. When they were granted audience before the great bodhisattva who had saved the king's life, they bowed low. Then the queen, sneaking a glance at the mutilated face of her husband's savior, screamed with horror as she recognized her own daughter, Miao Shan. The king fell at his daughter's feet and begged her forgiveness, but Miao Shan assured him that she had sacrificed nothing and would be made whole again. With this proclamation, the air was filled with the same fragrance of apple blossoms that had attended her birth. Beautiful flowers fell from the sky, and clouds of color swirled around all gathered. When the clouds parted, Miao Shan had been transformed into the Thousand-Armed and Thousand-Eyed Guanyin. She encouraged her parents to return home to their castle and ascended into heaven, leaving her mortal body behind. Her parents buried her body on the island and built a lovely temple above it to honor her. Then they returned to their castle where, with love and compassion, they brought the Buddhist teachings to all the kingdom.

Perceptions of Guanyin

People relate to Guanyin in two ways. For some, she is the goddess of compassion. As a goddess, Guanyin is approached in supplication to grant requests for healing, mercy, and protection. She is honored and celebrated for her compassionate interventions. Others consider Guanyin an archetype of mercy. Archetypes are instinctual patterns of character common to all people, such as the hero, villain, good mother, or fierce warrior. These patterns are largely unconscious and are consequently projected outside of the self, where they can be interacted with and expressed. As an archetype, Guanyin can be considered an externalized expression of the mercy and compassion common within all of humanity.[14]

Whether she is perceived as a goddess or an archetype, Guanyin's benevolent spirit remains the same. And just as it is possible to interact with the spirit of gratitude on Thanksgiving, it is possible to interact with Guanyin's mercy and compassion through celebration, chanting prayer, and meditation.

There are three annual celebrations of Guanyin, held on the nineteenth day of the second, sixth, and ninth lunar months. The first celebration acknowledges her birth from the Buddha's compassionate tear, or the eye of god. The second celebration marks her vow to forgo enlightenment until all sentient beings have reached it as well. The third celebrates her final ascension into nirvana. Celebrations on these feast days include chanting, prayer, the reading of sacred texts and meditation upon the virtues of compassion.

In the Mahayana Tradition of Buddhism, chanting is believed to prepare the mind for meditation, and also aids in ritual invocations. Four mantras, recited in their original Sanskrit form, are commonly used to invoke Guanyin. The best known of these mantras, *Om Mani Padme Hum*, translates as "praise to the jewel in the lotus." Common to many sects of Buddhism and present on many statues of Guanyin, this mantra is said to invoke Chenrezig, the Buddha of Compassion, and is believed to be as powerful as all of the teachings of the Buddha combined. The Venerable Thubten Chodron recalls her teacher Lama Yeshe insisting that "Even if you don't want to develop compassion, recitation of Om Mani Padme Hum will make compassion grow in your mind!"[15] Guanyin is said to have uttered this phrase at the moment of her genesis.

The most powerful chant honoring Guanyin, known as Te Pei Chow or the Dharani of Great Compassion, is *Namo Kuan Shi Yin P'u Sa* which means, "All hail to Guanyin, Bodhisattva!" Chanted three times slowly, it salutes Guanyin at the beginning and end of worship. Chanted more rapidly over a longer period of time, it invokes aid for specific purposes. Lesser known are the chants *Chiu K'u Chiu-Nan P'u Sa Lai* ("Save from suffering, Bodhisattva come!") used in emergency situations, and the single word *Hri*, which has no actual translation but is believed to capture the pure essence of Guanyin.

In many traditions, altars and shrines are constructed to bring symbolic form to otherwise intangible expressions of divinity. An altar can be as simple as a statue on a small table, or as elaborate as a three-tiered style with Guanyin, Buddha, and other enlightened beings on the top, representations of ancestors in the middle, and offerings of fruit, flowers, incense, and candles on the bottom. An altar to Guanyin can be used as a place to pay homage, chant, pray, and meditate. Prayer and meditation can be distinguished by the direction of their intentions. Prayers ask for help, give praise, or exclaim awe, often in the form of chants or other recitations. Meditation is a form of listening in stillness. Meditations specific to Guanyin are not as common as more generalized meditations on compassion, which appear to bring physiological benefits. EEG brain scans of a Tibetan lama performing a compassion meditation showed significant increases in the activity of the left frontal lobe—home to positive emotion—confirming Lama Yeshe's assertion that compassion is good for the mind.[16] Simple acts like the waving of a willow branch or the pouring of water can be viewed as rituals designed to embody and express Guanyin's protective and healing powers.

Conclusion

Guanyin is a sympathetic goddess, a being who has pledged to suffer together with humanity until all reach enlightenment. The word sympathy has its roots in the Latin *sympathia*, meaning "to suffer together." Guanyin has pledged to suffer together with humanity until all reach enlightenment. She is also an empathic goddess, feeling the pain of those who suffer as if it were her own. It is this capacity for empathy that underlies the mercy and compassion for which she is known.

Ultimately, Guanyin is an enigmatic goddess. Despite varied spiritual and social segregations of the time, she has been portrayed as bodhisattva and mortal, man and woman, princess and goddess. This transformative ability has helped her to prevail through changing religious systems and political across hundreds of centuries. Guanyin's endurance is a reflection of the universal and timeless desire of humanity to embody the principles of mercy and compassion.

Notes

1. Martin Palmer, Jay Ramsay, and Man-Ho Kwok, *Kuan Yin: Myths and Prophecies of the Chinese Goddess of Compassion* (London: Thorsons, 1995), 4.

2. David Leeming, *A Dictionary of Asian Mythology* (New York: Oxford University Press, 2001), 26.

3. Palmer, Ramsay, and Kwok, *Kuan Yin*, 5.

4. Chün-fang Yü, *Kuan Yin: The Chinese Transformation of Avalokitesvara* (New York: Columbia University Press, 2001), 6; Palmer, Ramsay, and Kwok, *Kuan Yin*, 7.

5. Palmer, Ramsay, and Kwok, *Kuan Yin*.

6. Palmer, Ramsay, and Kwok, *Kuan Yin*, 17.

7. Yung-t'ung T'ang, "On 'Ko-I,' " in *Radhakrishnan: Comparative Studies in Philosophy Presented in Honour of His Sixtieth Birthday*, by W. R. Inge et al. (London: Allen and Unwin, 1951), 276–286.

8. John Blofeld, *Bodhisattva of Compassion: The Mystical Tradition of Kuan Yin* (Boston: Shambhala, 1988), 23.

9. Koh Kok Kiang, *Guan Yin: Goddess of Compassion* (Singapore: Asiapac, 2004), 17.

10. Palmer, Ramsay, and Kwok, *Kuan Yin*, 39.

11. Ibid., 61.

12. Ibid., 63–78.

13. Ibid., 75.

14. Taigen Dan Leighton, *Faces of Compassion: Classic Bodhisattva Archetypes and Their Modern Expression* (Boston: Wisdom Publications, 2003), 27.

15. Bhikshuni Thubten Chodron, *Cultivating a Compassionate Heart: The Yoga Method of Chenrezig* (Ithaca, NY: Snow Lion, 2005), 156.

16. Daniel Goleman, *Destructive Emotions: How Can We Overcome Them?* (New York: Bantam Dell, 2004), 12.

Bibliography

Blofeld, John. *Bodhisattva of Compassion: The Mystical Tradition of Kyan Yin*. Boston: Shambhala, 1988.

Bolen, Jean Shinoda. *Goddesses in Older Women: Becoming a Juicy Crone*. New York: Quill, 2001.

Bonnefoy, Yves. *Asian Mythologies*. Translated by Wendy Doniger. Chicago: University of Chicago Press, 1993.

Boucher, Sandy. *Discovering Kwan Yin: Buddhist Goddess of Compassion*. Boston: Beacon, 1999.

Buswell, Robert E., ed. *Encyclopedia of Buddhism*. London: Macmillan, 2003.

Cabezön, Jose Ignacio, ed. *Buddhism, Sexuality, and Gender*. Albany: SUNY Press, 1992.

Chodron, Bhikshuni Thubten. *Cultivating a Compassionate Heart: The Yoga Method of Chenrezig*. Ithaca, NY: Snow Lion, 2005.

Chodron, Pema. *When Things Fall Apart*. Boston: Shambhala, 2002.

Gilbert, Paul. *Compassion: Conceptualisations, Research and Use in Psychotherapy*. New York: Routledge, 2005.

Goleman, Daniel. *Destructive Emotions: How Can We Overcome Them?* New York: Bantam Dell, 2004.

Inge, W. R. et al. *Radhakrishnan: Comparative Studies in Philosophy Presented in Honour of His Sixtieth Birthday*. London: Allen and Unwin, 1951.

Jones, Lindsay, ed. *Encyclopedia of Religion*. 2nd ed. Farmington Hills, MI: Macmillan Reference USA, 2005.

Kiang, Koh Kok. *Guan Yin: Goddess of Compassion*. Singapore: Asiapac, 2004.

Leeming, David. *A Dictionary of Asian Mythology.* New York: Oxford University Press, 2001.

Leighton, Taigen Dan. *Faces of Compassion: Classic Bodhisattva Archetypes and Their Modern Expression.* Boston: Wisdom Publications, 2003.

Monaghan, Patricia. *The Encyclopedia of Goddesses and Heroines.* Santa Barbara, CA: Greenwood Press, 2009.

Niwant, Nikky. *Buddhism for Today: A Modern Interpretation of the Threefold Lotus Sutra.* Tokyo: Kosei Publishing, 1976.

Olson, Carl. *The Book of the Goddess Past and Present: An Introduction to Her Religion.* Prospect Heights, IL: Waveland, 2003.

Palmer, Martin, Jay Ramsay, and Man-Ho Kwok. *Kuan Yin: Myths and Prophecies of the Chinese Goddess of Compassion.* London: Thorsons, 1995.

Paul, Diana Y. *Women in Buddhism.* Berkeley: University of California Press, 1985.

Reed, Barbara E. "The Gender Symbolism of Kyan-yin Bodhisattva." In *Buddhism, Sexuality and Gender,* ed. Jose Ignacio Cabezön, 159–180. Albany: SUNY Press, 1992.

Rissho Kosei-kai. *The Threefold Lotus Sutra.* Translated by Katō, Bunnō, Yoshirō Tamura, and Kōjirō Miyasaka. Tokyo: Kōsei Publishing, 1975.

T'ang, Yung-t'ung. "On 'Ko-I.'" In *Radhakrishnan: Comparative Studies in Philosophy Presented in Honour of His Sixtieth Birthday,* by W. R. Inge et al., 276–286. London: Allen and Unwin, 1951.

Wang, Sheila. "A Conceptual Framework for Integrating Research Related to the Physiology of Compassion and the Wisdom of Buddhist Teachings." In *Compassion: Conceptualisations, Research and Use in Psychotherapy,* ed. Paul Gilbert, 75–120. New York: Routledge, 2005.

Willson, Martin. *In Praise of Tara: Songs to the Saviouress.* London: Wisdom Publications, 1986.

Young, Serinity. *Encyclopedia of Women and World Religion.* New York: Macmillan Reference USA, 1999.

Yü, Chün-fang. "Feminine Images of Kuan-Yin in Post-T'ang China." *Journal of Chinese Religions* 18 (Fall 1990): 61–89.

Yü, Chün-fang. *Kuan Yin: The Chinese Transformation of Avalokitesvara.* New York: Columbia University Press, 2001.

11

Xi Wangmu: The Great Goddess of China

Max Dashu

One of the oldest deities of China is Xi Wangmu (commonly written as Hsi Wang Mu in older texts). She lives on Kunlun Mountain in the far west, at the margin of heaven and earth. In a garden hidden by high clouds, her peaches of immortality grow on a colossal tree, only ripening once every 3000 years. The tree is a cosmic axis that connects heaven and earth, a ladder traveled by spirits and shamans.

Xi Wangmu controls the cosmic forces, time and space, and the pivotal Big Dipper constellation. With her powers of creation and destruction, she ordains life and death, disease and healing, and determines the life spans of all living beings. The energies of new growth surround her like a cloud. She is attended by hosts of spirits and transcendental force. Xi Wangmu presides over the dead and afterlife, and she confers divine realization and immortality on spiritual seekers.

The name of the goddess is usually translated as Queen Mother of the West. *Mu* means "mother," and *Wang* "sovereign." But *Wangmu* was not a title for royal women. It means "grandmother," as in the *Book of Changes*, Hexagram 35: "One receives these boon blessings from one's *wangmu*." A classical glossary says that *wangmu* was used as an honorific for female ancestors. The ancient commentator Guo Pu explained that "one adds *wang* ["great," to the syllable *mu*, "woman"] in order to honor them." Paul Goldin points out that the ancient Chinese commonly used *wang* "to denote spirits of any kind" and numinous power. He makes a convincing

西王母莫知其始莫知其終

Figure 11.1 Xi Wangmu in her high mountain garden, surrounded by purple clouds, with her attributes of tiger, three-legged raven, ling zhi fungus, and peaches of immortality. (© 2000 Max Dashu.)

case for translating the name of the goddess as "Spirit-Mother of the West."[1]

The oldest reference to Xi Wangmu dates to the Shang dynasty, around 3300 years ago. It is inscribed on an oracle bone used in divinations: "If we make offering to the Eastern Mother and Western Mother there will be approval." The inscription pairs her with another female, not the male partner invented for her by medieval writers, and this linkage with an Eastern goddess persisted in folk religion. Suzanne Cahill, an authority on Xi Wangmu, sees her as one of the ancient "*mu* divinities" of the directions, "mothers" who are connected to the sun and moon, or to their paths through the heavens. She notes that the tiger images on Shang bronze offerings vessels may have been associated with the western mu deity, an association of tiger and West that goes back to the Neolithic.[2]

After the oracle bones, no written records of the goddess appear for a thousand years, until the *Zhuang Zi*, circa 300 BCE. The early Taoist text casts her as a woman who attained the Tao, the ultimate way of nature and source of all wisdom:

> Xi Wang Mu attained it and took her seat on Shao Guang mountain.
> No one knows her beginning and no one knows her end.[3]

These infinite and eternal qualities remain definitive traits of the goddess throughout Chinese history.

The *Shanhai Jing*

Another ancient source for Xi Wangmu is the *Shanhai Jing* ("Classic of Mountains and Seas"). Its second chapter says that she lives on Jade Mountain. She resembles a human, but has a tiger's teeth and a leopard's tail. She wears a head ornament atop her wild hair.[4] This is the *sheng* head-dress shown in the earliest representations of the goddess: a horizontal band with circles or flares at either end. The sheng is usually interpreted as a symbol of weaving. The medieval *Di Wang Shih Zhi* connects it to "a loom mechanism" that the goddess holds. Cahill states that the sheng marks Xi Wangmu as a cosmic weaver who creates and maintains the universe. She also compares its shape to ancient depictions of constellations—circles connected by lines—that correspond to the stellar powers of Xi Wangmu. She "controls immortality and the stars." Classical sources explain *sheng* as meaning "overcoming" and "height."[5]

The sheng sign was regarded as an auspicious symbol during the Han dynasty and possibly earlier. People exchanged sheng tokens as gifts on stellar holidays, especially the Double Seven festival in which women's weaving figured prominently. The festival, sacred to Xi Wangmu, was celebrated on the seventh day of the seventh month, at the seventh hour, when she descended among humans. Taoists considered it the most important night of the year, "the perfect night for divine meetings and ascents."[6] It was the year's midpoint, "when the divine and human worlds touch," and cosmic energies were in perfect balance.[7]

The *Shanhai Jing* goes on to say of the tigress-like Xi Wangmu: "She is controller of the Grindstone and the Five Shards constellations of the heavens."[8] The Grindstone is where the axial tree connects to heaven, the "womb point" from which creation is churned out. In other translations, she presides over "the calamities of heaven and the five punishments."[9]

For Guo Pu, this line referred to potent constellations.[10] The goddess has destructive power—she causes epidemics—but she also averts them and cures diseases.

The passage above also says that the tiger-woman on Jade Mountain "excels at whistling." This line is sometimes rendered as "is fond of roaring" or "good at screaming." The character in question, *xiao*, does not translate easily. It is associated with "a clear, prolonged sound" that issues from the throats of sages and shamans. (Perhaps it resembled Tuvan throat singing, a central Asian chant style that splits the voice into simultaneous high fluting and low growling registers.) Xiào was compared to the cry of a phoenix, a long sigh, and a zither. Its melodic sound conveyed much more than words and had the power to rouse winds and call spirits. Taoist scriptures refer to the xiào, and in the *Songs of Chu* it figures in shamanic rites calling back the souls of the dead.[11]

Chapter 12 of the *Shanhai Jing* returns to the goddess, seated on She Wu mountain: "Xi Wangmu rests on a stool and wears an ornament on her head. She holds a staff. In the south, there are three birds from which Xi Wangmu takes her nourishment. They are found to the north of the Kunlun mountains."[12] Three azure birds that bring fruits to the goddess often appear among her spirit hosts and emissaries in art and literature. Here the Western Grandmother appears on She Wu, or "Snake Shaman," mountain. *Wu* is the Chinese name for female shamans. Its written character depicts two dancers around a central pillar—the same cosmic ladder that recurs in the iconography of Xi Wangmu. The *Songs of Chu*, a primary source on ancient Chinese shamanism, describes Kunlun Mountain as a column connecting heaven and earth, endlessly deep and high.[13] It is the road of shamanic journeys between the worlds.

Xi Wangmu has shamanic attributes in the *Shanhai Jing*, which depicts her as a tigress, an animal connected to shamans in China and over much of Asia. Tiger-women and women dancing with tigers appear in Indus Valley seals circa 2400 BCE. *Yü* bronze offering vessels of the early Shang dynasty are shaped as a tigress clasping children in her paws, and tigers flank the head of a child being born on a colossal *fangding* bronze vat used in ancestral offerings. The *taotie* sign represents a tiger on innumerable Shang and Zhou offering vessels and masks. Of Xi Wangmu's tigress form, Mathieu Remi observes, "There are good reasons for thinking that here we have a description of a shaman in trance." He signals Chinese scholars who compared her staff to the sorcerers' staff. Cahill draws the same conclusion, calling attention to modern parallels: "The stool, headdress, and staff—still part of the shaman's paraphernalia in Taiwan today—reflect her shamanistic side."[14]

The *Shanhai Jing* returns to Xi Wangmu in the western wilderness in chapter 16. It describes "the mountain of Wangmu" in the country of the Wo people, who eat phoenix eggs. Whoever drinks the sweet dew of this place will be able to attain every desire. On the great mountain Kunlun is a spirit with a human face and a tiger's body and tail. Both are white, the color of the west. Finally, Xi Wangmu is again described with tiger teeth and tail, with new details: she "lives in a cave," on a mountain that "contains a thousand things." The *Daren fu* of Sima Xiangru agrees that Xi Wangmu lives in a grotto. In his account, the white-haired goddess is served by a three-footed crow and is unimaginably long-lived.[15] The first written reference to Xi Wangmu granting the elixir of immortality appears in the ancient *Huainan Zi*. She gives the potion to the Archer Yi, but his wife Chang E takes it and floats up to the moon where she becomes a toad and the lunar goddess.[16] Xi Wangmu grants longevity in the *Songs of Chu* and in numerous later sources.

Kunlun: Mountain of Mystery

The marvelous Kunlun Mountain lies somewhere far in the west, beyond the desert of flowing sands. Some said it was in the "heavenly" Tian Shan mountains of central Asia, or was the source of the Yellow River. But Kunlun is a mysterious place outside of time, without pain or death, where all pleasures and arts flourished: joyous music, dancing, poetry, and divine feasts.[17] Kunlun means "high and precarious," according to the *Shizhou Ji*, because "its base is narrow and its top wide."[18] It is also called Highgate or Triple Mountain. The *Shanhai Jing* names it Jade Mountain, after a symbol of yin essence. In the *Zhuang Zi*, Xi Wangmu sits atop Shao Guang, which represents the western skies. Elsewhere she sits on Tortoise Mountain, the support of the world pillar, or on Dragon Mountain. In the Tang period, the goddess was said to live on Hua, the western marchmount in Shaanxi, where an old shrine of hers stood.[19]

Fantastic beings and shamanistic emissaries inhabit the sacred mountain of the goddess. Among them are the three-footed crow, a nine-tailed fox, a dancing frog, and the moon-hare who pounds magical elixirs in a mortar. There are phoenixes and *chi-lin*, "azure lads" and spirits riding on white stags. A third-century scroll describes Xi Wangmu herself as kin to magical animals in her western wilderness: "With tigers and leopards I form a pride / Together with crows and magpies I share the same dwelling place." Medieval poets and artists show the goddess riding on a phoenix or crane, or on a five-colored dragon. Many sources mention three azure birds that bring berries to Xi Wangmu in her mountain pavilion or fly before her as she descends to give audience to mortals. For the poet Li Bo, three wild blue birds circling around Jade Mountain are "the essence-guarding birds" who fulfill the will of the goddess. Several poets described these birds as "wheeling and soaring."

The Jade Maidens (*Yü Nü*) are companions of the goddess, dancers and musicians who play chimes, flutes, mouth organ, and jade sounding stones. In medieval murals at Yongle temple, they bear magical *ling zhi* fungi on platters. In the "Jade Girls' Song," poet Wei Ying-wu describes their flight: "Flocks of transcendents wing up to the divine Mother."[20]

Jade Maidens appear as long-sleeved dancers in the shamanic *Songs of Chu* and some Han poems. The *Shuo wen jie zi* defines them as "invocators [*zhu*] . . . women who can perform services to the shapeless and make the spirits come down by dancing."[21] Centuries later, a Qing dynasty painting shows a woman dancing before Xi Wang Mu and her court, moving vigorously and whirling her long sleeves.[22]

Chinese art is full of these ecstatic dancing women. Tang poets describe Xi Wangmu herself performing such dances in her rainbow dress and feathered robe with its winged sleeves. In *The Declarations of the Realized Ones* she dances while singing about the "Great Wellspring," and the Lady of the Three Primordials replies in kind.[23] The Jade Maidens are messengers of the goddess and teachers of Taoist mystics. They impart mystic revelations and present divine foods to those blessed to attend the banquet of the goddess. But the *Book of the Yellow Court* warns spiritual seekers against "the temptation to make love to the Jade Maidens of Hidden Time."[24]

Sometimes Yü Nü appears as a single divinity, in connection with other goddesses. In Chinese Buddhism, she is the dragon king's daughter, presented to the bodhisattva Guan Yin. Or she is born from an appeal to Tian Hou ("Empress of Heaven"), a title posthumously bestowed on the coastal saint Ma Zi, who was syncretized with the Eastern goddess.[25]

The immortals journey to Kunlun to be with Xi Wangmu. The character for immortal (*xian*) reads as "mountain person," or alternatively as "dancing person."[26] The goddess lives in a "stone apartment" within her sacred mountain grotto—from which spring the underground "grotto heavens" of medieval Taoism. It is the paradise of the dead; a tomb inscription near Chongqing calls it a "stone chamber which prolongs life."[27]

Xi Wangmu is an eternal being who guides vast cosmic cycles. In her mysterious realm, the passage of time is imperceptible: "A thousand years are just a small crack, like a cricket's chirp." A visitor turns his head for a second, and eons have passed. When King Mu returns from his visit to her paradise, the coats of his horses turn white.[28] The Western Grandmother confers immortality, even as she presides over the realm of the dead.

Mirrors and Tombs

The goddess is richly portrayed in ancient bronzes, murals, painted lacquers, clay tiles, and stone reliefs. As befits her connection with the West, direction of death, most of this art is from funerary contexts. Xi Wangmu sits with hands tucked into voluminous sleeves, on a throne perched above an irregular stone pillar or a multitiered mountain. A lacquer bowl from Lelang depicts her on this high perch, in a leopard hat and on a leopard mat, with a Jade Maiden beside her.[29] In an important find near Tengzhou, Shandong, an incised stone depicts Xi Wangmu with a leopard's body, tail, claws, teeth, whiskers—and a woman's face, wearing the sheng headdress. Votaries make offerings to her on both sides. The inscription salutes *Tian Wangmu*: Queen Mother of the Fields.[30] This alternate title reflects her control of the harvests, a tradition attested elsewhere.[31]

At Suide in Shaanxi, a sheng-crowned Xi Wangmu receives leafy fronds from human and owl-headed votaries. The magical fox, hare, frog, crow, and humans attend her in a tomb tile at Xinfan, Sichuan. In this province, tomb art shows the transcendent goddess seated in majesty on a dragon and tiger throne.[32] She presides at the summit of the intricate bronze "divine trees" that are unique to Sichuan, with stylized tiers of branches representing the shamanic planes. Their ceramic bases often show Kunlun with people ascending.[33] Incense burners also depict the sacred peak with swirling clouds, magical animals, and immortals.[34]

Xi Wangmu also appears on circular bronze mirrors with concentric panels swirling with cloud patterns and thunder signs. She is flanked by the tiger and dragon, or the elixir-preparing rabbit, or opposite the Eastern King Sire, amidst mountains, meanders, "magic squares and compass rings inscribed with the signs of time."[35] Some mirrors are divided into three planes, with a looped motif at the base symbolizing the world tree. At the top a pillar rests on a tortoise—a motif that recalls Tortoise Mountain and the mystic pillar of the goddess.[36]

In Han times, people placed bronze mirrors in burials as blessings for the dead and the living, inscribed with requests for longevity, prosperity, progeny, protection, and immortality. Taoists also used mystic mirrors in ritual, meditation, and transmissions of potency. One mirror depicting

Xi Wangmu bears a poem on the transcendents: "When thirsty, they drink from the jade spring; when hungry, they eat jujubes. They go back and forth to the divine mountains, collecting mushrooms and grasses. Their longevity is superior to that of metal or stone. The Queen Mother of the West."[37]

The Goddess in Popular Movements

The *Han Shu* and other ancient histories indicate that the common people saw Xi Wangmu as a savior, protector, and healer. A popular movement devoted to the goddess arose and spread rapidly in a time of severe drought and political disorder. It reached its height in 3 BCE, as the *Monograph on Strange Phenomena* recounts: "It happened that people were disturbed and running around, passing a stalk of grain or flax from one to another, and calling it 'the tally for transmitting the edict.'" Commoners marched westward toward the Han capital. Many were barefoot and wild-haired, like their untamed goddess. People shouted and drummed and carried torches to the rooftops. Some crossed barrier gates and climbed over city walls by night, others rode swift carriages in relays "to pass on the message." They gathered in village lanes and fields to make offerings: "They sang and danced in worship of the Queen Mother of the West."[38]

People wore and passed around written talismans believed to protect from disease and death. Some played games of chance associated with the immortals.[39] There were torches, drums, shouting. Farming and normal routines broke down. This goddess movement alarmed the gentry, and the Confucian writer presented it in a negative light. He warned of the danger of rising yin: females and the peasantry stepping outside their place. The people were moving west—opposite the direction of the great rivers—"which is like revolting against the court." The writer tried to stir alarm with a story about a girl carrying a bow who entered the capital and walked through the inner palaces. Then he drew a connection between white-haired Xi Wangmu and the dowager queen Fu who controlled the court, accusing these old females of "weak reason." His entire account aimed to overthrow the faction in power at court.[40]

Change was in the air. Around the same time, the *Taiping Jing* (Scripture of Great Peace) described "a world where all would be equal." As Kristofer Schipper observes, "a similar hope drove the masses in search of the great mother goddess."[41] Their movement was put down within the year, but the dynasty fell soon afterward. Yet veneration of the goddess crossed class lines, reaching to the most elite levels of society—as it had since Shang times. Imperial authorities of the later Han dynasty raised altars to the goddess. But courtly ceremonies differed from rural festivals, and religious interpretations were contested. Unfortunately, the *Hanshu* is the only written account of folk religion, from a hostile Confucian perspective.[42] The literati did not value peasant religion, so they did not record it: "what is certain is that the religion of the common people, with its worship of holy mountains and streams, as well as the great female deities, was systematically left out."[43]

Patriarchal Revisions

From the Han dynasty forward, the image of Xi Wangmu underwent marked changes.[44] Courtly writers tried to tame and civilize the shamanic goddess, replacing her wild hair and tiger features with the image of a court lady in aristocratic robes, jeweled headdresses. Her mythology also shifted as new Taoist schools arose, shifting the old nature religion to more esoteric philosophical ground and increasingly absorbing Buddhist ideas. Xi Wangmu remains the main goddess in the oldest Taoist encyclopedia (*Wu Shang Bi Yao*). But some authors began to subordinate her to great men: she offers "tribute" to Emperor Yu, or attends the court of Lao Zi.[45] They displaced her with new celestial kings and imperial lords—but never entirely erase her power.

The spirit-trees of Sichuan show Xi Wangmu at the crest, with Buddha meditating under her, in a still-Taoist context.[46] By the Six Dynasties, paintings in the Dun Huang caves show the goddess flying through the heavens to worship the Buddha.[47] Her sheng headdress disappeared and was replaced with a nine-star crown.

Xi Wangmu held her ground in the Tang dynasty, when Shang Qing Taoism became the official religion. She was considered its highest goddess, and royals built private shrines to her. Poets called her the "Divine Mother," others affectionately named her Amah, "Nanny." But some literati demoted the goddess to human status, making her fall in love with mortals, mooning over them and despairing at their absence. In a late eighth-century poem she becomes "uncertain and hesitant" as she visits the emperor Han Wudi.[48]

Other poets portrayed the goddess as young and seductive.[49] Worse, misogynist writers openly disparaged her. The fourth-century *Yü Fang Bi Jue* complained about her husbandless state and invented sexual slurs. It claimed that she achieved longevity by sexually vampirizing innumerable men and even preying upon boys to build up her yin essence. But the

vigor of folk tradition overcame such revisionist slurs—with one important exception. The ancient, shamanic tigress side of Xi Wangmu, and her
crone aspect, were pushed aside. Chinese folklore is full of tiger-women: Old
Granny Autumn Tiger, Old Tiger Auntie (or Mother), Autumn Barbarian
Auntie. They retain shamanic attributes, but in modern accounts they
are demonized (and slain) as devouring witches. Two vulnerable groups,
old women and indigenous people, became targets.[50] Yet the association
of tiger and autumn and granny goes back to ancient attributes of Xi
Wangmu that are originally divine.

In another shift, the Han elite invented a husband for the Western
Queen Mother: the Eastern King Sire. Susan Lullo observed that there is
"no evidence in Han literature that the King Father ever existed in myth."
(The god of Tai Shan, the sacred mountain of the East, never seems to
be paired with Xi Wangmu.) The new husband was added to eastern
walls of tombs, opposite the Western Mother, for "pictorial balance"—
but also to domesticate the unpartnered goddess.[51] Attempts to marry
her off did not find favor in popular tradition. Two thousand years after
the Shang inscription to the Eastern and Western Mothers, folk religion
still paired Xi Wangmu with a goddess of the East. Often it was Ma Gu
or Ma Zi, goddess of the Eastern Sea, whose paradise island of Penglai
was equivalent to Kunlun. Ma Zi is another eternal being who oversees
vast cycles of time, as the Eastern Sea gives way to mulberry fields, then
changes back to ocean again. Xi Wangmu is said to travel to her blessed
Eastern Isle, or Ma Gu to Kunlun.[52] These goddesses share a title; like
Wangmu, the name Ma Zi means "maternal ancestor, grandmother."[53]

Another Eastern partner of the goddess was Bixia Yüanjün, sovereign
of the dawn clouds. She was the daughter of Mount Tai, and her sanctuary stood on its summit. Bixia Yuanjün oversaw birth as her counterpart
Xi Wangmu governed death and immortality.[54] A major shrine to the
Western Grandmother stood along the path up this mountain.[55] The poet
Li Bo referred to "the Queen Mother's Turquoise Pond" from which pilgrims drank while ascending Mount Tai. Stone inscriptions describe a rite
of "tossing the dragons and tallies" in which monks threw bronze dragons into the waters with prayers for the emperor's longevity.[56]

Taoist Mysticism and the Goddess

From very ancient times the Grandmother of the West was associated
with the tiger, the element metal, autumn, and the color white. These
associations were part of the Chinese Concordance, which assigned to

each direction (including the center) an animal, element, organ, emotion, color, sound, and season. Also known as Five Element or Five Phases, this concordance is the basis of Chinese medicine, astrology, and geomancy (*feng shui*).

Xi Wangmu is called *Jinmu Yüanjün*: "Metal Mother," "Primordial Ruler."[57] She is the great female principle, Tai Yin—which is also the name of the lung meridian in Chinese medicine, which governs autumn, death, and grief. The goddess governs the realm of the dead but is simultaneously the font of vital energy and bliss. A mural at Yongle Temple in Shanxi shows her with a halo, crowned with a phoenix and a Kun trigram that announces her as the Great Yin.[58]

The *Book of the Center* says that Xi Wangmu is present in the right eye. "Her family name is Great Yin, her personal name, Jade Maiden of Obscure Brilliance."[59] The *Shang Jing Lao Ze Zhong Jing* accords on these points and names her "So-of-itself," "Ruling Thought," and "Mysterious Radiance."[60] In Taoist mysticism the human body is the microcosm that reflects the terrestrial and celestial macrocosm. These themes are interwoven in traditions about the goddess. Kunlun is present in the body as an inverted mountain in the lower abdomen, at the center of the Ocean of Energies (*Qi Hai*). The navel is the hollow summit of the mountain, through which the depths of that ocean can be reached. This is the Cinnabar Field (lower Dan Tian), the "root of the human being." On the celestial level, the goddess also manifests her power through the Dipper Stars, a major focus of Taoist mysticism.[61] A Shang Qing text dating around 500 says that Xi Wangmu governs the nine-layered Kunlun and the Northern Dipper. The *Shihzhou ji* also connects Kunlun Mountain "where Xi Wang Mu reigns" to a double star in the Big Dipper known as the Dark Mechanism. The Dipper's handle, called the Jade Crossbar of the Five Constants, "governs the internal structure of the nine heavens and regulates yin and yang."[62]

Taoist texts repeatedly associate Xi Wangmu with nine planes: a nine-leveled mountain, pillar, or jade palace. She is worshiped with nine-fold lamps. She governs the Nine Numina—which are the original ultimate powers in Shang Qing parlance. The goddess herself is called Nine Radiance and Queen Mother of the Nine Heavens. Around the year 500, Tao Hung Jing systematized Taoist deities into two separate hierarchies, male and female, with Xi Wangmu ranked as the highest goddess. He gave her a lasting title: The Ninefold Numinous Grand and Realized Primal Ruler of the Purple Tenuity from the White Jade Tortoise Terrace. Other sources, such as the poet Du Fu, described her descending to the human realm enveloped in purple vapors.[63]

Teacher of Sages

Taoists recognized the ancient great goddess as a divine teacher and initiator of mystic seekers, and as the ultimate origin of their teachings and practices. She governs the Taoist arts of self-transformation known as internal alchemy: meditation, breath and movement practices, medicines and elixirs. The legendary shamanic emperors Shun and Yü were said to have studied with Xi Wangmu. Books also credit her as the source of wisdom that the Yellow Emperor learned from the female transcendents Xüan Nü and Su Nü. Eventually the goddess comes to be portrayed as a master of Taoist scriptures, with a library of the greatest books on Kunlun.[64]

Legend said that the Zhou dynasty king Mu (circa 1000 BCE) traveled to Kunlun in search of the Western Mother. Many ancient sources elaborated on their meeting beside the Turquoise Pond. The emperor Han Wudi was granted a similar audience in 110 BCE. The *Monograph on Broad Phenomena* reports that the goddess sent a white deer to inform him of her advent, and he prepared a curtained shrine for her. She arrived on the festival of Double Sevens, riding on a chariot of purple clouds and clothed in seven layers of blue clouds. She sat facing the east, while three big blue birds and other magical servitors set up the ninefold tenuity lamp. The goddess gave five peaches to the emperor. He wanted to save the seeds for planting, but she laughed, replying that they would not bear fruit for 3000 years.[65]

In a later account, the cloud carriage of the goddess is drawn by chimeric *chilin* in nine colors. She wears a sword, a cord of knotted flying clouds, and "the crown of the Grand Realized Ones with hanging beaded strings of daybreak." She grants the emperor a detailed teaching on how to attain the Tao—which he fails to follow. Instead of nourishing essence, preserving breath, and keeping the body whole, he loses himself in carousing and excess.[66]

Literature focuses on her meetings with emperors, but a deep and broad tradition casts Xi Wangmu as the guardian of women and girls. She was worshiped at the birth of daughters and protected brides.[67] Celebrations of women's fiftieth birthday honored the goddess. Women who stood outside the patriarchal family system were her special protegées, whether they earned their own way as singers, dancers, and prostitutes, or became nuns, hermits, and sages who attained the Tao.[68]

Though men greatly outnumber women as named and remembered Taoist masters—some of these were recorded only as "wife of"—in practice women acted as teachers and libationers (priestesses). Female instruction was built in to a greater degree than in any other "major" religion;

tradition demanded that a person of the opposite sex perform the initiation, and its highest degree "could only be obtained by a man and a woman together."[69] Many accounts show Xi Wangmu as the ultimate source of teachings transmitted by female sages and transcendents to mortal men. The *Zhen Gao* scroll lays out a complete spiritual matrilineage that begins with Xi Wangmu and enumerates clans and religious communities in the female line.[70] The female immortal Wei hua-cun was said to have transmitted teachings to the shaman Yang Xi. Shang Qing Taoism arose from her revelations, but it was understood that they were inspired by the Spirit Mother of the West.[71]

By the Ming dynasty, the mixture of Buddhism and Taoism gave rise to a new goddess with attributes of Xi Wangmu and Guanyin: Wusheng Laomu. This Venerable Eternal Mother "created the world in the beginning of time." She helps her children, who go to her western paradise at death. The visionary Tanyangzi, a devotee of Guanyin, received liberation from Xi Wangmu.[72]

The Western Spirit Mother lived on in women's embroidery. A favorite scene was the goddess flying on a phoenix toward her mountaintop garden, with the Jade Maidens welcoming her beside the Turquoise Pond. The Double Sevens festival sacred to Xi Wangmu drifted over the centuries toward the Weaver Girl. Because she neglected her weaving, the goddess separated her from Cowherd Boy by drawing her hairpin across the sky. Thus she created the Milky Way, a celestial river that separated the stars Vega and Aquila. Later, Xi Wangmu helped the lovers to reunite by sending 10,000 magpies to create a bridge. So they meet once a year, on the night of Double Sevens. In south China today, this holiday is named the Festival of Seven Sisters. Women propitiate them with magnificent altars adorned with offerings of lights, flowers, fruits, and fine needlework. The celebration culminates with a "wish-fulfillment banquet."[73]

Notes

Portions of this chapter are adapted from Max Dashu, "Xi Wangmu, the Shamanic Great Goddess of China," http://www.suppressedhistories.net/goddess/xiwangmu.html.

1. Paul R. Goldin, "On the Meaning of the Name Xi Wangmu, Spirit-Mother of the West," *Journal of the American Oriental Society* 122, no. 1 (January–March 2002): 83–85.

2. Suzanne E. Cahill, *Transcendence and Divine Passion: The Queen Mother of the West in Medieval China* (Stanford, CA: Stanford University Press, 1993), 12–13.

3. Gia-fu Feng and Jane English, *Chuang Tsu: Inner Chapters* (New York: Knopf, 1974), 125.

4. Mathieu Remi, *Etude sur la mythologies et l'ethnologie de la Chine ancienne: Traduction annotée du Shanhai Jing* (Paris: Institut des hautes etudes chinoises, 1983), 1:100.

5. Cahill, *Transcendence and Divine Passion*, 16–18, 45; Richard Strassberg, *A Chinese Bestiary: Strange Creatures from the Guideways Through Mountains and Seas* (Berkeley: University of California Press, 2002), 109.

6. Cahill, *Transcendence and Divine Passion*, 16, 167–168.

7. Catherine Despeux and Livia Kohn, *Women in Daoism* (Cambridge, MA: Three Pines Press, 2003), 31.

8. Cahill, *Transcendence and Divine Passion*, 16.

9. Strassberg, *A Chinese Bestiary*, 109.

10. Remi, *Etude sur la mythologies*, 102.

11. Sun Ji, "Wei-Jin shidai de 'xiao,'" in *Xunchang de jingzhi-Wenwu yu gudai shenghuo*, ed. Yang Hong and Sun Ji (Liaoning: Jiaoyu Chubanshe, 1996).

12. Remi, *Etude sur la mythologies*, 481.

13. Cahill, *Transcendence and Divine Passion*, 47.

14. Remi, *Etude sur la mythologies*, 100, 481; Cahill, *Transcendence and Divine Passion*, 19.

15. Remi, *Etude sur la mythologies*, 575–578, 481–482, 588.

16. Sheri A. Lullo, "Female Divinities in Han Dynasty Representation," in *Gender and Chinese Archaeology*, ed. Katheryn Linduff and Yan Sun (Walnut Creek, CA: Altamira, 2004), 270, 285.

17. Cahill, *Transcendence and Divine Passion*, 19–20, 77.

18. Despeux and Kohn, *Women in Daoism*, 28.

19. Cahill, *Transcendence and Divine Passion*, 76, 14–20, 60.

20. Ibid., 51–53; 99, 92, 51–53, 159; 99–100.

21. Jessica Rawson, "Tomb of the King of Nanyue," in *The Golden Age of Chinese Archaeology*, ed. Xiaoneng Yang (New Haven, CT: Yale University Press, 1999), 427.

22. Kristofer Schipper, "Taoism: The Story of the Way," in *Taoism and the Arts of China*, ed. Stephen Little and Shawn Eichman (Chicago: Art Institute, 2000), 36.

23. Cahill, *Transcendence and Divine Passion*, 165–166, 187.

24. Kristofer Schipper, *The Taoist Body* (Berkeley: University of California Press, 1993), 144.

25. Keith Stevens, *Chinese Gods* (London: Collins and Brown, 1997), 167.

26. Schipper, "Taoism," 36.

27. Wu Hung, "Mapping Early Taoist Art," in *Taoism and the Arts of China*, ed. Stephen Little and Shawn Eichman (Chicago: Art Institute, 2000), 83.

28. Cahill, *Transcendence and Divine Passion*, 47, 84, 114–115, 129.

29. Liu Yang, "Origins of Daoist Iconography," in *Ars Orientalis* (Ann Arbor: University of Michigan Press, 2001), 31:40.

30. Lullo, "Female Divinities," 271.

31. Cahill, *Transcendence and Divine Passion*, 13.

32. Liu, "Origins of Daoist Iconography," 40–43.

33. Wu Hung, "Mapping Early Taoist Art," 81–91.

34. Stephen Little, "Sacred Mountains and Cults of the Immortals," in *Taoism and the Arts of China*, ed. Stephen Little and Shawn Eichman (Chicago: Art Institute, 2000), 148.

35. Schipper, *The Taoist Body*, 172.

36. Wu Hung, "Mapping Early Taoist Art," 87.

37. Cahill, *Transcendence and Divine Passion*, 28–29.

38. Lullo, "Female Divinities," 278–279.

39. Cahill, *Transcendence and Divine Passion*, 21–23.

40. Lullo, "Female Divinities," 279–280.

41. Schipper, "Taoism," 40.

42. Cahill, *Transcendence and Divine Passion*, 24; Lullo, "Female Divinities," 277–281.

43. Schipper, "Taoism," 34.

44. Lullo, "Female Divinities," 259.

45. Cahill, *Transcendence and Divine Passion*, 34, 45, 121–122.

46. Little, "Sacred Mountains and Cults of the Immortals," 154–155; Wu Hung, "Mapping Early Taoist Art," 89, 154–155.

47. Cahill, *Transcendence and Divine Passion*, 42.

48. Ibid., 82–83, 58–69, 159.

49. Lullo, "Female Divinities," 276.

50. B. J. ter Haarm, *Witchcraft and Scapegoating in Chinese History* (Leiden: Brill, 2006), 55–76.

51. Lullo, "Female Divinities," 273–274, 261.

52. Cahill, *Transcendence and Divine Passion*, 118, 62, 77.

53. Schipper, "Taoism," 166; Stevens, *Chinese Gods*, 137.

54. Stephen Little, "Divine Manifestations of Yin: Goddesses and Female Saints," in *Taoism and the Arts of China*, ed. Stephen Little and Shawn Eichman (Chicago: Art Institute, 2000), 278.

55. Stevens, *Chinese Gods*, 53.

56. Cahill, *Transcendence and Divine Passion*, 1–2, 59.

57. Ibid., 68.

58. Little, "Divine Manifestations of Yin," 276, 281.

59. Schipper, *The Taoist Body*, 105.

60. Cahill, *Transcendence and Divine Passion*, 35.

61. Schipper, *The Taoist Body*, 106–107; 70.

62. Cahill, *Transcendence and Divine Passion*, 35–38.

63. Ibid., 68–69, 126; 33, 24, 168.

64. Ibid., 14–15, 44, 34.

65. Ibid., 48–55.

66. Ibid., 81, 149–153.

67. Stevens, *Chinese Gods*, 53.

68. Cahill, *Transcendence and Divine Passion*, 70.

69. Schipper, *The Taoist Body*, 58, 128–129.

70. Cahill, *Transcendence and Divine Passion*, 34.

71. Schipper, "Taoism," 44; Cahill, *Transcendence and Divine Passion*, 155.

72. Despeux and Kohn, *Women in Daoism*, 42–44.

73. Janice Stockard, *Daughters of the Canton Delta: Marriage Patterns and Economic Strategies in South China* (Stanford, CA: Stanford University Press, 1992), 42–44.

Bibliography

Cahill, Suzanne E. *Transcendence and Divine Passion: The Queen Mother of the West in Medieval China*. Stanford, CA: Stanford University Press, 1993.

Despeux, Catherine, and Livia Kohn. *Women in Daoism*. Cambridge, MA: Three Pines Press, 2003.

Feng, Gia-fu, and Jane English. *Chuang Tsu: Inner Chapters*. New York: Knopf, 1974.

Goldin, Paul R. "On the Meaning of the Name Xi Wangmu, Spirit-Mother of the West." *Journal of the American Oriental Society* 122, no. 1 (January–March 2002).

Little, Stephen. "Taoism and the Arts of China." In *Taoism and the Arts of China*, ed. Stephen Little and Shawn Eichman, 13–31. Chicago: Art Institute, 2000.

Liu, Yang, "Origins of Daoist Iconography." *Ars Orientalis*, vol. 31. Ann Arbor: University of Michigan Press, 2001.

Lullo, Sheri A. "Female Divinities in Han Dynasty Representation." In *Gender and Chinese Archaeology*, ed. Katheryn Linduff and Yan Sun. Walnut Creek, CA: Altamira, 2004.

Mann, Susan. *Precious Records: Women in China's Long 18th Century*. Stanford, CA: Stanford University Press, 1997.

Rawson, Jessica. "Tomb of the King of Nanyue." In *The Golden Age of Chinese Archaeology*, ed. Xiaoneng Yang, 410–437. New Haven, CT: Yale University Press, 1999.

Remi, Mathieu. *Etude sur la mythologies et l'ethnologie de la Chine ancienne: Traduction annotée du Shanhai Jing*. Vol. 1. Paris: Institut des hautes etudes chinoises, 1983.

Schipper, Kristofer. "Taoism: The Story of the Way." In *Taoism and the Arts of China*, ed. Stephen Little and Shawn Eichman, 33–55. Chicago: Art Institute, 2000.

Schipper, Kristofer. *The Taoist Body*. Berkeley: University of California Press, 1993.

Stevens, Keith. *Chinese Gods*. London: Collins and Brown, 1997.

Stockard, Janice. *Daughters of the Canton Delta: Marriage Patterns and Economic Strategies in South China*. Stanford, CA: Stanford University Press, 1992.

Strassberg, Richard. *A Chinese Bestiary: Strange Creatures from the Guideways Through Mountains and Seas*. Berkeley: University of California Press, 2002.

Sun Ji. "Wei-Jin shidai de 'xiao.'" In *Xunchang de jingzhi-Wenwu yu gudai shenghuo*, ed. Yang Hong and Sun Ji, 23–28. Liaoning: Jiaoyu Chubanshe, 1996.

ter Haarm, B. J. *Witchcraft and Scapegoating in Chinese History*. Leiden: Brill, 2006.

Wu Hung. "Mapping Early Taoist Art." In *Taoism and the Arts of China*, ed. Stephen Little and Shawn Eichman, 77–79. Chicago: Art Institute, 2000.

12

Yama no Kami: Mountain Mother of Japan

Denise Saint Arnault

In a Japanese myth from 1100 CE, the beautiful Okureha prays to the Japanese goddess of mercy for her mother's recovery. As she begins her decent from the mountain shrine, she is seized by a man. Despite her desperate cries for help, she realizes she is alone and hopeless to save herself.

> Suddenly, a piercing cold breeze came along, carrying the autumn leaves in little columns. . . . [The man] seemed to weaken to the cold wind. . . . In a few seconds, the man fell down as in a drunken sleep. Just then, [Okureha] saw, advancing towards her, a beautiful [young] girl . . . dressed in white, who seemed to glide. Her face was white as the snow . . . her brows were crescent-shaped . . . her mouth was like flowers. . . . "Be neither surprised nor afraid, my child. I saw that you were in danger, and I came to your rescue. . . . [Okureha fell on her knees to express her thanks]. . . . "I owe my deliverance entirely to you, holy lady."[1]

In this story, the girl encounters Yama no Kami in the form of a benevolent, beautiful, snow-white girl. The Kami is kind to her because Okureha is pious and comes to give prayers in the mountain, the place where the mountain deity resides. Yama no Kami is an earth mother deity that has been an important part of the indigenous Japanese religion, Shinto. Shinto literally translates to "the way of the deities" (*shin*, "deity"; *to*, "the way of") and is much older than Buddhism. In this chapter, Yama no Kami will be

Figure 12.1 Ascending mountain stairs to enter the dense, fearsome, and animated realm of Yama no Kami. (Photograph by T. Enami, ca 1898. Courtesy of the Rob Oechsle Collection.)

explored from the perspective of the Japanese indigenous religion of Shinto, Japanese cultural patterns, and from the perspective of the importance of geography of the Japanese islands.

Religious and Cultural Conceptions of the Mountain in Japan

Shintoism is a religion that venerates and worships all of the powers of nature and of the ancestors. Shinto teaches that all natural things have a spiritual force (animism), and that people are connected spiritually with the souls of all of their descendants, as well as the souls of those who are as yet unborn. *Yama* ("mountain") *no* (possessive connector) *Kami* ("deity") refers both to the animistic force of the mountains, as well as to the mountain itself as the deity. Volcanoes like Mount Fuji, as well as local mountains throughout Japan, are venerated by the Japanese people. Villages at the base of mountains often have a shrine at the entrance into the mountain, part of a pair of "companion" shrines, one at the base and one at the top of the mountain. Some mountains, especially after the advent of agriculture in Japan, became revered as sacred sources of water.

For Japanese farmers, this Kami is responsible for bringing forth water crucial to rice farming. People in these farming regions believe that the Kami resides in the mountain in the winter and comes down from the mountain in the spring, transforming into Ta no Kami (*ta*, "rice paddy," "deity of the rice paddy"). In some of these mountains, shrines are dedicated to Mi kumara no Kami (*Mi*, "water," *kumara*, "to distribute"), which roughly translates as "the mountain deity that distributes the blessed water in the form of rain, river or runoff."

Shinto practitioners did not tend to make statuary or give human form to Kami until the relatively later influence and integration of Buddhism from India and China from the sixth through the 11th century CE. Therefore, while Kami do not have male or female physical form, gender is implied in the way that they were described. For example, earth, and specifically the mountains, is described in terms similar to the great earth mother goddesses. Mountains were the powerful and majestic evidence of the supremacy and expansiveness of her protection and abundance. In addition, within mountains was earth-fire (symbolic of might, danger, anger, and destruction), caves (symbolic of the vulva and womb), and pure water runoff (symbolic of milk and nourishment).[2]

Within the Shinto religion, Kami are neither good nor evil; however, a deity could act either helpfully or destructively, depending upon the behavior of the humans in question. Japanese culture holds that human behavior is part of a relationship between humans and the divine, and the maintenance of a proper relationship is of utmost importance. Japanese culture is replete with taboos and rules for proper conduct. Propriety depends on one's gender, social position, occupation, and the specific situation. Language use, proper etiquette in addressing the deity, proper and consistent offerings, prayers, and talismans are central in the daily lives of the Japanese. Furthermore, Kami enforce these taboos, rules, and customs with rewards for proper conduct, warnings to make people do what is right, or punishment for improper behavior.

Shinto cosmology also holds that ancestor spirits move from the human realm into the realm of Kami through the passageway of the mountains. There is a Japanese concept of Shi de no yama (*Shi*, "death," thus "the mountain as the place of the voyage of the soul"). This concept conveys the idea that the spirit of the dead must go beyond the mountain before it arrives at the "Other World."[3] There are ancient stories of mountains as places of burial, and numerous Japanese mythological terms refer to the mountains as the places where souls go to rest. In some parts of Japan, two graves were built. One grave was situated in the cemetery of the local village for the corpse. The other grave was in a cave in the mountain and was the place where the villagers would go to worship the spirit of the deceased. Therefore, the dead go into a cave that is situated in the mountain and is the womb of the earth mother Yama no Kami. Birds and insects were believed to be messengers between the two worlds, or thought to be available to be possessed by ancestral spirits or Kami as a means of moving around in human places. There are legends and myths of sacred birds and insects, including the cuckoo and large red dragon-flies.[4] Perhaps influenced by the Buddhist concepts of the evolution of souls toward becoming gods, there is also a Shinto concept that ancestral souls can become Kami over time.

It is also helpful to explore the importance of the volcanic and moun-tainous landscape of Japan to appreciate the nature of Yama no Kami. None could convey the importance of this geography better than did Wal-ter Weston in his elegant 1924 address to the Royal Geographic Society:

> But it is the mountains of Japan that constitute its most striking feature and have exercised the most marked influence on the char-acter of its inhabitants. They occupy more than three-quarters of the total area of the country, and form the chief part of nearly every view. Nowhere do we find that intense love of freedom and independence always associated with mountain peoples so strongly marked as among the Japanese, for to those characteristics we have to add an intensely nationalistic spirit, inborn in an island people whose shores no conqueror has trod, since it became a nation. . . . [I]n many instances [one village would be] almost entirely cut off from its [nearest] neighbor[s] by high mountain barriers which not only made . . . [between village] communication difficult, but bred a strong disinclination for centralized government. It was in the seclusion of such inaccessible forest-clad hills and wild torrent val-leys that the fierce family feuds . . . persisted. . . . Nearly every mountain summit has its own guardian divinity [Yama no Kami], worshipped at some appropriate spot, and woe betide the careless or the contemptuous intruder on those sacred precincts at unpro-pitious seasons or in unhallowed ways![5]

The Mountain as the Place of Birth, Death, and Rebirth

The Japanese recognize the soul as being attached to the geographical place of its birth, as well as being a force that remains attached to the souls of its ancestors throughout time. The Japanese concept of *ie* roughly translates as "household." The ie includes all of the people who are currently living, those souls who are dead but who remain attached to the household, and those souls yet to be born into the household.[6] It is critical that families maintain good relationships with their ancestors, because these souls have a direct influence on the health and prosperity of the rest of the ie. Since souls reside in the mountains, maintaining a good relationship with Yama no Kami is central in security of the ie.

Throughout Japan, to this day, there are public festivals at appointed times of the year that honor and appease the ancestors. During these times of the year, the souls of the dead, who reside in the mountains, come down to visit. In rural Japan, it is common to find Yama no Kami shrines situated at the foot of the mountain, and the homesteads near these shrines hold special responsibilities to carry out certain rituals that will protect the village from the ancestral deities who reside within the mountain throughout the rest of the year.[7] During these festivals, most villages observe a custom in which a village or ie representative goes onto the mountainside to light a bonfire or torch in order to meet and welcome the spirits who are coming down from the mountain. Sometimes, torches are lit for the same purpose in cemeteries, at the village limits, or in high lanterns set in gardens.[8]

Related to the idea of souls residing within the mountains is the function of the Yama no Kami as mountain mother. Since the mountain contains the womb of the great mother, it is therefore the place where the sacred and mystical connection among life, death, and rebirth is dramatically enacted. Amaterasu omi Kami, the ancestral deity of the imperial family, is believed to bring down the "soul box" of the new emperor from the sacred mountain.[9] In her role as the great mother of birth, death, and rebirth, she holds all souls in a box. She is, therefore, sometimes known as the divine attendant goddess in childbirth, bestowing a soul into each new human being. Another popular belief is that Yama no Kami is a goddess who, once a year, gives birth to twelve children. She is called Juni sama (*juni*, "twelve"; *sama*, "sacred one"), and her twelve children symbolize the twelve months of the year.[10]

There is also a legend of the mountain maiden who tests the character of those men who hunt in the mountainous regions. The mountain maiden will give blessings depending on how the hunters respond to her needs. She presents herself to the hunters in the form of a young maiden called Yama no Shinbo, who has just given birth and she asks the hunters for food. In one tale, two brothers happen upon her. One brother is repelled by the fear of pollution by women after childbirth and refuses to help her. The other brother gives her his food, and she rewards him with success and happiness.

Other folktales paint a picture of an old woman called Yama Uba (*Yama*, "mountain"; *uba,* "grandmother" or "old woman"). In these stories, Yama Uba resides in a mountain hut and presents herself to wandering travelers in the guise of a young and beautiful girl while being, in reality, as old as time itself. Like other earth mothers, the role of Yama Uba is to work tirelessly to maintain the cycle of life of humans and the world itself. An example of this myth is the Noh play in a collection complied by Waley.[11] In this story, Yama Uba is the fairy of mountains that have been under her care since the world began. She has grown very old, and she has long, wild white hair, and an old, thin white face. In the play, Yama Uba tells her story:

> Round and round . . . from hill to hill, from valley to valley [I travel]. . . .
> In spring [I] deck the twigs with blossom, in autumn [I] clothe the hills
> with moonlight, in winter [I] shake snow from the heavy clouds. . . . On
> and on, round and round, caught in the Wheel of Fate. . . . On the Hill
> of Life, where men wander from incarnation to incarnation, never
> escaping [my] Wheel of Life and Death.

The conception of the mountain as goddess may have undergone transformation under centuries of Japanese patriarchal rule. In most of the popularly available folktales, the goddess is described as the vain mistress of the mountain, who dislikes women, especially young ones who would rival her beauty. Not unlike the wicked queen in the European folktale of "Snow White," she is said to appear to hapless, wandering young girls in the form of a hideous old woman. In these depictions, she is a trickster, trapping and killing the girls with a mouth that is like a slit cut from ear to ear. This conception makes reference to a story about Kuchi Sake Onna (*kuchi*, "cut"; *sake,* "face"; *onna,* "woman"), the vain wife of a samurai who punished her by slicing her face, and to the bitterness and revenge such a woman would direct toward those who are not disfigured. Some have suggested that people in villages may perform rituals of provide offerings that flatter this Kami by offering her items thought to be uglier than she, in order to gain favors and access to her dangerous and wild places. Others report stories of her being one-eyed and one-legged.[12] This mythological idea is also found in a contemporary horror movie, showing how enduring myths can be.

Mountain Mother as Guardian

Another type of Yama no Kami myth describes the mountain mother as a maiden with a son who helps humans navigate the wilderness and grants them permission to build houses or temples. Yama no Kami in her guardian aspect may appear as a snake, a dragon, or a centipede. There are stories of her as a wolf, fox, or monkey. These beings are general goblins of the mountains that have powers that include shape-shifting, communicating without speaking, reading human thoughts, and moving about without wings or walking. These beings are sometimes mischievous and operate to maintain proper social conduct by punishing those who are arrogant, vain, or misuse power.[13]

According to one legend a ninth-century monk named Kukai met a young hunter. The hunter's mother was named Nibutsu Hime, and she was the maiden goddess of the mountain. The monk was able to gain the favor of the maiden goddess, and this allowed him to build monasteries at Koya.

In the mountain, considered by the Japanese people to be a dangerous or wild place, lives Yama no Kami, acting as its protector or guardian. An example of this role is the myth told by Yanagita and translated by Fanny Mayer. In this tale, there was a blind flute player traveling at night in the mountain. Aware that he is in a sacred and potentially dangerous realm, he prays at the base of a sacred tree, saying: "Oh Mountain Spirit, since I have lost my way and night has come on, please let me stop here just for tonight. Therefore, although it may not be very pleasing to you, I will play a number on my lute, as is the custom of blind minstrels on a journey." After the man said this prayer, a voice reassured him that his offering of a song was accepted. Within minutes, the blind man heard footsteps and discovered a tray that contained a feast of foods. Again, the flute player offered his gratitude to the sacred tree and lay down to sleep for the night.

The next morning a hunter appeared to the blind man and said that he had been told to guide him to safety. The blind man reached out to find not a human, but a furry tail upon which to hold. Feeling confident from the blessings he had received the night before, the flute player held the furry tail and climbed down the hill. Hearing the sounds of village life, he knew he had made his way safely down the mountain. But then he also heard a child cry:

"There! There! Look over there! That blind minstrel coming down the mountain is hanging onto the tail of a wolf!" . . . [After hearing the minstrel's tale, a villager] struck his hands together and exclaimed, ". . . My little child suddenly spoke out strangely last night. 'I am the Mountain Spirit (Yama no Kami) . . . I have a special guest here tonight so make a feast and bring it to the mountain. Give it to the man resting under the great tree. If you are slow about it, I will take the life of this child.' " . . . The whole house was worried but somehow they hurriedly prepared a tray and sent it out to the mountain . . . [for] the guest of the Mountain Spirit.[14]

A different set of beliefs center on Yama no Kami as the goddess who works with those who hunt or cut trees in her domain.[15] In these myths, Yama no Kami is the mistress of the wild and defender of animals. One legend tells a story about the goddess of Mount Nikko, who was attacked by the goddess of the nearby Mount Akagi. The first goddess asked for help from a young hunter, Banzaburo, who was known for his skill in archery. Banzaburo shot out the eyes of the deity of Mount Akagi, who was disguised as a giant centipede. The goddess of Mount Nikko rewarded Banzaburo by giving him the right to hunt in every mountain and forest of Japan. Moreover, Banzaburo became regarded either as the ancestor of or the guardian deity of the hunting tribes, and in some cases he is celebrated as the son of the mountain maiden Yama-hime.[16] It is obvious that Yama no Kami is not a single deity, but that each mountain might have its own Kami. Finally, in relationship to this goddess, some scholars report that hunters would speak only in a secret language that conveyed their respect for their relationship with the goddess and their promise to also respect and protect her sacred animals.

The religious and cultural background provided shows the all-powerful and awesome nature of the mountain mother as the source of life, the place of the dead, and the source of rebirth. She is also a guardian and protector who brings water to nourish the soil for farmers and protects the trees and animals in her sacred realms. She is indeterminate and ambiguous, and therefore has no single representation. Yama no Kami can reward proper behavior, frighten people into restoring proper behavior, or punish improper behavior. She is alive and well in Japan, as shown by the persistence of festivals and daily life customs held to honor her and maintain relationship with her. Unfortunately, her nature has been corrupted in modern times and now she is represented as a frightening and vengeful character.

Notes

1. Anonymous, "The Perpetual Life-giving Wine," in *Ancient Tales and Folklore of Japan,* ed. R. G. Smith (Whitefish, MT: Kessinger Publishing, 2006), 178–179.

2. I. Hori, "Mountains and Their Importance for the Idea of the Other World in Japanese Folk Religion," *History of Religions* 6, no. 1 (1966): 1–23.

3. Y. Yagi, "Mura-Zakai: The Japanese Village Boundary," *Asian Folklore Studies* 47, no. 1 (1988): 137–151.

4. Hori, "Mountains and Their Importance."

5. W. Weston, "The Influence of Nature on Japanese Character," *The Geographical Journal* 63, no. 2 (1924): 106–119.

6. M. Ashkenazi, *Handbook of Japanese Mythology* (New York: Oxford University Press, 2008).

7. Yagi, "Mura-Zakai."

8. Hori, "Mountains and Their Importance."

9. H. O. Rotermund, "Mountains in Japan," in *Mythologies: A Restructured Translation of Dicionnaire des mythologies and des religions des societes traditionnelles and du monde antique,* ed. Y. Bonnefoy and W. Doniger, vol. 2 (Chicago: University of Chicago Press, 1991), 1051.

10. Hori, "Mountains and Their Importance."

11. K. Z. Ujinobu, "Yamauba (The dame of the mountains)," in *The Nōh Plays of Japan,* ed. A. Waley (Sydney: Allen and Unwin, 1921), 247.

12. F. H. Mayer and K. Yanagita, "Yanagita Kunio: Japanese Folk Tales," *Folklore Studies* 11, no. 1 (1952): i–97.

13. H. Iwai, "Yama no Kami," *Encyclopedia of Shinto,* Establishment of a National Learning Institute for the Dissemination of Research on Shinto and Japanese Culture, http://21coe.kokugakuin.ac.jp (accessed January 4, 2009).

14. Mayer and Yanagita, "Yanagita Kunio," 10–11.

15. C. Blacker, "The Mistress of Animals in Japan: Yamanokami," in *The Concept of the Goddess,* ed. S. Billington and M. Green (New York: Routledge; 1996), 178–185.

16. N. Naumann, "Yama no Kami," *Asian Folklore Studies* 22 (1963): 133–366.

Bibliography

Ashkenazi, M. *Handbook of Japanese Mythology.* New York: Oxford University Press, 2008.

Billington, S., and M. Green, eds. *The Concept of the Goddess.* New York: Routledge, 1996.

Bonnefoy, Yves, and Wendy Doniger, eds. *Mythologies: A Restructured Translation of Dicionnaire des mythologies and des religions des societes traditionnelles and du monde antique.* 2 vols. Chicago: University of Chicago Press, 1991.

Hori, I. "Mountains and Their Importance for the Idea of the Other World in Japanese Folk Religion." *History of Religions* 6, no. 1 (1966): 1–23.

Iwai, H. "Yama no Kami." *Encyclopedia of Shinto* Establishment of a National Learning Institute for the Dissemination of Research on Shinto and Japanese Culture. http://21coe.kokugakuin.ac.jp (accessed January 4, 2009).

Mayer, F. H., and K. Yanagita. "Yanagita Kunio: Japanese Folk Tales." *Folklore Studies* 11, no. 1 (1952): i–97.

Naumann, N. "Yama no Kami." *Asian Folklore Studies* 22 (1963): 133–366.

Smith, R. G., ed. *Ancient Tales and Folklore of Japan.* Whitefish, MT: Kessinger Publishing, 2006.

Waley, Arthur, ed. *The Noh Plays of Japan.* Sydney: Allen and Unwin, 1921.

Weston, W. "The Influence of Nature on Japanese Character." *The Geographical Journal* 63, no. 2 (1924): 106–119.

Yagi, Y. "Mura-Zakai: The Japanese Village Boundary." *Asian Folklore Studies* 47, no. 1 (1988): 137–151.

13

Re-membering the Cosmogonic Goddess of Cheju: Sôlmundae Halmang

Hea-Kyoung Koh

> All sacred things must have their place. It could even be said that being in their place is what makes them sacred for if they were taken out of their place, even in thought, the entire order of the universe would be destroyed.
>
> Claude Levi-Strauss, *The Savage Mind*

The goddess Sôlmundae Halmang is the creator of Cheju Island. Located in the southern tip of Korea, this island was geographically isolated until the last century. This long isolation has allowed the development and maintenance of a unique culture. Previous research found that the Cheju has been an egalitarian, "neither sex dominant" and "nonhierarchical" society. Sôlmundae Halmang is a giantess. The highest mountain on the island, Hanla Mountain (over 6000 feet), reaches below her elbow and the deepest river around her ankle. Her diarrhea created 360 hills and her urine formed the channel between Cheju Island and Udo, an auxiliary island. She is the land itself, and her presence marks the entire island.

Despite her explicit manifestation in the landscape, her cult has completely vanished. The fragmentary knowledge of Sôlmundae Halmang's myths is found throughout the island, with no apparent links among them. However, these fragments, each bound to a specific geographic site, are

Figure 13.1 Now available only through folktales about landscape features, Sôlmundae Halmang was once a powerful goddess of the Korean peninsula. (Photograph by Hea-Kyoung Koh.)

precious mythological gems that have never completely disappeared from the psyche of the Cheju Islanders. These skeletal remains can be the valuable foundation upon which the image of the age-old goddess can be built once more.

Weaving as the Dawn of Light

There stand many rocks of eccentric shapes in Sôngsanli Ilchulbong (the peak of the sunrise) among which there is a high soaring rock on which Sôlmundae Halmang put a lamp for her weaving.[1]

The Sôngsan peak, a 700-foot-high ocean cliff, stands marvelously on the eastern tip of the island. On top of the peak, a broad meadow of about thirty acres stretches inside the crater. Before electricity, a miniature Sôngsan peak called the *tûngkyôngsôk* was popular in Cheju households; it was a one-foot-tall cylindrical rock on the top of which pine resin was burned. Marie-Louise von Franz suggests that "[i]f we look at the folklore and mythology of the different crafts in more primitive societies . . . man never invented any craft or skill, but . . . it was *revealed* to him, . . . it is the Gods who produced the knowledge which man now uses if he does anything practical."[2] This suggests that the Cheju saw this lamp as invented by the goddess and shared it with humanity.

The sunrise or the moonrise over the cliff is not observable every day because of the rotation of the earth, but even when the sun rises just above the cliff, the mist from the ocean prevents people from witnessing this magnificent view. On the rare occasion when the sun rises above the cliff on a clear bright day, rays of light color the clouds and burn the air with red and golden flames above the contrasting black cliff. It must have been a numinous experience for Cheju's ancestors, for it still is. Perhaps this natural phenomenon, light sitting on the tall volcanic rock, inspired people to realize that if a cylindrical holder was prepared, the light would stay in the holder for use at home.

The dawn of the light is as literal as it is metaphorical. The encounter with the goddess's light in nature brought light into the consciousness of the Cheju inhabitants. When the sun rises above the horizon, rays of light penetrate into the living unity of the web of life. From this experience of nature, awakening into consciousness is frequently expressed as light: "illumination." Consciousness emerges like dawn from the dark unknown night. C. G. Jung states, "The longing for light is the longing for consciousness."[3]

Sôlmundae Halmang needed a lamp for her weaving. This association between light and weaving appears in various mythologies. The Greek Ariadne, who helps Theseus pass through the labyrinth by offering him a ball of thread, has a name that means "the most pure [light]."[4] Baba Yaga in the Russian fairytale is a spinner to whom Vasilisa goes to fetch light to her house. In the Japanese creation myth, when Izanagi descends to the underworld to search for Izanami, he makes a torch with the teeth of a comb used to pluck the wool from sheep and hackle the stems of flax and nettle in order to weave the divine gift, the cloth.[5] Light guides each step of the journey and illuminates the direction to move in as consciousness manifests. Weaving unfolds the mysterious web intangibly in the psyche as light makes everything vivid and understandable.

Weaving is the earliest human craft, as evidenced by stone implements and goddess figurines, and it also represents a giant leap of human consciousness, for the craft of weaving brings light into consciousness. The history of weaving began long before pottery, agriculture, and stock-breeding.[6] Recent archeological evidence shows that the oldest known twisted fiber is dated between 26,980 and 24,870 BCE.[7] Weaving seems to be the dawn of light by which the ancients transformed nature into culture.

The psychological association of weaving begins with discrimination, as Elizabeth Barber, an expert on prehistoric textile, points out: "true weaving involves two operationally different sets of elements":[8] warp and weft, vertical and horizontal, tension and flexibility, hardness and softness, right and left, giver and receiver, and nature and culture. This differentiation is the first step for the development of consciousness. The warp is stiffly fixed in the loom but the weft, the inserted set, needs to constantly flow up and down.

However, natural fibers and hairs are too short to weave so spinning is absolutely necessary. Sibylle Birkhauser connects spinning and mental activity, positing an ability to fantasize as "a prerequisite for creative achievement. The artist does his work through his connection with the great Spinning Woman who prepares all things in the unconscious."[9] One speaks of "spinning fantasy," "spinning wheels," and "spinning tales." Spinning is a circular movement around the center, constantly returning to the original source, twisting and drawing out the fine thread like unraveling a mysterious source from which a fine imagination comes alive. The artist works through connection with the great Spinning Woman who prepares all things in the unconscious.

Weaving is the celebration of the cosmic web and this enactment entails the renewal of the web. Sôlmundae Halmang weaves nature in Cheju and lifts the veil of darkness while bringing new life into existence. The whole world of Cheju may be on her loom that constantly spins around and weaves the web of living unity of Cheju.

Unfinished Underwear and Incomplete Bridges

> Sôlmundae Halmang had difficulty finding clothes because of her giant size. She proposed to the inhabitants of Cheju that if they made her underwear, she would build them a bridge to the mainland. Her underwear required one hundred *tong* [the unit to measure fabric] of silk but when all the silk was gathered there were only ninety-nine tong so unfortunately the clothes were not made for the Grandmother. Thus, the bridge building had to be stopped. The vestige of the bridge exists on the shore of Choch'ôn.[10]

Images of the clothes of a deity appear beginning in upper Paleolithic times. The Venus in Lespugue, from France and dated to 20,000 BCE, wears a skirt made of twisted strings hanging around her rear. Another Venus, from Gargarino in 20,000 BCE, wears a shorter skirt hanging in front under her breasts. These dressed figurines continue into the Neolithic and the Bronze ages. The figurine in Sipintsi western Siberia (3500 BCE) wears a pretty, long string skirt. Malta's "Sleeping Lady" wears a long skirt that reaches to her ankles. Barber stresses that from the Paleolithic through the Bronze Age string skirts are worn by goddesses and that they attract the eye precisely to specifically female sexual areas.[11] Because the emphasis lies on the power of the giver of life, the term "fertility" is preferable to "sexuality."

The skirts have special power that belongs to the deity. According to Barber, in the Greek Archaic period, many of the women wearing *peploi* on friezes and vase paintings are either goddesses or princesses. She explains the reason was economical, because of "the enormous time" that fiber work took.[12] Spinning and weaving are time-consuming and labor-intensive. The most difficult task makes the best offering for the deity because it requires painstaking effort and devotion. In Cheju offering clothes to the deity is still practiced. At shamanic shrines in both Sinchônli and Hadoli, the villagers offer clothes to the deities every year.

The Grandmother must have been acknowledged and venerated given the Cheju people's intention to make her underwear. However, the Cheju people are unable to compete with her. The task needs to be attempted but should not be completed. Probably the perfection, expressed by the number 100 in the myth, belongs not to mortals but to the Grandmother.

What the Grandmother promises as the prize for the Cheju people's devotion is a bridge. The natural shape of the land looks as if it has been stretched to reach another place, but it sinks into the ocean without reaching that objective. Nature allies herself with the Cheju people's longing for connection to unknown areas. Longing for the connection between one stage and another, known and unknown, visible and invisible, the world of the dead and that of the living, is a spiritual urge. The bridge, a major symbol in many religions, reveals how inextinguishable the desire for connection is. However, while a bridge offers a place for passage, at the same time it can be a place of trial. Psychologically, it is a place of transition where two contradictory ideas have not yet fully integrated but are hanging above a deep chasm. The fear of change is inevitable but the longing for expansion to the realm beyond is much stronger.

The vestige of the Grandmother's bridge building is the constant reminder of the age of Sôlmundae Halmang existing in nature. Telling the myth and remembering the event are psychological bridge-building between the Grandmother and the Cheju people, and the moments of her creation and the manifested world where the Cheju people live. In this regard, the bridge exists in the physical and metaphysical, and chronological and mythological realms, and weaves them all together.

Excreted Mountains

> In the time of Sôlmundae, once after eating millet porridge, the Grandmother had diarrhea which turned out 360 mountains on Cheju.[13]

The round curving discontinuous mountains are one of the outstanding beauties of Cheju. High and low, voluptuous and slim, symmetrical and asymmetrical, Cheju mountains stand separately, scattered sporadically on the horizon. The Cheju people have been told that these mountains originated from Sôlmundae Halmang's "anal birth," which means the production of feces by throwing it behind herself.[14]

Anal birth is the first natural way of creating things from a human body. When a baby pushes excrement out of its body, the baby sweats with hard labor to produce it, and the excrement becomes the baby's pride. Levi-Strauss introduces another example of anal birth in a Jivaro tribe: "the woman was so taken aback that she started to defecate here and there, and her excrement turned into banks of *nuwe* [potter's clay]." He associates excrement with the shapeless.[15] In medieval European alchemy it was considered as *prima materia* from which things can be formed.[16]

The farmer treats excrement as a prized treasure. Particularly in Cheju, not only human feces but also animal feces are highly valued for nurturing the soil. Human feces are eaten by pigs in the pigsty built under the outhouse, where the best pork is produced. In Cheju dung is preserved and mixed with organic trash as compost and brought to the fields once a year for increased production. Therefore, excrement is understood as concentrated biological power needed for regeneration.[17]

Excrement, as farmers realize, symbolizes natural abundance, which gives wealth. In the Germanic fairytale entitled "Ash-Maiden," if one wants to be rich, one needs to eat lentils, which will reappear as money or gold.[18] The association between dung and gold also appears in the Italian fairytale, "The *Excreta* of Gold."[19] Jung explains the association of gold to dung as the lowest value allies to the highest.[20]

Diarrhea, that flood of excrement, signifies abundance and the destructive power of the Unconscious. The awful dread of the erupting force and the ecstatic joy in creation are powerfully mingled. The 360 drops of Grandmother's spontaneous "holy shits" turned into golden beauties of Cheju's nature.

Majestic Urine

> Once upon a time, Udo [an auxiliary island] was not a separate island. One day when the Grandmother started to urinate her powerful urine which cut the land, it drifted in the majestic urine and became Udo. The chasm filled with her urine between the two pieces of land was so deep that whales and seals could live in it.[21]

Udo, an island that looks like a cow lying sideways, is located to the east of Cheju Island. Many fishermen who have crossed this channel for generations are mindful of the presence of the Grandmother and her dreadful urine, which jeopardizes their lives. Creation and destruction are two sides of the coin and represent two opposites of a single whole. The myth clearly shows that one cannot be separated from the other. The Grandmother's urination possesses the awesome power of the planetary force and nature's untamed creativity; the dynamic and vital outbreak of the generative force is frightfully destructive. This is, as Mircea Eliade depicts, "a festival of productive chaos."[22] It dismembers, dissolves, and transforms.

Urine is the essential material of the cosmos from which all that lives on Earth emerged. Water is the place of birth and at the same time of death because it is the solvent of dismemberment, dissolution, and transformation. Water is a metaphor for the depth of the psyche. In the depth of psychic water, unprocessed gems are hidden from the individuation process.

Three Legs of the Cooking Pot

> There are three rocks soaring toward the sky in Aewôl, which made the tripod on which the Grandmother put her pot for cooking.[23]

Three tall boulders about ten feet high stand in Aewôl in the northwest part of Cheju Island. The lower three bases seem to be one big rock mass because of heavy erosion but the three divergent pieces clearly stand high in the upper part. In the Cheju kitchen, the hearth, an assemblage of three rocks on which a cooking pot is placed, is exactly the same as the Grandmother's tripod.

The cooking pot and tripod have a special meaning for Cheju Island and the significance is well addressed by the taboos around them. The most important items when changing residence in Cheju are the cooking pot and the fire pot, and sometimes the chamber pot. One consults with a *simbang* (Cheju shaman) for the best date and time to move them. The Cheju Islanders believe that moving the pot to another place without consulting about the proper date can result in harm by the deity, specifically the kitchen goddess Jowang, who lives on the tripod. Many taboos surround Jowang's existence; "if one puts a scoop on the lid of a pot it will provoke the anger of Jowang." "It is harmful to put a cooking pot on the threshold."

These taboos contain the Cheju Islanders' belief and ideology. Stories say that Jowang is the wife of Munjôn-sin, the door deity who has a second wife, Chig-sin, the bathroom goddess. The two goddesses never get along, so the people do not exchange any items from the kitchen to the toilet and vice versa. Since the door deity stays at the threshold of the house, it demarcates the boundary between the kitchen inside and the toilet outside of the house. Cooking and metabolizing food are the same process in reverse order; food is first taken from the earth and placed in a clay container, then cooked by fire, then processed in the body. In the container of the body it is digested, burns oxygen, and is ejected as excrement back into nature.[24] The separation between kitchen and bathroom is aligned with the process of food going from nature to culture and the other way around. In this regard, not touching the cooking pot to the threshold seems logical in the clearly defined Cheju Islanders' space concept, since the pot belongs to the innermost center of the house rather than to the in-between space.

The domesticated fire in the hearth is directly associated with culture. Claude Levi-Strauss claims that "in the state of nature, earth was food; in its cooked form it becomes a vessel—that is to say, a cultural product."[25] Cooking is very much dependent on the pot, which allows the raw food to be contained and transformed into cooked food, a cultural product. Culture is the cooking of raw and formless material into form-bound and processed material. It is transformation and at the same time loss of freedom. The Grandmother myths of excrement and cooking address the two poles of culture and nature, which constantly interact.

The Fish in Her Womb

> One day Sôlmundae Halûbang and Sôlmundae Halmang were
> so hungry that they went out fishing in Sôpjigoji. When they
> arrived on the beach the Grandfather took off his trousers and
> jumped into the ocean between Sôngsan and Udo where the
> current was turbulent and the fish were abundant. As he started
> to churn the ocean all the fish rushed to the other side of the
> ocean where the Grandmother opened her legs as widely as
> possible and swallowed all of them into her vagina.[26]

Sôpjigoji is an inlet that is shaped like a leaf where the northbound ocean
current Tsushima passes by and moves toward the East Sea. Sôpjigoji is
well known among the villagers as an abundant source of fish. As is illustrated in the previous Sôlmundae myths, the sites where the myths arise
are related to the daily life of the Cheju Islander. Therefore it is not sur-
prising that the site of the Grandmother's fishing overlaps with that of
the Cheju fishers. However, the parts of aspects of a myth are never simple facts in themselves; each one holds symbolic meanings.

What does fishing symbolize? Primarily, the act of fishing gathers and
brings the hidden wealth from the unknown water to the surface. The
submerging into baptismal water, a major symbol of almost all religions,
purifies the polluted or unclean body-soul, and renews, reintegrates, and
harmonizes it again.

The fishing myth in which Sôlmundae Halûbang, a male god, suddenly
appears from nowhere is the only place where the grandfather emerges.
The Grandfather has the same name as the Grandmother, but in mascu-
linized form. It can be deduced that Sôlmundae is primarily as a goddess
who can also be a god because the original Sôlmundae has both feminine
and masculine attributes. The Grandfather Sôlmundae represents one
aspect of the Grandmother, for as Jung stresses, "the goddess came to
possess phallic symbols, even though the latter are essentially masculine.
Female lies hidden in the male, so the male lies hidden in the female."[27]
It seems the Grandmother Sôlmundae is originally an androgyne.

The attributes of the Grandfather are concentrated in phallic energy.
Literally the Grandfather stretches his lingam with which he churns the
ocean. His role is to create turmoil and vigorously stir up life energy.
Jung clarifies that "a phallic symbol does not denote the sexual organ,
but the libido, and however clearly it appears as such, it does not mean
itself but is always a symbol of the libido."[28]

The portrayal of fish within the womb of a goddess is found as early as prehistory. Marija Gimbutas introduced archeological evidence of this from Europe: a Boeotian vase from around 700–675 BCE, a Middle Minoan vase dated 2000–1700 BCE, and a Minoan sarcophagi 1100 BCE. She states "throughout prehistory the fish was homologized with the Goddesses' uterus."[29] The Native Americans in California, according to Levi-Strauss, describe fish as a female genital: "the body of the fish represents the uterus, while the tail is vagina."[30] The fish-uterus is associated with a new beginning and becoming.

As life on earth started in the ocean, so new life comes from the uterine water. The sea is the place where one returns to the primordial whole and is reintegrated into the formless one. The fish is another image of fecundity. The fish bears a profusion of eggs; the goddess Sôlmundae impregnates all fish in her fertile womb. Also in the myth, in the humorous image of the grandparents fishing, fish symbolize not only the uterine but also the phallic. The mobility of the fish sparks off the vital life force and generates procreation.

The Death of the Grandmother

> The Grandmother used to boast about her gigantic height. She tested whether there was any water on Cheju deep enough to cover her height. The water in Yongso (the lake where the dragon lives) was said to be quite deep but it barely reached around her ankles and the lake in Hongli her knee. At last, when she tried to test the depth of Muljangoli she was drowned because the water in Muljangoli was bottomless and so she sank down into the ocean.[31]

Muljangoli is a large, perfectly round lake on mountain Hanla, an ominous place where a *simbang* used to offer a pig as a sacrifice. The Cheju people say that speaking too loud in this area can invite a change of the weather. The Grandmother is taller than the tallest thing on Cheju. Enormously big and negligibly small are intimately related with human emotions. Enormously exaggerated emotions frequently appear as giants in literature.

Psychologically, when a giant appears in a story or a dream, humans shrink into a tiny size in contrast to the giant's overpowering force. A small person is vulnerable and exposed in the face of drastically destructive power. Victor Turner writes that this exaggerated expression is "a primordial mode of abstraction" and "this outstanding exaggerated feature is made into an object of reflection."[32] The size of the Grandmother signifies her gigantic influence on the people of Cheju. However, the overwhelming Grandmother dies in the myth.

Death symbolizes the most powerful transformation. The Grandmother's death in the Cheju psyche seems to signify that the Cheju people have grown up psychologically and the brutal and untamed force of nature that she symbolizes is not fatal anymore. However, her death is paradoxical. It gives freedom from the fear of engulfment, but at the same time creates the fear of separation and a longing for a return. Eliade points out that the narrative justifies "a new situation."[33] Probably the myth legitimizes this ambivalence of "the new situation" of the Cheju psyche.

The Grandmother enters into the bottomless hole in the ground and sinks down to the abyss of the sea. She returns to her own womb from which all beings are born. Sylvia Brinton Perera has written that "Libido runs from one pattern to another. . . . No part is static, it is all in process—death, sacrifice, decay, rebirth—as part of the dynamism of life's Great Round."[34] Nothing truly dies, but all is eternally transformed.

The Footprint and Footstep

> Grandmother was so tall that she reached in one step from Hanla Mountain to Pyosôn.[35]

Pyosôn is an inlet in the southeastern corner of Cheju Island. There are three more footsteps of the Grandmother in Ilchulbong in the eastern tip, Sanbang Mountain in the uppermost southwest part of the Island, Chuja Island, a small island north of Cheju. The four footprints in the four corners of Cheju seem to mark her territory. Since the farthest places are still located within one of her footsteps from the center of the island, the entirety of Cheju lies in her sovereignty. The footprint of the deity establishes not the vestige of a past presence but the living evidence of the certainty of the divine presence.

Grandmother's footsteps are her self-made imprint to verify her endurance and assure her presence on Cheju. Her long-inherited footsteps and myth continue to prove that she has left her impression on the psyche of Cheju. However, only personal tangible experiences makes this seem a living presence.

Sleep as an Act of Creation

> The Grandmother slept. Her head lay on the utmost north-
> erly section, Chuchado and her feet stretched to its southern
> tip, Sôpsôm.[36]

Her giant body stretches all the way from the northern to the southern
end of Cheju Island, which becomes the centrally located Hanla Mountain
that occupies 95 percent of the island. The goddess not only created the
island; she is the island. Creation is defined as the divine act by which the
world was created. Humans create worlds as mythological deities did,
mimicking the actions of those gods and goddesses. As Halmang sleeps,
the Cheju people sleep, and have a unique perspective of nighttime and
the time for sleeping.

Night is the time when the daytime "invisibles" emerge and animate
themselves; it is the time for spirits and souls to become active. Thus,
Cheju Islanders are careful not to trigger or animate these powerful spirits. There are many taboos: "If one makes metallic sounds at night the
ghost will come." "If people hang wet clothes to dry at night, they will
resurrect as thieves." "If one looks back during a night walk, the spirits
will be dishonored." "If the charcoal is painted on one's face while sleeping, that one will die soon." Nighttime taboos restrict human actions
because spirits initiate their actions at night. It seems both humans and
spirits share the same space but when one is active, the other is passive.

Because the Grandmother sleeps in a straight north/south direction,
the Cheju people have strict criteria for geographic directions while they
sleep that are directly associated with Cheju cosmology. North is the direction of Chilsông, which means the seven stars (the constellation Ursa
Major); it governs the life span of a mortal. Thus, the Cheju Islander sleeps
either toward the east or the south. In the beginning, the Grandmother
slept with her head toward the north because she is the immortal. The
Cheju Islanders, being mortal and not wishing to shorten their lives, never
sleep with their heads toward the north.

North and its full significance are apparent in the beliefs of Cheju.
Chilsông worship is the most grounded belief, which is predictably
related to the pole star, the highest point of the sky in the Northern
Hemisphere around which all the stars draw a mandalic circle every
night. This primal image of north is also a "symbolic direction" that the
Sufi calls "night of light"[37] toward which the soul ascends to widen and
deepen horizontal consciousness. The Grandmother's huge sleeping

body demonstrates where the soul is leading and points to the orientation of the soul's journey.

Conclusion

Sôlmundae Halmang, the creative and mythological force of Cheju Island, has gone deep within the unconscious in the psyche of Cheju. The thin thread of the limited source searching for the Halmang's image is another act of spinning and weaving to transform her mystery into a tangible texture from which her being can dawn in the living world. Re-membering her image itself is numinous and numen, as James Hillman points out, and refers to "the animation of image."[38] Animated and activated her image ensouls the world, which in turn will put humans back in touch with the heart of the creator, Sôlmundae Halmang again.

Notes

1. Yong-jun Hyun, *Chejudo Jonsol* (Seoul: Somunmungo, 1996), 24.

2. Marie-Louise von Franz, *Creation Myths* (Boston: Shambhala, 1995), 140–141.

3. Carl Gustave Jung, *Memories, Dreams, Reflections* (New York: Vintage, 1973), 269.

4. Kristina Berggren, "Prehistoric Symbols of Transformation," Ph.D. diss., Pacifica Graduate Institute, 2001, 83.

5. David F. Hadland, *Myths and Legends of Japan* (New York: Dover, 1992), 23–24.

6. Elizabeth J. W. Barber, *Prehistoric Textiles: The Development of Cloth in the Neolithic and Bronze Ages with Special Reference to the Aegean* (Princeton. NJ: Princeton University Press, 1991), 4.

7. Brenda Fowler, "Find in Europe Suggests That Weaving Preceded Settled Life," *New York Times,* May 9, 1995.

8. Barber, *Prehistoric Textiles*, 9.

9. Sibylle Birkhauser, "The Figure of the Spinning Woman in Fairy Tales," *Spring* (1963): 32.

10. Hyun, *Chejudo Jonsol*, 25.

11. Elizabeth Barber, *Women's Work: The First 20,000 Years* (New York: Norton, 1995), 44, 79.

12. Barber, *Prehistoric Textiles*, 364.

13. Song-jun Lee, "Solmundae Halmang Solhwayongu," *Kukmunhakbo* 10 (1990): 64.

14. Carl Gustave Jung, *Symbols of Transformation,* vol. 5 of *Collected Works* (London: Routledge, 1981), par. 279.

15. Claude Levi-Strauss, *The Jealous Potter* (Chicago: University of Chicago Press, 1988), 16, 20.

16. Jung, *Symbols of Transformation*, par. 276.

17. Jean Chevalier and Alian Gheerbrant, *A Dictionary of Symbols* (Oxford: Blackwell, 1994), 362.

18. Jung, *Symbols of Transformation*, 276n.

19. Stith Thompson, *Motif-Index of Folk Literature*, vol. 2 (Bloomington: Indiana University Press, 1955), 236 D1469.2.

20. Jung, *Symbols of Transformation*, par. 276.

21. Hyun, *Chejudo Jonsol*, 24–25.

22. Mircea Eliade, *Myth and Reality* (New York: HarperCollins, 1975), 57.

23. Hyun, *Chejudo Jonsol*, 26.

24. Levi-Strauss, *The Jealous Potter*, 175.

25. Ibid., 176.

26. Song-jun Lee, "Solmundae Halmang Solhwayongu," *Kukmunhakbo* 10 (1990): 54–77.

27. Jung, *Symbols of Transformation*, par. 324.

28. Ibid., par. 329.

29. Marija Gimbutas, *The Language of the Goddess* (New York: HarperCollins, 1991), 258–263.

30. Levi-Strauss, *The Jealous Potter*, 182.

31. Hyun, *Chejudo Jonsol*, 23.

32. Victor Turner, *The Anthropology of Performance* (New York: PAJ, 1988), 102.

33. Eliade, *Myth and Reality*, 21.

34. Brinton Perera Sylvia, *Descent to the Goddess* (Toronto: Inner City, 1981), 55.

35. Young-mi Moon, "Solmundae Halmang Solhwayonku," M.A. thesis, Yonse University, Seoul, 1999, 26.

36. Hyun, *Chejudo Jonsol*, 22.

37. Henry Corbin, *The Man of Light in Iranian Sufism* (Boulder, CO: Shambhala, 1978), 4.

38. James Hillman, *Healing Fiction* (Dallas: Spring, 1983), 74.

Bibliography

Barber, Elizabeth J. W. *Prehistoric Textiles: The Development of Cloth in the Neolithic and Bronze Ages with Special Reference to the Aegean.* Princeton, NJ: Princeton University Press, 1991.

Barber, Elizabeth J. W. *Women's Work: The First 20,000 Years.* New York: W. W. Norton, 1995.

Berggren, Kristina. "Prehistoric Symbols of Transformation." Ph.D. diss., Pacifica Graduate Institute, 2001.

Birkhauser, Sibylle. "The Figure of the Spinning Woman in Fairy Tales." *Spring* (1963): 31–45.

Chevalier, Jean, and Alian Gheerbrant. *A Dictionary of Symbols*. Oxford: Blackwell, 1994.

Corbin, Henry. *The Man of Light in Iranian Sufism*. Trans. Nancy Pearson. Boulder, CO: Shambhala, 1978.

Eliade, Mircea. *Myth and Reality*. New York: HarperCollins, 1975.

Eliade, Mircea. *The Sacred and the Profane. The Nature of Religion*. Trans. Willard R. Trask. New York: Harcourt, Brace and World, 1959.

Fowler, Brenda. "Find in Europe Suggests That Weaving Preceded Settled Life." *New York Times*, May 9, 1995.

Franz, Marie-Louise von. *Creation Myths*. Boston: Shambhala, 1995.

Gimbutas, Marija. *The Language of the Goddess*. New York: HarperCollins, 1991.

Hadland, David F. *Myths and Legends of Japan*. New York: Dover, 1992.

Hea-Kyoung, Koh. *In the Beginning Was the Goddess: Cheju's Cosmogonic Goddess Seolmundae*. Seoul: Hangyere Publications, 2010.

Hillman, James. *Healing Fiction*. Dallas: Spring, 1983.

Hyun, Yong-jun. *Chejudo Jonsol*. Seoul: Somunmungo, 1996.

Jung, Carl Gustav. *Memories, Dreams, Reflections*. Ed. Aniela Jaffe. Trans. Winston Richard and Clara Winston. New York: Vintage, 1973.

Jung, Carl Gustav. *Symbols of Transformation*. Vol. 5 of *Collected Works*. Ed. Sir Herbert Read and Michael Fordham. Trans. R. F. Hull. London: Routledge, 1981.

Lee, Song-jun. "Solmundae Halmang Solhwayongu." *Kukmunhakbo* 10 (1990): 54–77.

Levi-Strauss, Claude. *The Jealous Potter*. Trans. Benedicte Chorier. Chicago: University of Chicago Press, 1988.

Levi-Strauss, Claude. *The Savage Mind*. Trans. George Weidenfelf. Chicago: University of Chicago Press, 1966.

Moon, Young-mi. "Solmundae Halmang Solhwayonku." M.A. thesis, Yonse University, Seoul, 1999.

Perera, Sylvia Brinton. *Descent to the Goddess*. Toronto: Inner City, 1981.

Thompson, Stith. *Motif-Index of Folk Literature*. Vol. 2. Bloomington: Indiana University Press, 1955.

Turner, Victor. *The Anthropology of Performance*. New York: PAJ, 1988.

14

The Maiden with a Thousand Slippers: Animal Helpers and the Hero(ine)'s Journey

Doré Ripley

When [Rhodopis] was bathing, an eagle snatched one of her sandals from her maid and carried it to Memphis; and while the king
was administering justice in the open air, the eagle, when it arrived
above his head, flung the sandal into his lap; and the king, stirred
both by the beautiful shape of the sandal and by the strangeness of
the occurrence, sent men in all directions into the country in quest
of the woman who wore the sandal; and when she was found in
the city of Naucratis, she was brought up to Memphis and became
the wife of the king.[1]

Strabo recorded this happily-ever-after Cinderella story around 20 CE as
a rebuttal to the historian Herodotus who reported that one of the pyramids at Giza was the tomb of the Pharaoh's wife. In his *Geography*,
Strabo fills in Rhodopis's background, saying she was kidnapped from
her native Greece, where she was known as Doricha, and taken to
Egypt to become a household slave. But while she did attract the attention of the pharaoh, Amasis could not have built Rhodopis a pyramid
tomb because, as Strabo clarifies, she eventually left the pharaoh to
become the "beloved of Charaxus, [the poetess] Sappho's brother, . . .
who was engaged in transporting Lesbian wine to Naucratis for sale."[2]

Confirming the existence of this ancient love triangle, Herodotus writes, Rhodopis was a "fellow-slave of Aesop the fable writer . . . [and was rescued by] Charaxus of Mytiline, . . . brother of Sappho the poetess, [who] paid a large sum to redeem her from slavery. . . . When Charaxus returned to Mytilene after purchasing Rhodopis' freedom, he was ridiculed by Sappho in one of her poems":[3]

Lucky lady with luxuriant hair
And unfulfilled desire,
Even while rumor reports that
A god is leaving you to possess another,
At the same time another fate awaits you.

Thus Aphrodite, irritated by the sirocco,
Complains, with no hint of pride,
That somehow Doricha [Rhodopis] has once again
Attracted a youth her own age.[4]

Sappho insinuates that the Pharaonic god-king dumped the Greek courtesan for someone else, leaving Rhodopis free to pursue a wealthy wine merchant. From history's event horizon, Strabo and Herodotus's historic reports appear as myth, where an ancient kernel of truth grew into a local legend, but "[h]istory is more than merely a pileup of facts or a chronicle of the past; it is an art, and a very literary one at that"[5]—an art which, in this case, appears to be a battle of the ancient tabloids by some of the greatest writers of the classic world. The pharaoh did not record the story of Rhodopis, and Sappho's poetic commentary about ancient female opportunists is acknowledged in Herodotus's report of a courtesan who was honored with a pyramid tomb, compelling Strabo to rebut that claim with the story of the Cinderella Rhodopis who left the Pharaoh for a Greek wine merchant. Strabo's reporting offers modern-day readers a foundation of the Cinderella *ur märchen*—an early fairytale of unknown origin found all over the world.

Cinderella's thousand-year global circulation makes it the world's best-known fairytale, but no one can really say where it began or when Cinderella's magic slippers brought her to Europe. The earliest recorded European version was published in Italy in 1634,[6] with Perrault's familiar retelling produced in Paris in 1697. The fable is told in Scotland, Scandinavia, and Germany, from whence it was exported to North America and retold by pioneers and Native Americans. As Andrew Lang notes,

Similar institutions and a similar imaginative condition may give rise to similarities in tales, and even to some combinations of incidents, as often occurs in modern novels, while asserting, at the same time, that diffusion of those tales is perfectly possible and conceivable. As to the place and date of the very first tales, it may be Polar, pre-glacial. To seek such a date and place seems wasted labour.[7]

This assessment does not attempt to track the beginnings or even the likely migration of the Cinderella märchen; it looks at the earliest written texts of the Cinderella fable, those recorded by Herodotus and Strabo beginning in 440 BCE and the more complete märchen found in China in around 850 CE, to examine the hero(ine)'s quest.

Strabo's *Cinderella* story resembles the familiar märchen in two significant ways: magical slippers and an animal helper. Rhodopis's slipper is delivered to the pharaoh by an eagle, but the eagle is markedly absent from the Egyptian pantheon even though its representative iconography features "seventy-two different wild and domestic bird species."[8] Since the Egyptian civilization was located on the Nile, almost all the avifauna recorded by the ancient civilization is that of water birds, particularly ducks and geese, and to a lesser extent cranes. Waterfowl were mummified and entombed with various pharaohs whose crypt walls were decorated with friezes of duck hunting and trapping.

During the Ptolemaic period, 332–30 BCE, the Greeks not only headed the Egyptian state, but also brought the sacred eagle of Zeus to that land.[9] Strabo visited Egypt in 25–24 BCE with the Roman prefect, Aelius Gallus, on his expedition to Upper Egypt, shortly before Egypt became part of the Roman empire, but it was a thoroughly Greek Strabo who wrote the Egyptian fairy tale of Rhodopis in 20 CE.[10] While representations of the raptorial species are not rare in Egypt, the falcon, not the Greek or Roman eagle, tops the list.

The falcon, the sacred bird of Horus, is the most widely depicted of all avifauna in Egyptian iconography.[11] Of the many gods and goddesses inhabiting Egypt's pantheon, none adopt the eagle form. Geb wears a goose on his head, whereas Hathor wears a falcon on hers. Montu is often portrayed as falcon-headed, while Mut and Nekhbet are depicted as vultures.[12] Like Horus, Qebehsenuef and Ra are also falcon-headed. Vultures decorate coffins, geese decorate tomb walls, but in Strabo's reporting of the supposed fact-based prototype for the Cinderella story, he specifically names Rhodopis's helper as an eagle.

To the Greeks and Romans, the eagle represented power and justice and was associated with Jupiter and Zeus. Was Strabo creating a sensational story set in Egypt for his Roman audience, a contemporary tabloid sheet like the ones that now grace the checkout lines of every grocery store? Or was his story, complete with a sympathetic animal helper, a fable meant to recreate "the peaceful conditions of life enjoyed in the golden age" when animals and people lived in a "harmony from which human beings have progressively fallen away in the course of time"?[13]

The ancient Greeks, like later Christians, believed that during the golden age animals and humans lived in "peaceful coexistence . . . in a gardenlike paradise"—a paradise described in the writings of both Hesiod and Ovid. Pythagoras went so far as to "espouse an ethic of kinship with animals based on the doctrine of metempsychosis or transmigration of souls."[14] If one believes that souls can migrate among species, then humans "have a fundamental continuity with at least some nonhuman living beings" and as Empedocles states, "all things . . . have wisdom and take part in thinking." However in Plato's *Phaedrus*, Socrates disagrees, stating that humans were a higher form of life, because only they could be "seeker[s] after wisdom or beauty."[15] So when Aristotle rejected the animals' capacity for rational thinking, the ancient attitudes toward fauna changed. In *Anthropocentrism and Its Discontents*, Gary Steiner states, "the moral status of animals shifted fundamentally once it became a philosophical commonplace to assert that reason or understanding distinguishes human beings from 'the beasts.'"[16] Egyptian culture's polytheism, with its affinity to the animal world, is a striking contrast to the Greek pantheon's gods in human form. No wonder classical philosophers felt human enlightenment elevated them above the creatures of the land, sea, and air. The Romans emulated their Mediterranean peers and Strabo (a Greek in Roman toga) denies the Egyptian eagle-helper kinship with humankind. But not all peoples lost their empathy with the animal kingdom; half a world away in China, the fish was a particularly good omen, making it the perfect choice for the granter of wishes to aid Yeh-Shen, the Chinese Cinderella on her journey.

During the T'ang dynasty (618–907 CE), a Chinese Cinderella märchen was recorded by a court official who collected fables into an encyclopedic work.[17] His Cinderella fable includes all the main elements of the story: the death of the beloved father, the animal helper, the shoe motif, the evil step mother and sisters who try to keep Cinderella from the festival, and Cinderella's eventual recognition by the prince who marries her and thereby completes her heroic journey.

Cinderella's Heroic Journey

At the beginning of the 21st century, it is hard to imagine Cinderella a heroine appropriate to today's heightened hopes for women, but up until about 100 years ago, most women found the quest for a proper marriage the only journey open to them. Even today, Disney routinely recreates the marriage-as-female-quest in film. *Enchanted, Aladdin,* and *The Little Mermaid* each star a female protagonist searching for the perfect mate. From Shakespeare to Austen to modern-day Harlequin romances, the female obsession to find and procure a husband is portrayed much like Joseph Campbell's heroic cycle as outlined in his epic work, *The Hero with a Thousand Faces.*

The Cinderella märchen features a strong central character engaged on a heroic quest within the confines of the traditional female hearth to obtain a husband of her own choosing, and thereby gain entrance to the enchanted domestic space. It is this quest for the ideal mate that places Cinderella firmly on the wheel of Joseph Campbell's heroic cycle. The reluctance of Campbell and many other theorists to view marriage as an end to any hero's quest could leave Cinderella occupying the cold ashes of the traditional feminine hearth, but she's not easily daunted. Her animal helpers pick her up, dust her off, and magically propel her on her quest.

Traditionally, scholars believe the heroine's rare journey occurs when the new bride somehow becomes separated from her husband.[18] Other critics cannot imagine Cinderella engaging in a heroic journey at all. Bruno Bettelheim believes the Cinderella story conveys degradation and sibling rivalry leading to transference in child readers as they readily see themselves in Cinderella's position.[19] This seems plausible, but if Cinderella is an archetype Everychild, Bettelheim's assessment leads to a scathing indictment of family dynamics where it is easier for children to envision themselves as the victims of sibling rivalry or domestic abuse. Contrary to modern academic or psychological presumptions, this assessment suggests that the adolescent Cinderella struggles to get out of the house in order to go on a hero's journey to obtain her marriage to the prince.

In *The Hero with a Thousand Faces,* Campbell traces the steps of the archetypal hero's transformative journey. After the hero separates from the innocent world of childhood, he receives a call to adventure. Sometimes the hero refuses the call, but he eventually concedes, thereby gaining supernatural aid or guidance. Crossing the first threshold leads to

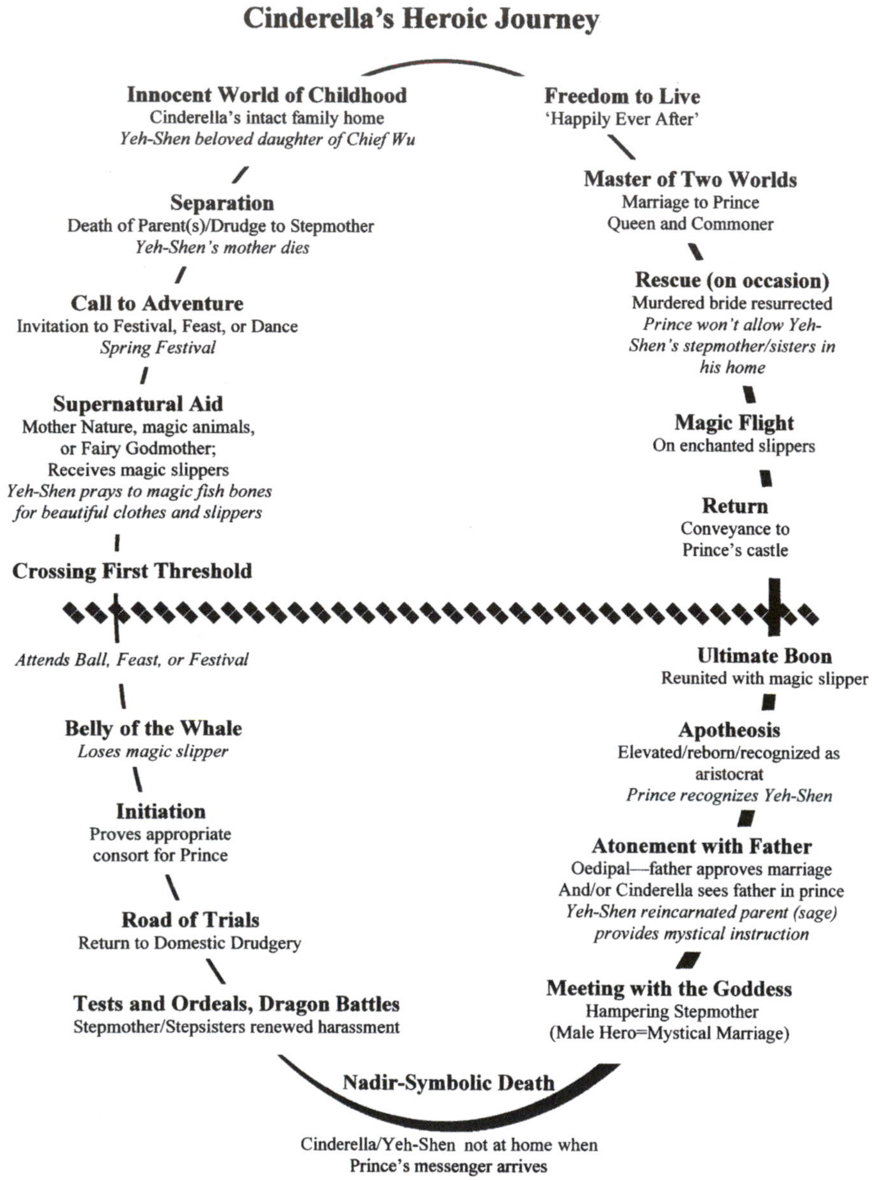

Cinderella's Heroic Journey

Innocent World of Childhood
Cinderella's intact family home
Yeh-Shen beloved daughter of Chief Wu

Freedom to Live
'Happily Ever After'

Separation
Death of Parent(s)/Drudge to Stepmother
Yeh-Shen's mother dies

Master of Two Worlds
Marriage to Prince
Queen and Commoner

Call to Adventure
Invitation to Festival, Feast, or Dance
Spring Festival

Rescue (on occasion)
Murdered bride resurrected
Prince won't allow Yeh-Shen's stepmother/sisters in his home

Supernatural Aid
Mother Nature, magic animals,
or Fairy Godmother;
Receives magic slippers
*Yeh-Shen prays to magic fish bones
for beautiful clothes and slippers*

Magic Flight
On enchanted slippers

Return
Conveyance to
Prince's castle

Crossing First Threshold

Attends Ball, Feast, or Festival

Ultimate Boon
Reunited with magic slipper

Belly of the Whale
Loses magic slipper

Apotheosis
Elevated/reborn/recognized as
aristocrat
Prince recognizes Yeh-Shen

Initiation
Proves appropriate
consort for Prince

Atonement with Father
Oedipal—father approves marriage
And/or Cinderella sees father in prince
*Yeh-Shen reincarnated parent (sage)
provides mystical instruction*

Road of Trials
Return to Domestic Drudgery

Tests and Ordeals, Dragon Battles
Stepmother/Stepsisters renewed harassment

Meeting with the Goddess
Hampering Stepmother
(Male Hero=Mystical Marriage)

Nadir-Symbolic Death

Cinderella/Yeh-Shen not at home when
Prince's messenger arrives

Figure 14.1 The familiar children's story of Cinderella made its way to Europe via Egypt but had its origin in China. The story exemplifies an archetypal journey of the heroine from her original family to the new family she will establish with her heroic prince. (Graph by Doré Ripley based on Joseph Campbell, *The Hero with a Thousand Faces* [Princeton, NJ: Princeton University Press, 1973], 245, and *The Hero's Journey*, http://hubcap.clemson.edu/~sparks/heroj.html.)

the region of adventure where the hero is thrown into the belly of the whale, completely cut off from his known world. Initiation begins on the road of trials, with the hero going through tests and ordeals, and ends with the hero's symbolic death. According to Campbell, the hero eventually meets with the goddess, sometimes engaging in a sacred marriage, which is often hampered by a temptress who tries to sway the hero from his quest. Along the way the hero achieves atonement with the father or some other powerful figure before the apotheosis of the hero or his rising above the corporeal world, where he receives the ultimate boon. The hero then sets out on the return journey, taking magical flight, and when he finally returns to the familiar world, he has the wisdom to become the master of two worlds: the supernatural or spiritual, and the mortal, where he can live freely.[20] Like Campbell's male heroes, Cinderella engages in a quest for a marriage to the prince that makes her the master of the enchanted domestic space where she can live happily ever after.

Campbell's hero's journey begins and ends in the same location but, like most women, Cinderella starts her journey in her father's (now stepmother's) house, with her odyssey ending in her husband's dwelling. Does this make Cinderella's realization of Campbell's journey impossible? As Melodie Monahan states, "Heading out is not going home" for the heroine. Starting out *is* going home for the male hero: he heads from a patriarchal home, out into a patriarchal society where his traveling is never questioned or seen as odd. By contrast, heading out and returning are problematic for the female. Just the act of crossing the threshold is seen as a female revolt, and a woman, once empowered by that success, "will resist subordination in a household."[21] But a thousand years ago a young woman's opportunity lay in a marriage contract, not the open road. Campbell's mythic beginning and ending of the hero's journey at the patriarchal home applies to a man who can travel abroad freely, not the woman relegated within domestic boundaries. And indeed, Cinderella does end where she begins. When she marries the prince, Cinderella recreates her father's house in her husband's home, while also reinforcing Campbell's Oedipal atonement, or reconciliation, with the father figure. This enables Cinderella to rule an enchanted domestic domain, thereby releasing her from the bonds of drudgery, even though she retains a subordinate position to the husband/father.

Cinderella in China

As previously noted, the oldest complete Cinderella variant was recorded in the ninth century by the Chinese scholar Tuan Ch'eng-Shih. He tells the story of a young girl whose call to adventure arrives during festival season with her stepmother forbidding her attendance. A reincarnated parent appears as a sage disguised as a koi fish, who acts as the familiar fairy godfather. The sage instructs Yeh-Shen to bury the bones of her murdered pet fish, thereby activating their magical properties. In order to go to the festival, she must pray to the fish bones, which magically provide her with splendid clothes and "the most beautiful slippers she had ever seen. . . . There was magic in the shoes" helping Yeh-Shen across the first threshold. On her way home after the festival, Yeh-Shen loses a slipper, immediately causing her beautiful clothes to disappear. This throws her into the belly of the whale and sets her on the road of trials, where Yeh-Shen is tested by ordeal at the hands of her stepmother. In the meantime, the king obtains the magic slipper and becomes fixated on finding the owner of the tiny shoe. The search begins. Yeh-Shen's filthy appearance makes her unrecognizable, manifesting her symbolic death but, even so, when the king sees Yeh-Shen he is struck by "the sweet harmony of her features" and demands the drudge try on the slipper. The shoe fits, reuniting Yeh-Shen with her magical slipper, the heroic cycle's ultimate boon, and the king finds true love, marrying the newly aristocratic Yeh-Shen. But Yeh-Shen could not complete her odyssey without her animal helper—magical fish bones.[22]

The fish is one of the earliest animal symbols found in China.[23] It "is an emblem of wealth, regeneration, harmony and connubial bliss," an apt choice in light of the Chinese Cinderella as the pet fish regenerates into the granter of wishes, leading to connubial bliss where reproductive powers are celebrated.[24] A brace of fish are often presented as "a betrothal gift to the family of the bride-elect because of its auspicious nature" and their reputation of swimming in pairs is further emblematic of a joyful union.[25] Further, the prince's wealth granted by the magic fish lifts Yeh-Shen's burden of drudgery, freeing her from all restraint— a fish symbolism carried forward with Buddhism. "As in the water a fish moves easily in any direction, so in the Buddha-state the fully emancipated knows no restraints or obstructions,"[26] and Cinderella's magical transformation frees her to embark on her hero's quest.

In Buddhism the fish is one of the propitious signs of the footprints of Buddha and is associated with the bird because of the similarity of their structures and the fact that they have adapted to the elements of water and air, differing from other creatures, causing "the Chinese [to] believe the nature of these creatures to be interchangeable."[27] In China the eagle would be an inappropriate animal helper for Cinderella because it is "a fearless and tenacious warrior on the side of right," while in

Greek religion the "eagle represents apotheosis and the power of the heavens."[28] It makes sense to have a Greek eagle drop a heavenly shoe in the lap of the Pharaoh Amasis, while its Chinese counterpart, a perseverant koi helper for Yeh-Shen, lifts her from bondage and poverty with the gift of magical gold slippers. Could a traveling merchant have provided a conduit whereby the Egyptian/Roman eagle dropped the sliver of a story into Chinese society allowing its animal helper to metamorphose into a fish, or did the story arrive on the sandals of an axial-age philosopher?

The German philosopher Karl Jaspers coined the term "axial age" as a period when "the spiritual foundations of humanity were laid, simultaneously and independently in China, India," and the Occident. Confucius was alive, and it was the age of Buddha. The philosophical trends of China were established at the same time that "Greece produced Homer" and the philosopher Plato. "Hermits and wandering thinkers in China, ascetics in India, and philosophers in Greece" roamed freely, but "what started out as freedom of movement became anarchy in the end." Ideas turned into dogma and "myths were transformed and infused with deep meaning in the very moment when the myth as such was destroyed."[29] The Cinderella myth could have arisen in China independently as Jaspers suggests, or it could have wandered into China because, as Campbell remarks, the hero's journey is found in "virtually all mythologies of the world."[30]

Joseph Campbell addresses the "rare" female quest, labeling Psyche's road of trials as "charming" partly because "all the principal [male/female] roles are reversed." Rather than addressing the historic subsuming of the mother goddess—the most ancient of global religions—Campbell only goes so far as to say that the earliest gods were androgynous. In Campbell's view, all women are representatives of the temptress, "the symbols no longer of victory but of defeat. . . . No longer can the hero rest in innocence with the goddess of the flesh; for she is become queen of sin." For the heroine, Campbell's midcycle "mystical marriage" marks the end of her quest and the man who finds her "fit to become the consort of an immortal" absorbs her. But while Cinderella's journey does end in nuptials, Cinderella does not run across the goddess and get married midjourney like her male counterparts. Instead, Cinderella's mystical marriage is the quest that makes her master of two worlds by recreating and elevating the home from which she fell. Cinderella's home is not that of the typical adolescent hero trying to escape the loving confines of the patriarch; rather, this home finds the heroine escaping the precinct of the matriarch, and she needs magical aid to do so.

The magic slippers enable Cinderella to cross the initial threshold, both literally and figuratively, but first she must get past the threshold guardian. In most cases, Cinderella's stepmother blocks her passage to the outside world. Campbell believes the guardian desires to remain within the "indicated bounds"; however, Cinderella's stepmother also wants to escape over the threshold in order to facilitate a meeting between her own daughter and the prince. The jealous stepmother blocks Cinderella's way because she knows Cinderella's nuptial qualifications far outshine her daughter's. Cinderella escapes in order to gain a new "zone of experience," while also facilitating her meeting with the prince. But once she escapes, Cinderella will face her nastiest trial in the belly of the whale.[31]

Cinderella's low point seems obvious, occurring when she loses her enchanted slipper, and causing her noble garments to dissipate in the breeze. Cinderella also loses her heroic identity and her noble manifestation—"the hero, instead of conquering or conciliating the power of the threshold, is swallowed into the unknown, and would appear to have died." Cinderella often hides a remaining magical slipper in order to prove her identity once its mate arrives in the hands of the prince. But before Cinderella's noble personality can be revealed, she must embark on a road of trials, which Campbell notes, is "a favorite phase of the myth-adventure . . . produc[ing] a world of literature of miraculous tests and ordeals."[32]

Unlike the hero, the heroine's journey is compressed spatially. The same character often plays different roles relevant to the heroic cycle. In this case, the stepmother not only provides the invitation, or call to departure, but also acts as the threshold guardian and troublesome goddess. Campbell asserts the meeting with the goddess is not always pleasant; sometimes she acts as the "hampering, forbidding and punishing mother."[33] The many attempts by Cinderella's stepmother to hinder the prince's search for the owner of the tiny shoe often creates the mistaken impression of Cinderella's death. She is hidden under filth and grime in Yeh-Shen and concealed by both dirt and doors in the familiar Perrault and Disney versions. Nonetheless, Cinderella's temperate performance scores, coupled with amulets and aid provided by her magical animal helpers, make the goddess's nasty attempts futile, clearing the way for Cinderella's atonement with father.

Cinderella's Oedipal atonement manifests with the young girl seeing her father in her future husband, while the daughter/wife must fight against the mother, which in Cinderella's case is a literal clash with the stepmother. According to Campbell, one must shatter his own ego in order to atone with the father, which Cinderella does by agreeing to marry the prince, thereby placing her trust in his mercy, and destroying her newfound individuation when she is reborn as the prince's wife. This secures Cinderella's apotheosis, as she reaches a "divine state to which the human hero . . . [goes] beyond the last terrors of ignorance."[34]

The most common vehicle of apotheosis in the Cinderella märchen is the shoe. In her Victorian tome, *Cinderella: Three Hundred and Forty-five Variants*, Marian Roalfe Cox points out that 157 of the variations contain not only a shoe, but a lost shoe.[35] The 20th-century Cinderella scholar Anna Brigitta Rooth traces the central motif of a small slipper reflecting the wearer's beauty to China, with Cox agreeing that the Orient generated the model of the lost "sandal or slipper."[36] This seems plausible since the fetish of tiny feminine "feet is peculiar and exclusive to the better classes of Chinese proper," making petite feet the mark of "beauty and gentility."[37] In the Orient's historic past, women wrapped their feet tightly in an effort to keep them from growing, leaving them crippled and often unable to walk. Even today women confine their feet in small awkward shoes—like boots sporting three-inch spike heels or platform espadrilles. The obsession of small, confined feet effectively imprisoned women in the confined space of the traditional home. In addition, Bettelheim believes "the female slipper, [i]s a symbol for that which is most desirable in a woman, arouses love in the male for definite but deeply unconscious reasons," making the shoe representative of a woman's vagina[38]—the definitive female space. But Cinderella's shoes exert magic, freeing her from the prison of her malevolent stepmother's abuse and restrictions, while taking her to the enchanted space of the prince. Cinderella's animal helper not only provides the heroine with supernatural aid, but also gives her a magic amulet. What else could a kitchen drudge want more than beautiful clothes and enchanted slippers?

To postmodern ears this sounds facetious, but until the beginning of the 20th century, the only wealth a woman could claim as her own was her clothing, and then only on a limited basis. Once a woman entered her husband's home, her property became his. A woman's fancy outer garments were her husband's capital since they could be marketed or pawned. Other than undergarments, a relatively new invention, the form-fitting shoe became a woman's most personal possession. The magic amulet of fancy clothes adds to Cinderella's natural beauty, giving her the opportunity to pass as an aristocrat, an appropriate step in Cinderella's circumstances due to her initial fall from grace. The tiny shoe sets Cinderella apart and acts as a catalyst for Cinderella's apotheosis.

Once past apotheosis, Cinderella again finds herself elevated to an aristocratic rank far above that of the normal individual. Her reunion with the magic slipper, the ultimate boon, elevates her to the position for which she is best qualified and is reminiscent of the position she held before her father died. At this point, Cinderella readily takes up her return journey in her magic slippers. Cinderella's husband literally lifts her over the final threshold, and her nuptials make her the mistress of two homes, that of the father/husband and husband/father; and commander of two worlds, that of the aristocrat/commoner and commoner/aristocrat creating her identity as queen of the domestic fairytale space, giving her the freedom to live happily ever after. But Cinderella pays a high price for her happiness, losing her identity as she is consumed by the hero and reincarnated as Mrs. Prince, the bearer of future generations. Unlike Campbell's hero who simply is, the heroine starts the heroic cycle anew as the creator of things becoming, because she is the bringer of life.[39]

Cinderella Today

Today Cinderella and its many ethnic variants dominate the children's section of any library. Not only do culturally authentic versions reflect an "original" Cinderella märchen, but they also display specific customs within the context of that community.[40] Illustrations culturally extend the hero's journey in Cinderella by depicting ethnic food, clothing and gender differentiation, hairstyles, homes and hearths, hierarchy, and ownership status.[41] Alien ingredients highlight unfamiliar lifestyles and, in Cinderella's case, foreign domestic spaces expand a child's literary experience. Illustrations add to these stories creating ethnic settings that help children understand and identify differences in world cultures while maintaining a homogenic connection through Campbell's heroic cycle. Christine Elmore of the Yale–New Haven Teacher's Institute believes multicultural fairy tales "help my third-graders develop insights into different cultures and their values."[42] While one can argue the ethnic authenticity of text and illustrations when comparing children's picture books to their Cinderella source märchens, what is apparent in the myriad manifestations of the tale is the hero's journey. Cinderella is aided by supernatural animals that provide her with magical accoutrements to embark on a trip, which until recent history was the only one available to women: the journey from her father's house to her husband's house. Today's society may find Cinderella's goal misogynistic, patriarchal, or even offensive, but Cinderella's journey was/is heroic; she must battle many obstacles in order to attain her magic castle and the enchanted domestic space. Whatever one's personal opinion, this journey marks an archetypal female historical event that is part of feminine culture and history and should therefore be respectfully recognized even while moving beyond its limitations.

Notes

Portions of this chapter are adapted from Doré Ripley, "Nature to the Rescue in the Hero(ine)'s Journey," http://www.ripleyonline.com/Under%20Discussion/Cinderella/Nature%20to%20the%20Rescue.htm.

1. Strabo, *The Geography of Strabo,* trans. Horace Leonard Jones (Cambridge: Harvard University Press, 1959), 17.1.33–34.

2. Ibid., 17.1.33.

3. Herodotus, *Herodotus Histories,* trans. Aubrey de Selincourt (Baltimore: Penguin, 1968), 155.

4. Sappho, "Lucky Lady with Luxuriant Hair," in *The Poems*, trans. Sasha Briar Newborn (Santa Barbara, CA: Bandanna, 2002), 26. Reprinted with permission.

5. Allen C. Guelzo, *Making History: How Great Historians Interpret the Past,* pt. 1 (Chantilly, VA: Teaching Co., 2008), 1.

6. Iona Opie and Peter Opie, "Cinderella," in *The Classic Fairy Tales* (New York: Oxford University Press, 1974), 119.

7. Andrew M. A. Lang, "Introduction" to *Cinderella: Three Hundred and Forty-five Variants of Cinderella, Catskin, and Cap O' Rushes, Abstracted and Tabulated, with a Discussion of Medieval Analogues and Notes* by Marian Roalfe Cox (1892; Germany: Kraus Reprint, 1967), xxii.

8. Patrick F. Houlihan, "A Bevy of Birds," in *The Animal World of the Pharaohs* (London: Thames and Hudson, 1996), 136.

9. Ibid., 137–141.

10. Strabo, 17.29.1; Lucia Gahlin, *Egypt: Gods, Myths, and Religion* (New York: Barnes and Noble, 2007), 7; *Oxford Classical Dictionary,* 3rd ed., s.v. "Strabo."

11. Houlihan, "A Bevy of Birds," 160.

12. Gahlin, *Egypt,* 24–27.

13. Gary Steiner, *Anthropocentrism and Its Discontents: The Moral Status of Animals in the History of Western Philosophy* (Pittsburgh, PA: University of Pittsburgh Press, 2005), 45.

14. Ibid.

15. Quoted in ibid., 46, 50.

16. Steiner, *Anthropocentrism and Its Discontents,* 53.

17. Opie and Opie, "Cinderella," 121.

18. Stephen L. Harris and Gloria Platzner, *Classical Mythology. Images and Insights,* 4th ed. (New York: McGraw-Hill, 2004), 355.

19. Bruno Bettelheim, *The Uses of Enchantment: The Meaning and Importance of Fairy Tales* (New York: Knopf, 1976), 236–237.

20. Joseph Campbell, *The Hero with a Thousand Faces* (Princeton, NJ: Princeton University Press, 1973), 49–238.

21. Melodie Monahan, "Heading Out Is Not Going Home: Jane Eyre," *Studies in English Literature* 28, no. 4 (1988): 589, 590.

22. Ai-Ling Louie, *Yeh-Shen: A Cinderella Story from China,* illus. Ed Young (New York: Philomel, 1982), n.p.

23. Hugo Munsterberg, *Symbolism in Ancient Chinese Art* (New York: Hacker, 1986), 153.

24. Harry T. Morgan, *Chinese Symbols and Superstitions* (South Pasadena, CA: Perkins, 1942), 40.

25. C. A. S. Williams, *Outlines of Chinese Symbolism and Art Motives: An Alphabetical Compendium of Antique Legends and Beliefs, as Reflected in the Manners and Customs of the Chinese,* 3rd ed. (Rutland, VT: Charles E. Tuttle, 1974), 185.

26. Lofcadio, quoted in ibid.

27. Ibid.

28. Nicholas J. Saunders, *Animal Spirits: The Shared World Sacrifice, Ritual, and Myth Animal Souls and Symbols* (Boston: Little, Brown, 1995), 115, 39.

29. Karl Jaspers, *Way to Wisdom: An Introduction to Philosophy,* trans. Ralph Manheim (New Haven: Yale University Press, 1951), 98–102.

30. Campbell, *The Hero with a Thousand Faces,* cover.

31. Ibid., 77–153.

32. Ibid., 90, 97.

33. Ibid., 111.

34. Ibid., 130–136, 151.

35. Cox, *Cinderella,* xxv, 505.

36. Anna Birgitta Rooth, *The Cinderella Cycle* (Lund: Gleerup, 1951), 106, 107; Cox, *Cinderella,* 109.

37. Photeine P. Bourboulis, "The Bride-Show Custom and the Fairy-Story of *Cinderella,*" in *Cinderella, A Folklore Casebook,* ed. Alan Dundes (New York: Garland, 1982), 98–109, 103, 104.

38. Bettelheim, *The Uses of Enchantment,* 269.

39. Campbell, *The Hero with a Thousand Faces,* 177, 196, 243.

40. Dana L. Fox and Kathy G. Short, "Why the Debates Really Matter" in *Stories Matter: The Complexity of Cultural Authenticity in Children's Literature* (Urbana, IL: NCTE, 2003), 3–24, 19.

41. Perry Nodelman, "Decoding the Images: Illustration and Picture Books," in *Understanding Children's Literature,* ed. Peter Hunt (New York: Routledge, 1999), 69–80, 74.

42. Christine Elmore, "Multicultural Fairy Tales—The Stuff of Magic," in *Yale–New Haven Teachers' Institute,* http://www.yale.edu/ynhti/curriculum/units/2004/2/04.02.01.x.html (accessed April 20, 2005).

Bibliography

Ai-Ling, Louie. *Yeh-Shen: A Cinderella Story from China.* Illustrated by Ed Young. New York: Philomel, 1982.

Bettelheim, Bruno. *The Uses of Enchantment: The Meaning and Importance of Fairy Tales.* New York: Knopf, 1976.

Campbell, Joseph. *The Hero with a Thousand Faces.* Princeton, NJ: Princeton University Press, 1973.

Cox, Marian Roalfe. *Cinderella: Three Hundred and Forty-five Variants of Cinderella, Catskin, and Cap O' Rushes, Abstracted and Tabulated, with a Discussion of Medieval Analogues and Notes.* 1892. Germany: Kraus Reprint, 1967.

Dundes, Alan, ed. *Cinderella: A Folklore Casebook.* New York: Garland, 1982.

Elmore, Christine. "Multicultural Fairy Tales—The Stuff of Magic." *Yale-New Haven Teachers' Institute.* http://www.yale.edu/ynhti/curriculum/units/2004/2/04.02.01.x.html (accessed April 20, 2005).

Fox, Dana L., and Kathy G. Short. "The Complexity of Cultural Authenticity in Children's Literature: Why the Debates Really Matter." In *Stories Matter: The Complexity of Cultural Authenticity in Children's Literature*, 3–24. Urbana, IL: NCTE, 2003.

Gahlin, Lucia. *Egypt: Gods, Myths and Religion.* New York: Barnes and Noble, 2007.

Guelzo, Allen C. *Making History: How Great Historians Interpret the Past,* pt. 1. Chantilly, VA: Teaching Co., 2008.

Harris, Stephen L., and Gloria Platzner. *Classical Mythology: Images and Insights.* 4th ed. New York: McGraw-Hill, 2004.

Herodotus. *Herodotus Histories.* Translated by Aubrey de Selincourt. Baltimore: Penguin, 1968.

The Hero's Journey. http://hubcap.clemson.edu/~sparks/heroj.html (accessed June 20, 2005).

Houlihan, Patrick F. "A Bevy of Birds." In *The Animal World of the Pharaohs*, 134–168. London: Thames and Hudson, 1996.

Hunt, Peter, ed. *Understanding Children's Literature.* New York: Routledge, 1999.

Jaspers, Karl. *Way to Wisdom: An Introduction to Philosophy.* Translated by Ralph Manheim. New Haven: Yale University Press, 1951.

Monahan, Melodie. "Heading Out Is Not Going Home: Jane Eyre." *Studies in English Literature* 28, no. 4 (1988): 589–608.

Morgan, Harry T. *Chinese Symbols and Superstitions.* South Pasadena, CA: Perkins, 1942.

Munsterberg, Hugo. *Symbolism in Ancient Chinese Art.* New York: Hacker, 1986.

Opie, Iona, and Peter Opie. "Cinderella." In *The Classic Fairy Tales*, 117–127. New York: Oxford University Press, 1974.

Rooth, Anna Birgitta. *The Cinderella Cycle.* Lund: Gleerup, 1951.

Sappho. *The Poems.* Translated by Sasha Briar Newborn. Santa Barbara, CA: Bandanna, 2002.

Saunders, Nicholas J. *Animal Spirits: The Shared World—Sacrifice, Ritual, and Myth—Animal Souls and Symbols.* Boston: Little, Brown, 1995.

Steiner, Gary. *Anthropocentrism and Its Discontents. The Moral Status of Animals in the History of Western Philosophy.* Pittsburgh: University of Pittsburgh Press, 2005.

Strabo. *The Geography of Strabo.* Translated by Horace Leonard Jones. Cambridge: Harvard University Press, 1959.

Williams, C. A. S. *Outlines of Chinese Symbolism and Art Motives: An Alphabetical Compendium of Antique Legends and Beliefs, as Reflected in the Manners and Customs of the Chinese.* 3rd ed. Rutland, VT: Charles E. Tuttle, 1974.

15

Sekhmet, Bast, and Hathor: Power, Passion, and Transformation through the Egyptian Goddess Trinity

Normandi Ellis

Three very powerful goddesses take a single form as the oldest divine being in ancient Egypt. They are the lion goddess Sekhmet, the cat goddess Bast, and Hathor, the beautiful woman who wears cow horns. All three goddesses can be found in the Old Kingdom of pharaonic Egypt (circa 3000 BCE) and may predate the First Dynasty (5000–3150 BCE).

Hathor originated in the predynastic cult of the sacred cow, which saw the Milky Way as the body of the sky goddess. All the stars that lay therein were souls of her children waiting to be born or returning to her in the afterlife. Sometimes Hathor the cow was called Mehurt, whose breasts flowed with milk. Images of the dancing horned goddess were carved on the rocks of the Egyptian savannah as early as 6000 BCE. The cow goddess appeared atop the Palette of Narmer, the first pharaoh of a united Upper and Lower Egypt. By the Fourth Dynasty, the face of the cow mother had turned into the sweet, beautiful face of a young maiden. In human form, she wore a crown of cow horns that cradled between them the gleaming disc of the moon or the sun. They called her "The Golden One." The diadem recalls Hathor's celestial home.

Figure 15.1 Three related Egyptian goddesses—Hathor, Sekhmet, and Bast—were all envisioned as embodied in feline form. Hathor was an especially beloved divinity, honored in huge public festivals each year. (Photograph © Patricia Haynes. Used by permission.)

She was, at various times, both mother and daughter of Ra, the sun god, and the consort of many divine beings whose temples flanked the Nile. Most notably, at the Temple of Edfu, she was the consort of the hawk god Horus, who was embodied in the living pharaoh while the pharaoh's queen embodied beautiful Hathor. Through all of her incarnations for more than 6000 years, Hathor remained the most frequently seen goddess in temples up and down the Nile. In some form or another, all goddesses drew upon her attributes; even the goddess Isis, whose appearance in Egypt coincides with the cow goddess, was often depicted wearing cow horns and was, at times, called the daughter of Hathor.[1] Two other ubiquitous goddesses embodied the duality of her nature— Sekhmet when she manifested solar attributes, and Bast in her lunar attributes.

Bast appeared dressed in green, the color of fecundity. A nurturing presence, she exhibited those feminine qualities associated with the moon. Her presence in the niches of most Egyptian homes was a peaceful, loving one. She tended her children, fed them, bathed them, loved them, and soothed their hurts. This cat-headed goddess was the tamed version of her bloodthirsty sister Sekhmet.

· Powerful Sekhmet wore a crimson robe. Fiery, fecund, and magical—the energy of life itself—the lion goddess protected the pharaoh. More statues of her remain in Egypt that of any other divinity. On the walls of Karnak temple, the lion goddess may be seen dashing alongside the chariot of pharaoh Ramses II as he entered battle. Sekhmet was considered a great spiritual warrior. She protected the temples and borders and exhibited in female form the solar qualities most identified with the sun god Ra. When the wicked of the world wearied the god, Ra sent his daughter Sekhmet to deal with them.

The Solar Origins of Sekhmet

Sekhmet's main feast day in Egypt was celebrated when the star Sirius in the constellation of Canis Major rose prior to sunrise during the month of August. The rise of Sirius signaled the coming change and renewal that occurs each year following the "Dog Days" of summer. After the thaw of snowcaps in central Africa's mountains, the annual Nile flood begins to wend its way northward, ending the summer drought and initiating the season of inundation.

In dramatic fashion, the rising Nile waters pushed the flood from Khartoum in Sudan, down through Upper Egypt, and finally all the way to the Delta in the north. When the inundation first trickled forth, the waters looked greenish before they turned an opaque, dark ruddy color from a type of red algae pushed out of the central African tributaries and downriver by the melting snow and floodwaters. The Arabs called this the Red Nile.

The red flow soon precipitated a burst of life-generating activity along the Nile banks. It may help here to realize that the Egypt of 10,000 BCE was a different place than today's land. Rather than being primarily desert, Egypt was a lush savannah, teeming with life. Some suggest that the overgrazing of cattle and climate change may have caused the Sahara savannah to turn into desert. After this change, around 6000 BCE, life in Egypt shrank to occupy primarily the Delta and the narrow strip of arable black earth washed down into the bottomland on either side of the Nile.

One of the many festivals that celebrated the flood and opened the Egyptian New Year was called "The Inebriety of Hathor." The beer- and wine-drinking festival that followed the first sign of flood was connected to the intoxicating drink that soothed the savage Sekhmet, a solar form of Hathor. The festivities that accompany the festival of "The Inebriety of Hathor" commemorated the saving of Egypt from the ravaging power of Sekhmet.

Ra, who created all things, ruled the earth in peace for thousands of years. But as he grew old, his human subjects forgot him and no longer offered their adoration. Outraged, the god summoned his council, soliciting their advice. Nun, god of primordial waters, suggested sending forth Ra's fiery solar eye, Sekhmet. The idea of sending his lioness daughter delighted Ra, who imagined irreverent humans fleeing, trembling in terror, and cowering in the mountains.

At her father's bidding, Sekhmet began to teach humankind a lesson by devouring every man, woman, and child who crossed her path. She ravaged all the land in both Upper and Lower Egypt, through the mountains and savannahs east and west of the river. She started in Nubia and ate her way north toward the Delta. The river ran red with the blood of those she had slain (a reference to the Red Nile flood). As the fierce goddess waded through the carnage, her feet turned red with the blood of her victims.

Ra looked down upon the havoc Sekhmet had created and felt immediate remorse. The thirst of his daughter for blood knew no bounds. He tried to rein her in, saying, "Come home. Thou hast done what I asked thee to do." But Sekhmet replied, "By my life, I love the taste of blood. My heart rejoices and I will work my will upon humankind." She would not be deterred.

Ra realized he had made a grave mistake, but neither god nor human could stop Sekhmet. But if she could not be stopped, perhaps her willful passions could be diverted. Ra turned to Thoth, god of wisdom. Thoth quickly sent his messengers to Elephantine Island, where the river burst forth from rocks. "Bring me the fruit that causes sleep," he said, "the fruit that is scarlet and its juice crimson as human blood." When the messengers returned, Thoth and Ra commanded the women in the city of Heliopolis to crush red barley and make beer. They mixed it with the juice of pomegranates and other magical ingredients, according to the recipe of Thoth. The women of Heliopolis made 7000 measures of this red beer.

At dawn, this soothing red brew was poured into a pool outside the city, where Sekhmet would find it. Thinking it was the blood of her victims, the lioness lapped up the mixture until it was gone. When the potion took effect, the heart of the fierce goddess was soothed. Sekhmet lay down and purred, no longer seeking revenge. She stretched out in the field for a sweet little sleep, having transformed herself into the gentle, nurturing, loving cat goddess, Bast.

This myth shows for the first time the emerging dual nature of Hathor. Bast is the sensual, purring, nurturing aspect, while Sekhmet is the roaring lion, a goddess with a temper. Bast reveals the nurturing mother of her kittens; Sekhmet shows herself the protector of her pride and her cubs. When Hathor's solar qualities are the focal point, the goddess assumes Sekhmet's lion form, and when her lunar qualities are at play, she appears as Bast the cat.

The beer that soothed Sekhmet was a staple of the Egyptian diet. Because the brewing and fermentation processes made the Nile water more potable and healthful, beer was offered at breakfast, lunch, and dinner. But wine was the favored drink of great celebrations. Whenever Hathor appeared as the "Queen of Happiness" and "Mistress of Drunkenness, Jubilation and Music" in one of more than forty festivals held in her temple at Dendera, alcoholic beverages were in plentiful supply. The sacred wine that induced a trancelike state may have contained psychotropic plants, says Robert Masters, possibly including belladonna, wormwood, or opium.[2] C. J. Bleeker believed that this sacred drunkenness was "the medium through which contact could be effectuated with the world of the gods."[3]

Triple Aspects of the Goddesses

Bast and Sekhmet are such tightly linked aspects of Hathor that the three goddesses were sometimes sculpted standing back to back on the handle of a cosmetic mirror. Because the ancestry of all three goddesses reaches back into the early dynasties of Egypt, they may be aspects of a single, superlative feminine divinity. The goddesses' names evoke that divine being by her attributes: Sekhmet (the powerful one), Bast (the soul of mother Isis), and Hathor or Het-hor (the house or shrine of the god Horus).

In later times, the Ptolemaic Greeks (circa 300 BCE) linked Hathor with Aphrodite, the goddess of love and beauty. Their reasoning is easy to follow, for Hathor's consorts were many. She was consort to Horus the Younger, the falcon god. She was linked as well to a number of gods, among them the crocodile Sobek, the ithyphallic Min, and the solar Ra. She shared her power equally with the gods but remained independent of them. Bleeker says, "Hathor always jealously guarded her independence and never allowed herself to be trapped in any mythological system that could detract from her true nature."[4] Hathor reigned as the supreme love goddess and a consort to nearly every other god in every pantheon throughout Egyptian history, but her connection to Sekhmet showed that she was a force to be reckoned with, especially in times of war, and especially when Sekhmet showed her powerful divine wrath.

The festival of "The Inebriety of Hathor" calmed that inner rage and provided Egypt's general populace with an outlet for their pent-up emotions. "Similar festivals were celebrated at the end of battle, in order to pacify the goddess of war, so that there would be no more destruction. On such occasions, the people danced and played music to soothe the wildness of the goddess."[5]

The Blood Mysteries

Together Hathor, Bast, and Sekhmet create a unified image of the divine feminine as maiden, mother, and crone. The three goddesses represent the stages of the blood mysteries that rule a woman's life as she moves across the roles of lover, mother, and elder. Beautiful Hathor is the consort of Egypt's gods and the perfect embodiment of the queen partnered with the pharaoh who embodies Horus. Bast is the mother protector of children, surrounded by her litter of kittens; she is also the bridge between the sensual young adult woman and the older, but still sexual wife and mother. Sekhmet embodies the cyclical blood that flows at birth and death; the blood that flows from mother to child in the womb; the blood on battlefields, and the menstrual blood or the blood of circumcision that separates the budding young adult from childhood. It is the cyclical red flood of the River Nile that became equated with the red, renewing menstrual blood that cleanses and prepares the way for renewal and regenesis. This blood is a kind of communion, in which humankind partakes of the divine drink of the gods. That is the mystery of transubstantiation.[6]

Blood held within was called the "wise blood," and menopause marked a time for women in ancient Egypt when the inner Sekhmet produced divisions and created magic. The red henna (or Egyptian privet) that adorned the heads of women in Egypt was a tribute to her and was said to be her "magic blood." Heads, hands, and feet were dipped in the colors of the goddess. Cheeks and lips were brushed with her paint. Even mummy cloths were sometimes dipped in henna as a sign of rebirth from the blood of the goddess.

To the left of the Temple of Karnak sits a small temple dedicated to the great trinity of Memphis—Ptah, Sekhmet, and their offspring Nefertum.

During the Eighteenth Dynasty the pharaoh Thutmose III refurbished the temple to honor the trinity. He made his annual harvest festival offering of "Feeding the Gods" at that smaller temple rather than at Karnak. To this day, inside that temple resides a large, black basalt statue of Sekhmet, who was said to be "great of magic." In fact more statues of Sekhmet can be found at Karnak than at any other temple and more statues exist in situ than any other divinity.

Thutmose III beseeched Sekhmet by calling her Mut, a word used to mean both "mother" and "death"; its hieroglyph of the vulture symbolized both. Not only does the vulture lay eggs, but it eats the dead. On a higher level, nurturance often demands sacrifice. The goddess feeds her people, who in turn feed the goddess. Thutmose III provided thrones of gleaming electrum for Ptah, Sekhmet, and Nefertum. He filled their temple with vessels of gold and silver, with "every splendid, costly stone," with fine linens and "ointments of divine ingredients." On the day of her feast, Thutmose stood before the altar and made the sacrifices that restore Egypt to "life, prosperity, and health." His gifts line the offering table: many jars of wine and jugs of beer, ducks and geese, a multitude of loaves of white bread, bunches of vegetables, baskets of fruits, and "offerings of the garden and every plant."[7]

The Healing Arts

The healing arts were part of the magical power of a wise woman, and Sekhmet was known as an important healing divinity. Inside one of the ten side rooms that surround the inner sanctuary at the Temple of Edfu, a medical library was kept, and in this place the healing priests, called *wab sekhmet*, conducted healings.[8] On the left side of the doorway was inscribed the magical, repeating image of a lion-headed cobra. A serpentine Sekhmet seemed to unwrap herself from seven coils and rise out of a shallow basket, her lioness head held high, her eyes glittering, and her tongue thrust between her teeth. Here the goddess appears as the life force itself.

While the priests and priestesses of Bast were adept at soothing jangled nerves and easing depression with herbal potions and music, the healers who were "great of magic" were more often high priests and priestesses dedicated to Sekhmet. They wore leopard skins to link them to her powerful feline energies. Because these goddesses understood the powerful visions brought by intoxication, both Sekhmet and Bast were said to bring healing dreams.

The Beneficent Role of Bast

The cat Bast offered the image of a kinder, more nurturing feline form. She often appeared as a woman with a cat's head carrying on her arm a basket with a litter of kittens. Mythologist Robert Briffault remarked upon the cat's great adaptability to motherhood and her ability to love substitute children equally with her own. Typically, cats who have lost a kitten willingly adopt the kittens from another litter.[9] In this area, Bast and Isis share the role of surrogate mother. Before Isis begat her son Horus, she mothered the jackal-headed god Anubis who had been abandoned in the desert.

A number of Egyptologists cite Greek sources that describe Bast as the "Soul of Ra"; like a cat that had nine lives, the sun god Ra had nine divine beings under his command. These nine primordial gods, called the Great Ennead, were generated from Ra's light substance. Other ancient Egyptians identified Bast with Isis as the true mother of all, whether she was mothering her own children or the abandoned children of others. Nearly every household with children had a wall niche devoted to Bast. Before her were laid fresh flowers, cups of milk, or other offerings. Statues of Sekhmet may have been the appropriate energy to guard the temples, the borderlands and the pharaoh, but Bast was the welcome guardian of the home. Little cat figurines of Bast with round head and pointed ears were produced in great quantities for private devotion. Families often owned a number of cats. Affectionate and graceful, they made great companions, and they kept away mice and snakes. When a cat died, it was mourned as a beloved family member, mummified in great ceremony, and buried with honor. Fifteen centuries later when the Suez Canal was being dug, workmen had to stop for weeks at a time to clear away the multitude of cat mummies they had uncovered in ancient pet cemeteries.

The cat goddess sometimes wore a necklace bearing the healing Eye of Horus, called the *wadjet*. At other times she wore on her breastplate the lion's head of her sister Sekhmet, a reminder of her fierce other self and of the mercurial ability of the feline goddess to change from lap kitty into warrior in the blink of an eye.

The dual nature of the goddess—her loving nature on the one hand and her wild anger and abandon on the other—are nowhere more tightly woven than in the myths of Bast and Sekhmet. Prayers to Hathor are quick to praise both aspects, lest one offend the other. This Hymn to Sekhmet-Bast appears in *The Egyptian Book of the Dead*:

Mother of the gods, the One, the Only . . .
Sekhmet is thy name when thou art wrathful,

Bast, beloved, when thy people call.
(Sekhmet) daughter of the sun, with flame and fury. . . .
Bast, beloved, banish all our fears.
Mother of the gods, no gods existed
Til thou . . . gave them life.[10]

In the Nile Delta Bast retained her stature from prehistory down to the reign of the Ptolemaic Greeks (343 BCE). According to the histories of Manetho, Bast's sacred city Bubastis, was active as early as 2925 BCE and influenced the theology of the priests of nearby Memphis, Heliopolis, and Sais.[11] During the Fourth Dynasty, pharaohs Khufu and Khafre kept laborers busy refurbishing and adding to Bast's main temple, in addition to building the pharaohs' grand pyramids. One royal inscription found on the Giza Plateau near Khafre's pyramid reads: "Beloved of the Goddess Bast and beloved of the Goddess Hathor."[12] Such an inscription linking Bast and Hathor is remarkable, since no other inscriptions of any kind occur elsewhere on the site.

During the Twenty-Second Dynasty, pharaoh Sheshonk I elevated Bast from local patron to the stature of a national heroine, chiefly because his lineage descended from her sacred city of Bubastis. By 930 BCE all Egypt adored Bast. King Sheshonk I, who considered himself a son of Bast, boldly moved the capital city from its long-standing home in Thebes to his hometown in Bubastis.

Although only a few crumbling walls remained in Bubastis, Sheshonk restored the Old Kingdom temples and erected new temples to honor the cat goddess. According to Herodotus, who visited the city around 600 BCE, no other temple compared with the grandeur of that of Bast. It was built in the very heart of the city, situated on an island enclosed by two divergent streams of the Nile that ran on either side of a single passageway. Each stream seemed 100 feet broad, and on the banks of the river were "fair-branched trees, overshadowing the waters with a cool and pleasant shade." A tall tower could be seen clearly from every part of the city. Inside the enclosure wall a beautiful garden of trees shaded the priests who carefully tended it. Part of the temple was said to have been built around an ancient sacred *persea* (avocado) tree. At the center of the temple stood a beautiful golden statue of the goddess Bast.[13]

Throughout the Delta in general, and at her sacred city Bubastis in particular, Bast was adored for her sensuality, congeniality, and loving nature. The Greeks especially loved her, and Bast festivals were never more popular than during the Graeco-Roman period. When migrating Libyans appeared in the Delta around 100 BCE, the population of the city soared once again.

Herodotus calls the "Great Festival of Bast at Bubastis" (April 15) one of the most important festivals in Egypt. At times bawdy, at times ecstatic, the festival celebrated Hathor as the consort, while it also celebrated Bast and her sister Sekhmet. The three were never found far apart. This may have been a result of the wine- and beer-drinking that accompanied nearly every feast day in Egypt, all the more so when one is reminded of the mystery of blood that transformed the ravaging Sekhmet into the purring Bast.

During the Great Festival visitors came from far and wide, clattering through the streets, clustering along the riverbanks, and crowding their boats onto the Nile. The festivals often drew over 700,000 people—including men, women, and children—and the days were filled with dancing, music-making, love-making, and wine-drinking. Drinking wine was viewed as a high religious sacrament, for its color was reminiscent of the blood of the divine and a reminder of spiritual renewal. Bubastis was the wine capital of ancient Egypt, its rich Delta soil providing large pharaonic estates bearing the choicest grapes. The white wines of Lower Egypt were called the Wine of Bast, while the red wines of Upper Egypt were called the Wine of Sekhmet.

Bast's island temple could only be reached by the crowded little ferry-boats that plied the waters of the Nile. Some of the larger boats filled with richly adorned noblemen and women sailed down river all the way from ancient Thebes. As they approached the little towns along the Nile, villagers heard the swelling strains of music coming from the flute play-ers and the women playing castanets. They heard the songstresses and sometimes trickles of laughter. Long before Bubastis was reached, the wine and beer had begun flowing. As the boats neared town, the villag-ers came down to the edge of the water to greet the entourage. If the boats stopped in town to freshen supplies, even more people crowded aboard to join the sailing party.

Herodotus said that more wine was consumed in Bubastis during the festival than at any other time of the year. Delicious foods included hon-eyed breads, raisin cakes, pomegranates, figs, roasted fowl, and meats. The streets fairly writhed with dancing, music playing, and singing all day and night.

Hathor: Goddess of Dualities

The ubiquitous goddess Hathor who reigned in heaven, on earth, and in the afterlife was the patron goddess of all women in whatever stage of life, but she is most beloved as the consort or divine wife. Her name Het-hor literally meant "the house" or "the shrine" of Horus, the falcon god. That shrine was her sacred womb.

In older myths, Hathor was the mother of Horus the Elder when he appeared as the solar child that the sky mother birthed onto the horizon. In later myths, Hathor became the beloved of Horus the Younger, whose mother was Isis. Whether she was connected to the elder or younger Horus, Hathor remained always eternally youthful and beautiful, even though she was older than Isis.

Her temples were found at Memphis, Thebes, the Sinai, and elsewhere. She was honored at Edfu, Kom Ombo, and Esna. The most important and well known of her temples was the Temple of Hathor at Dendera, which in its present condition is a Ptolemaic temple built around 332 BCE, but its inscription says it was built upon the previous site where the Fourth Dynasty King Cheops erected a temple to the goddess.[14] Its most famous attribute is its dramatic astronomical ceiling with symbols of the zodiacal signs that can clearly be recognized as the twelve familiar constellations. And yet, its pole star is not in Ursa Major but in Draco, the constellation that it would have appeared as pole star around 4500 BCE, an age that pre-dates the temple having been built by Cheops. This representation of the sky and the temple of the sky goddess Hathor seems to point to the dawning of ancient Egyptian civilization.

In her temple Hathor's statue was venerated and venerable, adored and adorned for thousands of years. Thus, the statue acquired the power to heal, to speak, and to bring dreams to her worshipers. Pure Nile water poured over the base inscriptions of her statue could heal diseased bodies, minds, and spirits. The pilgrims wrote stories of their miraculous healing in prayers, poems, and inscriptions through the Dendera temple.

As the oldest goddess in Upper Egypt, Hathor was assimilated into nearly every other goddess. Isis the mother and Hathor the consort become interchangeable. Wherever there was a temple that honored Hathor, there was also a smaller temple that honored Isis, and vice versa. In the Temple of Isis at Philae, the inscribed "Songs of Isis" praise the beauty and majesty of Hathor.

Oh, Lady of the Beginning, come thou before our faces in this her name of Hathor, Lady of Emerald, Lady of Aset, the Holy![15]

Because there were so many temples devoted to Hathor, many more women than men served in priestly offices engaged in her service, a custom unlike that of other temples in Egypt. At daybreak the pharaoh engaged in a ritual in which he broke the clay seal on the door of her shrine in order to gaze in silent adoration upon the beautiful face of the goddess. To the mistress of heaven he offered incense, the *menat* necklace, the sistrum rattle, and *ma'at*, the image of truth. These were among the pharaoh's gifts to his beloved, for Hathor was the goddess of the queen and thus coming before her was the culmination of a love story.

The sacred marriage of the pharaoh (as the embodiment of Horus) and the queen (embodiment of Hathor) was celebrated in May, during one of many harvest festivals. The festival began at the Temple of Hathor in Dendera and lasted about fourteen days, ending in Edfu at the Temple of Horus. During the festival, the statue of "The Golden One" was carried along the Nile by boat amid music, dance, and song. The union of the two most important lights in heaven was the culmination of the meeting of Hathor and Horus in Edfu. Their marriage took place precisely on the day of the new moon, when the sun (Horus) and the moon (Hathor) met in heavenly conjunction. The ancient Egyptians called this "The Day of the Beautiful Embrace."[16]

On the inner face of the east pylon of the Temple of Edfu is a description of the annual festival of the sacred union. The ritual marriage took place privately inside the temple where the divine couple remained for three days, consummating their holy marriage. Meanwhile outside the temple walls the entire population of Edu continued their celebration: drinking, feasting, singing, and dancing.

One song performed for the wedding celebration was called "Hymn to the Golden One." It was sung in chorus by several priestesses while the pharaoh enacted the offering rituals:

> The pharaoh comes to dance.
> He comes to sing for thee.
> O, mistress, see how he dances!
> O, bride of Horus, see how he skips! . . .
> He offers thee
> This urn filled with wine.
> O, mistress, see how he dances!
> O, bride of Horus, see how he skips![17]

The first record of a celebration of the sacred marriage appeared during the reign of the Middle Kingdom pharaoh Amenemhet I, around 2000

BCE. Linked with the harvest season rites, it commemorated the first fruits of the field and was held in honor of the ancestors.

In the union of the god and the goddess, all life had its regenesis. Of all the festivals in Egypt, this truly was Hathor's day. It was a festival in honor of the bride, for it is she who becomes mother of the holy child. The hierogamos or sacred marriage was a union of opposites. In this pair, Hathor is the divine mother, the sky, and Horus is the falcon god and the earthly king. It is a sacred marriage of sprit and flesh, heaven and earth. Every royal couple who ever lived reenacted the marriage sacrament as much for the renewal of the land and their people as for themselves.

Three days after the hierogamos was celebrated, the festival of the "Conception of Horus" occurred, which celebrated the seed that means the renewal of life. This was also considered the conception day of the pharaoh and of the child who would succeed him. From lovemaking came the heir to the throne. Here, father and son were merged into one. Hathor's love was sexual, maternal and spiritual. These triple aspects represent the deep passion for love, life, and light that runs through all her cosmic creation. Her powers generated "constant and ceaseless becoming." Her love for humankind was eternal.

Notes

1. Normandi Ellis, *Feasts of Light: Celebrations for the Seasons of a Woman's Life Based on the Egyptian Goddess Mysteries* (Wheaton, IL: Quest Books, 1999), 144.

2. Robert Masters, *The Goddess Sekhmet: Psychospiritual Exercises of the Fifth Way* (Woodbury, MN: Llewellyn Publications, 1991), 44.

3. C. J. Bleeker, *Hathor and Thoth: Two Key Figures of the Ancient Egyptian Religion* (Leiden, Netherlands: E. J. Brill, 1967), 91.

4. Ibid., 132.

5. Masters, *The Goddess Sekhmet*, 44.

6. See the "Cannibal Hymn of Unas" in Miriam Lichtheim, *Ancient Egyptian Literature*, vol. 1, *The Old Kingdom* (Berkeley: University of California Press, 1975), 36–38.

7. James Breasted, *Ancient Records of Egypt* (Chicago: University of Chicago Press, 1906), 2:225–248.

8. Normandi Ellis, *Dreams of Isis: A Woman's Spiritual Sojourn* (Wheaton, IL: Quest Books, 1995), 178.

9. Robert Briffault, *The Mothers* (New York: Macmillan, 1927), 594.

10. Margaret Murray, *Egyptian Religious Poetry* (London: John Murray, 1949), 103.

11. E. A. Wallis Budge, *The Gods of the Egyptians* (New York: Dover, 1969), 1:445.

12. Marilee Bigelow, "Bast," *Khepera* 2, no. 2 (March 1991).

13. Budge, *The Gods of the Egyptians*, 1:449.

14. Bleeker, *Hathor and Thoth*, 76.

15. James Teackle Dennis, *The Burden of Isis* (London: John Murray, 1918), 55.

16. Lucie Lamy, *Egyptian Mysteries: New Light on Ancient Spiritual Knowledge* (New York: Crossroads, 1981), 80.

17. "Hymn to the Golden One," in Bleeker, *Hathor and Thoth*, 99. Reprinted with permission.

Bibliography

Bigelow, Marilee. "Bast." *Khepera* 2, no. 2 (March 1991).

Bleeker, C. J. *Hathor and Thoth: Two Key Figures of the Ancient Egyptian Religion.* Leiden, Netherlands: E. J. Brill, 1967.

Breasted, James. *Ancient Records of Egypt.* 5 vols. Chicago: University of Chicago Press, 1906.

Briffault, Robert. *The Mothers.* 3 vols. New York: Macmillan, 1927.

Budge, E. A. Wallis. *The Gods of the Egyptians.* 2 vols. New York: Dover, 1969.

Dennis, James Teackle. *The Burden of Isis.* London: John Murray, 1918.

Ellis, Normandi. *Dreams of Isis: A Woman's Spiritual Sojourn.* Wheaton, IL: Quest Books, 1995.

Ellis, Normandi. *Feasts of Light: Celebrations for the Seasons of Life Based on the Egyptian Goddess Mysteries.* Wheaton, IL: Quest Books, 1999.

Lamy, Lucie. *Egyptian Mysteries: New Light on Ancient Spiritual Knowledge.* New York: Crossroads, 1981.

Lichtheim, Miriam. *Ancient Egyptian Literature.* Vol. 1, *The Old Kingdom.* Berkeley: University of California Press, 1975.

Masters, Robert. *The Goddess Sekhmet: The Way of the Five Bodies.* New York: Amity House, 1988.

Murray, Margaret. *Egyptian Religious Poetry.* London: John Murray, 1949.

16

Nut: Egyptian Night-Sky Goddess

Malgorzata (Margaret) Kruszewska

The image of the early Egyptian goddess Nut has been largely forgotten in favor of the better-known Isis whose temples and rituals survived into Greco-Roman times. Although temples were not exclusively devoted to Nut, her presence hovered over most sacred sites and decorated coffins, from that of King Tutankhamun to Queen Cleopatra's. To the uninitiated, it is possible to walk through an Egyptian temple and not recognize bits of her star body stenciled around the edges of doorways, along tunnels and passageways to tombs and in crevices where ceiling-sky meets pillar-tree. Because she is indefinite space, she can go unnoticed, yet it is her female body that gives shape to the cosmos.

Nut is the first goddess pictured in fully female form in the Egyptian genealogical systems later called the Enneads by the Greeks. Her mother, Tefnut, was described as moisture and, in her rare depictions, was represented with a lioness head. In iconography, Nut's body stretched naked, with visible pubic hair and full breasts with prominent nipples that emphasize her sex. Although sometimes conflated with the bovine Hathor or described as a sow mother, she did not possess the animal features as exemplified in such Egyptian goddesses as Sekhmet the lioness or Taweret the pregnant hippopotamus. Her face was not as distinct as Isis or Hathor, nor did she wear the royal crowns or carry the props that identified other goddesses. It is Nut's elongated female body that identifies her as holder of the myths and symbols of death and regeneration.

Figure 16.1 The Egyptian sky-goddess Nut stretched out above the earth and was depicted in the same posture above the deceased, painted on the inside of coffins. She was a powerful goddess in ancient times who, like many other such divinities, lost stature over the ages. (Photograph © Malgorzata (Margaret) Kruszewska. Reprinted with permission.)

Nut defined the contours of space with her exaggerated arms and legs, stretching into all directions. Sometimes she was bent, with fingertips touching the ground in front of her. Other times she stretched as if reaching for the extreme corners of the universe. Although her feet were often solidly planted in side profile on the ground, she was rarely pictured standing upright or sitting upon a throne in the stylized manner of many Egyptian deities. She suggests an action, process, or movement differing greatly from later male sky gods who became both passive and abstract. Nut is the "sky" as the site of the afterlife journey as well as the location of the daily birthing of the sun.

Geography and Dates of Nut's Worship

Although solar-focused worship is often attributed to northern Egypt (Lower Egypt) while an emphasis on stellar worship is associated with southern Egypt (Upper Egypt), Nut appears in both geographical locations.

Invocations and recitations to Nut are etched into funerary sites in both Upper and Lower Egypt, while images of Nut on temple ceilings are more prevalent in Upper Egypt. Over 100 invocations to Nut are inscribed along the ancient walls of the Pyramids at Sakkara near Cairo that date back to 2400 BCE. These oral recitations and chants date back to 3000 BCE.

At the Hathor Temple in Dendera, ceiling paintings of Nut appear in several different chambers. She is painted as either wearing a gown of stars or with the sun moving through her naked body. Although large sections of this temple have been identified from Roman times, it was built on top of an older goddess temple dating back to 4000 BCE. The prevalence of Nut imagery on mummy boards and coffin lids from 1550 BCE until well into Roman times provides ample evidence of her popularity.

The Myths of Nut

Nut as sky goddess was created from the union of Tefnut (moisture) and Shu (air). Pyramid text references describe her as already being "mighty" while in her mother's womb thus establishing her reign over the physical world.

> To say: Great lady, who did become heaven, you become (physically) mighty,
> You become victorious, you have filled every place with your beauty.
> The whole earth lies under you; you have taken possession of it;
> You encompass the earth and all things in your arms;
> May we become in you an imperishable star.[1]

While images of Tefnut are rare, Shu is often pictured as standing underneath the arch of Nut's body. Some scholars have interpreted Shu's lifted arms as holding up the sky-goddess but one text clearly describes her supremacy.

> To say: High one over the earth, thou art above thy father Shu, who hast the mastery over him.
> He has loved thee in that he has set himself under thee; all things are thine.[2]

Nut was called "She Who Gives Birth to All Gods" because she began the Egyptian mythic dynasty by giving birth to Isis, Osiris, Nephthys, Seth, and, in some myths, Horus. The birth myth is significant in that it begins with Nut as a regenerative goddess, not a reproductive goddess. Nut swallows the sun and allows the orb to travel through her body every evening. In some myths, the sun enters between her legs and rides through the hours along her back. Although Nut gives birth to the deities, she is not a fertility goddess. In fact, it is her reputation for "swallowing" souls that creates the "birther-mother" myth.

The Roman historian Plutarch recorded a myth about Nut's power to swallow the deceased and turn them into stars, an ability that angers and threatens the sun god who curses her by not allowing her to give birth to any children during the year, which was constructed as 360 days. Thoth, in his role as keeper of records and scribe, adds five extra days, during which time Nut births the five deities Osiris, Horus, Seth, Isis, and Neph-thys. Thus she begins the genealogy that continues through Isis to all the Pharaohs. The myth of Nut's creatiom of the cosmos was eventually altered so that the central character was the male creator Atum. Nut was then demoted to granddaughter and the sun god became the source of kingly power.

Nut's most obvious function is as keeper of time, as she regulates sun-rise and sunset, the seasonal movement of the sun, and even the celestial heavens. A striking image painted on the ceiling of an upper chamber at the Dendera temple shows her in a fully outstretched pose next to a detailed round zodiac calendar known as the Dendera Zodiac. Although the Dendera Zodiac dates to a much later Roman period, the image of Nut's body as a celestial map occurs much earlier as seen in paintings on the inside of coffin lids. Papyri paintings also show a double image of Nut, with her two backs aligned designating night and day movements. Underneath other paintings of Nut's elongated U-shaped body are detailed drawings of each hour as the sun and stars move through her back. She was the gatekeeper of these movements of the constellation.

Nut was often also thought of as the Milky Way, as described in a funerary text.[3] Analyzing the placement of constellations and planets drawn on her body may reveal an astoundingly precise astrological map used for navigation, ceremonies, and prediction of seasonal flooding pat-terns. Astronomer Ronald Wells has calculated the positions of the stars and planets that occurred around the vernal equinox near Cairo around 3500 BCE and then nine months later on the winter solstice; he notes that the pattern suggests the hieroglyph for a female giving birth. Nut not only births the daily sun but also controls the reemergence of yearly light. Writ-ten on her body is the celestial calendar, a directional compass, and pre-cise patterns of solar and stellar positions.

Perhaps most poetic are the frequent references in myths and invocations describing the stars on Nut's body as the souls of all deceased beings. In later myths, it was precisely this aspect of Nut's abilities that the sun deities wish to control. In these myths, Nut is portrayed as a sow goddess who "eats" her children by swallowing them back into the sky where they live as celestial stars. While still acknowledging Nut's domain in the afterlife, the great pharaohs identified with the power of the sun as the source of their religio-political powers. Kings of Egypt were then said to be of divine birth and called Sons of Ra despite the obvious source of their divine power originating through matrilineal inheritance.

Images of the Goddess

Nut is found in ceiling paintings at temples devoted to Isis, Hathor, or Osiris/Horus. Her shape follows the architectural features of the temple, with her body defining the square or rectangular ceiling. Despite abundant painted images of Nut, no known carved statues or figurines exist. Her presence is understood to be time and space as she instead hovers above and around sacred temples and in coffins.

Nut's image appears in several of the chamber rooms at the Dendera Temple north of Luxor on the west bank of the River Nile. On the ceiling of a small side temple possibly designated for New Year or healing rituals, Nut's body curves around a square ceiling. Her fingertips, back, feet, and head are positioned at the four corners. A large orb rests in front of her lips, touching her nose and chin. A second orb rests between her thighs and belly and radiates triangles of lines toward the face of Hathor on the ground below. The last ray touches a plant growing from the ground, possibly a sycamore, later associated with both goddesses. She wears a zigzag-patterned gown that begins just below her breasts, which are of the same color and material as the sun orb and her arms. A long line runs from her nipple to the ground, suggesting nourishing milk flowing from her body. Her long arms extend over her head in such a way that they appear to be radiating from her eyes and forehead. Nut's face is in side profile with exposed ear and prominent nose and full lips.

An elongated Nut spans the ceiling of the large hall at Dendera Temple. She is in the familiar bent pose commonly seen on smaller square ceilings but here she fills the architectural space of an extended rectangular form. Underneath her body are hundreds of detailed figures travelling in processional rows of boats. The round sun orb appears not only from the curve around her vagina but also just outside her calf and near her lips. Extending from the circle around her lips are large wings that run parallel to her outstretched arms. Below her breasts are double wings. Several long wave-like patterns adorn the lower bodice of her gown while the upper bodice is covered in teardrop and floral patterns.

Paintings of Nut inside or on top of coffins vary greatly. In the coffin of "God's Wife Ankhnesneferibreto" (possible date of 525 BCE), Nut is shown naked in full frontal pose with arms stretched over her head and a dark orb attached to her conspicuous V-shaped vulva. Similar sarcophagi paintings of Nut show her with either a single orb (sun) at her belly or orbs at her heart and throat.

A Middle Kingdom Sakkara sarcophagus from the Thirteenth Dynasty (approximately 1790–1649 BCE) is adorned with a detailed painting of Nut in the bent pose with her body as the dome. This sarcophagus contains approximately 25,000 hieroglyphs and thousands of figures traveling through Nut's body in detailed scenes of the voyage in the afterlife. Below her rounded body is another symbol of Nut, two arms forming a platform holding a huge circle that includes two side profiles of the goddess with long raised arms. Underneath Nut's arched body is the bovine mask of the goddess Hathor.

References to Nut's outstretched arms occur in many invocations including those inscribed on King Tutankhamun's shrine IV:

Mother Nut, may you spread your wing to my face.
May your two arms embrace me in health and in life, that I may exist
    inside you, and that you may provide my protection![4]

Although feathered arms are frequently associated with Isis or Maat, the image also appears directly above hieroglyphs invoking Nut's name. This motif was frequently painted on the exterior of coffin lids underneath the head painted as a funerary mask that creates an illusion of double wings spreading from the breasts over the heart. The heart was protected because it was believed to be the holder of memory and imagination.

Nut is also painted wearing a diaphanous dress covered with stars and, in some paintings, her face is that of Hathor with large ears and stylized hair. Hathor's face is often merged with the body of other goddesses such as Isis and Nut when emphasizing their maternal aspects. In written invocations, Nut is also described as having braided hair[5] associated with a woman preparing for childbirth. However, it may also identify Nut with a certain region or locality.

A funerary papyrus from the Twenty-First Dynasty (1025 BCE) shows Nut's body arched over a side reclining ithyphallic Geb. Descriptions of this composition often ignore the sexual placement of Shu's one hand on top of Nut's breast as the other hand points to her darkened vulva. A feather from Shu's headdress brushes Nut's navel. Shu is thus not only the intermediary between earth and sky, but is also entreating Nut and making sure she receives sexual pleasure. Shu both interferes with and acknowledges Nut's desire to be united with Geb. In some myths, Nut and Geb are only in union while creating the deities, while in others Nut's erotic wishes are fulfilled as she lies down alongside Geb every night.

Nut's image is perhaps the most erotic of all Egyptian goddesses. Not only is she often beautifully naked but her female shape, darkened nipples, and triangular vulva are emphasized. Images of the great sky goddess differ greatly from the flattened bodies usually associated with Egyptian paintings. She is fully human and gloriously, unambiguously female.

Coffin images of Nut are also highly erotic with references to her embracing arms and body such as that found inside the coffin of Anknas-Neferibre:

I am thy mother Nut,
I spread myself over thee in my name "sky";
thou enterest my mouth, thou comest out of my thighs, like Re every day.[6]

Nut is thought to be not only the womb-tomb but also the transporter into the next realm awaiting those who know her power. She carries the deceased from earth, where Geb is holding them as prisoners in the ground. Spell 181 describers Nut as protector during this journey:

Your mother Nut has put her arms about you that she may protect you,
and she will continually guard you,
even you the high-born.[7]

During the New Kingdom (1554–1075 BCE) Nut is also described and painted as a sycamore tree. Spell 59 of *The Book of the Dead* entitled "Spell of breathing air and having power over water in the realm of the dead" invokes Nut with "Oh you sycamore of the sky, may there be given to me the air which is in it."[8] Funerary papyri show the deceased bowing to a full sycamore tree. Nut's arms extend out from the tree with blessing of water symbolized by long wavy lines streaming above and below. In some images the deceased offers water to Nut for the afterlife. Another significance of Nut being a tree goddess is that burial in a wooden coffin that contained her image meant a return to the goddess. Some scholars note that the prevalence of Nut's image on coffins shows her as a key goddess in assisting the deceased on the journey through the netherworld.

Nut's clear and unchanging identity as both birther of the gods and receiver of the dead spans over 3500 years, from predynastic times until the Roman empire. Remarkably well-preserved myths, invocations, and visual depictions of Nut indicate a persistent presence throughout Egyptian culture. Nut stretches across time and space, birth and death, holding all within her female body. She is both the road that all souls move through and the energy that sustains the daily, monthly, and yearly cycles of celestial planets and beings. Her arms are not the cradling, nurturing arms of Isis the mother, but instead offer strong, direct pathways on the journey in the afterlife.

Notes

1. Raymond O. Faulkner, trans., *The Ancient Egyptian Pyramid Texts* (Oxford: Clarendon Press, 1969), 142.

2. Ibid, 143.

3. Raymond O. Faulkner, trans., *The Egyptian Book of the Dead: The Book of Going Forth by Day*, ed. Eva von Dasso (San Francisco: Chronicle Books, 1994).

4. Barbara S. Lesko, "The Sky Goddess Nut," in *The Great Goddesses of Egypt* (Norman: University of Oklahoma Press, 1999), 40.

5. Ibid., 39.

6. Alexander Piankoff, "The Sky Goddess Nut and the Night Journey of the Sun," *Journal of Egyptian Archaeology* 20, nos. 1/2 (June 1934): 58.

7. Faulkner, trans., *Egyptian Book of the Dead*, 133.

8. Raymond O. Faulkner, trans., *The Ancient Egyptian Book of the Dead*, ed. Carol Andrews (Austin: University of Texas Press, 1972), 68.

Bibliography

Antelme, Ruth Schumann, and Stephanie Rossini. *Sacred Sexuality in Ancient Egypt: The Erotic Secrets of the Forbidden Papyrus*. Rochester, VT: Inner Traditions, 1999.

Baring, Anne, and Jules Cashford. *The Myth of the Goddess: Evolution of an Image*. London: Arkana Penguin Books, 1991.

Billing, Nils. "Nut—The Goddess of Life in Text and Iconography." Ph.D. diss., Uppsala University, 2003.

Bonnefoy, Yves. *Greek and Egyptian Mythologies*. Chicago: University of Chicago Press, 1991.

Capel Anne K., and Glenn E. Markoe, eds. *Mistress of the House, Mistress of Heaven: Women in Ancient Egypt*. New York: Hudson Hills Press, 1996.

C. L. R. "A Late Egyptian Sarcophagus." *The Metropolitan Museum of Art Bulletin* 9, no. 5 (May, 1914): 112–120. http://www.jstor.org/stable/3253860.

El-Sharkawy, Iman. *Ancient Egyptian Religion*. Cairo: Lehnert and Landrock, n.d.

Etz, Donald V. "A New Look At the Constellation Figures in the Celestial Diagram." *Journal of the American Research Center in Egypt* 34 (1997): 143–161.

Faulkner, Raymond O., trans. *The Ancient Egyptian Book of the Dead*. Edited by Carol Andrews. Austin: University of Texas Press, 1972.

Faulkner, Raymond O., trans. *The Ancient Egyptian Pyramid Texts*. Oxford: Clarendon Press, 1969.

Faulkner, Raymond O., trans. *The Egyptian Book of the Dead: The Book of Going Forth by Day*. Edited by Eva von Dasso. San Francisco: Chronicle Books, 1994.

Hollis, Susan Tower. "Women of Ancient Egypt and the Sky God Nut." *Journal of American Folklore* 100, no. 398 (October–December 1987): 496–503.

Lesko, Barbara S. "The Sky Goddess Nut." In *The Great Goddesses of Egypt*, 22–44. Norman: University of Oklahoma Press, 1999.

Piankoff, Alexander. "The Sky Goddess Nut and the Night Journey of the Sun." *Journal of Egyptian Archaeology* 20, nos. 1/2 (June 1934): 57–61.

Wells, Ronald. "It's Later Than You Think: The Origins of Egyptian Calendars and Their Modern Legacy." Synopsis written by Al Berens as corrected by Ronald Wells of lecture presented for ARCE/NC American Research Center in Egypt, Northern California, Berkeley California, n.d.

Wilkinson, Richard H. *The Complete Gods and Goddesses of Ancient Egypt*. London: Thames and Hudson, 2003.

17

The Queen of Sheba: Transformation of an Ancient Cosmology of Interconnectedness

Miri Hunter Haruach

Legends concerning the Queen of Sheba are retold here by weaving together the various known stories. This is followed by an examination of the story's elements to demonstrate how the Queen was used as an example, by the patriarchy, for other women and other cultures. The composite of legends is drawn from traditional East African and South Arabian folklore, as well as the Qu'ran, the *Tanakh*, the Christian Bible, and the *Kebra Nagast*.

Once upon a time, in the Land of Sheba, there lived a fierce and terrible dragon. The dragon was feared by all of the inhabitants of the land, but especially by young girls, whom the dragon always took away from their families. One day, a peasant decided that he was brave enough to fight and kill the dreaded dragon. He had a son and a daughter, and he did not want his daughter snatched away by the dragon. So off he went. He wrestled and defeated the dragon. The people of the Land of Sheba were so delighted that they made him king. He ruled for many years and then died, leaving his throne to his son. After a very short reign, the son took ill and died. Since the son had no heirs, the throne passed to his sister, Makeda.

When she was twenty-two, she heard of a wise king who lived in the north, named Solomon. One of her merchants, Tamrin, told her that he was the wisest man on earth. Makeda, wise herself, was intrigued by this information and decided to test Solomon's wisdom. She prepared her caravan and made preparations for the arduous six-month journey. Meanwhile Tamrin had started out ahead of his queen's caravan with orders to let Solomon know the queen's plans. When Solomon heard this news, he set about to make her stay a pleasant one. He told his *djinns* (magical spirit helpers) to build a palace for the Queen of Sheba.

The djinns got together to discuss the situation. They realized it was possible that Solomon would fall in love with the queen, and then there would be two rulers for whom the djinns would be forced to work. So they came up with their own plan. The djinns had heard that the queen had hairy legs. They decided to build the palace but to make floors of glass above a lake, so that when the queen saw the floor, she would be tricked into thinking that she was crossing water and then raise her skirts. Solomon would see her hairy legs and be repulsed.

On the day that the queen arrived, Solomon escorted her to her new palace. Upon seeing the floor, the queen raised her skirts and revealed her hairy legs. Solomon was so repulsed that he called upon the djinns and asked if they knew of any remedy for the queen's hirstute condition. First, the djinns said that she should shave. Solomon thought it inappropriate for a woman to shave her legs as a man shaves his face. So the djinns devised a sticky ointment called gypsum. Applied to the queen's legs, the ointment removed the hairs. This accomplished, Solomon agreed to have an audience with the queen. Makeda began to test Solomon's wisdom.

In the first test, a room was filled with thousands of flowers, handcrafted to look real and then perfumed with flower essences. Only one real flower was in the room. Makeda challenged Solomon to find it. He opened a window and allowed a bee to buzz in. The bee went directly to the real flower.

In the second test, Makeda presented male and female youths dressed alike and asked Solomon to distinguish boys from girls. Solomon had plates of roasted corn and nuts brought to the youth. The males began eating eagerly with their bare hands while the females ate slowly, revealing gloved hands.

Makeda then asked Solomon to identify the following:

Seven there are that issue, and nine that enter; two yield the draught, and one drinks. Said he to her, Seven are the days of a woman's menstruation, and nine the months of pregnancy; two are the breasts that yield the draught, and one the child that drinks it.[1]

She also asked riddles of Solomon that pertained to the story of Lot, which he answered correctly. After he successfully met her tests, the king and queen felt that they had met their equals and fell madly in love. The queen stayed for six months being wined and dined by the king. Solomon gave her the Gaza strip as a present. They discussed trade routes and territorial boundaries. This was especially important since Solomon was building a fleet of ships that could navigate the seas. The building of this fleet would have meant that the queen, whose realm had a monopoly on the land routes of the spice trade, would have faced economic downfall if Solomon completed his fleet.

At the end of six months, the queen prepared to take her leave of Solomon. The king was heartbroken and attempted to coax her into staying. She was firm, stating that she must return to her people. Solomon proposed that she share his bed with him on her last night in Jerusalem. The queen refused. The king seemed resigned to not being able to physically consummate this relationship. He prepared a lavish and spicy feast for the queen's last meal. As the two retired, the king told her that if during the night she should take anything of value from him that he would then be entitled to sleep with her. The queen assured him that there was nothing that she desired of him.

Both went to their respective beds. Solomon only pretended to sleep. In the middle of the night the queen arose from her bed to relieve her thirst from the evening's feast. As she was drinking, Solomon came up to her and said that he now had the right to have his way with her. The queen answered by saying that she had not taken anything from Solomon. He responded by asking her what could be more valuable to the king of an arid country than water. Still, the queen refused his bed and offered her handmaiden in her stead. Solomon accepted this offer. After his liaison with the handmaiden, he returned to the queen. They spent the rest of the night together. The queen left the next morning with her entourage for her homeland of Sheba.

The Ethiopian story continues to say that the queen returned to her homeland and gave birth to a son, Menelek. When Menelek came of age, he went to visit his father. Knowing from a revelatory dream that his kingdom was doomed because he had chosen to worship the deities of his wives rather than the one god of Israel, Solomon renamed him David II, after his own father, and anointed him King of Zion. In a Yemeni story, the queen's brother was too young to be king when their father died. Upon returning to her home, the queen abdicated her throne to her brother. In both stories, there is clearly a passing of women's power to a male.

There are variations of the above story. The first is a folktale from Tigray, a province in Northern Ethiopia. It says that there was a girl named Eteye Azeb (Queen of the South), who was to be sacrificed to a dragon. Just as she was to be killed, seven saints appeared and saved her life. The saints also killed the dragon and in this process some of the dragon's blood dropped onto the girl's foot. The foot became a donkey's hoof (or perhaps a dragon's foot). The townspeople were so delighted with the death of the dragon that they made the girl queen. Eventually the Queen traveled to Solomon who cured her foot. Another Ethiopian folktale states a girl was sacrificed annually to the dragon, which was finally killed by the brave queen-to-be.[2]

Another legend regarding the Queen's hoofed foot says that once there was a mother bird, the *neser*, whose child was taken off by a predator. The mother bird flew to the Garden of Eden and took a branch from the Tree of Life. She carried the limb in her beak to where her child was held, then dropped the limb onto the predator and killed him. She then took her child to safety. Years later the Queen of Sheba was traveling to Solomon's court. Solomon, having heard about her foot, wanted to cure her. He ordered the bird to lay the branch from the Tree of Life across a small pond. When the Queen arrived, she touched her hoofed foot to the branch and her foot was transformed.

Another tale tells how Adam, on his deathbed, persuaded his son Seth to return to the Garden of Eden and to beg Gabriel for the oil of mercy. Gabriel took a branch from the tree of which Adam and Eve had eaten and gave it to Seth. The tree had dried up since the couple had left the Garden. When Seth returned to Adam, Adam had already died. Seth planted the branch on Adam's grave. There it grew into a mighty tree.

> Solomon cut it down to build, but it always changed shape and was thrown down as a bridge. When the Queen came to cross the water, she knelt in adoration at the sacred wood and prophesized that it would be used to nail a world savior who would defile and end the Jewish heritage.[3]

The Queen forms a bridge: a bridge between the Old Testament and the New Testament; a bridge between the past and the future. She serves as the link, to what was and what is.

The Elements

The dragon story is a remnant of a matrifocal culture. The Queen's slaying of the dragon parallels her statement from the *Kebra Nagast*, that a woman will never rule Ethiopia again.[4] It shows the changeover from matrifocal to patriarchal culture. Women's knowledge and power are not deemed important by the emerging patriarchy. In short, she herself puts an end to the matristic society by killing the dragon (abdicating the throne to a son or a brother). In the patriarchal overlay of the Queen's story, she is shown as a betrayer of other women as she clearly states that no other women will rule. With this betrayal, women in her realm became subjugated to the expansion of patriarchal culture.

In another legend, the queen-to-be is rescued from the dragon by Christian saints. After her rescue she is crowned. Undoubtedly, her allegiance would be to those that saved her life. Psychologically, to betray or in any way threaten the loss of those who have saved your life would be dangerous. Even though the saints rescued her, it is never mentioned whether or not Makeda had a positive or negative connection to the dragon. Since the dragon was worshiped in premonotheistic Ethiopia,[5] Makeda's "rescue" consisted of replacing the values of premonotheism with the values of her "rescuers."

Another version of the Queen of Sheba story states that each year the Queen saved a girl from being sacrificed to the dragon. This is another indication of societal changes. The original sacrifice would have been the king/consort of the Queen. In pagan cultures, each year the Queen selects a king/consort, who is sacrificed during the summer solstice. It should also be noted that pagan sacrifice is symbolic, not literal, and represents the waning of the light of the sun.

The adult Sun King embraces the Queen of Summer in the love that is death because it is so complete that all dissolves into the single song of ecstasy that moves the worlds. Then the Lord of the Light dies and sets sails across the dark seas of time, searching for the isle of light that is rebirth.[6]

Important in interpreting this story is the way in which Makeda's last evening with Solomon is always romanticized. Solomon prepared a lavish going-away celebration for her, but only with the intent to trick her into his bed. Not only does she take the religion of Solomon to the Land of Sheba, but she also abdicates her throne to her son who was conceived through an act of coercion.

The Queen has hairy legs or, in some versions, an animal's hoof for a foot. The hair must be removed or the queen's deformed foot cured.

Both instances suggest that the Queen was magical. "Curing" her is another way of taking her power. The power of a woman's hair has been linked to love spells as well as forces for creation and destruction. From folklore to St. Paul to the Rastafarians, hair is synonymous with character. The first book of Corinthians states that hair symbolizes strength, the ability to control spirits and wealth. A Rastafarian story states that one should not keep a lock on his or her money, but one should keep locks on his or her head. Witches were known by their hair. Medusa's hair was said to be made of serpents. To remove Makeda's hair was to take her power.

The above collage of tales represents themes and ideas that have been told regarding the Queen of Sheba. Within these stories, her original role appears as priestess to her people. The importance of the Land of Sheba and of the Queen herself cannot be denied. Why else were she and her people chronicled by all three major monotheistic religions? She is used in these stories as an example of patriarchal womanhood. In each story she submits, her power is removed, she is coerced into bed with her conqueror, she gives birth to a new order. But behind all this is the notion that this woman and the women who ruled before her were powerful—too powerful to coexist with patriarchy.

The History of the Sabean/Sheban People

The Sabeans began in what is now Ethiopia and spread out in four directions: Arabia to the north, the Sudan to the west, India to the east, and south throughout Africa. There are legacies of the Queen of Sheba in places such as Zimbabwe, Chad, India, and Nigeria. The Sabeans, who went into Arabia, settled there. Those that traveled to the west became wanderers, spending just enough time in a region to leave behind a cultural or religious legacy. Eventually the wandering Sabeans traveled into Egypt and Canaan and Sumer, then made their way into southern Arabia, where they encountered members of their original tribe. They settled there until they were forced by invading tribes from the north to move back across the Red Sea. They left Arabia for the city of Axum. From Axum, they moved further south into the mountains of Gondar, finally settling in modern-day Ethiopia.

Sertima gives the following history for Queen Makeda, the Queen of Sheba: "The dynasty that Makeda belonged to, according to tradition, was established in Ethiopia in 1370 BC. It was instituted by Za Besi Angabo and lasted 350 years." Sertima further states that Makeda followed her grandfather and father on the throne. Her brother, Prince Noural, died at an early age leaving the throne to his sister. Makeda assumed the throne in 1005 BCE. She ruled for fifty years over a land of unknown size. "The various lands ascribed to her empire included parts of Upper Egypt, Ethiopia, parts of Arabia, Syria, Armenia, India and the whole region between the Mediterranean and the Erythraean Sea."[7] During her reign, she established extensive trade relations to maintain the economic status of her empire. Her throne was passed on to her son Menelek I, first ruler of the Solomonic dynasty. The Solomonic dynasty consisted of rulers of Ethiopia who were descended from the lineage of Makeda and King Solomon of Israel. The last ruler of the Solomonic dynasty was Haille Selassie, who died in 1975 CE. Makeda died in 955 BCE. The ruling city of the Solomonic dynasty was, by then, Axum. Axum lies in the modern-day Tigray region of Ethiopia.

In *The African Origin of Civilization*, Cheikh Anta Diop states:

the Adites, descendants of Cush from the line of Ham, lived originally in Arabia. Cheddade, a son of Ad and builder of the legendary "Earthly Paradise" mentioned in the Koran, belongs to the epoch called that of the "First Adites." This empire was destroyed in the 18th century BC by an invasion of coarse, white Jectanide tribes, who apparently came to settle among the Blacks.[8]

Diop states that the Adites soon regained power and that the Jectanides were absorbed into the Adite cultural and political climate. The saga continues in the eighth century BCE when the Jectanides again seized power and control over the Adites. This, according to Diop, occurred at the same time that the Assyrians were gaining control over Babylon. Diop asserts that the Babylonians were also Cushites. After the Jectanide victory in Arabia, many of the Adites crossed the Red Sea and settled in what is modern-day Eritrea, while

the other remained in Arabia, taking refuge in the mountains of Hadramaut and elsewhere. This is the source of the Arab proverb: 'As divided as the Sabeans,' and why Southern Arabia and Ethiopia became inseparable linguistically and ethnographically.[9]

He continues:

During the reign of the Queen of Sheba in the 10th century BC, the land enjoyed an unparalleled time of prosperity. Perhaps because the Queen of Sheba and her people worshipped the Sun, the Moon, the stars and the planets, they were able to use their appreciation of these natural elements in their own kingdom."[10]

Sheba was rich and prosperous, a prosperity due to monopoly over the spice trade and a strategic location around the trade routes to and from countries further east. When ships began to navigate the Red Sea, the Sabean monopoly along the trade route was broken, thus ending their economic success and cultural prosperity.

Despite the decline of the Sabean culture, the story of the Queen of Sheba survived, holding a connection to a lost matrifocal culture. In Ethiopia, her greatness has been codified into a national document that has shaped the history and culture of a nation. Demonized by Christianity, Islam, and Judaism, she was nonetheless a queen who held sway over the greatest king of Israel, Solomon. It was to her heir that Solomon transferred the Ark of the Covenant, a container built to hold the original Ten Commandments given to Moses and the Israelites at Mount Sinai. Wherever the Ark was stored was the seat or the home of the Jewish people, the people of Zion. In Islam, the Queen submits to the God of Solomon, not by choice, but by trickery.

Language contains and maintains cultural elements that clearly depict a link, a code, to a prepatriarchal time. The ancient language of the Queen of Sheba's realm was Himyaritic, which evolved into the East African language called Ge'ez. Ge'ez is the parent language of the modern Ethiopian language Amharic. Amharic is the language of the ruling class of Ethiopia called the Amharas. All of these languages are considered to be part of the Semitic family of languages, which also include Hebrew, Aramaic, and Arabic. The word *Saba/Sheba* is analogous to the word *Sabbath*, the day of rest observed by all three major monotheistic religions. It is also the name of the seventh day of the week in Hebrew. The word *Sheba* has been translated into English as "south." This, however, is an incomplete translation that occurred because the Land of Sheba was south of Israel as well as of Europe. The following analysis suggests a more accurate definition. Semitic words have three-letter roots. The root of *Sheba* (transliterated into Latin letters) is Sh (s), B(v), and ah. This root corresponds to the word *Sheba/Saba*.

The following words have that same three-letter root: *Sabbatical*, an extended period of rest; *Shavua*, Hebrew word meaning week; *Sheva*, Hebrew word for the number seven; *Saba* Amharic word for the number seventy; and *Shayba*, Arabic word meaning old woman.

According to Ethiopian Jewish tradition Sabbath or *Shabat* is not a day or a number, but the name of the daughter of God. The Ethiopian Jewish book, entitled *Teezaza Sanbat* (Commandment of the Sabbath), tells of the creation, but primarily the book is focused on the "greatness and glory of the Sabbath of Israel, her adventures, acts, punitive expeditions and intercession with God. She is described as the daughter of God, a divine princess, to whom all angels pay homage and who is exceedingly loved by God Himself."[11]

Compare this to the description of Sumerian Nisaba, goddess of grain, writing, and wisdom (see Vol. 2, Chap. 1). The prefix *Ni-* means "Lady" or "Queen," so *Ni-Saba* means Queen or Lady of Sheba. It was the role of this goddess to give wisdom to kings. Further, Nisaba is depicted as the "Lady of the Mountain." Numerous hymns were composed in her honor that describe the totality of her functions:

> O Lady coloured like the stars of heaven, holding the lapis lazuli tablet born in the great sheepfold by the divine Earth . . . born in wisdom by the Great Mountain (Enlil), honest woman, chief scribe of heaven, record-keeper of Enlil, all knowing sage of the gods.[12]

Again looking at the Sumerian texts of hymns to Nisaba, we find references to her as a woman born in the mountains; "You who are granted the most complex wisdom"; "dragon emerging in glory at the festival"; and Aruru (mother goddess) of the land.

As mentioned earlier, the word *Sheba/Saba* is also connected with the number seven, which has a long, complex history as a spiritual number. The Pythagoreans, who considered the number seven holy and divine, specifically state that Sheba (the number 70) is divine and holy. Makeda's title, the Queen of Sheba, refers to a tradition of mysticism and sacredness. Sheba, Saba, Ni-Saba are all names of the goddess. The Sabeans of Arabia and East Africa, the Sumerians, and even the Israelites and Canaanites worshiped this figure in one form or another. Bathsheba, mother of King Solomon, may be read as one of her priestesses, for her name translates as "daughter of Sheba."

The consciousness of the Queen of Sheba is emerging at the beginning of the new millennium as human consciousness as a planet is turning or re-turning to values that exemplify the concepts of respect and honor for the feminine, for nature and for the planet. There is a desire to re-turn to the ancient cosmology of interconnectedness.

Notes

Portions of this chapter are adapted from articles written by Miri Hunter Haruach for http://www.projectsheba.com.

1. Barbara Black Koltuv, *Solomon and Sheba* (York Beach, ME: Nicolas-Hays, 1993), 84.

2. Joachim Chwaszcza, *Yemen* (Singapore: APA Publications, 1992), 84, 85.

3. James B. Pritchard, ed., *Solomon and Sheba* (New York: Praeger, 1974), 21.

4. Miguel Brooks, trans., *Kebra Nagast: The True Ark of the Covenant* (Lawrenceville, NJ: Red Sea Press, 1995), 25.

5. Graham Hancock, *The Sign and the Seal* (London: British Printing Company, 1992), 141.

6. Starhawk, *The Spiral Dance* (San Francisco: Harper and Row, 1979).

7. Ivan Van Sertima, ed., *Black Women in Antiquity* (New Brunswick, NJ: Transaction Publishers, 1988), 16, 17.

8. Cheikh Anta Diop, *The African Origin of Civilization: Myth or Reality* (Chicago: Lawrence Hill Books, 1974), 124.

9. Ibid., 125.

10. Koltuv, *Solomon and Sheba*, 29.

11. Wolf Leslau, *Falasha Anthology* (New Haven, CT: Yale University Press, 1951), 19.

12. Tikva Fryman-Kensky, *In the Wake of the Goddesses* (New York: Fawcett Columbine, 1992), 42.

Bibliography

Budge, E. A. Wallis, trans. *The Queen of Sheba and Her Only Son Menyelek*. London: Oxford University Press, 1932.

Chwaszcza, Joachim. *Yemen*. Singapore: APA Publications, 1992.

Diop, Cheikh Anta, and Mercer Cook, trans. and eds. *The African Origin of Civilization: Myth or Reality*. Chicago: Lawrence Hill Books, 1974.

Doe, Brian. *Southern Arabia*. New York: McGraw-Hill, 1971.

Finch, Charles, et al. *African Origins of the Major World Religions*. London: Karnak House, 1988.

Fryman-Kensky, Tikva. *In the Wake of the Goddesses*. New York: Fawcett Columbine, 1992.

Gray, John. *Near Eastern Mythology*. New York: Peter Bedrick Books, 1969.

Hancock, Graham. *The Sign and the Seal*. London: The British Printing Company, 1992.

Jackson, John G. *Ethiopia and the Origin of Civilization*. Baltimore: Black Classic Press, 1939.

Koltuv, Barbara. *Black Solomon and Sheba*. York Beach, ME: Nicolas-Hays, 1993.

Lassner, Jacob. *Demonizing the Queen of Sheba*. Chicago: University of Chicago Press, 1993.

Leslau, Wolf. *Falasha Anthology*. New Haven, CT: Yale University Press, 1951.

Marcus, Harold. *A History of Ethiopia*. Berkeley: University of California Press, 1994.

Mercier, Jacques. *Ethiopian Magic Scrolls*. New York: George Braziller, 1979.

Patai, Raphael. *The Hebrew Goddess*. Detroit: Wayne State University Press, 1978.

Phillips, Wendell. *Qataban and Sheba: Exploring the Ancient Kingdoms on the Biblical Spice Routes of Arabia*. New York: Harcourt, Brace and Co., 1955.

Pritchard, James B., ed. *Solomon and Sheba*. New York: Praeger, 1974.

Sertima, Ivan Van, ed. *Black Women in Antiquity*. New Brunswick, NJ: Transaction Publishers, 1988.

Starhawk. *The Spiral Dance*. San Francisco: Harper and Row, 1979.

Townes, Emilie M., ed. *Embracing the Spirit: Womanist Perspectives on Hope, Salvation and Transformation*. Maryknoll, NY: Orbis Books, 1997.

Westcott, W. Wynn. *The Occult Power of Numbers*. Hollywood, CA: Newcastle Publishing, 1984.

18

The Goddess Auset: An Ancient Egyptian Spiritual Framework

C. S'thembile West

The Pyramid Texts, "the most ancient body of literature known," were "inscribed on the walls of pyramids and pharaonic tombs during the Fifth and Sixth Dynasties of the Old Kingdom (2464–2355 BCE)," according to Normandi Ellis, translator of the ideograms referred to as the "Holy Writing"[1] called *Mdw* (word) *Ntr* (god) or *medu neter* (scholars agreed to add vowels to facilitate pronunciation) in ancient Egypt, known as Kemet to its residents. Scholars who have studied these representational ideograms offered diverse interpretations. In light of the contextual nuances of Kemetic life, specific philosophical and spiritual concepts will be highlighted herein.[2]

Background and Foreground

The story of the goddess Auset provides a window to better understand the fundamental philosophy of Kemetic society and the critical role that women played in the maintenance and renewal of the social order. Auset's story contains metaphysical and ethical concepts, creative and transformative, that reflect Nile Valley civilization's gifts to world culture. According to linguist, historian, and anthropologist Cheikh Anta Diop, Nubia gave birth to Egypt:

This is quite logical if one considers the likelihood that the Nile Valley was peopled by a progressive descent of the Black peoples from the region of the Great Lakes—the series of lakes in the heart of Africa that lie south of the Nile River, particularly Lake Victoria and Lake Albert, as well as Lake Tana which run into the White Nile and Blue Nile respectively—the cradle of *Homo sapiens sapiens.*[3]

Lake Tana, situated in the Ethiopian Mountains, floods every summer and causes the erosion and movement of fertile silt into the Nile Valley.

University of Chicago researcher Keith Seele, supported by UNESCO, excavated the Qostul cemetery in Nubia in 1963–1964, before the construction of the Aswan Dam and the flooding of the area. The remnants of Nubian culture found there validate that Nubia, located south of contemporary Egypt, was indeed home to a rich civilization. The excavation that Diop chronicles is important because it uncovered essential markers for royalty in Nubia that would also appear in ancient Egypt, called Kemet and spelled *Kmt* in ancient times. The engravings on the incense burner or censer revealed, according to Diop, that "Nubian monarchy is the oldest in the history of humanity." And Nubian monarchal lineage was vested in the queen-mother. Hence, some scholars have come to understand "the matriarchal essence of Egyptian royalty and the importance of the role of the Queen-mother in Nubia, Egypt, and the rest of Black Africa."[4] Auset embodies the concept of the queen-mother.

As protectors of the royal line, women played a critical role in the systematic maintenance of upper-class life in ancient Egypt. It was not unusual for a young girl to marry her brother or a half brother by the same father to preserve royal lineage. The story of the goddess Auset mirrors this practice.

In Pharaonic Egypt, the pharaoh was perceived as a representative of the divine on earth. As such, his presence was a reminder of the sacred trust, governed by the core, social, ethical, life principle of *ma'at*—truth, justice, beauty, balance—that rulers pledged to their constituents. In that Auset restores the body of her brother/lover Ausar, through perseverance and cooperation with the ancestral and spirit worlds, her story demonstrates the central role of ma'at in ancient Egyptian culture as well as women's critical contribution to sustaining not only the social order, but also life itself. The myth is an anchor for social relations as well as complementary relations between women and men.

Framing the Context of Scholarship on Ancient Africa

Rarely does one find reference to Auset in written records of mythology from ancient Egypt in the Common Era (CE). Only in the highly politicized writings of African-centered scholars, which gained recognition in the late 20th century, does Auset's name appear. Many readers may recognize Auset by the popular Greek referent, Isis, a name that reflects Greece's conquest of Nubia in the fourth century CE.

Contemporary scholarship continues to use Greek referents for classical African civilization, an emphasis that illuminates the power of conquerors to identify, name, and define cultural markers, as well as to shape the discourse of conquered, often-devalued populations and cultures. As such, it is necessary to provide a framework for the story of Auset. She is part of the critical project to reconstruct and value the philosophical legacy, worldview, and social perspective of ancient Egypt or Kemet.

Perhaps best known for the creation of Kwanzaa ideology in 1966, philosopher and African-centered scholar Maulana Karenga provides a contrast to the standard or European-centered approach to discussions of early civilization,

> a privileging of Greece and Judeo-Christian emphases is defined, as suggested above by its assumption of cultural and religious superiority and its correlative assumption that ancient Egypt's religion is essentially a pagan project, undeveloped, prelogical, mythopoeic and without serious cultural depth or intellectual and ethical insight.[5]

Ancient Egypt has been perceived primarily as a place for archaeological study and inquiry rather than a "suitable subject for modern religious and ethical discourse."[6] This chapter seeks to remedy this historical reality by emphasizing that larger-than-life, meta-mythological characters, with origins in ancient Egypt, are best understood within the worldview of their architects, the Kemetic peoples. Moreover, the goddess Auset, with her definitive human qualities, is meant to be distinctively metaphorical and, thereby, easily integrated into the daily lives of the people. Traditional Kemetic depictions of gods and goddesses function in the service of everyday life; in this way, their status is elevated beyond that of myth. Their personal qualities are meant to provide examples of the moral standards for daily living.

The Story Begins: Ausar as God/Man

Akbar refers to the "Myth of Ausir and Black Awakening."[7] The story begins with Ausar (referenced as Ausir in some sources), who had divine origin. Not unlike other myth-based, human-like and simultaneously god-like personalities in ancient Egypt, Ausar came from heaven and lived among humans. Ausar was the first to teach religion and cultivation of the land as well as science, for in Kemet science and religion were merged. Schools were housed in temples because spirituality and knowledge were perceived interdependently. Every pursuit was sacred. A knowledgeable person was a spiritual person and conversely, a spiritual person had highly developed intellectual skills. As such, it was appropriate that Ausar reign over both science (i.e., farming) and religion (that is, spirituality).

Ausar was the first "teacher of worship of the Gods." However, it is extremely important to understand that "gods" to Kemetic peoples referred to the *neters* or forces of nature. It is also critical to note that the *Mdu Ntr* or *Medu Neter*, a pictorial or diagrammatic communication, was the script that the Greeks called hieroglyphs. This concept is important because of the intricate relationship among neters, human beings, stories, and rituals in an African-centered social setting. Moreover, Ra Un Nefer Amen confirms that the neters refer to both seen and unseen phenomena, the subjective and objective realms in which energy/matter are formless and "ordered into forms or objects," respectively.[8] Ausar understood the common and the "celestial." Hence, Ausar is a meta-character in the worldview constructed by the ancients. Ausar embodies ma'at and, thereby, represents good, right action, justice, and order.

Dichotomies of good versus evil abound in the story. For Ausar, the embodiment of heaven and earth, his antagonist is Set ("who later became Satan," "Shaitan" or "Devil").[9] Set, allegedly Ausar's twin brother, whose nature was oppositional to good, wanted to destroy him. As the foremost enemy of truth, Set is the embodiment of deception, trickery, and falsehood. Akbar notes that Ausar was led to his death through trickery. Set threw a party and invited Ausar as well as seventy-two co-conspirators. Then Set fashioned a chest—literally a coffin—specifically to match Ausar's dimensions. Each of the guests was invited to see if they could fit into the chest. Ausar was the last to attempt it. The conspirators sealed the chest and threw Ausar into the river where he drowned, and the currents took the coffin out to sea. The drowning of Ausar introduced the concept of death into the world. Finally, a mighty tree "consumed" the chest and grew around it. That tree became so beautiful that a king noticed it, cut it down, and carried it off to his land. The king built a castle around the tree, the actual "tomb of Ausar."

The Goddess Auset's Family Origins

Linguist and historian Yosef ben-Jochannan relates how the goddess of the sky, Nut, and Geb had five children: Ausar, Auset, Set, Nephthys, and Horus the Elder. Ausar, eldest son of Geb, inherited kingship of the earth. Auset, Ausar's sister, had been loved by him, even in the womb.

After Ausar's imprisonment in the coffin, Auset, "the spirit of truth, comfort, diligence, perseverance, and determination,"[10] according to Akbar, sought her beloved's body. Her search ended when she found the tree that held the coffin of Ausar. She claimed the body. However, Set, the symbol of evil waiting to challenge good, discovered that Auset had found Ausar's body. Set found it and vowed to "mutilate" Ausar. Set cut the body into fourteen pieces and threw them into the river.

Undaunted by Set's treachery, Auset embarked on a search for the scattered pieces of Ausar's body. With the inexplicable tenacity that she represents, Auset miraculously found all the body parts, except the phallus, allegedly swallowed by a fish. Nonetheless, with the help of Tehuti (Thoth in Greek), the dismembered phallus was restored. Ausar, in his restored form, was then resurrected into the heavens where he became the judge of the souls of those who left the earth.

Variations of the Ausar/Auset Myth

According to ben-Jochannan, after Auset found Ausar's body, Set grabbed it and cut it up, then flung the pieces all over Egypt. The pieces of Ausar's body became relics for shrines in ancient Egypt. Then, ben-Jochannan asserts, Auset and her sister Nephthys searched the land, retrieving the pieces and reuniting them with the help of Anubis, the god of mummification. In this version of the complex myth, Auset took the form of a kite and flew over the land in search of Ausar's scattered pieces. It is not clear how her sister accompanied her. Nonetheless, Ausar's body was restored, and he was resurrected.

Greek historian and biographer Plutarch (40–120 CE), telling the story more than 2000 years after its origin, alleged that Ausar's body washed up on the shore of Syria, at Byblos. He too said that a tree grew around Ausar's body. Unlike the original version, Plutarch suggests that the king of Byblos noticed the tree and took it. According to Plutarch, Auset gained favor with the king and persuaded him to allow her to take the body of her husband/brother back to Egypt. This version of the myth does not make clear how Auset found the body.

Auset: Message and Meaning

Despite diverse interpretations of an essentially oral tale, the metaphorical intent of the original myth remains intact. Dependence on communal relations to support viable existence was integral to ancient Egyptian thought and to the story. Sustaining communal life with dynamism and vitality depended upon human negotiation of seen and unseen forces, objective and subjective realities, nature and beliefs. Any discussion of Auset's significance must be balanced by a meaningful interpretation of Ausar's behaviors, to reflect the complementary between and the interdependence of social values and behavior, a tangible demonstration of ma'at in the community.

Auset represents truth, nurturance, and the persistence of the human spirit, while Ausar embodies the spirit of rejuvenation and regeneration. However, his restoration is impossible without Auset's determination, knowledge, and alliance with her sister Nephthys, as well as the powerful Tehuti, who assisted in restoring Ausar's phallus. Ra Un Nefer Amen says, "Tehuti is the source of the intuition that shows the way to achieve the equilibrium between the interest of the whole, and of the person."[11] In this context, Auset's understanding that Ausar's body must be completely reconstructed, to restore balance in the social order heightens awareness that community viability and renewal depend upon complete regeneration, wholeness.

With Ausar's return to wholeness, Auset's personal desire is achieved and balance in the community is restored. Consequently, a critical balancing ma'at returns. The restoration of harmony within the human family supports balance in the larger universe. In sum, the myth demonstrates the interdependence of humans and gods, reason and passion, seen and unseen forces. The metatext of the myth is best understood in the balanced matrix of birth, rebirth, renewal, and daily life in ancient Egypt. Within the nexus of a social system that seeks to balance universal, political, social, and personal domains in the context of everyday living, Auset and Ausar represent benchmarks for human behavior as understood in ancient Egypt. Auset illuminates the critical value of family, the extended family of spirits and ancestors, and community coherence. Her actions confirm that no bond is more important than kinship ties, and that no value is greater than love.

Contemporary Reflections of Auset/Ausar

Ra Un Nefer Amen leads the Ausar Auset Society, a community-based spiritual organization designed to promote effective, spiritual living based on Kemetic principles, in African diaspora neighborhoods in New York City. He distinguishes between spiritual cultivation and religion: "I am using the concept of 'spiritual cultivation' as an alternative to the concepts of 'religion' and 'religious systems'."[12] Nefer Amen argues that religious systems and worth can be measured by the "degree of spiritual growth" among the constituents. Spiritual growth is evident in how one lives, which has everything to do with the cosmology—worldview and perspective—that undergirds a philosophy of being in the world or ontology among ancient Africans.

Both Karenga and Nefer Amen concur that the ethical mandate—ma'at—articulated by ancient Egyptians exists in the context of an African cosmology. An African worldview weds human beings—young and old, those yet-to-be-born and those who have passed on—with animals, plants, and objects in a never-ending cycle of interdependent energy exchange. Human interaction with the diverse elements of the physical/objective and spiritual/subjective worlds created a profoundly spiritual orientation for Africans. This spiritual orientation to living is a pervasive presence in the African diasporic continuum.

Karenga agrees with diverse scholars that "substantial myth" is present in ancient Egyptian religion as in Judaism, Christianity, Hindu, and Chinese traditions: "What I am posing as problematic is the tendency to overstress myth and cult and deny ancient Egypt's genuine theology and ethics in the process." Embedded in the myths and stories are core life principles and social values. "The need, then, is to treat such narratives and propositions as is done with Jewish and Christian myths, i.e., as sources of philosophical insight and as points of departure for developmental discourse in religion and ethics."[13] As such, the story of goddess Auset and her brother/husband offers meta-ethical as well as practical lessons for daily living. A brief interrogation of an African cosmology provides the frame and context for the messages embedded in Auset's story.

African Cosmology: A Foundation for Constructive Living

African cosmology focuses on a balance among natural, human, and supernatural forces. The interdependent relationship between humankind and the environment is perceived as normative and instructional. According to John S. Mbiti, an African way of being or ontology is culturally constructed around five critical components: god/spirits, ancestors, human beings, animals and plants, and finally inanimate objects. The universe is viewed from the perspective of humans. Through rituals, both rites of passage and daily practices, human beings order, manipulate, and direct the varying components of being in the world. By honoring life force or energy in the natural world—trees, plants, and animals that are sacrificed for human survival—human beings facilitate balance between their daily lives and nature. In the context of ritual, song-dance-chant that includes stories, songs, prose, poetry, dance, and drama, humans acknowledge their interdependence with nature. Moreover, god, ancestors, humans, plants, animals, and objects infused with life force through human manipulation constitute the circle of life. Hence life, in the most traditional African sense, never ends. Death is simply another beginning, and those-yet-to-be-born are part of the living.

In such a cosmology, human behaviors either support or disrupt harmonious living, coexistence and peace. The songs, the dances, the chants, call and response, poetic orations, and multilayered musical instrumentations with their rhythms, sounds, and nuances are meant to enhance, heighten, and intensify the energy inherent in natural phenomenon. Cultural rituals are intended to support daily living. The day-to-day practices of human beings are meant to reflect the co-creative enterprise of living with the spirit/god-force in them. In fact, the refinement of a human being's ability to negotiate natural phenomenon in ways that support ongoing spiritual cultivation within daily community life is, indeed, testimony to an African cosmology, worldview and perspective.

In sum, the cosmology functions in the service of daily life. As such, the idea of spirit—an aspect of the divine—is intricately woven into every fiber of daily life. In this context, the goddess Auset's ability to act in consort with spirit or spirit representatives, as she demonstrates keen human insights, mirrors an ancient Egyptian cosmological vision. The spiritual and the secular are not at odds in an African-centered worldview. It is in a nexus where the sacred and secular meet that human beings can reach the height of spiritual cultivation. This concept of human life as an ongoing negotiation with spirit/s as well as natural phenomenon illustrates how the ethical center of ancient Egyptian society, ma'at, gives shape to daily human activities.

Myth as Metatext: A Context for Constructive Living

Myths are often thought to present guiding principles for existence as they make sense of human life and emotion. African-centered scholar and psychologist Na'im Akbar says that contemporary humans have "lost an appreciation for the power of the myth."[14] Like Karenga, who suggests that myth served as a source of philosophy and ethics within Kemet, Akbar highlights the value of myth and emphasizes how it has been constructed not only as an organizing principle of ancient African life, but also as a profound demonstration of the seamless merging of philosophy and science among ancient Africans.

Akbar discusses how the ancients examined and thought about the universe, god, and nature. He explored the implications of these realms in science and daily life. Akbar notes: "The brilliant minds of those people pursued science as far as it could take them. They finally found that science ran out. They took theology and philosophy as far as they could take them, and they found out that all logic ran out." In sum, Akbar postulates that the ancients surmised: "If we can't put these descriptions into reality, let's see if our descriptions can transcend reality."[15] Hence, the ancients created myths to function as guides to understand existence and daily life. Mythmaking was central to an ethical social system that promotes self-reflection, identity formation, and harmonious communal living. In the Auset/Ausar metatext, the moral qualities and behaviors of the goddess Auset are meant to be guides for constructive living.

African Humanism and Ma'at

Herodotus noted in his annals that people with "burnt skin and woolly hair" developed Nubian culture. At the confluence of the Blue and White Nile rivers, deep in the heart of Africa, Nubian civilization spawned the cosmological and ethical principles of ancient Egyptian civilization. Ma'at was the cornerstone of the sociospiritual structure. The unifying idea of ma'at acts as a bridge connecting god, society, nature, and the universe. These critical connections support the philosophical foundation for daily life in traditional African cultures. In community settings, actions are judged by how well they enhance community coherence, relationship viability, kinship ties, and the ethical mandate of ma'at that undergirds all actions. In sum, ma'at is a composite life principle that guides and sets a standard for right behavior.

Ways of knowing and being in the world, directly influenced by cosmology—the ideological concepts about how one ought to behave—require an ongoing balance among spiritual, intellectual, creative, and natural phenomena in an African worldview. In ancient Egypt, so-called rational thinking acknowledged the interdependence of spiritual, natural, and relational contexts and was illuminated in rituals. By contrast, in the Platonic and Aristotelian tradition, reason is separate from concepts of spirit. Moreover, the hierarchal relationship of a mind/body dichotomy re-enforces the separation between intellectual and physical, reason and passion, spirit and nature. Auset embodies reason and passion, spirit and nature and, thereby, personified not only the presence of spirit in human interaction, but also the profound connection between seen and unseen forces.

The story of Auset demonstrates how human beings can wed spiritual beliefs with the driving force of ma'at. Auset, like the body of a dancer in the nexus of song-dance-chant communication, becomes sacred when she engages with Tehuti to connect the dismembered parts of her beloved. In this context, sacred and secular merge, one indistinguishable from the other. Wisdom culled from observations of natural phenomena like sunrise, sunset, weather and plant cycles, birth and death, demonstrate and support a mandate for human beings to act responsibly in relation to the environment and other human beings.

In bringing human action into alignment with natural phenomena, African humanism fosters living in harmony with nature, other human beings, and unseen forces. No hierarchal distinctions are made between the living, those yet-to-be-born, and ancestors. Hence, diverse realms are joined philosophically, physically, and emotionally in the daily lives of the people. Daily rituals are linked not only to maintaining a balance between humans and unseen forces, but also humans and ancestors, those who have passed on. Rituals of song-dance-chant serve as integral reminders of the importance of family legacies, kinship ties, and intergenerational links. In this worldview, ma'at functions as a strong organizing principle.

In conclusion, scholar Theophile Obenga, whose work highlights the extensive borrowing of myth and legends from Africa by the Greeks, articulates the complexity of ma'at and provides an overarching paradigm or model to understand its function as an organizing principle of daily living. Obenga states that "the notion of Maat is complex and rich" and notes four areas of manifestation: universal, political, social and personal domains. Ma'at reflects the "totality of existence";[16] it is right action and antithetical to injustice; it underscores "duty in a communal context"; it acknowledges cosmic order in oneself. Ma'at represents the spiritual and the divine, as well as the social, physical, and tangible components of existence. As such, its conceptualization, in the context of everyday life, reflects a holistic approach to living within African cultures. The goddess Auset epitomizes this perspective. The journey Auset undertakes to restore the dismembered body of Ausar illuminates how personal integrity and perseverance are vital components of social cohesion, as well as personal development and spiritual cultivation. As such, Auset's story provides a comprehensive example of African humanism, ma'at in action.

Notes

1. Asa G. Hilliard, Nia Damali, and Larry Williams, *The Teachings of Ptahhotep: The Oldest Book in the World* (Atlanta: Blackwood Press, 1987), 8.

2. The concepts and explanations discussed herein reflect the scholarship of Cheik Anta Diop, Maulana Karenga, Normandi Ellis, Ra Un Nefer Amen, Yosef ben-Johannan, Theophile Obenga, and Ivan Van Sertima.

3. Cheikh Anta Diop, *Civilization or Barbarism: An Authentic Anthropology* (New York: Lawrence Hill Books, 1991), 103.

4. Ibid., 105.

5. Maulana Karenga, *Maat, the Moral Ideal in Ancient Egypt: A Study in Classical African Ethics* (New York: Routledge, 2004), 13.

6. Ibid.

7. Na'im Akbar, *Light from Ancient Africa* (Tallahassee, FL: Mind Productions and Associates, 1994), 49.

8. Ra Un Nefer Amen, *Metu Neter: The Great Oracle of Tehuti and the Egyptian System of Spiritual Cultivation* (New York: Khamit Corp., 1990), 1:49.

9. Akbar, *Light from Ancient Africa*, 49.

10. Ibid.

11. Amen, *Metu Neter*, 245.

12. Ibid., 125.

13. Karenga, *Maat*, 15.

14. Akbar, *Light from Ancient Africa*, 47.

15. Ibid.

16. Theophile Obenga, *Ancient Egypt and Black Africa* (London: Karnak House, 1992).

Bibliography

Akbar, Na'im. *Light from Ancient Africa*. Tallahassee, FL: Mind Productions and Associates, 1994.

Amen, Ra Un Nefer. *Metu Neter: The Great Oracle of Tehuti and the Egyptian System of Spiritual Cultivation*. Vol. 1. Bronx, NY: Khamit Corp., 1990.

Ani, Marimba [Dona Richards]. *Let the Circle Be Unbroken: The Implications of African Spirituality in the Diaspora*. Trenton, NJ: Red Sea Press, 1980.

Ani, Marimba [Dona Richards]. *Yurugu: An African-Centered Critique of European Cultural Thought and Behavior*. Trenton, NJ: Africa World Press, 1994.

Asante, Molefi Kete. *The Egyptian Philosophers: Ancient African Voices from Imhotep to Akhenaten*. Chicago: African American Images, 2000.

Assmann, Jan. *The Mind of Egypt: History and Meaning in the Time of the Pharaohs*. New York: Metropolitan Books, 2002.

ben-Jochannan, Yosef A. A. *Africa: Mother of Western Civilization*. Baltimore: Black Classic Press, 1988.

Bernal, Martin. *Black Athena: The Afroasiatic Roots of Classical Civilization*. Vol. 1: *The Fabrication of Ancient Greece, 1785–1985*. New Brunswick, NJ: Rutgers University Press, 1987.

Diop, Cheikh Anta. *Civilization or Barbarism: An Authentic Anthropology*. Brooklyn, NY: Lawrence Hill Books, 1991.

Ellis, Normandi, trans. *Awakening Osiris: The Egyptian Book of the Dead*. Grand Rapids, MI: Phanes Press, 1988.

Hilliard, Asa G., Larry Williams, and Nia Damali, eds. *The Teachings of Ptahhotep: The Oldest Book in the World*. Atlanta: Blackwood Press, 1987.

Ife, Zadia. "The African Diasporan Ritual Mode." In *The African Aesthetic: Keeper of the Traditions*, ed. Kariamu Welsh-Asante, 31–52. Westport, CT: Praeger, 1993.

James, George G. M. *Stolen Legacy*. Newport News, VA: United Brothers Communication Systems, 1980.

Karenga, Maulana, trans. *Maat, the Moral Ideal in Ancient Egypt: A Study in Classical African Ethics*. New York: Routledge, 2004.

Karenga, Maulana, trans. *Selections from the Husia: Sacred Wisdom of Ancient Egypt*. Los Angeles: University of Sankore Press, 1989.

Mbiti, John S. *African Religions and Philosophy*. 2nd edition. Portsmouth, NH: Heinemann Educational Books, 1989.

Obenga, Theophile. *Ancient Egypt and Black Africa*. London: Karnak House, 1992.

Van Sertima, Ivan, ed. *Egypt Revisited*. New Brunswick, NJ: Transaction Publishers, 1991.

Williams, Chancellor. *The Destruction of Black Civilization: Great Issues of Race from 4500 B.C. to 2000 A.D.* Chicago: Third World Press, 1987.

19

Ogbuide: The Igbo Lake Goddess

Sabine Jell-Bahlsen

Water is life. Without water there is no life. When astronauts venture to the moon in search of extraterrestrial life, they return empty-handed, with no evidence of water. People in the industrialized world tend to forget such existential basics. But indigenous people of Africa have long held this knowledge sacred and attributed divine qualities to their life-giving sources of fresh water. In the words of Nigeria's "First Lady of Letters," Oguta-born novelist Flora Nwapa, "water is the life-giving thing."[1]

The Riverine Oru-Igbo worship Oguta Lake as the awesome goddess Ogbuide, also known as Uhammiri.[2] Her husband is the river god Urashi, and the divine pair embodies procreation. Moreover, the water goddess occupies an eminent position in the Igbo pantheon of gods and goddesses. Locally, Ogbuide's importance equals that of the earth goddess, Ani/Ala, who is more widely known to the outside world, and whose supreme importance for Igbo custom has been vividly illustrated by the renowned novelist Chinua Achebe.[3]

The priesthood of the preeminent female Igbo deities, earth and water, is traditionally hereditary, vested within specific patrilineages and reserved for initiated men.[4] However, additional avenues of priesthood are open to both men and women through vocation. This type of nonhereditary priesthood is commonly known as honoring Mammy Water. In the past, many Mammy Water priestesses were prominent women, even though some

Figure 19.1 The popular image known as Mammy Water (Mami Wata) throughout West Africa is used by local worshippers to represent the lake goddess Ogbuide, one of a number of water divinities who are connected with the powers of fecundity but also, paradoxically, death and rebirth. (Photograph by Sabine Jell-Bahlsen.)

Mammy Water priests were male. A popular imported poster known as Mammy Water is locally used to portray Ogbuide. It replaces older, more archaic sculptures in many places, and has become an icon throughout West Africa, causing much speculation among art historians.[5]

Mother Water in Igbo Cosmology

The Igbo supreme God is known as Chi-Ukwu, the great Chi, who is vast, beyond limitation, shape, age, and gender, and too grand to be contained in temples or manmade images. The word *chi* can roughly be translated as "soul," "spirit," "life force," "essence," or all of the above. Chi-Ukwu, then, means "Great Soul/ Great Spirit/ Great Life-Force/ Supreme Being."[6] Chi-Ukwu has created, determines, and leads the universe, manifests in many different ways, and is supplemented by a pantheon of lesser deities, ancestral forces, and forces of nature, preeminently Mother Water or Nne Mmiri, who is associated with childbirth.[7]

The Divine Forces of Nature

Historically, there were no temples, shrines, or priests dedicated to Chi-Ukwu. People would pray to Chi-Ukwu in private and seek out mediators to address the Supreme Being.[8] The messengers are deities served at their own shrines by dedicated priests, who may act as intermediaries. The pantheon of deities below Chi-Ukwu consists of three major sets: the forces of nature's male and female divinities, the ancestors, and the mythical heroes and other messengers.[9] More conservative, static entities of this universe are challenged by more creative and dynamic ones. In 1914–1916, Talbot characterized the binary opposition between "Water Spirits" and "Land Spirits" as a major theme in the religious beliefs of the Igbo, Kalabari, and Ijaw people of the Niger Delta.[10] This view is corroborated by Robin Horton and by this author's field research among the Riverine Igbo, and also resonates in Chidi Osagwu's notion of "truth and chaos."[11] Two female deities—the supreme[12] earth goddess Ani/Ala and the supreme water goddess Nne Mmiri—take the lead among the forces of nature. In the Oguta area, the lake goddess Ogbuide is venerated as the supreme water goddess who sanctions and is constantly invoked to explain custom and its behavioral and especially reproductive norms.

In this universe, human beings must struggle to find their ways in a powerplay of deities associated with the forces of nature, ancestors, and other vectors. Diverse powers may confront, challenge, or support human beings. In order to keep healthy, sane, and productive, people must maintain equilibrium among self and other supernatural, social, and natural forces in a delicately balanced triad. Since the complexities of Igbo cosmology are not always transparent to everyone, diviners (*dibia*) are important to help people sort things out.[13] The diviner's undertaking is comparable to that of a psychotherapist.

Water the Birth Giver

According to Chinwe Achebe, "Mother Water" Nne Mmiri is a generic notion[14] or generalized idea of the Igbo water goddess, an abstract concept combining several local deities associated with individual waters, such as Ogbuide, Idemili, or Ava, and those water spirits found by P. A. Talbot as early as 1914.[15] Ogbuide is first of all a fertility goddess comparable to Talbot's generic birth-giving water goddess, M[m]iri Omumu, "water the birth giver," or Onitsha's birth-giving water goddess in Kay Williamson's Igbo-English dictionary.[16] Ogbuide is believed to give life and children and is identified with wealth.[17] But she is also ephemeral, harbors change, embodies fluidity and transition, and plays a decisive role in negotiating a challenging, ever-changing world.

The life-giver Ogbuide is adored but also feared, for she may not only give but also take life. Her worshipers sing, "*Mmiri di Egwu*" ("Water is awesome!"). She controls the crossroads in the eternal transitions between life and death. She may give, challenge, or destroy life. She is evasive and ephemeral, may sponsor ambivalent gender, and can protect transgressors of reproductive norms.[18] Ogbuide may either reconfirm or change one's destiny—at a price. She plays a decisive role in the eternal cycle of life.[19]

Birth, Death, and Reincarnation: The Eternal Cycle

Ogbuide's supreme importance becomes clear from the Igbo belief in reincarnation and the cyclical, rather than linear, concept of time. Two proverbial prayer stances offered at the goddess's shrine on the occasion of thanking her for the birth of a baby boy illustrate this concept:

Ani du mu uzo echi. "World/Earth, show me the road back"[20] (referring to reincarnation)
Nmanyi na enwe uge, ndu aka enwedi. "Drinks normally have a last drop, life does not"[21] (meaning that life continues forever).

Each human being has his or her own *chi*, an individual force derived and endowed by the Supreme Being, Chi-Ukwu. The individual chi leaves the human body at death to reunite with Chi-Ukwu poised to reincarnate in another body at a later stage of the eternal life-cycle—provided the person was properly buried in ancestral land. Ancient African worldviews including Igbo cosmology perceive the soul as indestructible, moving in an eternal cycle of life through circular time and reincarnation, rather than straight to heaven or hell. An individual may eventually reincarnate, when the departed chi returns to earth in another human body.[22]

The ideas of a continuous cycle of life, reincarnation, and the indestructible soul/life force are closely interrelated. The notion of the soul's eternal movement in circular time is diametrically opposed to the linear model. In Igbo art, the circle is a recurrent theme, symbolizing eternity, circular time, and the continuous transitions of life to death to life.[23]

The major stages of life are birth, naming (coinciding with entry into human society and childhood), puberty and initiation (associated with the metaphorical death of the child and the birth of an adult), adulthood

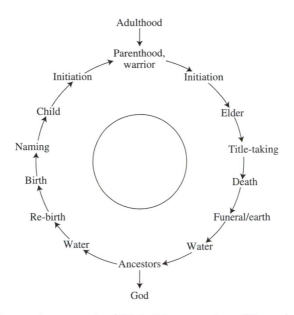

Figure 19.2 The continuous cycle of life in Igbo cosmology. (Illustration by Sabine Jell-Bahlsen. Reprinted with permission.)

(associated with marriage, parenthood, title taking and being a warrior), old age (associated with acquisition of wisdom, more advanced title taking, dignity, and priesthood), loss of spouse, death (both associated with funerary rites and taboos), and rebirth.

Each of these stages involves a transition through initiation into a new stage of life, whereby the individual receives a new name or title. Each initiation is an existential transition, metaphorically associated with the death of the old person and the birth of a new one. Passing through the different stages of life on earth, acquiring accumulative names and titles, reaching old age with many children, grandchildren, wealth, titles, priesthood, social recognition, and other personal achievements is the life goal to be crowned only by a correct, splendid, and expensive funeral, a burial in ancestral earth leading through water to the reunion with the ancestors and Chi-Ukwu, and ultimately—and again through water—to reincarnation.

However, there are certain preconditions attached to an Igbo person's successful reincarnation. In order to reincarnate, the individual must have received a proper burial in ancestral land—something denied to those who have committed an abomination or a serious crime, suffered from certain diseases, broken reproductive norms, or died an unnatural death, such as in childbirth or suicide.[24] It is believed that only when an individual has been properly buried may his or her chi reincarnate in another human being and eventually be reborn.

The water goddess poses yet another challenge to an individual's reincarnation and renewed life on earth, for it is believed that an individual must cross water not only once, at death, but also before reincarnating. At each of these watery transitions, Ogbuide confronts the human being first before entering this world and again when exiting. Upon reincarnation, the soon-to-be-born person must sort out and may change destiny, *akarakara*, with the help of the water deity. If accepting her help at this critical transitory points to change in one's destiny, then that person must worship the goddess or her husband later in life. Failure to do so can have devastating consequences for one's physical or mental health and the well-being and even life of one's immediate family.[25] Furthermore, while the water goddess may bring children, wealth, and good fortune, the parents of a newborn must take care to properly determine who has reincarnated the new being to avoid the potentially fatal mistake of offending a reincarnating water deity or ancestor.[26]

Healing and the Water Goddess

Because Ogbuide is positioned so crucially in the Igbo universe between life and death, and because she is so essential in the eternal life-cycle, the goddess may endow her followers with sacred priesthood and with the gifts of divination and healing. Some of her priests and priestesses are diviners who address personal issues and can help an individual sort out the complexities of existence. Diviners and herbalists attend to a host of health issues including mental, gynecological, and other illnesses. Healing may entail initiation, priesthood, and training to become a herbalist.[27]

On an herbalist's signboard, the python reminds viewers of the snake winding around the staff of the ancient Greek gods of medicine, Asclepius and Hygeia. The python prominently signals the goddess's faculty endowed on her priestess to heal illness that situates humans between the worlds of the living and the dead.[28] The sacred creature announces Ogbuide's divine power over life and death. The goddess is credited with granting children and bringing the gift of life, wealth, and medicines. But the python also indicates the lake goddess's binary faculties. Her pythons may bring a message of fortune or doom, and they may also act as avengers.[29] Ogbuide is unpredictable: She may change human destiny; she may create, heal and preserve life; but she may also take both life and fortune. Ogbuide may either bring or avert death.

Visual Representations and Colors

The color white is associated not only with the paleness of a newborn, but also with that of a dying person. All transitions, such as birth, naming, initiation, title-taking, death, and rebirth are critical transit points in an individual's existence and ritually marked with white chalk. The color white represents transition from and into another stage of life/death/ time. Igbo elders, priests, and mediums alike use white limestone, *nzu,* to communicate across the dividing lines of here and there, life and death, divinities and humans, to call on the extramundane, to invoke the ancestors or the spirit world, and God. Nzu is found underwater, a gift of the water goddess whose emblem is the color white. White chalk (or its urban, diasporic substitute, talcum powder) indicates spirit involvement and is used to signal visionary status, mark the body in ritual dedication and prayer, feed the spirits, draw sacred signs and symbols on the ground or body, and cool the feverish body and mind. The color white symbolizes Ogbuide, who controls the watery crossroads into and from this world. Ogbuide's worshipers wear white costumes to honor her in ritual.[30]

White chalk, nzu, is ritually combined with yellow chalk, *edo,* representing the color red of Ogbuide's husband, the river god Urashi. The combination of the two colors signals procreation and conveys life. Water worshipers wear costumes in the two colors and adore the water deities' sacred sites in red and white in honor of the divine pair, celebrating male and female, conjugal cooperation, procreation and balance as a precondition for the continuity of life. Igbo culture is life-affirming and values fertility and children as human beings' greatest asset. The divine pair personifies the need for power sharing and reciprocity as essential for procreation, continuation of life, and society at large. This view underscores the creative power of equilibrium as a core value of society. The virtue of balance is voiced in Igbo proverbs, such as "When something stands, something else stands beside it," and "The buttocks touch reciprocally and harmoniously when moving."[31] Rituals in honor of the water deities celebrate, teach, reaffirm, and reinforce the virtue of balance and cooperation of the sexes as the basic value of Igbo culture. Meandering or entwined pythons illuminate this concept.[32]

The Sacred Python

Throughout most of Igboland and much of West Africa, the royal python is a messenger of God and may even represent the supreme being. The sacred creature must not be killed by humans.[33] The python is also closely associated with the water goddess and her life-giving qualities, pro-creation, death, and eternity. In her region, the python is Ogbuide's sacred totem and emblem. The python reveals itself in two distinct ways: (1) as meandering or entwined pair, and (2) as a circle. The two appearances carry opposite messages: (1) procreation and life, or (2) death and eternity.

The red and white color symbolism of procreation and its expression in zigzag lines or a meandering pair of snakes has been described above. The coiled python corresponds to the symbolism of the color white and represents continuous transitions in a circle that symbolizes the cycle of life and death, reincarnation, and the indestructible soul/life force. In a circular appearance, the python signals transition, such as death, reincar-nation, and eternity.[34]

The python indicates Ogbuide's binary divine power to give and take life. The snake is also a key in its antithesis to Christian-Muslim beliefs alike. To the traditional Igbo, the python is a religious symbol of divine power, reincarnation, eternity, and cyclical time. The python and Mammy Water, the woman who carries snakes, have both become objects of spite and aggression by Christians and Muslims. Christians associate the snake with the biblical temptation of Eve; Muslims refer to the Hausa myth of origins that alludes to the defeat of female rule, the imposition of male dominance, and the introduction of Islam into Northern Nigeria, around 800 CE.[35] Likewise, some Christians demonize indigenous African beliefs in the water goddess, her sacred creatures, and other divinities, and attack priestesses and even children as witches in contemporary Nigeria.[36]

Ogbuide's Hair: Symbol of Fecundity

Another prominent element identifying Ogbuide is her long, thick, at times twisted hair. Following Frazer, abundant hair symbolizes female fecundity and reproductive taboos—the water goddess's domain; hair-styles, which express ideas of beauty and identity, are taken very seriously in Nigeria.[37] Igbo women and men customarily groom their hair very carefully. If an individual no longer grooms, cuts, or ties his or her hair, it grows very long and twisted. This is known as "dreadlocks" in Europe and America, and as *dada* among the Oru-Igbo—a stark contrast to "nor-mal" African hairstyling portrayed in classic African art and on barbers' signboards. Growing dada is rarely deliberate and never taken lightly. It can happen to an individual man, woman, or even a child. Dada signals an existential crisis, a special state of mind, water spirit calling, or mental illness.[38]

Dada has an added significance to women's transition to mature womanhood that may involve initiation, female circumcision, symbolic death and rebirth. Individuals who cannot live up to reproductive norms—such as Igbo women giving birth to twins, or who resist female circumcision, or marriage—may turn dada. To the locals, Ogbuide's long hair signals excessive fertility, conflict of mind and body, resistance, change, and nonconformism, and is expressed in dreams, visions, prophesies, and extraordinary behavior.[39]

Conclusion: Ogbuide as Female Potency

The lake goddess Ogbuide represents the female side of the Igbo universe. Her domain is the crossing between the worlds, for she controls the entry into and exit from life through water in the eternal cycle of life and death, known as *ebibi* in Igbo. Water and women are revered as lifegivers and preconditions for life. The lake goddess is believed to favor balance and to heal disorder. She defines reproductive norms, aids procreation, and brings life and wealth. But she also takes life and fortune, protects the unusual, is awesome, dynamic, and volatile, and may bring about change. The python is her totem animal, messenger, and avenger. Unlike Eve, who was human, succumbed to the snake's temptation, and caused human expulsion from paradise, Ogbuide is a life-affirming goddess who carries pythons as sacred emblems of two-pronged African religious beliefs.

Notes

1. Sabine Jell-Bahlsen, "An Interview with Flora Nwapa," in *Emerging Perspectives on Flora Nwapa*, ed. Marie Umeh (Trenton, NJ: Africa World Press, 1998), 647.

2. The Igbo are a major ethnic group of the West African country of Nigeria, comprising about 30 million living mostly in the country's southeast. As a result of the slave trade and Nigeria's civil war over Biafra, the worldwide Igbo population including the Diaspora amounts to approximately 100 million today. The Igbo are a heterogeneous people, but share a common language and certain cultural traits. Their culture is democratic, rejecting monolithic power structures, and made up of many subdivisions. Igbo society consists of independent communities based on large patrilineages, or extended families, with notable exceptions described by Uchendu, Ottenberg, and Manfredi. Yam farming, trade, fishing, and hunting provided the traditional economic basis. Despite local variations, most Igbos historically share certain pre-Christian religious beliefs and associated values

including a desire for balance, religious worship of the ancestors, the earth goddess, and the male-gendered staple vegetable, the yam, as well as the ritual significance of kola hospitality. Most prominently Igbo culture is characterized by a veneration of female fecundity and motherhood. The supreme value attached to motherhood is expressed in the Igbo name *Nneka*, "Mother is Supreme." The Oru-Igbo are a subdivision of the Riverine Igbo, one of several Igbo subgroups. See also Catherine Obianuju Acholonu, *Motherism: The Afrocentric Alternative to Feminism* (Owerri, Nigeria: Afa Publications, 1995); and Obinkaram T. Echewa, *I Saw the Sky Catch Fire* (Philadelphia: Amadi Press, 2002).

3. Sabine Jell-Bahlsen, *The Water Goddess in Igbo Cosmology: Ogbuide of Oguta Lake* (Trenton, NJ: Africa World Press, 2008); Chinua Achebe, *Things Fall Apart* (London: Heinemann, 2008).

4. Sabine Jell-Bahlsen, "Female Power: Water Priestesses of the Oru-Igbo," in *Sisterhood, Feminisms, and Power: From Africa to the Diaspora,* ed. Obioma Nnaemeka (Trenton, NJ: Africa World Press, 2009); Jell-Bahlsen, *The Water Goddess,* chaps. 1, 2, and 10.

5. An exemplary archaic image of the divine pair of water deities is the seated pair of clay sculptures representing the river goddess Ava and her husband at Ukanna near Nsukka. Jell-Bahlsen, *The Water Goddess,* p. 74, fig. 32; Sabine Jell-Bahlsen, "Eze Mmiri di Egwu: The Water Goddess Is Awesome: Unraveling the Mammy Water Myths," in *Queens, Queen Mothers, Priestesses, and Power: Case Studies in African Gender,* ed. Flora Kaplan (New York: Annals of the New York Academy of Sciences, 1997), 103–134; Jill Salmons, "Mammy Water," *African Arts* 10, no. 3 (1977); Henry Drewal, "Performing the Other: Mami Wata Worship in West Africa." *The Drama Review* T 118 (1988): 160–185.

6. Chinua Achebe, "Chi in Igbo Cosmology," In *Morning Yet on Creation Day* (Garden City, NY: Anchor Books, 1975); Achebe, *Things Fall Apart.*

7. Chinwe Achebe, *The World of the Ogbanje* (Enugu: Forth Dimension Publishers, 1986), 13–15.

8. This practice has obviously changed with the advent of foreign missionaries and priests who claim the name *Chukwu* for the Christian God worshiped in their churches.

9. E. B. Idowu, *African Traditional Religion: A Definition* (London: SCM Press, 1967).

10. P. Amaury Talbot, *Tribes of the Niger Delta: Their Religion and Customs* (New York: Barnes and Noble, 1967), 32.

11. Robin Horton, *Patterns of Thought in Africa and the West: Essays on Magic, Religion, and Science* (New York: Cambridge University Press, 1997), 217–218; Jell-Bahlsen, *The Water Goddess;* see also Chidi G. Osuagwu, "Truth and Chaos: Dynamics of Truth within Igbo Cosmology," paper presented at the Owerri International Symposium on Religion in a World of Change organized by the Whelan Research Academy, Owerri, Nigeria, October 2002.

12. The supreme earth goddess and the supreme water goddess are general deities, each of whom is supplemented by a pantheon of more localized earth and water deities, such as the earth goddess of a compound or a piece of land, or the goddess of a creek or a stream.

13. John Anenechukwu Umeh, *After God Is Dibia: Igbo Cosmology, Divination, and Sacred Science in Nigeria* (London: Karnak House, 1997.

14. Achebe, *The World of the Ogbanje*.

15. Talbot, *Tribes of the Niger Delta*.

16. Kay Williamson, *Igbo English Dictionary* (Benin City: Ethiope Publishing Co., 1972), 421.

17. In this agrarian society, children were once regarded as identical with wealth, a notion expressed in the Igbo name, *Kego*, "Child is better than money."

18. Igbo traditional reproductive norms are extremely important locally and contested by some feminists including Flora Nwapa. However, Igbo gender norms are not as rigid as commonly perceived and may even be flexible beyond Western imagination. Ifi Amadiume, *Male Daughters, Female Husbands* (London: Zed Books, 1987); Leslye Amede Obiora, "Reconsidering African Customary Law," *Legal Studies Forum* 7, no. 3 (1993): 217–252.

19. Achebe, *The World of the Ogbanje*.

20. In this case, Ani is the earth goddess of an individual compound.

21. This prayer was offered by the late hereditary priest of Uhammiri/Ogbuide, Obiadinbugha, Uzor Ohaka of Umudei on behalf of Chief Francis Ebiri and his family, at Orsu-Obodo, Oguta II, in July 1979. Jell-Bahlsen, *The Water Goddess*, 85.

22. Marcel Griaule, *Conversations with Ogotomelli: An Introduction to Dogon Religious Ideas* (London: Oxford University Press, 1970); Robert F. Thompson, *Flash of the Spirit* (New York: Vintage Books, 1983); Patrice Malidoma Somé, *Of Water and the Spirit: Ritual, Magic, and Initiation in the Life of an African Shaman* (New York: Putnam Books, 1994); Jell-Bahlsen *The Water Goddess*.

23. Chike Aniakor and Herbert Cole, *Igbo Arts: Community and Cosmos* (Los Angeles: Fowler Museum of Art, 1984); Thompson, *Flash of the Spirit;* Jell-Bahlsen, *The Water Goddess;* Roy Sieber and Roslyn Adele Walker, eds., *African Art in the Cycle of Life* (Washington, DC: Smithsonian Institution Press, 1988).

24. Victor Chikezie Uchendu, *The Ibo of Southeast Nigeria* (New York: Holt, Rinehart and Winston, 1974); Jell-Bahlsen, *The Water Goddess*.

25. As in the case of Eze Nwata and others. Sabine Jell-Bahlsen and Georg Jell, *Eze Nwata—The Small King* (video) (New York, 1983); Jell-Bahlsen, *The Water Goddess*.

26. Sabine Jell-Bahlsen, "Names and Naming. Instances from the Oru-Igbo," *Dialectical Anthropology* 13 (1989): 199–207; Sabine Jell-Bahlsen, *Mammy Water: In Search of the Water Spirits in Nigeria* (video) (Watertown, MA: Documentary Educational Resources, 2009); Jell-Bahlsen, "Circular Time, Reincarnation, and Multiple Names," chap. 5 of *The Water Goddess*, 85–104.

27. In her last manuscript, Flora Nwapa illustrates this option in the story of Ona, whose life and career is inspired by Nwapa's interviews with real-life herbalists and priestesses of Ogbuide in the Oguta area. Flora Nwapa, *The Lake Goddess* (Trenton, NJ: Africa World Press, forthcoming); Jell-Bahlsen, *The Water Goddess*, chap. 20.

28. Uchendu, *The Ibo of Southeast Nigeria*; Jell-Bahlsen, *The Water Goddess.*

29. Chinua Achebe, *Anthills of the Savannah* (New York: Anchor Books, 1986), 96.

30. The ritual use of white chalk and costumes associated with Ogbuide are documented on video in Jell-Bahlsen, *Mammy Water.*

31. Obioma Nnaemeka, "Prologue," in *Sisterhood, Feminisms, and Power* (Trenton, NJ: Africa World Press, 1998); Nnaemeka, personal communication.

32. Jell-Bahlsen, *The Water Goddess*, chaps. 18 and 20, and p. 202, fig. 73; *Mammy Water* (video).

33. Chinua Achebe, *Things Fall Apart* (London: Heinemann, 1959); Achebe, *Anthills of the Savannah*; Achebe, *The World of the Ogbanje*; O. Catherine Acholonu, *The Igbo Roots of Olaudah Equiano* (Owerri, Nigeria: Afa Publications, 1984), 14; Geoffrey Parrinder, *African Mythology* (London: Hamlin, 1967); Robert F. Thompson, *Flash of the Spirit* (New York: Vintage Books, 1983); Aniakor and Cole, *Igbo Arts*; Jell-Bahlsen, *The Water Goddess*, chap. 13.

34. Jell-Bahlsen, *The Water Goddess*, 197 fig. 70. In this chalk drawing on the ground, the water deity's priest, Palmer has drawn a cycle representing the python to signal the imminent death of one of his patients.

35. According to the Hausa myth of origins, a man named Baghida arrived at Daura from Baghdad. There he killed the snake that dominated the town's well—synonymous with fertility—and married Queen Daurama. Their seven children founded the original Hausa cities. This mythical event is commemorated in a relief plaque at the entrance gate to the emir's palace at Daura to this day. Jell-Bahlsen, *The Water Goddess*, 172 fig. 66; Sabine Jell-Bahlsen, *Tubali: Hausa Architecture of Northern Nigeria* (video) (Watertown, MA: Documentary Educational Resources, 2009).

36. Obodimma Oha, "The Rhetoric of Nigerian Christian Videos: The War Paradigm of *The Great Mistake*," in *Nigerian Video Films*, ed. Jonathan Haynes (Jos, Nigeria: Nigerian Film Institute, 1997), 93–98; Sabine Jell-Bahlsen, "Let Her Song Prevail. Reflections on the Life of the Late *Ogbuefi, Eze Mmiri*, Madame Martha Mberekpe of Orsu-Obodo," paper presented at the fourth WAAD conference at Abuja, August 2009. "Slaughter of the Gods," *The Nation*, September 21, 2008; *Saving Africa's Witch Children*, a television documentary by the UK Channel 4 titled *Calabar: Saving Africa's Witch Children*, aired on November 12, 2008.

37. Sir James Frazer, *The Golden Bough: A Study in Magic and Religion* (London: Macmillan, 1955); see also Walter Andritzky, "Ethnomedizin und das Wallfahrt-sphaenomen: ein oekopsychologischer Ansatz zur kulturvergleichenden Evaluation—Dargestellt am Beispiel der Magdalenen-Wallfahrt in Latzfons/ Tirol," *Ethnopsychologische*

Mitteilungen 5, no. 2 (1996): 179–188. Andrew Magnin, ed., *J. D. Okhai Ojeikere Photographs* (Paris: Scalo, 2000).

38. Jell-Bahlsen, *Mammy Water*, and *The Water Goddess*.

39. Jell-Bahlsen, *The Water Goddess*, "Dreams and Divination" (chap. 18), 265–275, and "*Ogbuide*'s Healing Therapies" (chap. 20), 285–320.

Bibliography

Achebe, Chinua. *Anthills of the Savannah*. New York: Anchor Books, 1986.

Achebe, Chinua. "Chi in Igbo Cosmology." In *Morning Yet on Creation Day*. Garden City, NY: Anchor Books, 1975.

Achebe, Chinua. *Things Fall Apart*. London: Heinemann, 1959.

Achebe, Chinwe. *The World of the Ogbanje*. Enugu, Nigeria: Fourth Dimension Publishers, 1986.

Acholonu, Catherine Obianuju. *The Igbo Roots of Olaudah Equiano*. Owerri, Nigeria: Afa Publications, 1989.

Acholonu, Catherine Obianuju. *Motherism: The Afrocentric Alternative to Feminism*. Owerri, Nigeria: Afa Publications, 1995.

Amadiume, Ifi. *Male Daughters, Female Husbands*. London: Zed Books, 1987.

Andritzky, Walter. "Ethnomedizin und das Wallfahrtsphaenomen: ein oekopsychologischer Ansatz zur kulturvergleichenden Evaluation—Dargestellt am Beispiel der Magdalenen-Wallfahrt in Latzfons/ Tirol." *Ethnopsychologische Mitteilungen* 5, no. 2 (1996): 179–188.

Aniakor, Chike, and Herbert Cole, eds. *Igbo Arts: Community and Cosmos*. Los Angeles: Fowler Museum of Arts, 1984.

Drewal, Henry. "Performing the Other: Mami Wata Worship in West Africa." *The Drama Review* 118 (1988): 160–185.

Echewa, Obinkaram T. *I Saw the Sky Catch Fire*. Philadelphia: Amadi Press, 2002.

Frazer, Sir James. *The Golden Bow*. London: Macmillan, 1955.

Henderson, Helen K. *Ritual Roles of Women in Onitsha Igbo Society*. Berkeley: University of California Press, 1973.

Horton, Robin. *Patterns of Thought in Africa and the West: Essays on Magic, Religion, and Science*. New York: Cambridge University Press, 1997.

Idowu, E. B. *African Traditional Religion: A Definition*. London: SCM Press, 1967.

Jell-Bahlsen, Sabine. "Female Power: Water Priestesses of the Oru-Igbo." In *Sisterhood, Feminisms and Power*, ed. Obioma Nnaemeka, 102–137. Trenton, NJ: Africa World Press, 2009.

Jell-Bahlsen, Sabine. "An Interview with Flora Nwapa." In *Emerging Perspectives on Flora Nwapa*, ed. Marie Umeh, 633–663. Trenton, NJ: Africa World Press, 1998.

Jell-Bahlsen, Sabine. *Mammy Water: In Search of the Water Sprits in Nigeria* (video). Watertown, MA: Documentary Educational Resources, 2009.

Jell-Bahlsen, Sabine. "Names and Naming: Instances from the Oru-Igbo." *Dialectical Anthropology* 13 (1989): 199–207.

Jell-Bahlsen, Sabine. *Tubali: Hausa Architecture of Northern Nigeria* (video). Watertown, MA: Documentary Educational Resources, 2009.

Jell-Bahlsen, Sabine. *The Water Goddess in Igbo Cosmology; Ogbuide of Oguta Lake.* Trenton, NJ: Africa World Press, 2008.

Jell-Bahlsen, Sabine, and Georg Jell. *Eze Nwata—The Small King* (video). New York: Ogbuide Films, 1983.

Kaplan, Flora Edouwaye, ed. *Queens, Queen Mother, Priestesses, and Power: Case Studies in African Gender.* New York: New York Academy of Sciences, 1997.

Magnin, Andre, ed. *J. D. Okhai Ojeikere Photographs.* Paris: Scalo, 2000.

Manfredi, Victor. "Igbo Initiation: Phallus vs. Umbilicus." *Cahiers d'etudes africaines* no. 145 (1997): 157–211.

Nnaemeka, Obioma, ed. *Sisterhood, Feminism, and Power.* Trenton, NJ: Africa World Press, 2009.

Nwapa, Flora. *Efuru.* London: Heinemann, 1961.

Nwapa, Flora. *Idu.* London: Heinemann, 1966.

Nwapa, Flora. *The Lake Goddess.* Trenton, NJ: Africa World Press (forthcoming).

Obiora, Leslye Amede. "Reconsidering African Customary Law." *Legal Studies Forum* 7, no. 3 (1993): 217–252.

Oha, Obodimma. "The Rhetoric of Nigerian Christian Videos: The War Paradigm of *The Great Mistake*." *Nigerian Video Films,* ed. Jonathan Haynes, 93–98. Jos, Nigeria: Nigerian Film Institute, 1997.

Osuagwu, Chidi G. "Truth and Chaos. Dynamics of Truth within Igbo Cosmology." Paper presented at the Owerri International Symposium on *Religion in a World of Change* organized by the Whelan Research Academy, Owerri, Nigeria, October 2002.

Ottenberg, Simon. *Double Descent in an African Society: The Afikpo Village Group.* American Ethnological Society Monograph Series. Seattle: University of Washington Press, 1968.

Parrinder, Geoffrey. *African Mythology.* London: Hamlin, 1967.

Salmons, Jill. "Mammy Water." *African Arts* 10, no. 3 (1977): 8–15.

Sieber, Roy, and Roslyn Adele Walker, eds. *African Art in the Cycle of Life.* Washington, DC: Smithsonian Institution Press, 1988.

Somé, Patrice Malidoma. *Of Water and the Spirit: Ritual, Magic, and Initiation in the Life of an African Shaman.* New York: Putnam Books, 1994.

Talbot, Amaury P. *Tribes of the Niger Delta: Their Religion and Customs.* New York: Barnes and Noble, 1967.

Thompson, Robert F. *Flash of the Spirit.* New York: Vintage Books, 1983.

Uchendu, Victor Chikezie. *The Ibo of Southeast Nigeria.* New York: Holt, Rinehart and Winston, 1974.

Umeh, John Anenechukwu. *After God Is Dibia: Igbo Cosmology, Divination, and Sacred Science in Nigeria.* London: Karnak House, 1997.

Umeh, Marie, ed. *Emerging Perspectives on Flora Nwapa.* Trenton, NJ: Africa World Press, 1998.

Williamson, Kay. *Igbo English Dictionary.* Benin City, Nigeria: Ethiope Publishing Co., 1972.

20

Òşun: Yoruba Goddess in Nigeria and the African Diaspora

Diedre L. Badejo

For centuries, a plethora of indigenous women's organizations have guided various aspects of their sociopolitical, cultural, and daily lives of Africa's richly diverse cultural regions. Throughout Africa, in fact, women's organizations remain as living testimonies to their complex roles in ancient and contemporary histories. Even today, oral narratives celebrate women's roles in the founding of towns, on the battlefield as warriors, and, of course, at the crossroads of life as mothers and mourners. African women have, as Gwendolyn Mikell notes, "a quixotic relationship to traditional and modern political systems." Mikell identifies three "indigenous models of gender, polity, and state" that existed in various forms throughout much of the continent. These indigenous models are (1) corporate, based on kinship that emphasized the group or corporate entity over the individual; (2) dual-sex, based on occupational and ritual organization that emphasized "sex complementarity" and age-group status; and (3) gender-bias, or gendered processes that slowly eroded indigenous women's royal authority over time.[1]

From the late 19th century onward, colonialism greatly impacted these sociopolitical structures, partly by transforming and/or co-opting the authority of the region's cultural elite, and partly by undermining and diverting their accountability to their respective populations. This diversion, especially to culturally elite African men or male-dominated colonial structures, particularly weakened women's organizations that had existed for hundreds of years. Perhaps the most egregious intrusion resulted from the collusion between colonialist authorities and African patriarchal systems that intentionally weakened the control of women's institutions. Such collusion is characterized by Mikell as "benign female exclusion."[2] Nevertheless, indigenous cultures managed to survive and in some cases survive as a means of cultural preservation. In West Africa and the African Diaspora, the Yoruba are among the most adept at self-preservation, and the Òşun mythology exemplifies that strength.

Yoruba Creation Narrative

The Yoruba goddess tradition, which extends from western Nigeria to the Republic of Benin and the southern coastal region of Togo, is one of West African's most intriguing and complex traditions. Like the land it covers, the imagery of the Yoruba goddess traditions reflects the natural environment that traverses diverse coastal, forest, and savannah landscapes. Rivers, lagoons, lakes, violent thunderstorms and rainfall, droughts and pestilence, maternal and infant deaths, weddings and funerals flow throughout the region and the people's lives. Most Yoruba deities, male and female, are associated with the natural environment, and their narratives reflect local histories and challenges to their very existence.

Òşun is such a deity. She is associated with the river that bears her name in western Nigeria. She is also known as the founder and patron of Osogbo Township, a crossroads for trade, cultural pluralism, creative arts, and safe haven for disparate travelers and refugees from wars, famines, and other hardships. Osogbo Township and the deity Òşun are celebrated for protecting women, children, and refugees as well as traders, farmers, and the fish and animals that occupy the Òşun Grove.

In Yoruba cosmology, Òşun is the only female among the original seventeen deities or Irunmole, assigned by Olodùmare, the creator, to prepare the world for human habitation. When the other sixteen male deities exclude her from their planning sessions, Òşun uses her talents and powers to disrupt the implementation of their plans. When the male Irunmole complain to Olodùmare, they are rebuffed. Olodùmare reminds them that seventeen deities were sent to organize the world for human beings, and their neglect of the only woman among them is the cause of their failure. They are also reminded that each of them including Òşun was given his or her own special *ase* (power/abilities/talent) that taken together facilitate successful existence. Olodùmare reprimands them and tells them to beg forgiveness from Òṣun. They comply, and she demands the inclusion of powerful women like her in all worldly affairs. The Irunmole agree, and she releases the covenant that binds their works.

Her actions and victory over the male Irunmole underscore critical perspectives about the source and efficacy of women's power and the delicate social cultural balance that such power is meant to maintain. Òṣun's narrative emphasizes a divine source for all power and abilities and admonishes the sexist exclusion in the planning and engagement with life itself. Òṣun represents balance between male and female power and capabilities. Nor is unbridled female power accepted. In several narratives, Òṣun suffers the consequences of her missteps or misbehavior. Nonetheless, her ability to impede the work of a very select group of powerful deities suggests that within Yoruba thought the fact that women's bodies create and sustain life, and can also forestall it, is a great source of power. This concept resonates through diverse narratives, and finds corroboration in other Yoruba traditions and practices.

Òṣun Orature and Ontology in Performance Space

Oral literature, often referred to as orature in Africa, is a formidable avenue for accessing the continent's knowledge of itself and its understanding of that knowledge. Africa's diversity of languages and cultures contributes to its diversity of oral literary styles, narratives, and worldviews. In ritual and ceremony, in public and private, in sacred and secular settings, oral literature codifies the sociocultural archive of most ethnolinguistic sociocultural organizations. The format, venue, and raison d'être for spoken word performances are as diverse as the oral literary genres themselves. African orature can be intoned, chanted, sung, prayed, orchestrated, and staged across a spectrum of large and small environments. Its presentation in performance is guided by cultural norms and aesthetics that reflect West African and Sahelian worldviews generally and are differentiated by the peculiarities and preferences of each given society specifically.

Annual Yoruba festivals galvanize communities around their historic and cultural achievements, inform the young about their heritage and the meaning of life, and celebrate their rich traditions. During festivals such as these, important historic events are performed, traditional poetry and epics are narrated, and the oral praise poems known in Yoruba as *orile oriki* are chanted. Collectively, these activities remind the ruling families like the Ataoja of Osogbo and the Iya Òṣun as well as others of their individual and civic responsibilities. Festivals are tapestries of music, song, dance, mime, costuming, fine arts, and narrative performances. In their preparation, they employ the talents and training of numerous skilled artisans and cultural professionals. Carvers, smiths, weavers, cultural historians, poets, musicians, and dancers carefully plan and prepare for annual celebrations and ritual performances. The Òṣun Festival occurs over sixteen days and, like other Yoruba festivals, takes place at designated sacred venues. Festivals often become the focal point for reuniting community members and for family gatherings, especially the local rulers and their extensive organizations, to reconnect with their constituencies.

Annual festivals create forums for oral literary production and performance. For the Yoruba, ritual performance, public festivals, and family gatherings are among the most popular venues for assuring the continuity of cultural knowledge, recounting sociopolitical history, and celebrating the icons of Yoruba identity. In a ritual context, festivals often become a time of communal and individual healing or settling of disputes, a time of spiritual renewal and thanksgiving. The Òṣun Festival's songs and poetry, music and dance, epic narratives and iconography are pathways to understanding the Yoruba goddess Òṣun. Her narrative and worship resembles the dual human and divine nature of Yoruba orisa traditions and cultural ideals of leadership.

The Òṣun Festival usually occurs in August, and the entire Osogbo Township becomes the stage for the annual celebration as the whole town follows their political and spiritual leadership from the palace to the center of town to the Òṣun Grove. The festival celebrates Òṣun as the foundress of Osogbo, and as one of the wives of Sango, the fourth king of Old Oyo who reigned around the 16th century. Osogbo grew into a bustling commercial center that served, and continues to serve, as an intersection between Ife, Ibadan, Ijebu, and Ilorin. The Òṣun Festival celebrates her role as a woman of keen business acumen, a dyer, an owner of brass, parrot feathers, and beads. It celebrates her protection of refugees, traders, childless women, animals, and fish that live in her forest. As a sacred image of female rulership and icon of women's power, Òṣun represents the quintessential portal of human existence through which life emerges and thrives. She possesses a cool female principle whose nature balances the fiery male principle of Sango, one of her husbands and lovers.[3]

Yoruba performance arts are organized by genre, purpose, and frequently by the status of the performer(s). The *oloriki* or praise singers are among those who are trained to celebrate Òṣun's sacred history, her worship, and the Ataoja's rulership of Osogbo in Òṣun State. The oral literary narratives and poems provide invaluable historical data, but their most intrinsic cultural value lies in the energy ignited in ritual and civic performance spaces. Excerpts from Òṣun narratives and poetry illustrate her importance in Yoruba thought.

The Òṣun Narrative

The *Oriki Òṣun* or Òṣun Praise Poetry is chanted a capella in three sections during both sacred and secular occasions in her honor. Section 1 presents Òṣun's many appellations, attributes, and townships historically associated with her or her worship. Section 2 elaborates on her prowess and her chief characteristic as Yéyé, the good mother. Section 3 captures her spiritual essence and cosmogenic authority from which Òṣun worshipers derive their own authority and strength. The *Oriki Òṣun* denotes the possibility of an aboriginal past that is both matrifocal and dual gendered in its ontology and leadership structure. This is a clear departure from the universal view of gender inequity and female oppression as the dominant paradigm in traditional West African cultures. Second, although both women and men worship Òṣun, the *Oriki Òṣun* are maintained and intoned by women who are trained as professional praise singers. They are the guardians of the oral texts, the stylistic integrity, and the performance aesthetics of the Òṣun oral literature.

Phase 2 of the chant (distinct from section 2 mentioned earlier, and excerpted here) builds on complex metaphors and layered meanings. In its oral recitation, the highly stylized chanting evokes images of the power and "coolness," core images for Òṣun. In this section, Òṣun's sacred and secular metonyms signal that she is a giver of life, a healing mother, a wealthy woman, a ruler, and a wife of Sango, another powerful deity. Òṣun's ability to "deliver" townspeople and women from life's challenges is signified by allusions to the majestic flow of her body, which is analogous to the River Òṣun, and her corulership with the Ataoja, the traditional ruler in Osogbo. In the poem, Òṣun conquers with ease and grace while remaining vigilant as well as energetic. For the women and men who worship her, she is the epitome of female power and femininity whose alluring characteristics suggest central aspects of a feminine ideal in Yoruba culture.

This section of the poem also provides historical as well as political illusions suggesting that Osogbo as well as other Yoruba towns may have female origins and rulers. For example, one of her praise names or cognomens, Solagbade, alludes to a wealthy person who wears a crown. Since only rulers or those who hold the authority to rule wear crowns, her praise name signifies her rulership of Osogbo, and ties female rulership to such towns as Ara, Ijesa, Efon, and Anke which are identified in the poem as Òşun towns. References to extinct towns such as Anke indicate that the poem and its origins are rooted in antiquity. These references also name towns where Òşun is worshiped and/or through which her river flows. Indeed, the breadth of Òşun's characteristics and Òşun worship depicts a cultural perspective that values abundance and variety among human beings.

Phase Two of the Praise Poem for Òşun (*Oriki Òşun*)
Òşun Osogbo ooo
The child is secretly created, Òşun Osogbo!
The one who in flowing majestically along hits her body against the grass.
The one who in flowing majestically along hits her body against the rocks.
Praise-worthy owner of the secrets of life.
The wealthy one who wears a crown! The effervescent one!
I salute the Great Mother Òşun, Òşun Osogbo.
My Mother, Òşun Osogbo,
Who gives birth with ease and grace,
My mother, please deliver and rescue me!
The wealthy one who wears a crown! The effervescent one!
I cried "deliverance" through the water,
Òşun Osogbo, please deliver me!
I cried "deliverance" to you!
Òşun Osogbo ooo!
My Mother is the giant cock (rooster)
Who climbed to the top of the palm nut tree to build her house.
Yes, it is from there that she calls the King of Ara with a loud voice.
I stand to wait for Òşun's blessings, my hands are not deep enough (to hold them).
Òşun Osogbo!
Òşun Osogbo greetings, I spread my cloth,
I will certainly receive more.
Solagbade, she who scopes sand, and scopes sand to hide money!
Come and look at Òşun Osogbo!
My Mother, Owner of the medicinal healing pot.
Oloro, Ruler of Ijesa!
In the dead of night, please do not sleep!
I salute the Great Mother, Òşun!
(. . . . .)
The wealthy one who wears a crown! The effervescent one!

I salute the Great Mother Òṣun!
Who does not know that Òṣun helps the Oba (ruler) to manage and rule
Osogbo?
Òṣun Osogbo is the one who will help me
Accomplish my goals.
Òṣun Osogbo is the one who will definitely help me
Accomplish what I cannot accomplish on my own!
Because of children she eagerly listens to noise!
Because of Sango she masters the art of cooking amala!
My father of the house, my husband!
Because of children she cultivates nutritious spinach!
The wealthy one who wears a crown, the effervescent one![4]

The Metanarrative of Òṣun

Yoruba mythology is a complex metonymic system that serves as a
method for preserving and retrieving Yoruba cultural history, ideology,
and epistemology.[5] The ritual words chanted to invoke Òṣun belong to a
class of specialized orature that is found at the matrix of musical and
poetic forms. These works are distinct from the nonspecialized communal songs that address the transition through various rites of passage or
states of being in subject, form, and style. Philosophically speaking,
women guard and regale the coming and going of life. From birth to
death, women celebrate, nurture, and mourn the capriciousness of human
existence.

Interlacing narratives and iconography portray Òṣun as knowledge
keeper and propagator, mother and warrior, wife and confidante, healer
and protector, divine and woman being. As noted above, Òṣun is the only
female deity present at the creation of the world, aye.[6] In Osetura, a major
odù Ifá (Ifá chapter), Olódùmarè confers the leadership of the àjẹ́ (powerful beings) as well as the authority to give or withhold children to Òṣun.
As leader of the àjẹ́ and giver of children, Òṣun preserves human life and
watches over the covenants of the àjẹ́, or powerful beings. An àjẹ́ herself,
she is the one among the 401 òrìṣà in the Yoruba pantheon. Occasionally
referred to as the seventeenth òrìṣà (Abiodun),[7] Òṣun is also the one who
stands between the 200 òrìṣà on the left (osi) and the 200 òrìṣà on the right
(otun). With her perfectly carved beaded comb, Òṣun Sèègèsí Òlòyá-íyùn,
she parts the pathways that lead from the world of the unborn (orun) to
the world of the living (aye).

According to some of her songs, she is also eégun, an ancestor to those
who answer her call and to those who seek her. She is seer and confidante,

knowledgeable in the vagaries of life itself, a defender of humanity who witnesses the power of both constructive and destructive forces in the polydimensional world of the Yoruba. In her manifestations, she is both divine and human, and as such, she shares in the pleasures and pain of both forms of being. Òṣun is healer, diviner, and warrior whose transmutability of form and substance canonize a "dialogical" view in Yoruba thought. Her evanescence serves as a key to understanding her image as living energy (aṣe) and cultural synergy (àjẹ́) in the long history of humanity, deity, and the universality of change. She is Yéyé, the universal womb, mysterious and awesome in its potentiality. Òṣun presides over the world, ayé and children, ọmọde, good and bad.

Human Relations and the Yoruba Social Order

Òṣun's oral literature shares its beauty and linguistic complexity with a cornucopia of Yoruba verbal/visual and artistic performance traditions. Her images represent a centralizing woman-presence positioned at the vortex of creation as well as life itself. Her praise-name, Òṣun Sèègèsí Òlòyá-íyùn, is a critical motif that idealizes her primary position among the principal òrìsa in the pantheon. It alludes to her as owner of the womb wherein the secret pathways and knowledge of human life unfold. In Yoruba cosmology, that secret life of the womb mirrors the awò or secret life of the living. The symbiotic nature of the unborn and the living converge with her power as an àjé, an awesome combination that serves as a metonym for her guardianship over the birth and destiny of human beings. As Yéyé, she protects the life she gives, often employing her powers as àjé to do so. Her physical presence is envisioned as a robust woman whose very body exudes sensuality, quintessential motherhood, and prowess.

Often praised, Òṣun's sensuality finds expression in several odù Ifá and oríkì Òsun in Yoruba orature. References to her passion for oils, bathing, clothes, and beautification along with references to brass, swords, calabashes, and agbò pots lead those familiar with Yoruba cultural and aesthetic acumen to evoke images, meaning, and presence of Òsun in diverse environments. The odù Ifá refers to her as the one who carves the pathways of human destiny with her perfectly carved beaded comb, a complex symbol of her feminine prowess, her patronage of the arts, her desire for perfection, and her sense of beauty. As a river, she is the one whose body handles the soft beauty of grass and the hard edginess of stone with equal ease and grace. Even in elusive passages where she remains unnamed, interconnecting images and narratives make her presence known.

She is identified with the numbers five (*aárùún*), sixteen (*meríndìnlógun*), and seventeen (*metádìnlógun*) with parrot feathers, birds, cowries, cool waters, and honey.

Although Òsun is Aje and owner of the beaded comb, she demonstrates patience, an indication of her character, as she observes their arrogance and lack of character. Similarly, she presides over the covenant of both malevolent and benevolent forces that are constantly stirring the pot of human affairs. In silence, she watches activities of both humanity and divinity alike, waiting like a good mother to assist them when they so desire by appealing to her properly. Unquestionably, Òsun's maternal pathway is a dominant characteristic reflected variously in her roles as warrior, lover, friend, and confidante. Consider the following refrain from another more extensive odù Ifá:

> *Yemese o pa 'ni loni!*
> *O pa 'gun ra!*
> *Òsun Apara pa 'gun ra loni!*
> *O pa 'gun ra!*
> *Òsun Apara pa 'gun ra loni o!*
> *O pa 'gun ra!*

> Yemese killed for total destruction today!
> She waged a war for destruction;
> Òsun Apara waged war for destruction today!
> She waged a war for destruction;
> Òsun Apara waged war for destruction today!
> She waged a war for destruction.[8]

During several interviews, Yemi Eleburuibon, Ifá priest and Ogun devotee, recited several odù Ifá including this one where Òsun manifests as male energy taking on a warrior modality. In some of these manifestations, she presents as female and in others she presents as male. In both cases, she emerges in defense of a town and its people. In a Yoruba worldview where gender is associative, roles become transmutable irrespective of biological design. In the odù Ifá Ereti Alao, Òsun is captured with other members of Osogbo Township and led away from their home. The frightened townspeople turn against her because she refuses to raise her sword against their enemies. She continues to tell the captives that they must be patient until the right time; however, they continue to abuse her and to grumble and complain. Nonetheless, she waits patiently until they reach a particular place before she reaches inside of herself and unsheathes a sword to cut down their captors. She advises the astonished townspeople that when she falls down to become a river, that they must follow the flow of her river if they are to return to their original township. This act of "falling down" to become a river path signals her leadership of Osogbo Township, and the call to its people to emulate her path as warrior and transmutable being. It is also a call to become a devotee, to follow her spiritual path as conserver of human life and culture. The seeming contradiction between being warrior and devotee dissolves in Òsun's cool waters of amelioration and healing.

In contrast to this warrior image, Òsun is also peacemaker. She entices Ogun, the orisa of war and iron, to re-engage with the community of beings, just as she playfully captures the town of women who revolt against the men. Here, her honey-sweet words and sensuality persuade the errant orisa and womenfolk to re-engage themselves in the market-place of life; for the forges and the bellows will not work without Ogun's fiery essence and life cannot continue without the regenerative powers of women. These *pa itan* or narratives illustrate that one of Òsun's functions in Yoruba thought is to mediate dialogical discourse. Her cosmogenic metonym stresses balance, orchestrates the vagaries of life, and places sacrifice at the crossroads of restitution, cleansing, and healing. Images of *eyele* (birds) on Osanyin's staff or the *Opa Oba* or the *Adé Oba* signify the key spiritual position that Òsun holds while alluding to her own prowess as healer, ruler, and aje. Òsun's pathways simultaneously encompass the generative kinesis of worldly existence and the potency of human and divine synergy.

The Feminine in Òṣun's Voice

As the owner of the universal womb, Òṣun is the metaphor and dialectic of Yoruba thought. Her dynamic energies activate the principles of human and divine existence in swirling, ebb and flow among multiple layers of being. She mediates constructive and destructive impulses with patience, ease, and grace. She is an ultimate female with the potential to unleash devastating male energies of destruction. Òṣun is metaphorically the epitome of secrecy and the source of knowledge. In her most profound essence, she completes the cycle of life as both ancestor and mother, acknowledging the interrelatedness of birth and death. With respect to the Irunmole, they derive the art of divination from her in the form of the meríndinlogun through which she also consults and speaks. Her synergy embraces the artfulness of life and the dynamic art of engagement the energy of life itself.

In several *oriki*, Òṣun, her synergistic images signify the fusion of diverse energies that encompass her persona. An excerpt from *Ijo Orunmila* summarizes Yoruba perspectives about women—as well as about knowledge, secrecy, and power.

Òṣun, oYéyé ni mo . . .	Òṣun, who is full of understanding,
O wa yanrin wayanrin kowo si . . .	Who digs sand and buries money there.
Obinrin gbona, okunrin nsa . . .	Woman who seizes the road and causes men to flee,
Òṣun abura-olu . . .	Òṣun, River that the king cannot exhaust . . .
	One who does things without being questioned,
Ogbadagbada loyan . . .	One who has large, full-bodied breasts,
Oye ni mo, eni ide kii su . . .	One with fresh palm leaves, who never tires of wearing brass.
Gbadamugoadamu obinrin ko Se gbamu . . .	Enormous, powerful woman who cannot be subdued.
Ore Yéyé o . . .	Most gracious Mother,
Onikii, amo-awo maro . . .	Onikii, who knows the secret of cults but never discloses.
Yéyé Onikii, obalodo . . .	Gracious mother, Queen of the Mighty River,
Otutu nitee . . .	One who has a cool, fresh throne,
Iya ti ko leegun, ti ko leje . . .	Mother, who has neither bone nor blood . . .[9]

Like the Ifá corpus and the *merindinlogun* system themselves, Òṣun's synergy resides at the crossroads, vibrating intensely with a unity of opposites found in her oriki and her odù. This dialogical thought underlies notions of mutability and transmutability of Yoruba thought from its ancient past to its diverse present and its global future. This Yoruba dialogical worldview speaks its authority and generative identity pulsating from its African source throughout a complex global manifestation. Once inside the flow of her river, Òṣun's cool synergistic vision sweetly and wisely guides a multitude of pathways for human beings to choose to follow.

Òṣun and the Flow of Humanity

Òṣun is a quintessential image of mother who speaks to women through their common identity as biological, surrogate, and communal mothers. In Yoruba worldview, motherhood is associated with power and mystery, with transformative abilities, and with the authority to activate or suspend life itself. Motherhood is the esteemed gateway to lineage, rulership, and personal immortality. Òṣun's image is a metanarrative and cognate for women's organizational power and authority. Oblique and direct references to her form a common identity and common cause. Through

Òṣun's narratives, motherhood serves as a source of power, an icon, and status symbol for Yoruba women's social, political, economic, and spiritual roles. In Yoruba cosmogenic terms, motherhood is shrouded in divine awe and mystery at the same time that it is infused with human agency. Sociopolitically, motherhood is a negotiable asset through which women organize and manipulate or are manipulated by family, social institutions, and/or other women. In any case, Yéyé holds court over human affairs, and sometimes, over the other divinities as well.

Her cosmogenic signature is the active principle by which human beings get on with the business of living. Òṣun along with the other orisa proposes a spectrum of divine within rather than the divine unreachable and outside of the self. As one of her cognomens suggests, Òṣun is Ìyálóde, mother of the marketplace of the world. Known for her business acumen, Òṣun engages humanity vigorously in ayé, the world. Iyalode is a metaphor for communal organizing and the catalyst for familial, social, economic, and political transformation. Motherhood was, and is, undoubtedly as much a socioeconomic institution as political one. It signifies more than the responsibilities of childbirth and childrearing; here, motherhood also engenders a network of similarly obligated female, and by extension, male relatives and their dependents. In certain environments, motherhood translates into the control of a large number of workers on farms, in the marketplace, or within the domestic sphere.

As an institution, motherhood worked because women function as an interest group through a network of mothers—biological, surrogate, and communal—who also exchanged mutual services within a given sociocultural environment.[10] For these women, motherhood allowed for the distribution of particular roles and responsibilities by reconfiguring multiple female identities as daughters, sisters, wives, and grandmothers when necessary. For those more enterprising women, these multiple identities were often used to wield influence and power in their natal or marital homes. In the Yoruba Diaspora, Òṣun and other female deities continue to serve as reminders of these multiple roles. Motherhood also worked for surrogate mothers and co-mothers because children are trained from birth to reciprocate certain roles, responsibilities, and obligations within the family, for their parents, and most especially for their mothers. This is especially true in the ways that sons differentiate between their responsibilities to their mothers and wives.

Òṣun in Yoruba cosmology captures the complex understanding of women and their roles in the society. From a mythical perspective, the Òṣun narratives reflect social ideals while simultaneously acknowledging human foibles through both human and divine agency. Her narrative reifies the creative power of the womb, emphasizing how women can halt the flow of humanity not only by withholding children, but also through their agency and abilities as human beings.

Notes

1. Gwendolyn Mikell, *African Feminism: The Politics of Survival in Sub-Saharan Africa* (Philadelphia: University of Pennsylvania Press, 1997), 10–16.

2. Ibid., 16.

3. D. L. Badejo, *Òṣun Seegesi: The Elegant Deity of Wealth, Power, and Femininity* (Lawrenceville, NJ: Africa World Press, 1995); Badejo, "Sango and the Elements: Gender and Cultural Discourses," in *Sango in Africa and the African Diaspora,* ed. Joel Tishken, Toyin Falola, and Akintunde Akinyemi (Bloomington: Indiana University Press, 2009), 111–134.

4. Badejo, *Òṣun Seegesi.*

5. Badejo, "Sango and the Elements."

6. Badejo, *Òṣun Seegesi.*

7. Rowland Abiodun, "Verbal and Visual Metaphors: Mythical Allusions in Yoruba Ritualistic Art of Ori," *Word and Image: A Journal of Verbal/Visual Inquiry* 3, no. 3 (1987): 252–270.

8. Ifá Yemi Eleburuibon, personal interviews, 1982.

9. Fashina Falade, *Ijo Orunmila* (Lynwood, CA: Ara Ifa Publishing, 1998) 47–48.

10. Tuzyline Jita Allan et al., *Women Writing Africa: West Africa and the Sahel* (New York: Feminist Press, 2005), 54.

Bibliography

Abiodun, Rowland. "Verbal and Visual Metaphors: Mythical Allusions in Yoruba Ritualistic Art of Ori." *Word and Image: A Journal of Verbal/Visual Inquiry* 3, no. 3 (1987): 252–270.

Abiodun, Rowland. "Women in Yoruba Religious Images." *African Languages and Cultures* 2, no. 1 (1989): 1–18.

Allan, Tuzyline Jita, et al. *Women Writing Africa: West Africa and the Sahel.* New York: Feminist Press, 2005.

Badejo, D. L. *Òṣun Seegesi: The Elegant Deity of Wealth, Power, and Femininity.* Lawrenceville, NJ: Africa World Press, 1995.

Badejo, D. L. "Sango and the Elements: Gender and Cultural Discourses." In *Sango in Africa and the African Diaspora,* ed. Joel Tishken, Toyin Falola, and Akintunde Akinyemi, 111–134. Bloomington: Indiana University Press, 2009.

Bascom, William. *Sixteen Cowries: Yoruba Divination from Africa to the New World.* Bloomington: Indiana University Press, 1980.

Euba, Akin. *Yoruba Drumming: The Dundun Tradition.* Bayreuth, Germany: Eckhard Breitinger, 1990.

Fashina Falade. *Ijo Orunmila.* Lynwood, CA: Ara Ifa Publishing, 1998.

Mikell, Gwendolyn. *African Feminism: The Politics of Survival in Sub-Saharan Africa.* Philadelphia: University of Pennsylvania Press, 1997.

Okpewho, Isidore. *The Oral Performance in Africa.* Ibadan: Spectrum Books, 1990.

Olajubu, Chief Oludare. "Yoruba Oral Poetry: Composition and Performance." In *Oral Poetry in Nigeria,* ed. Uchegbulam N. Abalogu, Garba Ashiwaju, and Regina Amadi-Tshiwala, 71–85. Lagos: Nigeria Magazine Special Publications. 1981.

Pemberton, John, and Funso S. Afolayan. *Yoruba Sacred Kingship: "A Power Like That of the Gods."* Washington, DC: Smithsonian Institution Press, 1996.

Steady, Filomena Chioma. "African Feminism: A Worldwide Perspective." In *Women in Africa and the African Diaspora*, ed. Rosalyn Terborg-Penn, Sharon Harley, and Andrea Benton Rushing, 3–24. Washington, DC: Howard University Press, 1987.

Yai Olabiyi Babalola. "In Praise of Metonymy: The Concepts of 'Tradition' and 'Creativity' in the Transmission of Yoruba Artistry over Time and Space." In *The Yoruba Artist: New Theoretical Perspectives on African Arts,* ed. Rowland Abiodun, Henry Drewal, and John Pemberton, 107–117. Washington, DC: Smithsonian Institution Press, 1994.

21

Iyami Osoronga: Primordial Mothers of Yoruba Spirituality

Aina Olomo

The celestial powers of the primordial mothers came to earth in human incarnations at the town of Ota located in the part of Yorubaland that is now Nigeria. Societies of "witch-women" who honored the "Great Mother" in central and northern Nigeria extended into land-locked Western Africa and the country of Niger. In these societies men and women are members but women are the main titleholders. In Nigeria and the People's Republic of Benin the heads of these groups are known as *Iyalase* and *Iyalaje*; in Nupe the leader is *Lelu*.

As early as the 16th century, West African people who shared a common language and many traditions were described as Yoruba by another African group, the Hausas. One of the commonalities among these groups is the belief in the existence of female powers, an idea that continues to be supported throughout Yorubaland. The Yoruba are the largest ethnolinguistic group in Africa and number more than 20 million people and include many subethnic groups: the Anago, Yagba, Aku, Egba, Ikiri, Ijumu, Abinu, and Igbede are a few. Other African countries with Yoruba populations are Senegal, Sierra Leone, Niger, Bukino Faso, Ghana, and Togo. In Africa's Vodoun and in parts of the Yoruba Diaspora, the religious traditions of the "Great Mothers" are still retained orally and expressed ritually. Ceremonies and sacred scriptures reflect the belief that the goddesses are married to, or the polarities of, the deity who presides over destiny. This union represents the Yoruba concept of duality as it is in all of creation.

The pantheon or multileveled group that frames the divine feminine principle of the Yoruba is referred to by many names, including Iyami Osoronga, Iya N'la, Aje, Odu, Na, Gbadu, Eleiye, Iya Won, Iya Agba, and Iya Wa. These figures are individual and collective; they can exist one at a time or simultaneously. The primordial mother's powers and her names are fluid and interchangeable. Throughout this chapter any or all of these names may be used to describe the great mother energies. These participants in the female functions of the universe are a collective, believed by the Yoruba and Diasporic Yoruba to be the primordial mothers of creation. The title of this chapter, "Iyami Osoronga" (My Mother the Sorceress), is one of the most common indicators of divine feminine energy.

The sacred names of the primordial mother include Aje, physical incarnations of a society of powerful women; Eleiye, bird master and custodian of its mysteries; Awon Iya Wa, "Our Mother" of all; Iya Agbe, the bottom of the calabash which is a symbol for earth; Iya Aiye, the "Mother who controls the World"; Iya Imole, the "Mother of the divinities"; Iya N'la, the great and bearded mother; Nana Buruku, the terrible mother. A further significant word, *Oso*, refers to wizards and sorcerers who are male members of a society that worships the mothers.

Iyami, Orunmila, and Esu

The Yoruba sacred oracle is not contained in any one "holy book," for the transfer of sacred spoken words to literal text is recent. The spirituality and methods of divinations continue to be retained and transmitted orally. Stories of Iyami Osoronga are preserved in oral and limited written sacred texts known as *Ifa* in Nigeria, *Fa* in the Republic of Benin, and *Afa* in Togo, West Africa. All of these divination methods and texts can be referred to as *Ifa* throughout the Yoruba Diaspora. Ifa is a collection of Holy Scriptures that hold within it history, ethics, and the cultural traditions of the Yoruba. These sacred texts are composed of 256 chapters or *odus* that are accessed through detailed processes of divination.

Orunmila is the divinity who presides over the process of divination. He is described by adherents as being the *Elerin-ipin* or the divinity who witnessed creation. Orunmila is important to the understanding of the primordial mother because he is one part of her dual harmonies. This duality was joined by another deity, Esu; together they make an important triad that regulates humanity. This group of three moves the male powers of destiny and the feminine powers of cosmic justice through the universe.

Orunmila, Iyami, and Esu are the liaison between the supreme being, who is the dual-sexed male-female creator divinity, with the earth and its creatures. Esu, the divinity who rides the pendulum between the creator and the divine feminine principal, is the impartial guardian of the threshold. An important aspect of Esu is that his powers allow for the materialization of spirit on earth; he opens the doors between one end of creation's extremes and the other.

Because Esu knows everything that happens on both sides of the doorway, he allows portals to swing open and close intermittently. Esu makes it possible for the will and wishes of humanity to enter higher realms, thereby altering human perception and reality. By closing these pathways or openings he keeps out whatever he deems necessary to remain on the "other side" of divine tracts. Esu acts as the enforcer of both polar opposites, Orunmila and Iyami; Esu is the entryways to their wisdom.

Oracles of the Primordial Mother

Due to many historical and cultural reasons, verses of Ifa that contain the stories, taboos, and powers of the primordial mothers are not widely published. As a result, practitioners of Yoruba-based spiritualities rely on the willingness of their elders to transmit the information orally. This has meant that many elders and other notable priests and priestesses may or may not have an in-depth understanding of the placement and ethos of "Our Mother the Sorcerer." Pierre Verger, a Frenchman who traveled extensively throughout West Africa and Brazil, researched and documented most of the available information on Iyami Osoronga.[1]

There are sixteen primary or main odus that combine to produce 240 distinct subdivisions. Each of these chapters or odus is a divinity with a name and a hieroglyphic type mark or sign. The content of each odu contains numerous legends, parables, medicines, and sacrifices; the keys to abundance and good character are inherent principles in each segment. Verger cataloged the narratives of how Iyami came to earth despite the fact that very little was known about the Iyami and her cosmic functions before the 19th century. Verger's groundbreaking work produced a literal record of what was held in words in the following odus: Osa Meji, Idi Meji, Irete Meji, Irete Ogbe, Ose Tura, Ofun Meji, Irete Oworin, Oturopon Meji, Oworin Ogunda, Ose Oyeku, and Ogbe Sa. The understanding of Iyami as the "holder" or owner of the calabash of creation or the *Igba Iwa* and *Gbadu* are in the odu texts of *Ejiogbe* and *Orangun,* the first and the last odu. Priests and priestesses of Orunmila spend a lifetime memorizing and learning the material.

How Iyami Came to Earth

The great mother came to earth in the stomach of the divinity of destiny, Orunmila, when the planet was first formed. Iyami and Orunmila arrived in the astral container of the odu Osa meji. Of all the 256 odus only Osa meji was willing to transport the mothers to earth. On coming to earth the great mothers were given power over Orisanla, the divinity associated with internal aspects of the planet's creation.

When the supreme being was bringing the earth into existence, areas of work and responsibilities were delegated to the divinities. But none were given to Gbadu, the great mother. After these assignments were distributed the great mother asked the supreme being, 'What would be my work? What would be my power?' Iyami reminded the supreme being that all the supernatural beings that had been sent to earth were male and she was the female among them. The creator admitted that she had been neglected when the tasks for the divinities had been given out. As compensation, Gbadu was made the mother of all; whatever she said would become manifest. As an expression of her power she was given a weapon, a terrestrial bird that could do good or wickedness but would always obey the instructions of the mother. The Eleiye aspect of the primordial mother became the bird master. It is she who would be owner of the powers of the birds and of the calabash known as earth.

She has been angry ever since she was initially left out of the divine plans for the earth. Iyami collected the feminine rage of the ages. She, as the mother of creation, is giver and taker of life. Iyami is always angry when there is injustice; she does not hesitate to use her destructive powers to restore balance. The screams of women in labor, the tears a woman sheds from the pains of abuse and neglect, have all been stored in this divine feminine consciousness, to be periodically unleashed on those who perpetrate horrors against women and break her laws.

The Power of Iyami

Although Orunmila and the primordial mother understand the destinies and the balancing processes of everything in creation, they are also polar extremes of existence. Orunmila knows the innate destiny and the ethical behavior that help human beings make the most of an incarnation.

The great mother, by contrast, defends and responds to any offenses committed against natural laws. In order to become a member of a society organized to honor and placate the primordial female a person has to have been the psychic cause of at least one death. Punishments heaped on humanity related with the mothers include decay of internal organs because mother devours them, malicious incidents that disrupt normal life, and death. Blindness, illness, misfortune, obstacles, impotence, infertility, earthquakes, drought, and famine are only some of the plagues humanity faces when the mother of the earth comes to visit.

Iya N'la, the great ancestral mother of "witches" who come to earth as humans, incarnates in human form at will. Owners of the terrestrial birds and members of Iyami societies gain the goodwill of Iyami Osoronga through sacrifice and worship. Those who worship the primordial mother are referred to as "witches." It is important to note the specific African interpretation of the term *witch*. In parts of Yorubaland *all* women are suspected of having psychic power, interpreted as witchcraft. Husband-death and infertility are often blamed on "witches" or more accurately community mothers, sisters, and wives. It is widely known among the Yoruba that the pantheon of Iyami will always respond readily to disrespect, jealousy, and disobedience. These elders of the night send out birds to dispense justice and dole out punishment. While women who are identified with the powers of the mothers are feared and ostracized in Yorubaland, their function is understood to be a necessary component for a stable society.

Why Is the Primordial Mother Still Enraged?

It is through the body of mothers that each person comes to the world and from their breasts everyone receives the first taste of life's sweetness; the mothers have been the containers of power that elevate the consciousness of kings to divine status; as devout spiritual mentors they lead rituals that give people divine access. Neither victim nor perpetrator gains when men and women are polarized. When the volume and frequency of the collective soul is diminished by inharmonious acts, the rage of the mothers is energized.

Women have paid a price for real or suspected power, so the pantheon of Iyami no longer has to have an immediate provocation. Iya'Nla establishes the laws that she wants humanity and deities to follow, and she decides when they have been violated. People are not always aware of what Iyami's prohibitions are because her bans are not always announced. Oral stories remind Yoruba people that when Iyami did not want the deities to pick a specific kind of fruit, use a particular leaf, or carry out certain behaviors she first persecuted and then punished them. Behavior, good or bad, can provoke the response of Iyami.

Male and Female Incarnations of the Divine Feminine

Although the stigma of being a "witch" applies most often to women, there are male sorcerers and wizards. Men equipped with supernatural talents are called *Oso* and the females are known as *Aje*. Oso and Aje are the disciples of the Iya N'la. When children are suspected of having psychic and ancestral connections to the primordial powers of women they are called *Obanje*. While Oso(s) are dangerous, they are thought to be less violent than the females. Obanjes can bring good or bad fortunes to their families. For example, it is alleged that the females will not hesitate to kill members of their families and babies while Oso(s) seldom declare war on members of their family. These men do not cause bodily harm to each other or confront the more powerful Aje. When they do wage an attack it is often done openly or with bravado. This oracular chant acknowledges the powers of the great mother; even Yoruba men sing it.

> Pay tribute to women.
> . . . if they pay tribute to women,
> the earth will be tranquil.
> . . . You bend the knee, bend the knee for women.
> Women brought you into the world this is what makes us humans.
> Women are the intelligence of the earth, bend your knee for women.[2]

Yoruba people believe in multiple souls and believe that the spiritual power of the primordial mothers is drawn from an accumulated composite of one of humanity's souls; the gender soul. Osoronga, Iya N'la, Aje, Odu, Na, Aje, Gbadu, Eleiye, Iya Mole, Iya Won, Iya Agba, and Iya Wa embody female power and physically incarnate as female mystics and sorcerers. The mothers own the information and wield power as it has been revealed, used, and lived by women and nature. The personality of this archetype is well known for its temper and destructive tendencies, but she also has nurturing qualities and exhibits well-honed defense responses for her children.

Elderly Women

An exploration of Yoruba ideas concerning the roles of the divine feminine would not be complete without mentioning the fear of the elder mothers within Yoruba culture. This fear is one of the contradictions within the philosophy of Yoruba. Oral traditions maintain that elderly women not only own and dispatch the mystical bird from the sacred cala- bash; they can also turn themselves into birds of the night in order to consume their victim's blood and organs. They are also suspected of con- ducting meetings in the forest with other members of their societies to plan malicious deeds. Wise women within other groups who are devoted to many of the divinities of the Yoruba are often suspected as being car- riers of Iyami power; without doubt some of them are punished for manipulating and directing the destructive magical powers of Iyami.

Despite the fear that surrounds the capabilities of elderly women, they are culturally indispensable. Such women are beyond the social restric- tions usually imposed upon females of childbearing age. Powerful elderly women crown kings, who wear the symbol of their birds on top of their crowns. In order for a king to rule, he must have the sanction of the Iyami. Therefore elder women are essential in the rituals conducted in the coronation of a new monarch. Elder mothers not only participate in these coronations; they also actively take part in deposing unsuitable rulers. They are integral to many of the rituals that govern, build, and hold the established social order together.

As women age in Yorubaland they are feared; it is believed that is when women have extraordinary power. In parts of Africa elderly women have been the scapegoats for epidemics and other societal crisis that develop, including mass deaths. The powers of Iya N'la and her aging daughters are granted by the creator. Consequentially they are only held accountable by the ultimate consciousness in which they share; this unique status spearheads their connection with the supranatural. In indig- enous society, older women continue to impact the daily workings of society because they exercise influence over the children they have borne and nurtured. Elder women are one of the strings that weave generations together, connecting the past to the present and setting the patterns for the future with the lives they have lived.

Persecution of Iyami

The spiritual work of the women who belong to the societies that retain the traditions of the mothers has gone underground. Yoruba peo- ple are afraid of civil and ritual death, so many women have been killed because they were suspected of having or actually having destructive authority. Political and cultural movements such as *Atinga* swept through

West Africa after the Second World War. Atinga was first called *Tigere* when it started in 1940 in an area that is now known as Ghana. Members paraded around mimicking trance-like states common to members of an Iyami association. Once these hunters of powerful women identified the chief of the "witches," they ordered her to bring forth her pot or calabash that contained the carcass of her bird familiar. From the Northern Gold Coast of Africa, Atinga moved south, then eastward to Togo, Dahomey, now Benin, and then to Nigeria until the assassinations of women were prohibited by the British government in 1951. Once outlawed, these movements changed their names in order to camouflage and continue their purpose.

The Child's Right and Rehabilitation organization of Nigeria has documented that more than 15,000 children have been victims of witch-hunts. "Between 2004 and 2007 CRARN registered a total of 820 incidents of children branded as witches in Akwa Ibom State, Nigeria."[3] In many parts of Yorubaland, it does not matter whether a female is young or old. The possibility always exists that she will have to endure political and social restrictions because of gender and age. Indigenous adherents to Yoruba spirituality have not been exempt from their own forms of violence. For example, the cyclical masquerade of *Oro* was used in Nupe to uncover and kill "witches." Seraphim sects of Yoruba Christians are still very active as "witch"-hunters. The need to destroy powerful women is supported by prominent and wealthy Muslims and Christians. The Ketu of Southwestern Nigeria circumcise young women and conduct public rituals aimed at females who have been judged to have committed errors against the group ethos. In Oyo, an empire of Nigeria, shrines were destroyed and women's powers were suppressed. There was a focus on the societies devoted to certain deities, particularly the ones that had large numbers of women as members.

The Era of the Great Mother

Dominated by men, Islam was introduced into Yorubaland in the 1200s and the Christian missionary hierarchy 600 years later. Islam, Christianity, and anthropologists have had a tremendous influence on the interpretations of religious female functions. Most have attempted to define and describe their encounters with the indigenous shrines through the matrix of "good and evil" and the responses of the supreme being of their respective religions. Conversions to foreign religions and misinterpreted observations concerning the ancient roles of Yoruba women and men have caused a social response of fear at the mere mention of the word *Iyami*. This fear of female power continues to be supported by Yoruba adoption of foreign religious beliefs, as well as cultural indoctrination, and is maintained by religious persecution.

During the first years of Yoruba conversions to Christianity in the late 1800s, the Christian Missionary Society (CMS) made use of their ethno-centric gender constructions to interject their own cultural ideals and begin the process that would change the role and status of women in the society and culture of the Yoruba. These supposedly complementary roles between men and women in the early church were different than the roles of "mother" and "father" held within indigenous religious practices. Men and women acquired status based on their spiritual acuity, and both were equally respected for the work they did among their religious bodies. Prior to slavery and colonization, humane and divine feminine power was valued alongside those of their male counterparts.

The establishment of this new order gained its footing and a cultural blow swept across the West Coast of Africa and struck Yorubaland at its womb. Consequently a society that was organized around the concepts of family, lineage, and spirit began to be dismantled, only to be replaced by a civil society that challenged and undermined the authority of the family and spiritual leaders. Slowly an allegiance to the developing state and the ever-expanding authority of the merchant master and colonizer created two groups of people: one group, the merchants, who controlled the lives of the many so the wealth of the few could increase, while the other group, the newly created government, perpetuated the slave culture that had taken root in the minds and spirits of the victims. As a result of all the aforementioned persecutions and attempts at suppressing the powers of the divine feminine forces of the universe, the diversity of life on earth that the primordial feminine energy sustains is endangered. The great mother has begun to strike back in response to being left out of the equations of humanity. She is rallying all parts of herself including the uniting of her daughters and sons as the earth prepares for its next evolutionary shift.

Notes

1. Pierre Fatunmbi Verger, *Articles Volume 1* (Montclair, NJ: Black Madonna Enterprises by Arrangement with the Fundacao Pierre Verger, 2007). As a result of the intimate relationships Verger had with various societies of worshipers in the Yoruba Diaspora he compiled what is considered the first and

most authentic account of Ifa oracles in regard to the so-called "witches," and their practices and the sacred theology.

2. Ibid., verses: 362:367, 147.

3. CRARN—Child's Right and Rehabilitation Network (2009), Adesuwa Initiatives, http://www.adesuwainitiatives.org/page/index.php?id=34.

Bibliography

Alcamo, Iyalaja Ileana. *Iyanla, Primordial Mother.* Brooklyn, NY: Althelia Henrietta Press, 2006.

Apter, Andrew. *Black Critics and Kings: Hermeneutics of Power in Yoruba Society.* Chicago: University of Chicago Press, 1992.

Bascom, William. *Ifa Divination: Communication between Gods and Men in West Africa.* Bloomington: Indiana University Press, 1969.

Chuku, Gloria. *Nigeria in the 20th Century: Women and the Complexity of Gender Relations.* Durham, NC: Carolina Academic Press, 2002.

Drewal, Henry J., and Margaret T. Drewal. *Gelede: Art and Female Power among the Yoruba.* Bloomington: Indiana University Press, 1983.

Edemodu, Austin. "Odyssey of an American Female Babalawo." *The Guardian* (Lagos, Nigeria), October 27, 2002.

Franklin, Wink, "Review of *Forgiveness, Loving Kindness, and Peace,* by Jack Kornfield." *IONS,* December 2002.

Lawal, Babatunde. "Ejiwapo: The Dialectics of Twoness in Yoruba Art and Culture." *African Arts* 41 (2008). http://www.thefreelibrary.com/Ejiwapo:+the+dialectics+of+twoness+in+Yoruba+art+and+culture.-a0175443008.

Lawal, Babatunde. *The Gelede Spectacle: Art, Gender, and Social Harmony in an African Culture.* Seattle: University of Washington Press, 1974.

Matory, J. Lorand. *Sex and the Empire That Is No More.* Minneapolis: University of Minnesota Press, 1994.

Olomo, Aina. "African Spirituality, Identity, Racism and Conflict." In *Global African Spirituality, Social Capital, and Self Reliance,* ed. Tunde Babawale and Akin Alao, 2000–2220. Lagos, Nigeria: Malthouse Press, CBAAC, 2008.

Olomo, Aina. *Core of Fire A Path to Yoruba Spiritual Activism.* Brooklyn, NY: Althelia Henrietta Press, 2002.

Olomo, Aina. "First Commentary: Accepting Destiny." In *Ifa: The Yoruba God of Divination in Nigeria and the United States,* ed. Louis Eason and Djisovi Ikuomi. xix. Trenton, NJ: Africa World Press, 2008.

Peel, J. D. Y. *Religious Encounter and the Making of the Yoruba.* Bloomington: Indiana University Press, 2000.

Verger, Pierre Fatunmbi. *Articles Volume 1.* Montclair, NJ: Black Madonna Enterprises by arrangement with The Fundacao Pierre Verger, 2007.

About the Editor and Contributors

PATRICIA MONAGHAN is professor of interdisciplinary studies at DePaul University in Chicago and Senior Fellow at the Black Earth Institute in Wisconsin. She is the author of more than a dozen books, including *The Encyclopedia of Goddesses and Heroines* (Greenwood) and *The Red-Haired Girl from the Bog* (New World Library). She is an officer of the Association for the Study of Women and Mythology. Monaghan has published four books of poetry and has won numerous prizes for her literary work, including a Pushcart Prize.

KELLY D. ALLEY is alumni professor of anthropology at Auburn University. She has carried out research in northern India for over fifteen years, focusing on public culture and environmental issues. Her book, *On the Banks of the Ganga: When Wastewater Meets a Sacred River*, explores Hindu interpretations of the sacred river Ganga in light of current environmental problems. Alley worked on the "Ganga Radio Series," a series of features and documentaries about the culture and ecology of the river Ganges in India and Bangladesh that has aired on National Public Radio. Alley and M. C. Mehta, an environmental lawyer from Delhi, directed a project to facilitate professional exchanges among environmental lawyers, scientists, and NGOs to solve river pollution problems in India.

LAURA AMAZZONE holds a master's degree in philosophy and religion, with an emphasis in women's spirituality, from the California Institute of Integral Studies. Over the past ten years she has written and taught about the myths and rituals of the Kaula and Shakta Tantra tradition and goddesses in India, Nepal, and Southeast Asia. Amazzone's book, *Goddess Durga: Sacred Female Power,* is forthcoming. She teaches at Loyola Marymount University in Los Angeles.

DIEDRE L. BADEJO, Dean of Letters, Arts, and Social Sciences and professor of English at California State University–East Bay, has been an American Council on Education Fellow, a Fulbright Senior Research Scholar, a Rockefeller Fellow, and the recipient of many honors and recognitions. She was also senior editor and head of the editorial department at Ahmadu Bello University Press in Nigeria. Recent published works include *Sango and the Elements: Gender and Cultural Discourses* and *Osun Seegesi: The Elegant Deity of Wealth, Power, and Femininity.*

MAX DASHU teaches global women's history and goddess traditions. In 1970 she founded the Suppressed Histories Archives to research female shamans, mother-right cultures, and the history of domination. Drawing on her collection of over 15,000 slides, she presents visual talks at universities, conferences, museums, and community centers. She is completing the first volume of *The Secret History of the Witches,* which looks at priestesses, oracles, goddesses, and ceremony in ancient Europe.

NORMANDI ELLIS is the award-winning author of six books of poetry, fiction, and nonfiction, including three on ancient Egypt, *Awakening Osiris* (translations from the hieroglyphs of *The Egyptian Book of the Dead*), *Dreams of Isis,* and *Feasts of Light: Celebrations for the Seasons of Life.* She is also a facilitator of workshops on creativity, spiritual autobiography, and hieroglyphic and symbolic thinking, and as a leader of sacred travel in Egypt. Her most recent work is forthcoming in the anthology *The Modern Day Alchemist.*

ELINOR GADON, in her book *The Once and Future Goddess: A Symbol for Our Time,* chronicles the sacred female and her re-emergence in the cultural mythology of our time. Her most recent work for publication in collaboration with Rita Ray is a sociocultural analysis of data from five years of fieldwork in the villages of Orissa. Her work in progress is an analysis of the relationship of mythology of masculinity to violence in American culture. She is a resident scholar at the Women's Studies Research Center, Brandeis University.

JUDY GRAHN is a poet, woman-centered cultural theorist and early contributor to literature of women's spirituality. Her book *Blood, Bread, and Roses: How Menstruation Created the World* outlines an origin story of culture blossoming from women's blood rituals, especially menstruation. Her latest poetry collection is *love belongs to those who do the feeling.* A prose and poetry collection, *The Judy Grahn Reader,* covers forty-five years of her work. She also wrote *Another Mother Tongue: Gay Words, Gay Worlds,* a cultural and spiritual history of "gayness." Grahn is editor of *Metaformia: A Journal of Menstruation and Culture* (www.metaformia.com). She co-directs the Women's Spirituality Master's Program at the Institute of Transpersonal Psychology and teaches in the Writing, Consciousness, and Creative Inquiry Program at the California Institute of Integral Studies.

MIRI HUNTER HARUACH is a scholar, actor, and singer/songwriter. She has toured nationally with her one-woman shows "Grandmothers of the Universe" and "The Queen of Sheba? Yes I Am." She is adjunct professor at the California Institute of Integral Studies in San Francisco and president and founder of Project Sheba. She is also the media program director and producer for Jewish Life Television.

SABINE JELL-BAHLSEN is an anthropologist and documentary film-maker. She holds an MA from the Free University in Berlin, Germany, and a PhD from the New School University in New York, and has taught at the Rhode Island School of Design, Ball State University, and the University of Technology in Papua New Guinea. She has carried out extensive field research in Nigeria, lectured widely, and published numerous articles in journals and anthologies, and the book, *The Water Goddess in Igbo Cosmology: Ogbuide of Oguta Lake.* Her ethnographic films include *Mammy Water: In Search of the Water Spirits in Nigeria.*

BETZ KING is a clinical psychologist in suburban Detroit. She is an adjunct faculty at the Michigan School of Professional Psychology and has a clinical practice specializing in psychospiritual women's empowerment. Betz was ordained as a Spiritualist minister, Reiki Master and priestess of the Western Mystery Tradition before completing her doctoral degree.

HEA-KYOUNG KOH received her PhD in mythological studies from the Pacifica Graduate Institute; she also earned an MA in culture and creation spirituality from Holy Name College, Oakland, and an MS in Paleontology from Kyoung-Pook National University, Korea. She was an adjunct faculty at the Intercultural Institute of California and a member of the faculty at The Catholic University in Korea. She is president of the Myth and Dream Association in Korea. She is the author of *Why Did Heavenly Maiden Leave the Woodcutter?: A Depth Psychological Interpretation of Korean Fairytales.*

MALGORZATA (MARGARET) KRUSZEWSKA teaches at Santa Rosa Junior College in California and is also a seminar leader at Sonoma State University, California, in the Depth Psychology Program. Her published topics and presentations include: female-centered spiritual practices in yogic traditions, the Black Madonnas of her native Poland, and feminist methodologies in religious studies. She is also a published poet and playwright and produces a radio hour titled *Sacred Sounds with Saraswati.*

JEFFREY S. LIDKE is associate professor of religion in the Department of Religion and Philosophy at Berry College where he also chairs the Asian Studies Task Force and Interfaith Council. Lidke's research interests include Hindu and Buddhist Tantra, philosophy of aesthetics, the intersections of religion and ecology, and cultural semiotics. His publications combine textual sources with ethnographic data from several years of research in Nepal, India, Bhutan, and Southeast Asia.

JUNE McDANIEL is a professor of history of religions at the College of Charleston. Her books include *The Madness of the Saints: Ecstatic Religion in Bengal; Making Virtuous Daughters and Wives: An Introduction to Women's Brata Rituals in Bengali Folk Religion;* and *Offering Flowers, Feeding Skulls: Popular Goddess Worship in West Bengal.* She has done fieldwork in India on grants from the American Institute for Indian Studies, and on the Fulbright Senior Scholar Research Grant. At the American Academy of Religion, she has been co-chair of the Ritual Studies Group and the Mysticism Group, and was founding co-chair of the Anthropology of Religion Group.

VICKI NOBLE is a healer, writer, wisdom teacher, and artist, co-creator of the original Motherpeace tarot cards and author of eight books, including *Motherpeace, Shakti Woman,* and *The Double Goddess.* For three decades, she has spoken and taught in the United States and internationally, leading tours to sacred sites and facilitating workshops for women. Her books are published in German, Italian, Spanish, and Portuguese. She teaches in the Women's Spirituality Masters program at the Institute for Transpersonal Psychology in Palo Alto, California, and has a private practice in astrology and as a tantric mentor.

AINA OLOMO, the Ajidakin of Ife, is a Yoruba chief with more than thirty years of Yoruba spiritual traditions. She has been installed in Ile Ife, Nigeria. While in Benin, she received the title Her Excellence Igbo Iyalase along with the mask and guardianship of Gelede. She ritually received a stool made from the sacred Iroko tree of the Great Mother that honors her connection to the Iyami. She is also an ordained interfaith minister.

RITA RAY is chair of the Sociology Department, Utkal University, Bhubaneswar, Orissa, India. Since 1982 she has been active as consultant on development projects in India for the state government, the government of India, the Ford Foundation, and the World Bank. Her special interests have been issues of gender and displacement which have been the subject of her numerous publications. Her works in progress include a book, *Beyond Resettlement and Rehabilitation*.

CONSTANTINA RHODES teaches in the Program in Religion at Hunter College of the City University of New York. She has served as president of the American Academy of Religion/Southeast and is a founding member of the Society for Tantric Studies. A translator of Sanskrit poetry, she is the author of *Shaiva Devotional Songs of Kashmir and Invoking Lakshmi: The Goddess of Wealth in Song and Ceremony*. She is in private practice as a Certified Intuitive Consultant and offers private consultations as well as workshops on the development of intuitive states of consciousness.

DORÉ RIPLEY is a lecturer at California State University–East Bay and Diablo Valley College, where she teaches intensive reading and writing. She is on the board of directors for the Humanities Education and Research Association (HERA), a group devoted to promoting the worldwide study, teaching, and understanding of the humanities across a range of disciplines. She has published several articles and papers on topics ranging from Shakespeare's women to Peter Pan.

DENISE SAINT ARNAULT is associate professor in nursing and anthropology at Michigan State University. She is an anthropologist who focuses on women's studies, especially gender and cultural meanings in Asian and

Native American communities. She has also studied Japanese deities, priestesses in Japan and Korea, the mother goddesses of Turkey, and the goddesses of Hekate and Artemis.

MIRANDA SHAW holds a PhD from Harvard University and is the author of *Passionate Enlightenment: Women in Tantric Buddhism* and *Buddhist Goddesses of India*. Her field research and writings focus on Buddhism, women's spirituality, and goddess traditions in India and the Himalayas. She is currently bringing her third book, *Buddhist Goddesses of Tibet and Nepal*, to press.

C. S'THEMBILE WEST earned a PhD in African American studies at Temple University, Philadelphia. She has published poems in the *Journal of Feminist Studies in Religion*, and more recently in *The New Rain Series*. Her article, "Honoring the Body: Rituals of Breath and Breathing," appears in *Faith, Health, and Healing in African American Life*, edited by Emilie Townes and Stephanie Mitchem. She teaches in the Department of Women's Studies, Western Illinois University.

Index